Operation Valuable Fiend

The CIA's First Paramilitary Strike
against the Iron Curtain

ALBERT LULUSHI

Arcade Publishing
New York

First Edition

Arcade Publishing books may be purchased in bulk at special discounts for sales
promotion, corporate gifts, fund-raising, or educational purposes. Special editions
can also be created to specifications. For details, contact the Special Sales Department, Arcade Publishing, 307 West 36th Street, 11th Floor, New York, NY 10018
or arcade@skyhorsepublishing.com.

Arcade Publishing® is a registered trademark of Skyhorse Publishing, Inc.®,
a Delaware corporation.

Visit our website at www.arcadepub.com.
Visit the author's website at www.valuablefiend.com.

10 9 8 7 6 5 4 3 2 1

Library of Congress Cataloging-in-Publication Data is available on file.
Library of Congress Cataloging-in-Publication Control Number: 2014004159

ISBN: 978-62872-322-9
Ebook ISBN: 978-1-62872-394-6

Cover design by Owen Corrigan

Printed in the United States of America

To Enit, Alex, Anna, and Tereza

"I am very strongly of the opinion that the lessons which are daily being borne in upon us by the development of this Project are to a considerable extent being neglected in favor of rapidly growing vested interests, and that as a result we stand a very good chance of being faced with a failure the nature and causes of which will be confused in an exchange of recriminations."

—From CIA memorandum "Current Status of Project BGFIEND," August 16, 1949

"One general feature, which seems to be common to many instances of controlled operations, is the unconscious effort on the part of all concerned to rationalize the appearance of security checks when used to indicate control. Such a reaction is natural when considered in terms of the case officer's identification with the Agent. Obviously, however . . . such a rationalization negates the entire purpose of such checks."

—Chief, Communications Security Division, CIA, January 13, 1954

"It's part of a writer's profession, as it's part of a spy's profession, to prey on the community to which he's attached, to take away information—often in secret—and to translate that into intelligence for his masters, whether it's his readership or his spy masters. And I think that both professions are perhaps rather lonely."

—John le Carré, September 25, 1977

Contents

List of Maps and Documents   *ix*

Acknowledgments   *x*

Introduction   *xi*

List of Acronyms   *xvi*

List of Cryptonyms and Pseudonyms   *xviii*

Note on the Pronunciation of Albanian Names   *xxi*

Prologue   1

1 The Office of Policy Coordination   4

2 Albania between 1912 and 1949   13

3 Genesis of Operation Fiend   40

4 The National Committee for Free Albania   57

5 Philby in Washington   73

6 First Infiltrations of 1949   77

7 Reevaluation of Project Fiend   89

8 Labor Services Company 4000   99

9   Odyssey of the First CIA Paramilitary Team   109

10 Philby's Exit   123

11 Propaganda and Psychological and Economic Warfare   131

12 Adverse Developments in the Infiltration Program   146

13 A Bucket of Diamonds and Rubies   163

14 A Rich Harvest of Bitter Fruit   173

15 King Zog Overstays His Time in Egypt   208

16 Planning the Fondest Dream   217

17 The American Backers Are Obliged to Withdraw   230

18 Lessons and Legacy of Project Fiend   243

    Epilogue   260

    Notes   271

    Bibliography   297

    Index   318

List of Maps and Documents

Albania circa 1950   *xxvi*

The last note of the US mission in Albania
to the Foreign Ministry   30

Minutes of meeting between Zog I, King of the Albanians,
and Burton Y. Berry, from the Office of Policy
Coordination, in Alexandria, Egypt, on May 5, 1949   48

Itineraries of the 1949 infiltration teams in southern
Albania   83

CIA-distributed leaflet about Soviet aid to
Albania   133

CIA-distributed leaflet featuring Nastradini,
the sage in Albanian folklore   134

CIA map indicating the status of teams in Albania
by the end of October 1951   160

CIA map indicating the area of operations of
Apple team and the spot where the covert plane was hit
by antiaircraft fire on October 24, 1953   203

Operational map showing the movement of forces
during the CIA-planned coup d'état in Albania   222

Acknowledgments

I am grateful to all those who made it possible for me to write this book. They include: employees at the National Archives in College Park, Maryland, who helped me track hundreds of hardcopy and electronic documents from the CIA and Department of State archives; Alex Rankin and Laura Russo at Boston University's Howard Gotlieb Archival Research Center for facilitating access and research of the McCargar and Burke collections; Breanne LaCamera at Columbia University Center for Oral History for tracking down interview transcripts of Col. Gratian M. Yatsevitch; and my friends in Albania Anton Ashta and Xhevdet Shehu for locating material from Albanian archives and sources.

I received tremendous help and encouragement from those who read early drafts of the book and provided invaluable suggestions that improved the end product. They include Astrit Lulushi, Elez Biberaj, William E. Ryerson, Frank G. Wisner II, Ellis Wisner, Wendy Hazard, Gratian M. Yatsevitch III, Monica Morrill, Rose Dosti, Nicholas Pano, Marguerite Ulmer-Power, Jon Lieb, and David Robarge.

A big thank you goes to my editor at Skyhorse Publishing, Cal Barksdale, who saw the value of the book from the beginning and provided great guidance throughout the editing and publishing process.

Last but not least, infinite thanks to Enit, Alex, Anna, Esmeralda and "Slim Shady" who put up with my writing schedule and created a warm and cozy environment so I could finish the project, even when the feat seemed so far from possible.

Introduction

In 1949 a newly minted branch of the CIA, flush with money and burning with determination to roll back the Iron Curtain, embarked on the first paramilitary operation in the history of the agency. Theirs was an elaborate plan, coordinated with the British Secret Intelligence Service, aimed at detaching the weakest of the Soviet satellites in Europe, Albania, from Moscow's orbit. The operation suffered a dismal failure and the CIA substantially shut it down by 1954.

I had heard the story growing up in Albania in the 1970s and 1980s, where the Communist propaganda machine trumpeted it as a triumph of the Albanian secret police, the Sigurimi, over the "reactionary forces of internal and external enemies." All of these enemies, the story went, were controlled by the CIA and its numerous subordinate foreign intelligence agencies, including the British, Greek, Yugoslav, and Italian services. Until the fall of the Communist regime in 1992, a museum of the Sigurimi in Tirana prominently displayed clothes, parachutes, radio transmitters, and weapons of the so-called "diversionists" together with gruesome pictures of those who were killed next to pictures of those who were captured and put on show trials between 1949 and 1954.

When I came to the United States in the early 1990s, I read the version of the story recounted by Nicholas Bethell in his book *Betrayed*, in which he places the blame for the failure of the operation on Kim Philby, the most famous Soviet mole inside the British Secret Intelligence Services. Philby had served as the joint commander of the operation in its early days. It sounded like a reasonable explanation, and I didn't think much about it until the fall of 2012, when I reread Bethell's book over the Thanksgiving weekend. Going over the sequence of events, I realized that Philby had been involved with the effort only until the summer of 1951 when he fell under suspicion, whereas the operation sustained most of its casualties afterward. It was logical to think that other factors must have been in play to cause the compromise.

I began researching what others had written about the story, only to find that most authors had retold Bethell's version of the events or had treated the subject in a cursory fashion, based on a limited set of primary sources that had become available over the years. To satisfy my intellectual curiosity, I made a list of questions I wanted answered about this story: Why did the CIA choose to conduct an operation of this kind? Why did they pick Albania? Who were the key players in the operation, from all sides? Where did they come from and how did their background influence their choices and actions during the operation? What happened to them afterward? What were the lessons the agency learned from the Albanian operation? What were the warning signs that were missed, and did they have an effect on other operations that followed? Ultimately, how are we to judge the outcome and legacy of the operations conducted at the time from today's perspective?

I began a journey of research and discovery in order to answer these questions. It took me to the National Archives, where I found a surprisingly large number of CIA documents—declassified as of 2007—about the operation BGFIEND, also known as Project Fiend, which thoroughly detail how the agency planned and conducted their activities. Given the usual reluctance of the CIA to reveal sources and methods of operations, I found these documents fascinating in that they provide a unique insight into the actions of the paramilitary arm of the agency—the precursor of today's National Clandestine Service—in the early and formative years of its existence.

Further insight into the character and thoughts of a number of CIA officers who participated in the events came from materials I found in personal archives of James McCargar and E. Michael Burke located at Boston University, as well as from interviews with sons and daughters of Frank Wisner, Gratian Yatsevitch, Joseph Lieb, and Alfred Ulmer.

Albanian nationalists who participated in the operation spoke or wrote very little about their activities in those years, in order to protect family members trapped in Albania from the continued wrath and persecution by the Communist government. Nevertheless, I was able to capture a glimpse of their feelings about the operation from conversations with family members of Hasan Dosti, from transcripts of interviews with Abaz Ermenji by Robert Elsie, and from other material that I found in the McCargar and Burke archives.

I also tried to research and incorporate in the story the perspective of the Communist opposition to the operation. Unfortunately, primary source documents remain mostly locked away in the Sigurimi archives. When the political will and resources allow these archives to be opened, we may learn exactly how the Sigurimi learned about specific details of the operation, the role of Soviet advisers in the conduct of the operation, the interrogation techniques that the Sigurimi used against captured agents, and other aspects of this story that remain in the dark.

Nevertheless, I was able to leverage interviews and memoirs published in Albania since the fall of Communism by members of the Sigurimi. These accounts continue to glorify Sigurimi's role in crushing any opposition to the Communist regime in its early days; therefore, I filtered them rigorously in order to separate pertinent facts from diatribes and praises to a bygone system. The result is a multi-faceted story, which presents elements of the operation from the perspective of both sides: those who participated on the American side and their Communist opponents.

In the early phases of writing the book, I reached out to a family member of one of the CIA officers that directed Project Fiend with some questions about his father's role in it. After several days of silence, I received a one-line response: "I am surprised that anyone is interested in the events in Albania so many years ago." We began a long exchange of emails in which I explained that this particular project, while small compared to other efforts undertaken by the agency—his father had participated in a number of them—was important in a unique way.

The agency used the Albanian operation, the first paramilitary action in its history, as the proving ground for developing and honing future plans, organizational structures, and methods of operations. It harvested the experience collected from engaging the adversary in a new front—covert paramilitary actions—and drew lessons, good and bad, which left the imprint on the planning and execution of other Cold War paramilitary actions that followed, including coup d'états in Iran and Guatemala, and the Bay of Pigs invasion in Cuba, to mention a few.

Our exchanges were fruitful and I received not only answers to all my questions but also additional input that strengthened the book. But his one-line response in the first email remained in my mind. It has kept me thinking of the value that the story continues to have today, over and above what we expect to learn from it as a historical account covering the CIA, the Cold War, intelligence, espionage, the Balkans, and other similar topics.

Physicists working to understand how the universe works today and how it will evolve tomorrow often reach back into the depths of time, as close to the Big Bang as possible, for clues and information. The paradigm applies equally well to the study of history. *Operation Valuable Fiend* takes us in the past, to a crucial moment in the late 1940s when the US intelligence community had a requirement to fight a new kind of war, the Cold War, and it realized that it needed to develop new capabilities beyond intelligence collection, analysis and reporting. It then shows how the CIA, still in its early days at the time, went about developing these capabilities and taking the fight to the adversary.

The world is very different today with new threats that range from global terror and nuclear proliferation to narco-trafficking and the rise of China. But the core processes by which the agency identifies mission gaps, develops new capabilities, and takes them into operations remain the same. As a case study of an early application of these processes, *Operation Valuable Fiend* helps us understand their complexities and the myriad of ways in which the best-intentioned efforts can get derailed or produce unforeseen results.

I hope then that *Operation Valuable Fiend* becomes a solid source of information for you, dear reader, with an interest in the history of the CIA in its early days, its attempts to roll back the Communist threat around the world, and the consequences—intended and unintended—of these attempts.

And if you are simply looking for an intertwined set of characters—refugees, lawyers, officers, politicians, spies, kings, traitors, farmers, writers, Ivy Leaguers, illiterates—who pushed, pulled, supported, mocked, loved, hated, betrayed, respected, pursued, and killed one another, then read on.

Albert Lulushi
Oakton, Virginia

List of Acronyms

ACEN	Assembly of Captive European Nations
ADPC	Assistant Director for Policy Coordination
BBC	British Broadcasting Company
BK	Balli Kombëtar, the National Front
BKA	Balli Kombëtar Agrarian, a leftist splinter group of Balli Kombëtar
BKI	Blloku Kombëtar Indipendent, the National Independent Bloc
BKO	Balli Kombëtar Organization, a conservative splinter group of Balli Kombëtar
CIA	Central Intelligence Agency
Cominform	Communist Information Bureau
DCI	Director of Central Intelligence
DDP	Deputy Director of Plans
DOD	Department of Defense
DZ	Drop zone
EUCOM	US Army European Command

FBI	Federal Bureau of Investigation
GNA	Greek National Army
ICJ	International Court of Justice
IRO	International Relief Organization
JCS	Joint Chiefs of Staff
KGB	Komitet Gosudarstvennoy Bezopasnosti, the Committee for State Security in the Soviet Union
LNÇ	Lëvizja Nacional Çlirimtare, the Albanian National Liberation Movement
NCFA	National Committee for Free Albania
NCFE	National Committee for Free Europe
NSC	National Security Council
OPC	Office of Policy Coordination
OSO	Office of Special Operations
OSS	Office of Strategic Services
OTP	One-time Pad
PSB	Psychological Strategy Board
RFE	Radio Free Europe
Sigurimi	Drejtoria e Sigurimit të Shtetit, the Albanian Directorate of State Security
SIS	Secret Intelligence Services
SOE	Special Operations Executive
VOA	Voice of America
W/T	Wireless transmitter

List of Cryptonyms and Pseudonyms

For obvious reasons, the original CIA documents used to reconstruct the story recounted in this book are full of cryptonyms and pseudonyms. To the extent possible, I have avoided them from the main body of text in order to maintain the narrative flow for the reader. They appear more frequently in the notes and bibliography, where I cite original titles of memos and documents. The CIA often used multiple cryptonyms for the same entity to strengthen operational security and maintain compartmentalization of the information.

In the CIA nomenclature, cryptonyms always appear in capital letters. The first two letters were used for cryptographic security and were based on factors such as the geography or type of operation. The rest of the cryptonym was a word selected randomly from a dictionary, in principle with no particular relation to the place or person the cryptonym was supposed to mask. However, it is not difficult to imagine tongue-in-cheek CIA officers picking words like "wahoo" for Albanian, "drink" for Greece, "credo" for Rome, "gypsy" for Communist, "roach" for Yugoslavia, "crown" for United Kingdom, "steel" for Soviet Union, and "metal" for Washington, DC.

BGBRAWL	Cryptonym for Egypt
BGFIEND	Cryptonym for the OPC Albanian operation between 1949 and 1952

BGGYPSY   Cryptonym for Communist

BGSPEED   Cryptonym for the operation to purchase and outfit a vessel in the Mediterranean to be used for broadcasting black propaganda into Albania

CHARITY   Cryptonym for the intelligence-gathering operation in northern Albania financed by the OSO and run by Italian Navy Intelligence between 1949–1952

DECADAL   Cryptonym for Xhafer Deva

FONTANA   Cryptonym for the intelligence-gathering operation in southern Albania financed by the OSO and run by Italian Navy Intelligence in 1949

HBBASIS   Cryptonym for the covert site in Germany where the OPC trained Albanian and Bulgarian agents for infiltration missions in 1950 and 1951

HBPIXIE   Cryptonym for Albania. "Pixieland" referred to Albania, and "Pixies" to Albanians

HTGRUBBY   Cryptonym for clandestine radio station Voice of Free Albania

HTNEIGH   Cryptonym for the National Committee for Free Albania

JBALERT   Cryptonym for the US Air Force

JBPARSON   Cryptonym for the operation that maintained about two hundred Albanians as potential reserve for armed operations under the cover of Labor Company 4000 near Frankfurt, Germany

KMWAHOO   Cryptonym for Albania or Albanian. "Wahoos" referred to Albanians

LAWBOOK   Cryptonym for the operation to parachute Kosovar followers of Xhafer Deva in northern Albania financed by the OSO and run by Italian Navy Intelligence between 1949–1952

LCBATLAND   Cryptonym for Albania

LCDRINK   Cryptonym for Greece

Malament, Henry R.	Pseudonym for Hasan Dosti
Murat, Nelson J.	Pseudonym for Enver Hoxha
OBDURATE	Cryptonym for the operation to control BKI elements in Rome
OBHUNT	Cryptonym for the operation that sponsored infiltration of agent teams in Albania
OBLIVIOUS	Cryptonym for the operation that provided support and guidance to the NCFA
OBOPUS	Cryptonym for the CIA Albanian operation that replaced BGFIEND in 1952
OBSIDIOUS	Cryptonym for the operation that sponsored the infiltration of agent teams in Albania between 1954 and 1956
OBSTACLE	Cryptonym for the operation to control BKI elements in Rome between 1952 and 1954
OBTEST	Cryptonym for the operation to run the clandestine radio station Voice of Free Albania
Pilgrim	Pseudonym for Frank Wisner
QKPALING	Cryptonym for NCFA newspaper *Shqipëria*
QKSTAIR	Cryptonym for the operation against Bulgaria that the OPC launched in early 1950
RNCASTING	Cryptonym for King Zog
RNLUMPIT	Cryptonym for Archibald Lyall
RNPUTLOG	Cryptonym for Hamit Matiani
TPROACH	Cryptonym for Yugoslavia
VALUABLE	Cryptonym for British SIS Albanian operation between 1949 and 1953
XNMALEDICT	Cryptonym for Balli Kombëtar Agrarian
Yarborough	Pseudonym for King Zog
ZRMETAL	Cryptonym for Washington, DC

Note on the Pronunciation
of Albanian Names

In order to maintain the accuracy and authenticity of the story, I have used the Albanian language representation for names of Albanian characters or geographical locations in Albania. The pronunciation of Albanian is phonetical and comes quite naturally to English speakers once they learn the thirty-six basic Albanian sounds, which also make up the letters of the Albanian alphabet. The list below contains the letters of the Albanian alphabet, their corresponding English sounds, and a pronunciation example.

Letter	Sound	Pronunciation Example
A, a	a	t<u>a</u>r
B, b	b	<u>b</u>oy
C, c	t͡s	ra<u>ts</u>
Ç, ç	t͡ʃ	<u>ch</u>ur<u>ch</u>
D, d	d	<u>d</u>oor
Dh, dh	ð	<u>the</u>
E, e	ɛ	<u>e</u>nd
Ë, ë	ə	m<u>u</u>rder

F, f	f	<u>f</u>ast
G	g	<u>g</u>um
Gj, gj	ɟ	<u>j</u>oin
H, h	h	<u>h</u>at
I, i	i	t<u>ee</u>
J	j	<u>y</u>es
K, k	k	<u>k</u>it
L, l	l	<u>l</u>ost
Ll, ll	ɫ	ba<u>ll</u>
M, m	m	<u>mom</u>
N, n	n	<u>n</u>o
Nj, nj	ɲ	El Ni<u>ñ</u>o
O, o	o	<u>o</u>pen
P, p	p	<u>p</u>ot
Q, q	t͡ʃ	su<u>t</u>ure
R, r	ɾ	<u>r</u>ope
Rr, rr	R	ba<u>rr</u>el
S, s	s	<u>s</u>ong
Sh, sh	ʃ	<u>sh</u>arp
T, t	t	<u>t</u>en
Th, th	θ	<u>th</u>ick
U, u	u	f<u>oo</u>t
V, v	v	<u>v</u>an
X, x	d͡z	Go<u>dz</u>illa
Xh, xh	d͡ʒ	<u>J</u>ohn
Y, y	y	déjà v<u>u</u>

Z, z	z	zoom
Zh, zh	ʒ	treasure

Here are the pronunciations for some of the names that appear in this story:

Enver Hoxha: *Enver Hoja*
Koçi Xoxe: *Kotchi Dzodze*
Abas Kupi: *Ah-bas Koopee*
Abas Ermenji: *Ah-bas Ermeñee*
Tahir Premçi: *Ta-heer Pram-tshi*
Halil Branica: *Haleel Branitsa*
Ismail Vërlaci: *Ees-mah-eel Ver-la-tsi*

Operation
Valuable Fiend

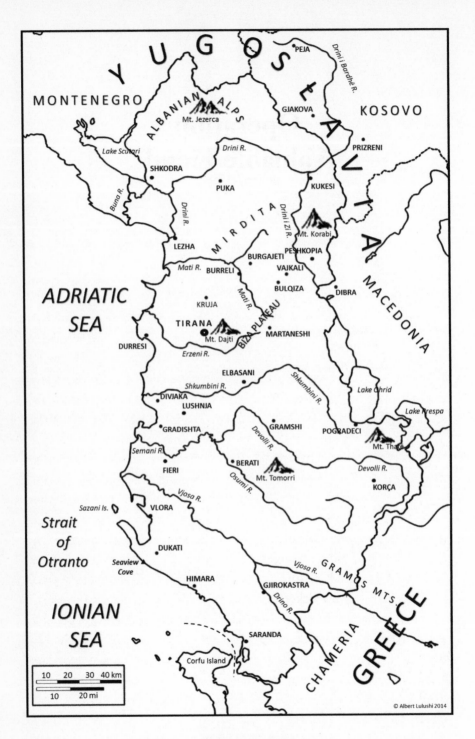

Albania circa 1950

Prologue

In late afternoon on November 11, 1950, a rickety truck pulled up next to a Douglas C-47 Skytrain airplane parked on the tarmac of a small military airstrip located twelve miles northwest of Athens, Greece. The plane was all black and lacked any insignia or identification numbers on its body. Nine men jumped from the truck, unloaded seven bundles, and then climbed aboard the C-47 with the help of the pilot and four members of the crew, all veterans of the pre–World War II Polish Air Force contracted by the Central Intelligence Agency to fly dangerous covert missions over denied areas in the Balkans.

The men were in their early thirties and dressed alike in clothes made of military-grade material, but without distinguishing marks that would identify them with any known military force. They were suited up to survive in rugged terrain and cold weather. Each man wore a leather helmet on his head, a scarf tied around his neck, a shirt and a wool sweater under a snow jacket, heavy trousers over long underwear, socks, boots, and gloves. Each man had a German Schmeisser submachine gun strapped to his chest, three magazines of ammunition attached to the belt, together with a Walther P38 pistol and magazine, commando knife, jackknife, map, compass, and flashlight. Each man carried $100 to $150 worth of local currency and forty gold napoleons in money belts under the layers of clothes.[1]

The nine men were the first team of paramilitary agents that the CIA was parachuting into Albania. Four of them would operate in the

Kukësi region in the northeast mountains of Albanian near the Yugoslav border. The other five would be parachuted into the mountains of Martaneshi farther south. Their mission was to represent the National Committee for Free Albania among the population, to give hope to their countrymen that the day of liberation from the Communists was approaching fast, to collect information about the situation in the country, and to stay in touch with their case officer in Athens in order to receive more supplies and additional agents. Even though they were on a reconnaissance and intelligence-gathering mission, the men knew they were going against ruthless enemies who would show no mercy if they captured them. A thin glass ampule containing liquid potassium cyanide, known as an L-pill, was sewn into the collar of the snow jacket in such a way that the man wearing the jacket could reach down and bite on the ampule even with his hands tied behind his back. Death would follow in ten to fifteen seconds and would save the agents from the horrendous tortures that awaited them if the enemy captured them alive.[2]

The plane took off from the airstrip at 1940 hours. It headed west over the Gulf of Corinth, turned north by northwest over the Ionian Sea, and flew along the Greek coast past the island of Corfu. When it reached the Straits of Otranto, it banked to the right and followed a northerly course parallel with the Albanian coastline. It entered Albania at 2227 hours at the junction of the Yugoslav border and the sea at the southern extremity of Buna River valley, south of Shkodra. There, the plane turned onto a northeasterly course, flying in a straight line until its path intersected with the Drini i Zi River.

The navigator tried his best to orient himself using landmarks, especially riverbeds in the narrow valleys below. But it was a moonless night, and in the complete darkness ground checkpoints were unrecognizable. "A matter of black sameness and all streams looked alike," the crew would report when they returned to Athens.[3]

They reached the target zone for the first drop near Kukësi at 2251. There was no one on the ground to signal, so the plane circled the area for approximately one hour with the navigator unable to find the precise drop point. The Kukësi team conferred with the pilot, who assured them that at least they were not over Yugoslavia. Not wanting to abort the mission, the men decided to go. Four men and three bundles parachuted in a single run at 2350.

After the drop, the plane set on a southerly course and headed to the second target in the mountains of Martaneshi. The navigator was not able to recognize the drop zone there either, making it necessary to circle the general area for nearly an hour. Finally, he spotted a suitable clearing and at 0045 the party of five jumped from 1,200 feet above the ground. The plane circled back and discharged four bundles of equipment. Then, it set its course west in a line north of Tirana and Durrësi straight out to sea. It departed the Albanian coast at 0150 and landed in Greece at 0345 hours. Total time of flight was eight hours ten minutes. Total time over Albania: three hours twenty-three minutes.[4]

* * *

Upon their return to Athens, the Polish aircrew reported no flares, no antiaircraft fire, no interception attempts, and seemingly no detection. The morale of the drop parties had been especially high. Their physical condition was good—the flight had been in smooth air and no one became airsick. During the journey, the nine men displayed normal curiosity about ground scenery below and a nervous excitement when the aircrew fastened the static lines and opened the cabin door. In the case of both drops, the jumpmaster pushed the leader of each team through the door to get things going—the rest followed very quickly. Any momentary balking was purely an instinctive reaction. The richly experienced aircrew was generally satisfied with the whole operation.[5]

News of the successful parachute drop reached Washington the next day and caused a great deal of enthusiasm in the hierarchy in the Office of Policy Coordination (OPC) at the CIA. The OPC was one of the youngest and most activist components of the United States intelligence community at the time, in charge, despite its innocuous name, of aggressive actions to combat Communism and to counteract the "vicious covert activities of the USSR."[6]

The drop of November 11, 1950, was the first paramilitary action of Project Fiend, the OPC's ambitious operation aimed at breaking the weakest link in the chain of Soviet satellites, Communist Albania.

CHAPTER I

The Office of Policy Coordination

On July 26, 1947, President Harry S. Truman signed the National Security Act, which laid the foundations of the modern national security establishment, based on the experience gained during World War II and the challenges presented by the intensifying Cold War. It created the National Security Council (NSC) to advise and assist the President on national security and foreign policies; established the office of the secretary of Defense, led by a civilian presidential appointee to coordinate the activities of the separate Departments of Army, Navy, and Air Force; and instituted a Joint Chiefs of Staff (JCS) organization responsible for the unified strategic direction, command, and integration of land, naval, and air forces. It also created the Central Intelligence Agency (CIA), the first peacetime coordinated and comprehensive intelligence service in the nation's history.[1] As the Congress wrote the National Security Act initially, the CIA's mandate was very similar to that of its predecessor, the Central Intelligence Group, which President Truman had created in January 1946 by presidential directive. The CIA's mission was to collect intelligence by secret or overt means, perform research and analysis, and produce intelligence summaries and estimates.[2]

The first few months of the CIA's existence coincided with an escalation of Communist activities throughout the world and particularly in Europe. The Soviet Union leveraged both the good will created by its fight against the Nazis during the war and the presence of its armies in a number of European countries after the war to inspire and support local Communist parties by open means or behind the scenes. In Czechoslovakia, the Communists had won only 38 percent of the votes in the 1947 elections and held a minority position in the government and parliament. But they controlled the police, security apparatus, and armed forces, which they used to engineer a coup in February of 1948. A government purged of non-Communists came to power, and the parliament quickly approved a new constitution proclaiming Czechoslovakia a People's Democracy, effectively placing it in the Soviet orbit.

A similar scenario risked being repeated in Italy, which had scheduled parliamentary elections for April 18, 1948. The Italian Communist Party, the strongest Communist party in Europe outside the Soviet Union, had outperformed the Christian Democrats in municipal elections in 1946 and 1947. Supported by millions of dollars funneled "in black bags of money directly out of the Soviet compound in Rome,"[3] they were poised to win the parliamentary elections. Almost forty years later, Gianni Agnelli, the Italian industrial mogul and head of the Fiat conglomerate, described the effects of a Communist electoral victory in Italy as follows: "[It] would have been a tragedy for Italy; . . . would have been a tragedy for Europe; . . . would have been a tragedy for the Mediterranean; and it would have been a setback for America."[4]

The United States took a number of steps to ensure a favorable outcome of the elections. Significant economic and military aid available under the Marshall Plan was directed to Italy; the large Italian-American community in the United States sent millions of letters, postcards, and telegrams urging their friends and family back home to reject the Communists. The Voice of America and commercial radio stations in Italy broadcast hours of programming designed to influence the vote, with the Voice of America featuring prominent personalities like Frank Sinatra and Gary Cooper to pitch their message.

However, there was a need to act more decisively with direct but clandestine support that would help the Christian Democrats and their coalition partners get over the top. The CIA's Office of Special Operations (OSO) was the natural choice for the job. The OSO was the intelligence-gathering arm of the CIA that controlled the overwhelming majority of the agency's personnel and assets at the time. Most of the OSO officers had learned their tradecraft during World War II, serving in military intelligence units or in the Office of Strategic Services (OSS), created by William J. "Wild Bill" Donovan in 1942 to collect intelligence and conduct sabotage operations against Axis targets in Europe and parts of Asia.

James Angleton, the OSO station chief in Rome, took charge of the CIA operation to influence the Italian election. Angleton had been instrumental in rebuilding the Italian intelligence services after the war and had unfettered access to their hierarchies, which he used to channel all available OSO assets toward supporting the Christian Democratic candidates and their allies. F. Mark Wyatt, a young CIA officer assigned to the operation recalled:

> We had bags of money that we delivered to selected politicians, to defray their political expenses, their campaign expenses, for posters, for pamphlets, what have you. And we did many things to assist those selected Christian Democrats, Republicans, and the other parties that were completely reliable—that could keep the secret of where their funds came from.
>
> We would like to have done this in a more sophisticated manner. Passing black bags to affect a political election is not really a terribly attractive thing. But we only had a few months to do this, and that was the principal thing that we did.[5]

In the end, Alcide De Gasperi's Christian Democrats and their coalition partners were able to beat Palmiro Togliatti's Communist-Socialist alliance thanks to the strong anti-Communist get-out-the-vote effort supported by the Catholic Church and financed by the CIA.

* * *

The legal cover for the CIA's conduct of the Italian operation had been provided by NSC directive 4-A of December 17, 1947, which directed the director of Central Intelligence (DCI) to "Initiate and conduct, within the limit of available funds, covert psychological operations designed to counteract Soviet and Soviet-inspired activities which constitute a threat to world peace and security or are designed to discredit and defeat the United States in its endeavors to promote world peace and security."[6]

An increasing number of people in the national security establishment came to the realization that countering the Soviet threat in a cold war required a broader spectrum of covert actions, more than just psychological operations like those undertaken to influence the outcome of the Italian elections. NSC directive 10/2 of June 18, 1948, authorized the CIA to conduct broad *covert* rather than merely *psychological* operations, defining them as:

> All activities . . . which are conducted or sponsored by this Government against hostile foreign states or groups or in support of friendly foreign states or groups but which are so planned and executed that any US Government responsibility for them is not evident to unauthorized persons and that if uncovered the US Government can plausibly disclaim any responsibility for them.
>
> Specifically, such operations shall include any covert activities related to: propaganda; economic warfare; preventive direct action, including sabotage, anti–sabotage, demolition and evacuation measures; subversion against hostile states, including assistance to underground resistance movements, guerrillas and refugee liberation groups, and support of indigenous anti-Communist elements in threatened countries of the free world.[7]

The Office of Policy Coordination was created on September 1, 1948, to organize and manage these covert operations. As envisioned by NSC 10/2, the OPC took direction from the State Department in peacetime and from the military in wartime. The OPC was placed organizationally under the CIA "for *housekeeping and logistics only* [italics in original]."[8] It had a direct line reporting and access to the State Department and military hierarchies, with only a "dotted line" dependency on the director of Central Intelligence, who was Roscoe H. Hillenkoetter, rear admiral, US Navy.

The engine behind the creation of the OPC and the man assigned to lead it was Frank Gardiner Wisner, a forty-year-old lawyer who came over from the State Department with the title of assistant director for policy coordination. The higher echelons of the CIA and the State Department at the time were full with ambitious and bright northeasterners educated at Ivy League schools. While equally ambitious and brilliant, Wisner came from the south and his alma mater was the University of Virginia. He was born and raised in Laurel, Mississippi, into a family that had moved there from Iowa after the Civil War to start a successful lumber business and therefore did not owe its prosperity to the slave-owning plantation economy of the antebellum South. Although he grew up in one of the most segregated states of the union, Wisner was proud of the enlightened role his family and especially his sister, Elizabeth Chisholm, had played in discovering the talents and supporting the musical education and career of Leontyne Price, the world-renowned African American soprano.[9]

After attending public high school in his hometown, Wisner enrolled in the all-boys Woodberry Forest School in Orange, Virginia, and then went on to complete undergraduate studies and law school at the University of Virginia. After graduating, Wisner worked on Wall Street and then enlisted in the US Navy six months before Pearl Harbor. Things got interesting for him when he transferred to the Office of Strategic Services (OSS) in July 1943. His first assignment was in Cairo, Egypt, and then from there to Istanbul, Turkey.

In August 1944 Wisner was transferred to Romania on the heels of the retreating German army in order to coordinate the safe evacuation of hundreds of Allied airmen held there as prisoners of war. In Romania, Wisner witnessed from up close the focused efforts of the Soviet Union to establish a Communist regime. The plight of King Michael and the privileged, fervently anti-Communist Romanian elite convinced Wisner that the Soviet Union was gearing up to exploit its power and undermine US interests in Europe and beyond.[10] Wisner was among the few officials at the time to raise concerns about the dangerous enemy that the Soviet Union was becoming, concerns that George F. Kennan, the US deputy chief of mission in Moscow, had articulated most vocally. In his famous "long telegram" from Moscow in February 1946, Kennan had advocated strongly for a new attitude in US policy toward America's wartime ally.

After the war, Wisner went back briefly to his legal career in New York City before joining the State Department in 1947, where he and

Kennan, then the head of the Policy Planning Staff, agitated for new ways to counter the Soviet threat, which eventually lead to the creation of the OPC.

Wisner envisioned the OPC as a focal point within the government able to render services to the entire government through its ability to consider problems and get things done where more overt agencies were unable to act. Wisner understood that achieving this vision would result in an unprecedented power in the hands of his organization, which in turn demanded the highest quality of personnel to wield that power responsibly and intelligently.[11] In the weeks and months immediately following the creation of the OPC, Wisner focused his efforts on building an organizational structure and finding the best and the brightest people that would enable him to accomplish his vision.

In its initial days, the OPC comprised about fifteen people, most of them inherited from a previous organization known as Special Projects Group, whose primary function was the conduct of propaganda activities. The OPC's first organizational structure had two main divisions, Operations and Plans & Projects, with foreign branches under each division. The Operations division included branches covering broad geographical areas under the overall direction of the chief of operations. In the early days, there were so few people working for the OPC that only the branches handling Germany, Austria, and the Balkans were actually operating. The branch covering the Balkans and Southeast Europe, Foreign Branch B Section I, or FB-I, was responsible for Albania, Bulgaria, Greece, Hungary, Malta, Romania, and Yugoslavia. It also covered the Free Territory of Trieste, an area on the northern shores of the Adriatic disputed between Italy and Yugoslavia, which, like Berlin, had been one of the fault lines between the Western Allies and the Soviet Union in the early days of the Cold War. The allies partitioned the territory into two zones in 1947. Zone A included the port city of Trieste and a narrow strip of coastline surrounding it; it remained under the administration of the US and Great Britain until 1954, when it became part of Italy. Zone B included parts of the Istria peninsula under the control of Yugoslavia, which went on to incorporate it into its own borders in 1954.

The first chief of FB-I was James McCargar, a Foreign Service officer with deep knowledge of the Soviet Union and Eastern Europe who had taken a temporary assignment with the CIA in 1948 as a case officer in Genoa, Italy, before moving over to the OPC in February 1949.[12] A graduate of Stanford University, McCargar had worked briefly as a reporter for the *San Francisco Call-Bulletin* before joining the Foreign Service in 1942. His first assignment was in Vladivostok in the Russian Far East, where he served as vice consul. In 1943, he moved to Moscow as secretary of embassy. In 1944, McCargar received a commission in the Naval Reserve and served in Alaska through the end of the war as a liaison between the Soviet Navy and the US Merchant Marine. After the war, McCargar returned to the Foreign Service and went to Budapest, Hungary, first as secretary of legation, and then as chief of the political section. In 1946, McCargar established and ran an escape network through Soviet-occupied territory that saved over sixty Hungarian and Romanian pro-Western political personalities and their families from the arrests, imprisonments, and executions that ravaged Eastern Europe at the time.[13]

Soon Franklin Lindsay joined the OPC as McCargar's boss overseeing all the OPC East European projects. Lindsay had been second in command in the OSS mission attached to Tito's partisans in Yugoslavia during World War II. He brought to the job firsthand experience in guerrilla actions and understanding of the Balkans and partisan warfare principles.[14]

In those early days, Wisner surrounded himself with like-minded former OSS operatives, most of whom he personally recruited with a direct and passionate pitch that went along these lines: "I'm setting up a new organization inside the CIA called the Office of Policy Coordination, and it'll be something different, maybe something up your alley. OPC won't just gather intelligence. We'll be what America needs in this Cold War, an action arm. You're a man of action, aren't you . . . ?"[15]

Once the new recruits were on board, Wisner pushed them to compete and produce actionable projects. He managed the OPC like a law firm: the more clients, the more cases, the more rewards.[16] He judged the performance of individuals by the importance and number of projects they initiated or managed. No idea was too far-fetched as long as it was useful in subverting the Soviet influence anywhere in the world.

For example, a new staff office created in late 1949 to conduct propaganda and psychological warfare activities included an eclectic mix of writers, financiers, Hollywood producers, and movie agents, who in 1950 acquired the movie rights to George Orwell's *Animal Farm* and financed the production and release of the film in 1954. They chose to create an animated movie that parents and children alike could watch and designed the script carefully to convey a clear anti-Communist message. Attention to all the necessary details, including a full complement of jokes and a happy Disney-like ending that was a departure from Orwell's original book made the film a success at the box office. Similarly, they produced another antitotalitarian movie based on Orwell's *1984*, which they released in 1956. No one outside the agency had any idea that the CIA financed the movies.[17]

Wisner's energy and focus caused the Office of Policy Coordination to grow rapidly within the CIA, often at the expense of the older and more established Office of Special Operations, whose espionage and counterintelligence activities were important but not as exciting to the CIA customers in the White House, State Department, and the Pentagon. Whereas the OSO was generally content to collect, analyze, and disseminate intelligence, Wisner was eager to put intelligence to work. During the course of 1949, the OPC gradually built up its budget to $4.7 million and its staff increased to 302 people assigned to seven overseas stations, in London, Frankfurt, Vienna, Rome, Athens, Istanbul, and Cairo, who covered countries in Europe and the Near East.

The rest of the world began to receive coverage as the organization began sucking in additional staff and budget. Foreign Branch A covered Western Europe; B was extended to cover the Soviet Union and all its satellites and was later renamed the Eastern Europe division; C covered the Middle East and Africa; D covered China, Japan, Southeast Asia and the Pacific Rim; and E covered the South America, Central America Mexico, the Caribbean, and Canada. Curiously, there was a Foreign Branch F initially, which covered the United States—a reorganization that took place in May 1950 put an end to it, although the CIA would continue to conduct operations in the United States until the Congress explicitly forbade it in the mid-1970s.

The OPC established stations under cover at overseas embassies and consulates. These stations operated side by side with existing OSO

stations, which often became a source of friction among compartmentalized personnel who kept each other at arm's length, although nominally they all belonged to the same agency. By the beginning of 1952,
the OPC had 2,812 employees and 3,142 contract personnel working
in forty-seven stations around the world and a budget of $82 million,
which quickly climbed to $200 million a year.[18]

From the inception of the OPC in September 1948 until October 1950, when General Walter B. Smith, US Army, became director
of Central Intelligence, Wisner enjoyed a great degree of autonomy.
Direction from the State Department and the Joint Chiefs of Staff was
broad and vague, which allowed him considerable flexibility to develop
and pursue projects. In late 1948 and early 1949, as Wisner, Lindsay,
McCargar, and others in the OPC worked eagerly to take their organization off the ground, they were looking for an opportunity to engage
the Soviet adversary quickly and decisively. Yet they realized that,
logistically and organizationally, the OPC was not prepared to implement large-scale operations. The consensus was that only a narrowly
defined and focused operation would provide the impetus required to
expedite the development of the OPC structures, processes, and procedures necessary to run larger efforts. They needed a pilot project
that would serve as a pioneer for the OPC and would provide invaluable lessons for future operations.[19]

They found the target for such a project in Albania, a small country in the Balkans, nestled between Yugoslavia and Greece, only fifty
miles from Italy across the Adriatic Sea but "nonetheless as remote as
any corner of Europe."[20]

CHAPTER 2

Albania between 1912 and 1949

H istorically, the strategic significance of Albania derives from its position on the eastern shore of the Straits of Otranto, at the entrance to the Adriatic and astride the land route between the Adriatic and the Aegean. It is one part of the parcel of earth where Europe meets Asia Minor. In this position, Albania had long been a focal point of conflicting interests and the battlefield where those interests often squared off. In the middle ages, under the leadership of Gjergj Kastrioti Skënderbeg, Albanians shielded Christian Europe from the Ottoman Muslim juggernaut led by two of their most powerful sultans, Murad II and Mehmed II, the Conqueror. Forced into submission, they sought to avoid complete annihilation by embracing in large numbers the religion of the invader, which made them a target of their Christian neighbors, whose national identities flourished in the nineteenth century, including Greece, Italy, and the Slavic nations of the Balkans.

As an independent national state, Albania was more a creation of Great Powers politics than it was an expression of national will and power of its people, who declared its independence on November 28, 1912, when the Ottoman Empire was in its last throes. Great Britain, France, Germany, Russia, Austria-Hungary, and Italy drew Albania's boundaries in 1913 to balance out conflicting claims of the neighboring countries rather than based on the ethnicity or national affiliation of the population living the area. As a result, almost half of Albanians remained outside the borders of Albania proper and lived in its neighboring countries.

The Great Powers established the independent Albania as a monarchy under their protectorate. They offered the throne to Prince William of Wied, a German aristocrat, who was crowned as prince of Albania on March 7, 1914, in the port town of Durrësi in central Albania. Wied's rule came under fire immediately from all directions. The Greek army occupied most of southern Albania, which Greece had claimed historically as part of its territory under the name of Northern Epirus. A peasant insurrection broke out, led by Muslim fundamentalists who wanted to overthrow the Christian monarch and return Albania to the dominion of the Ottoman Empire. His prime minister, Essad Pasha Toptani, attempted a coup at the instigation of Italy. In the meantime, World War I broke out. On September 3, 1914, after only six months on the throne, Wied left Albania, which quickly became the crossroads for opposing armies in the great conflict.

The Paris Peace Conference of 1919 ensured the independent existence of the country at the time, thanks in no small part to President Woodrow Wilson's refusal to allow Greece, Yugoslavia, and Italy to partition Albania between them. Although nominally still the monarch of Albania, Wied, who had been on the losing side of the conflict, found no support among the participants at the Peace Conference in his efforts to return to the Albanian throne. Essad Pasha Toptani, his former prime minister, was equally unsuccessful in his efforts to establish himself as the ruler of Albania. He cut a deal with the Italians, promising them the port of Vlora and the island of Sazani in return for their support to his claim to power. The Albanian public was dismayed when they learned about this deal. A young schoolteacher by the name of Avni Rustemi traveled to Paris from Libohova, a small town in southern Albania, and in June 1920 shot and killed Essad Pasha in front of Hotel Continental, today the Westin Paris-Vendôme, in rue de Castiglione. The French police arrested him on the spot and he stood trial accused of pre-meditated murder, but a French court acquitted him in December 1920 after his lawyer passionately described Rustemi's act as the spontaneous action of a patriot incensed by the machinations of an oriental pasha against his country. Rustemi returned to a hero's welcome in Albania, where a jubilant electorate sent him to the newly formed Albanian parliament.

Throughout the early 1920s, the national politics of the Albanian state were dominated by a tiny upper class, mostly landowners and tribal chieftains, as well as elements from a small middle class who could afford an education abroad. Political parties in the Western sense did not exist, and people rallied around personalities driven by family relations, tribal affiliations, or economic bonds. The best known among such personalities was Ahmet Zog. He was born in 1895 to a landowning family with feudal authority granted by the Ottoman Empire over the region of Mati, in central Albania. He spent his boyhood years in Istanbul, where he received his early education at a military academy.[1] On November 28, 1912, he represented his district as one of the youngest delegates in the assembly that declared Albania's independence in Vlora. During World War I, he volunteered for the Austro-Hungarian army but fell out of favor with the authorities who confined him in Vienna for the last two years of the war.

Between 1921 and 1924, Zog was a member of the Albanian parliament, leading the caucus of conservative landowners who elected him, and served in a succession of higher posts: minister of interior, head of Albanian armed forces, and prime minister. Zog used his increasing powers with a heavy hand not only to suppress opposition to his rule but also to settle old personal scores and family feuds. In April 1924, his agents assassinated Avni Rustemi, the liberal member of the parliament with whom Zog was në gjak, in blood debt. Essad Pasha was Zog's uncle on his mother's side, and it was Zog's tribal duty to avenge his death.

Rustemi's murder caused an outcry in the country. Theofan S. Noli, the highest bishop of the Albanian Orthodox Church and a political ally of Rustemi, delivered a heartfelt eulogy at Rustemi's funeral held in Vlora. A Harvard graduate and master of the written and spoken word, Noli used his speech to stir the passions of the population against Zog, forcing him to flee in Yugoslavia for his safety. Noli became prime minister of a democratic liberal government in June 1924. However, his political and governing skills were far weaker than his rhetoric skills. A series of missteps in the next few months caused Noli to lose support of the liberal base that had brought him to power.

His move to recognize the Soviet Union and exchange ambassadors with Moscow ensured that he would get no support from the outside either.

Zog used Noli's errors to his advantage. With the support of the Yugoslav and British governments,[2] Zog financed and organized a shock force of several hundred supporters complemented by White Russian mercenaries. In December 1924, Zog returned from exile, forced Noli to flee, and thoroughly cleaned the country of any remaining opponents, murdering some and forcing the rest into exile. On February 1, 1925, the Albanian parliament elected Zog president of the newly established republic. On September 1, 1928, that same legislative body proclaimed him Zog I, king of the Albanians.

While generally ruling as a constitutional monarch, Zog maintained control of nearly all aspects of Albania's government and political life, physically eliminating, imprisoning, or forcing into exile a number of opponents and making many enemies in the process. It is said that he survived fifty-five assassination attempts, one in front of the Vienna State Opera, where he drew a pistol he always carried with him and shot back at the would-be assassin—the only known case in history of a head of state fighting back during an assassination attempt.

Zog's rule had all the characteristics of a personal dictatorship, but during this period Albania progressed considerably. The unification of the country under a strong central government, the gradually increasing impact of Western influences, and the vitality and patriotism of the Albanian people brought about improvements in many fields. Modern methods slowly replaced the old Turkish administrative system that had survived since the time when Albania was under Ottoman rule. Zog outlawed *hakmarrja*—the particularly bloody Albanian vendetta—and the tradition of carrying arms, prevalent especially in the highlands, even though he risked alienating some of his strongest supporters, including his own tribesmen. The government began collecting taxes and recruiting young men for the army—measures traditionally disobeyed by the Albanian population even at the height of the Ottoman period. The parliament approved a penal code based on the Italian model in 1928. A new civil code, patterned on Napoleonic law, went into effect in 1929; it eliminated the dualism of religious (Sharia) and civil courts inherited from the Ottoman Empire. From then on, only state courts judged civil questions. The new code abolished polygamy among Muslims, which resulted in the improvement of the legal position of women.

Zog took measures to improve the education and living conditions of the population. A network of roads built with Italian loans enhanced communications and trade among several parts of the country. The Vocational School in Tirana, founded in 1921 by the American Junior Red Cross, began to offer the first courses in agriculture. From 1931, the Albanian Government and the Near East Foundation of New York jointly ran the Albanian-American Agricultural School of Kavaja, in central Albania. Italian companies using local labor laid a pipeline to carry oil from wells in south central Albania to the port of Vlora. There was enough oil for the internal needs of Albania and for exportation to Italy.

The government also showed a greater interest for the health of the people. After a preparatory study, the Albanian government and the Rockefeller Foundation concluded an agreement, whereby both parties would share in equal proportion the expenses for a campaign to eradicate malaria. The work started in 1929 and resulted in the opening of anti–malaria stations in Tirana, Durrësi, Shkodra, Berati, Elbasani, and Vlora. Beginning with 1932, the government established health centers in various towns for the protection of mothers and children.[3]

* * *

Zog was a bachelor when he came to the throne. His envoys prospected among European royal houses for a suitable queen—without success, given the reluctance of some of the most eligible and wealthy candidates to marry the self-proclaimed Muslim monarch of a somewhat backward kingdom. Then, in 1937, Zog met Geraldine Appony, twenty years his junior and daughter of Count Julius Nagy-Appony of Hungary and Gladys Virginia Stewart of New York. Despite her aristocratic pedigree, Geraldine had no fortune and at the time was selling postcards in a Budapest art museum.[4] In a sort of Cinderella story, she agreed to marry Zog after a brief courtship and after receiving assurances that she would raise the future offspring of the marriage as Catholic.

Zog's marriage was celebrated in Tirana on April 26, 1938, a date chosen to coincide with the 487th marriage anniversary of Albania's medieval hero, Gjergj Kastrioti Skënderbeg, whose descendant Zog claimed to be. The bride wore her wedding dress of ivory satin, which Zog's sisters had chosen from Chanel in Paris, with a high crown of orange blossoms and a train five yards long heavily encrusted with flowers worked in diamonds and pearls. She wore several jewelry pieces designed specifically for the event by the Ostier Jewelers of New York, including a diamond diadem topped with a miniature version of Skënderbeg's battle helmet surmounted by the head of a mountain goat. The king wore the heavily decorated uniform of a general.

The ceremony was strictly civil and lasted only six and a half minutes—carefully avoiding religious symbols, given that the king was Muslim and the bride was Christian. One of the official witnesses who signed the marriage certificate was Count Galeazzo Ciano, Fascist Italy's foreign minister and Mussolini's son-in-law, who presented himself as a great friend of Albania and Zog. Ciano gave the newlyweds a silver table centerpiece on behalf of himself and his wife, Edda. Mussolini's wedding gift was a yacht and four bronze vases. Hitler gave an enormous Mercedes Benz with a removable roof, Albert Lebrun, president of France, a Sèvres vase, Admiral Miklós Horthy, regent of Hungary, four Arab horses, and the king of Italy an antique figure of a dragon.[5] The president of the United States, Franklin D. Roosevelt, sent a telegram of good wishes to the king that said, "May Albania continue to prosper under Your Majesty's reign."[6]

In the afternoon of their wedding day, King Zog and the new queen, Geraldine of Albania, left Tirana under a shower of confetti dropped by Italian airplanes droning overhead. In the shiny red Mercedes from the Führer, they drove toward the coast to spend the honeymoon at the summer palace that the people of Durrësi had given Zog when he was president of the Albanian republic. The palace, known as Zog's villa, still exists today on a promontory overlooking the city and bay of Durrësi.

To mark the occasion of his marriage, Zog granted a wide amnesty to his political opponents jailed in Albania or in exile, including Bishop Fan Noli, who had emigrated to the United States and settled in Boston, Massachusetts. At the same time, the marriage was the final blow to his relations with Shefqet Vërlaci, Albania's wealthiest landowner and a former supporter. In the mid-1920s, Zog had promised to marry Vërlaci's daughter but broke the engagement when he became king in 1928 to the great humiliation of Vërlaci, who moved to Italy with his son Ismail, determined to do everything in his power to undermine Zog's rule.

Besides being an official witness to the wedding, Ciano was the highest-ranking foreign dignitary in attendance. He had overshadowed the wedding festivities with a triumphal arrival from Italy two days before. Clad in uniform and smiling broadly, Ciano stepped from a Savoia plane at the Tirana airfield to the rapturous reception of a throng of supporters wearing black shirts and carrying Italian flags. He inspected the Albanian honor guard before speeding in a car toward the royal palace, while Fascists chanted, "Duce, Duce!" Later, Count Ciano inaugurated the construction of a new highway from Tirana to Durrësi.[7]

During his trip to Albania, Ciano finalized a plan he had been developing for months to bring an end to Zog's rule and annex Albania to the Italian crown in pursuit of the Fascist dream of rebuilding the Roman Empire. Almost a year later, at the end of March 1939, Mussolini gave final approval to the execution of the plan. Italian troops began massing in the southern Italian ports of Brindisi and Bari, while the Italian minister in Tirana, Francesco Jacomoni, presented Zog with a draft agreement to turn Albania into an Italian protectorate. Although the whole country would stand behind the king if he chose to resist the invader, Zog decided that opposition would be futile and prepared to flee the country. Queen Geraldine was nine months pregnant and due to deliver any day. In order not to jeopardize the future heir's claim to the throne, Zog remained in Albania until the baby was born, on April 5.

Sounds of celebratory canon rounds announcing the birth of the heir, Prince Leka, mixed with the noise of Italian planes flying low over the skies of Tirana and reverberations from the shelling of the Albanian coast by the Italian navy. On April 7, Good Friday, Italian forces began landing in all of the major ports of Albania. Staying one step ahead of them, Zog crossed the Greek border into exile, followed by a large retinue that included his extended family and officers of the

Royal Guard. Officially, the king was going abroad to defend the rights of the nation, a duty bestowed on him by the National Assembly. He took the gold reserves of the Albanian National Bank, estimated at three million gold coins,[8] and the crown jewels, which were part of the national treasure, as well as personal and family treasures. After a harrowing journey through Greece, Turkey, Romania, Sweden, and France, Zog and his entourage eventually made their way to England. The British government did not recognize Zog as a deposed monarch in exile and allowed him to settle to England on condition that he not engage in political activities. Zog obliged and spent the war years "settled in bucolic exile at Henley-on-Thames,"[9] far removed and disassociated from events in Albania.

* * *

The Italian Army occupied Albania with relative ease. Small groups of Albanian soldiers and gendarmes, such as those in Durrësi, led by the commandant of Gendarmerie Abas Kupi, fought on their own initiative but were not able to impede the landing and advance of the Italians for more than a few hours. On the morning of April 8, Italian forces entered Tirana and occupied all the government buildings. Within a few days, they had extended their reach throughout the country. On April 12, the Albanian National Assembly directed Shefqet Vërlaci, Zog's archrival who had returned to Albania with the Italian troops, to form a new government. At the same time, the assembly abolished the constitution of 1928 and offered the crown to the Italian monarch, Victor Emmanuel III. In return for acquiescing to the Italian annexation, a handful of Albanian leading figures received positions in various Italian institutions, including Shefqet Vërlaci who became a member of the Italian senate.[10]

For the next couple of years, the Italians ruled the country with relative ease. Italy used Albania to launch an attack against Greece on October 28, 1940. It was an adventure that quickly turned into a disaster. The Greek army under the command of General Alexandros Papagos repulsed the initial assault and then launched a counteroffensive, pushing the Italian armies out of Greece and occupying the major cities in southern Albania. To rescue an embarrassed Mussolini, Hitler sent his armies into Greece and Yugoslavia in April 1941 and effectively brought all the countries in the Balkans under the Axis domination.

In May 1941, after the German occupation of Greece and Yugoslavia was complete, the Italians took over most of the Albanian-populated regions of Yugoslavia, including Kosovo, parts of Macedonia, and pockets of Montenegro, and placed them under the control of the Albanian quisling government. The Germans placed the Albanian populated region of Çamëria in Greece under the command of an Albanian high commissioner, although it remained under the jurisdiction of the German military command in Athens. This arrangement lasted throughout the Italian and German occupation and offered Albanians for the first and only time in their history the political reality of a greater, or ethnic Albania. It went a long way toward achieving its intended purpose: creating goodwill for the Axis powers among members of the Albanian ruling class and keeping them from organizing the population into active resistance against the occupying armies.

* * *

The British government, in line with its prewar policy of appeasement, accepted the annexation of Albania to the Crown of Italy after the invasion of April 7, 1939. The United States, on the other hand, following the Wilsonian principles of respect for democracy, sovereignty, liberty, and self-determination, considered Albania a victim of Axis aggression and withdrew its mission to Tirana. When World War II started in earnest, the US and its British allies encouraged and supported the resistance of the Albanian people against Fascist and Nazi forces of occupation. Beginning in 1943, missions from the British Special Operations Executive (SOE) and the US Office of Strategic Services (OSS) began to infiltrate in Albania and to provide active support in the fight against the Axis forces and their collaborators.

To avoid chain-of-command issues and operational overlaps between the British and American missions, the two sides agreed upon a division of labor from the beginning. The SOE provided money, arms, and ammunition, most of it American in origin, as well as training to resistance fighters. They also engaged in active fighting, blowing up bridges, calling in Allied air strikes, and setting up ambushes. The

OSS had the job of gathering intelligence about the enemy and rescuing Allied airmen shot down during their bombing runs to Romanian oil fields and elsewhere in the vicinity. OSS teams in Albania reported to their headquarters in Bari, where the Albanian Section was headed by Harry T. Fultz, who in civilian life had lived in Albania for many years before the war as director of the American Red Cross Vocational School and who had a solid understanding of the country.[11]

One grouping that fought effectively against the Axis forces and received ample support from the Anglo-American missions was the National Liberation Movement, or Lëvizja Nacional Çlirimtare (LNÇ). Created in September 1942, it was initially a coalition between the Communist Party, led by Enver Hoxha, and other nationalist elements, including Zog supporters such as Abas Kupi. From the beginning, however, the Communists dominated the LNÇ, under the guidance and close supervision of Tito's envoys from the Communist Party of Yugoslavia.

A consummate politician, Hoxha "successfully used his combative instincts and skills to win the internal battles for leadership of the Communist Party of Albania. He could be ruthless and he could be charming, depending on whether a competitor needed to be destroyed or won over."[12] Hoxha also understood the suggestive power of image for the masses. From the early days, and for the rest of his life, he cultivated his natural good looks and tall stature into an appearance that was always impeccable, clean cut, and well groomed. Whether dressed in military uniforms supplied by the Allies during the war or in custom-tailored suits imported from France afterward, Hoxha always projected confidence and leadership to the poor and uneducated majority of his followers. Here is how OSS personnel assigned to Hoxha's headquarters portrayed him in a 1945 biographic profile:

> 6'3", 235 lbs. Churchillesque in sleeping and working habits. Impatient, vain, egotistic; despite mountain experience, his habits are sedentary; likes luxury; great personal ambition—politically, a "climber;" good sense of humor, not necessarily always serious. Tends to subordinate interest in femininity to hard work. Well-modulated, appealing voice in public appearances and speeches. Is at ease in company but is

not socially inclined; however, is effusively concerned with observing the rules of etiquette he knows. Moderate drinker, heavy eater. Attitude toward US—Anti, though expresses himself as pro.[13]

In reaction to the LNÇ, in November 1942 Albanian anti-Communist elements announced the formation of the National Front, or Balli Kombëtar (BK), an organization dedicated to preserving Greater Albania, preventing a Communist takeover of the country, and barring King Zog from returning to the throne. The leadership of BK included a mix of large landowners, such as Ali Klissura, and intellectuals, such as Mithat Frashëri and Hasan Dosti. Born in 1880, Frashëri descended from the family of the leading organizers of the Albanian National Renaissance, a nationalistic movement in the late nineteenth century, and had been a member of Albania's first cabinet after its independence in 1912. Later, he became minister to Greece, represented Albania at the Paris Peace Conference in 1919, and then became minister to France and Albania's representative in the League of Nations. In 1926, he resigned following disagreements with Zog's government.[14] A fervent republican in his convictions, Frashëri withdrew from public life under Zog's monarchy and eked out his living from the proceeds of a bookstore in Tirana, which the Communists confiscated after he went into exile in 1944.[15]

Hasan Dosti was born in 1895 and was a preeminent intellectual and scholar, having earned degrees in law and political science from the University of Paris, Sorbonne. He returned to Albania in the late 1920s to practice law but ran afoul of Zog's administration who imprisoned him several times for his opposition.[16] Under the Italian occupation, he served as minister of justice in 1942, with the knowledge and agreement of Mithat Frashëri, who favored arrangements under which elements of BK served from inside the quisling governments as a "constitutional opposition to the Italians."[17]

Initially, LNÇ and BK tried to collaborate in the fight for liberation. Delegates from both organizations reached an agreement in Mukaj, outside Tirana, in August 1943 to join forces against the Italians, only to see it repudiated days later by Enver Hoxha at the instance of the Yugoslav envoys, who saw the agreement as an acceptance by LNÇ of BK's vision of Greater Albania. Abas Kupi, who had been part of the negotiations and instrumental in forging the agreement, pulled his supporters out of the LNÇ and created a new political grouping called Legaliteti, or Legitimacy, whose aim was the restoration of the monarchy.

The collapse of the Italian administration in September 1943 and the immediate occupation of Albania by the German Wehrmacht sharpened the differences between the Communist-dominated LNÇ partisans and the nationalist groupings in the country. Pressing the social revolution side of the Communist agenda, in October 1943 Hoxha ordered LNÇ partisan units to "attack and destroy the forces of the Balli Kombëtar wherever they might find them, even if it should mean suspending operations against the Germans."[18] Mithat Frashëri gave similar instructions to his followers. Citing the "urgent need of the country for order and discipline," he ordered all BK formations to suspend military operations against the Germans for the time being and to respond in kind to all attacks from the Communists.[19] In the ensuing civil war, the superior discipline and better equipment of the LNÇ prevailed. The partisans drove the BK forces into areas controlled by the Germans, which put them temporarily out of the reach of the partisans but opened them up to accusations by Communists of collaboration.

The LNÇ continued fighting against the Germans, although they did so initially on a small scale, with token actions aimed at convincing the Allies to provide them with arms and subsidies, a goal they achieved. Bolstered by assistance from the British and the Americans, LNÇ increased in strength and numbers and began engaging the Germans directly, especially as the Wehrmacht began withdrawing its units from the Balkans. At the same time, the civil war raged and, as a British officer later observed, "out of every one hundred rounds which we [Allies] sent them, ninety would be fired against Albanians."[20]

Until September 1944, BK was not able by and large to find a way to resist the LNÇ attacks and fight the Germans at the same time. For their part, the Germans succeeded in drawing segments of the BK into fighting their common enemy, either openly in direct support of Wehrmacht units or indirectly as part of the administration governing the Albanian state. During joint German-BK mop-up operations in

January 1944, BK forces surrounded the British staff in Albania. They captured and turned over to the Germans the highest-ranking British officer in Albania, Brigadier Edmund F. Davies, chief of the SOE military mission to the Albanian partisans.[21] His chief of staff, Lieutenant Colonel Arthur Nichols, was wounded but managed to evade capture, only to die later of his wounds and frostbite.

The monarchist Legaliteti took a wait-and-see attitude, never deciding until the end whether to fight the Communists or the Germans. Throughout 1944, Abas Kupi pressed Colonel William Mac-Lean and Major Julian Amery—the British SOE representatives sent to his movement—for arms to fight both the Germans and the Communists; the British in turn insisted he take action against the Germans first before receiving assistance.

A pocket of resistance against the Italians and Germans that was decidedly anti-Communist existed in Kosovo, under the leadership of three brothers, Gani, Hasan, and Said Kryeziu, and supported by a British SOE mission under the command of Major Tony Simcox. By the end of summer 1944, they found themselves actively fighting against the Germans while at the same time fending off approaches by Yugoslav and Hoxha's partisans to co-opt them into their movements. Once the Germans retreated, the Kryeziu brothers faced the wrath of the Communists on both sides of the border. Albanian partisans arrested Gani Kryeziu and handed him over to the Yugoslavs, who put him on trial as antirevolutionary and sentenced him to five years of hard labor "for exposing the people to German reprisals."[22] Albanian partisans also captured Said Kryeziu, but he managed to escape and flee to Italy in October 1944.[23] Yugoslav partisans lured Hasan Kryeziu into their headquarters where he disappeared without a trace. The Albanian partisans took Major Simcox in "protective custody," escorted him south in handcuffs, and unceremoniously asked the British mission to return him to Bari, Italy.[24]

In September 1944, the war was coming to a close in Albania. Germans abandoned all but the main cities and the principal roads necessary to evacuate their troops from Greece. The LNÇ, having already established firm command of the southern part of the country, pushed into nationalist-held territory in central and northern Albania. They branded all anti-Communist elements not affiliated with LNÇ as Nazi

collaborators and eliminated all nationalist leaders the partisan formations could capture.

By the end of September, the Allied governments had given up
hope that any other group outside the LNÇ would engage the Germans head-on in fighting actions in Albania. Belated actions by BK and
Legaliteti elements against the Germans at the time were not sufficient
to change that opinion. The British headquarters ordered MacLean
and Amery to abandon the Legaliteti and to evacuate to Bari, Italy, at
the end of October 1944. They sent explicit orders not to bring Kupi
or any of his followers out of Albania for fear of angering Hoxha. A
few days later, Kupi, his two sons, and three companions landed in
Brindisi, Italy, on their own boat after being lost at sea for seven nights
and six days with only rainwater to drink and one night's worth of food
supplies for subsistence.[25]

Other nationalist elements also found the means to escape to Italy,
including Mithat Frashëri, Ali Klissura, Hasan Dosti, and about one
hundred leading members of the BK.[26] Elements who were compromised by their collaboration with the Axis embedded in and evacuated
with the German army as it began its retreat from Albania. The largest group of nationalists, made up primarily of rank-and-file elements,
remained behind and tried their best to disappear into the countryside
and make their way back home. A handful of them, especially in the
northern and central areas of the country, took to the mountains to
continue fighting the Communists.

* * *

Enver Hoxha entered Tirana on November 28, 1944, at the head
of the provisional government and a day later declared Albania liberated from the Germans. The Communists began a campaign of terror
aimed at the physical elimination of all real or potential opponents of
the future regime. The 70,000-man-strong partisan army that came
out of the war was unleashed against the countryside in pursuit of anti–
Communist elements and their supporters. Mehmet Shehu, the most
successful and feared partisan commander, coordinated the mop-up
operations.

Shehu had honed his fighting skills in the Spanish Civil War, where
he had fought on the Republican side. He returned to Albania in 1942

and applied his military knowledge in successful engagements against Italians, Germans, and nationalist elements. During the war he earned a reputation for being ruthless, not just during combat operations but especially in the treatment of prisoners and civilians afterward. After the battle for the liberation of Tirana, which Shehu led personally, OSS operatives noticed there were very few wounded among the German prisoners and reported to their base in Bari that partisan policy was to "have no wounded German prisoners." They simply killed the wounded outright, without showing any mercy.[27]

In 1945, Shehu went to Moscow for high-level staff training at the Voroshilov Military Academy. During his stay in the Soviet Union, he met with Stalin, who seemed to take a liking to him.[28] Upon his return to Albania, Shehu became chief of staff of the army and zealously pursued anti-Communist elements by enthusiastically applying Soviet methods from the ruthless Stalinist terror of the 1930s, such as summary judgments by mobile three-man courts, extrajudicial sentencing of opponents, and internment of their family members and relatives.

While Shehu led the military in its operations against anti-Communist resistance still active in the countryside, Koçi Xoxe, the minister of interior, directed the terror against the large populated centers of the country. Deeply frustrated with his humble origins and lack of education—he had been a tinsmith by profession—Xoxe was particularly harsh against intellectuals, whom he despised and pursued relentlessly. One example that speaks for all is the persecution of the Kokalari family. Two brothers, Mumtaz and Veisim, who had been neutral and unaffiliated with any political party throughout the war, were executed extrajudicially in November 1944 when Shehu's forces entered Tirana. Their only fault was that they owned one of the few Albanian publishing houses of the time, which had printed a pamphlet promoting the idea of Kosovo being the cradle of Albanian nationalism.

Their sister, Musine Kokalari, was the first Albanian woman writer in history. She was one of the founders of the Albanian Social Democratic Party in 1944, which existed for only a few months and counted only a handful of members in its ranks. In November 1945, she cosigned a memorandum addressed to the American and British Missions in Tirana, requesting their intervention to postpone the

upcoming elections in which the choice for candidates was limited
to the Communist-led Democratic Front members only. For this,
the Communists arrested her in January 1946 and put her in a public
show trial in June, together with thirty-six other defendants—a number of whom were members of the parliament elected on the Democratic Front ticket who had decided to form an opposition group to
the Communist-led majority.

In a telegram reporting on the atmosphere of the trial, Joseph E.
Jacobs, the head of the American mission in Albania, wrote: "Yesterday after trial crowd attacked prison van and beat up defendants badly.
Kokalari, one of two female accused, had most of her hair torn from
her head. Guards stood idly by."[29] Musine Kokalari's sentence was
twenty years in prison, which she served in the notorious prison of
Burreli, in the Mati region. After her release, she spent nineteen years
in internment, isolated from her family until she died in 1983.

Another group that Xoxe singled out for particularly harsh
treatment was the Roman Catholic clergy, who from the beginning
had been an unapologetic opponent of the Communists and their
Yugoslav backers. Out of seven bishops and archbishops that Albania had in 1944, only one remained alive in a concentration camp
in 1949: the Communists had killed three outright and expelled
one as a foreigner; two more died in detention. Only a handful of
priests survived in hiding by 1950, after the Communists killed twenty-three, put in prison thirty-five, and expelled thirty-one. They also
imprisoned or sent to hard labor camps forty-three nuns, expelled
eighty-five, and forced the remaining eighty to abandon the habit
and return to civilian life.[30]

* * *

Neither the United States nor the United Kingdom recognized
the Hoxha government that came out of the war right away. On May
8, 1945, VE Day, an informal American Mission arrived in Albania
tasked to survey the situation in the country before accepting Hoxha's
request for recognition of his government. The US placed two conditions before granting recognition: the holding of free elections and
affirmation of the validity of treaties and agreements in force between
the United States and Albania on April 7, 1939.

The State Department considered the first condition satisfied after the elections in December 1945, despite the fact that only Democratic Front candidates were on the ballot. With regards to the second condition, the Albanian authorities were willing to accept multilateral treaties but declined to honor bilateral agreements between the two countries that King Zog's governments had negotiated. Finding no way to overcome the impasse and in face of the hostile treatment of the mission members and their employees, the United States withdrew its mission from Albania on November 14, 1946.

The US Navy sent two vessels, the light cruiser *Huntington* and accompanying destroyer *Noah*, to pick up the State Department personnel from the port of Durrësi, but they stopped just outside the three-mile limit of the territorial waters because the Albanian government had not allowed them to dock at the port. A tugboat evacuating the personnel almost capsized in rough seas but managed to bring everyone safe aboard the destroyers.[31] Shortly after the withdrawal of the US mission, the Albanian authorities staged in Tirana a public show trial of several engineers and technicians accused of sabotaging drainage works. Throughout the trial, they accused Harry T. Fultz, attaché of the mission, of recruiting the defendants as spies on behalf of the American intelligence.

The relations of the British with the new Albanian government were even more contentious. Hoxha had come out of the war with a deep hatred for the British SOE emissaries, who, he felt, had not supported him wholeheartedly and had double-crossed him by continuing to back Abas Kupi and Legaliteti until the moment they fled Albania. Postwar trials in Tirana mentioned regularly members of the British Military Mission as supporting anti-Communist elements in the mountains. Faced with continued attacks in the press for inciting sabotage and terrorist actions, the British withdrew their mission from Tirana on April 6, 1946.

A month later, Albanian shore batteries fired upon but did not hit two British cruisers navigating between the Albanian and Greek coasts in the three-mile-wide Corfu channel.[32] Over the next few months, the Albanian and British governments exchanged diplomatic notes, with the British demanding an apology and the Albanians claiming that British ships should not be in their territorial waters. The situation

Mission
xxxxxxxx

No. 79

N O T E   V E R B A L E

The American Mission presents its compliments to
the Ministry of Foreign Affairs and has the honor to
request that exit visas be issued to the following
members of the Mission who will depart on November 14:

    Miss Lydia Young FitzGerald
    Mr.   Harry T. Fultz
    Miss Joan Fultz
    Mr.   George D. Henderson
    Mrs. George D. Henderson (Agnes L.)
    Mr.   Rudolph Marinschak
    Mr.   William A. Notbohm
    Miss Martha Ann Shoemaker
    Mr.   Anthony Stevens
    Miss Martha Vaughan Winn

The corresponding passports or travel documents
are attached to this end.

At the same time, the Mission desires to request
clearance for two United States Navy vessels, the
light cruiser HUNTINGTON and accompanying destroyer
NOAH, to enter Albanian territorial waters at Durres
in order to take out the members of the Mission,
their effects and certain articles which are the
property of the United States Government. It is
desired that the HUNTINGTON be allowed to anchor off
the bar at the entrance to the harbor, and that the
NOAH be authorized to enter the harbor to pick up
the personnel of the Mission. The USS HUNTINGTON
has one stack, the NOAH two, and both ships are
painted gray.

The American Mission takes this opportunity to
express its appreciation to the Ministry of Foreign
Affairs for its cooperation in the past.

    Tirana, November 9, 1946.

Enclosures:
    9 Passports
    1 Travel Document

To the
    Ministry of Foreign Affairs,
        Tirana.

GDHenderson/mas/vw

*The last note of the US mission in Albania to the Foreign Ministry, requesting exit
visas for its staff and permission—which was not granted—for two US Navy vessels
to enter Albania's territorial waters to assist with the evacuation*

escalated when two British destroyers, the *Saumarez* and the *Volage*, struck mines on October 22, 1946, as they were passing through the Corfu Channel. Both destroyers were heavily damaged, one beyond repair; forty-four sailors were killed, and forty-two more were injured by the explosions.

In November 1946, the British navy conducted minesweeping operations in the area and found irrefutable evidence that the mines were recent and not left over from World War II. Albania had no navy to speak of and no technical capabilities to have planted the mines, so the suspicions fell on its Communist big brother, Yugoslavia. Karel Kovaćić, a lieutenant commander with the Yugoslav navy who defected to Italy in July 1947, testified that he had seen two Yugoslav mine-sweepers fully loaded with mines leave their base toward Albanian waters shortly before the October 22 explosions and return empty just afterward.

The British government took the position that the Albanian authorities should have known what was happening in such proximity of their shores. A meeting of the UN Security Council discussed a resolution blaming Albania for the British loss of life, which the Soviet ambassador to the UN Andrei Gromyko promptly vetoed. The United Kingdom took the case to the International Court of Justice in The Hague, which on April 9, 1949, found that "Albania was responsible for the explosions and for the resulting damage and loss of human life suffered by the United Kingdom." The court also found that the mine-sweeping operation by the British navy conducted in the aftermath of the explosions had violated Albanian sovereignty.

The court awarded £843,947 (slightly over $2 million at the time, about $20 million today) to the United Kingdom in damages.[33] The Albanian government rejected the verdict and refused to pay. For a long time, it would be the only instance when a party to a case adjudicated by the International Court of Justice had failed to carry out a decision of the court.[34] In retaliation, the British sequestered 1,574 kilograms (almost 3,500 pounds) of gold the Germans had taken with them when they retreated from Albania. The Allies had captured the gold at the end of the war and had deposited it in the Bank of England in the trusteeship of a US-British-French commission pending transfer to the Albanian government. The deadlock between the British demanding liquidation of damages and Albania claiming the return of its gold lasted until the mid-1990s, when the post-Communist Albanian government normalized its relations with the West.[35]

* * *

The newly established Communist regime in Albania considered Greece as a major threat from the very beginning, and not just for ideological reasons. The Greek government maintained that Albania had been a party to the 1940 attack against Greece by the Italians and considered Greece and Albania to be in a state of war. It publicly advertised its aim of detaching from Albania and attaching to Greece a band of land comprising roughly a fifth of the total Albanian territory, which Greeks called Northern Epirus and had historically claimed as theirs. The Hoxha government forcefully rejected any such claims. In his first speech as head of the provisional government in Tirana on November 28, 1944, Hoxha promised defiantly that, "Albania is ready to fight to preserve southern boundaries fronting Greece."[36]

The renewal of hostilities in the Greek Civil War in 1946 exacerbated the tensions. Albania, together with Yugoslavia and Bulgaria, supported the Communist Greek guerrillas by opening up their territories for safe haven and resupply purposes. Regular skirmishes occurred along the border between armed groups from each side as they made incursions on the opposite side against military targets and quite often against the civilian population.

This support helped prolong the conflict to the point where Stalin had to step in. In a meeting with Bulgarian and Yugoslav leaders in Moscow on February 10, 1948, Stalin ordered: "The uprising in Greece has to fold up. . . . They have no prospect of success at all. What do you think, that Great Britain and the United States—the United States, the most powerful country in the world—will permit you to break their lines of communication in the Mediterranean Sea! Nonsense. And we have no navy. The uprising in Greece must be stopped, and as quickly as possible."[37]

For all intents and purposes, the Greek government did not distinguish between the Albanian government and the Albanians. It treated Albanians in Greece, including those who had fled the Communist regime, with a tolerance little above that accorded to enemy aliens during hostilities. Consequently, many Albanians living there felt, with reason, that the Greek government was not so much against the Communist Albanian government as anti-Albanian.[38] US diplomats tried persistently to steer the Greek administration instead to a policy that was unequivocally anti-Communist alone.

The United States had informed the Greeks that it did not support their territorial claims against Albania, which it considered as having "no ethnic, little strategic and less historical basis."[39] The State Department directed its ambassador to Athens and the rest of the diplomatic personnel assigned to Greece to "bring up in informal talks with Greek Foreign Office officials the subject of the Greek official attitude toward Albania, and to reiterate the US position with regard to the Greek pretensions."[40]

* * *

Yugoslavia was the country with which Albania had the best relations in the years after the war. Building on their wartime influence over key Albanian Communist leaders, the Yugoslavs established a firm grip on the postwar Albanian state. In 1946, during a state visit in Moscow, Tito received the green light from Stalin to control the country on behalf of the Communist bloc.[41] Next year, the Soviet Union sent another signal that it saw Albania as a mere Yugoslav dependency. Albania was the only Communist-controlled country that Stalin did not invite into the Communist Information Bureau, or Cominform, an organization he created in 1947 to coordinate policies of the Soviet Union, the emerging East and Central European Communist nations, and the leading West European Communist parties. Yugoslavia represented Albania at Cominform meetings.

A considerable number of Yugoslav advisers and technicians went to Albania under the guise of helping to administer the aid provided by their government, but their role was effectively to build and direct the Albanian state, military, and security apparatus at all levels. At the same time, the Albanian leaders lost no opportunity to extoll the virtues of their Yugoslav friends and allies. Between 1946 and 1947 a series of political, social, economic, and military agreements concluded between the two countries in effect turned Albania into a complete dependency of Yugoslavia. There was a brief power struggle in the ranks of the Communist leaders between the pro-Yugoslav faction, led by Koçi Xoxe, minister of interior, and the pro-Soviet faction led by Nako Spiru, in charge of economic planning. It was resolved in favor of the Yugoslavs when Spiru committed suicide in November 1947, after finding himself isolated and abandoned by Hoxha.

Fully aware of what was happening in Albania, Stalin requested that a Yugoslav delegation go to Moscow to bring into harmony the policies of Yugoslavia and Soviet Union regarding Albania. Milovan Djilas, one of Tito's top lieutenants at the time, traveled to Moscow in January 1948 and met with Stalin and Molotov to discuss the issue. Recounting the meeting in his memoirs, Djilas wrote: "Stalin said: 'We have no special interest in Albania. We agree with Yugoslavia swallowing Albania!' At this, he gathered together the fingers of his right hand and, bringing them to his mouth, he made a motion as if to swallow them. . . . 'Yes, yes. Swallowing! You ought to swallow Albania—the sooner the better.'"[42]

Once they received Stalin's blessing, the Yugoslavs moved swiftly to capitalize on the situation. At a plenum of the Albanian Communist Party's Central Committee in February to March 1948, the Xoxe faction purged the leadership ranks of all those who were not fervently pro-Yugoslav. They expelled the pro-Soviet Mehmet Shehu, an ally of Nako Spiru, from the Central Committee and demoted him from his position as chief of staff of the army. They accelerated measures put in place to incorporate Albania as a seventh republic in the Yugoslav Federation. Hoxha's position became even more precarious when Yugoslavs demanded the deployment of two Yugoslav divisions in Albania under the pretext of defending it in case of an attack from Greece. Hoxha played perhaps the only card he had left by informing the Soviet government of the request and asking for advice on handling the matter. Reports that came out later indicated that at this critical juncture Hoxha also sounded out a certain Western power—most likely France, which was the only Western country with a legation in Tirana at the time—about the possibilities of sanctuary.[43]

* * *

Hoxha's plea for help reached Moscow at a time when the Soviet perspective toward Yugoslavia had shifted dramatically. For several months Moscow had tried to curb the Yugoslavs' independent streak and force them into the vassal position in which all the other Eastern bloc countries had fallen. Stalin's acquiescence to Yugoslavia swallowing Albania had clearly been a gesture of goodwill toward Tito to convince him to accept Soviet domination. When Tito failed to respond, Stalin displayed his fangs. In letters sent to the Yugoslav Communist Party between March and May, Stalin and Molotov accused the Yugoslavs of denigrating the Red Army and Soviet Union and admonished them to correct their mistakes. Facing stubborn opposition from the Yugoslavs, Stalin expelled them from the Cominform on June 28, 1948.

The news caused an immediate about-face in Albania's position toward Yugoslavia. All its leaders, including Xoxe, lined up on the side of the Kremlin denouncing the "Trotskyite" Tito and his followers. They gave Yugoslav advisers in Albania forty-eight hours to leave the country and closed the border between the two countries. They also promptly abrogated all bilateral agreements binding Albania to Yugoslavia and launched a virulent anti-Yugoslav campaign in the media. Over the next several months, Hoxha's followers purged the ranks of the party, military, and government from Yugoslav supporters. In a reversal of fortune, Mehmet Shehu sacked Xoxe and took his place as minister of interior. Not long after that, Xoxe was arrested, convicted in a secret trial in May 1949, and executed. The subsequent anti-Titoist purges in Albania brought the liquidation of fourteen members of the party's thirty-one-person Central Committee and thirty-two of the 109 People's Assembly deputies. Overall, the party expelled about 25 percent of its membership.[44]

The Soviets took the place of the Yugoslavs in Albania, and by the middle of 1949 they had approximately three thousand advisers in the country. Dimitri Chuvakhin, the Soviet minister in Tirana, coordinated their work and was reported to be "the actual boss of the country."[45] A Soviet military mission of about one hundred officers, under the command of Major General N. J. Pavlov,[46] advised the Albanian Army at the corps and division levels; Bulgarian officers provided guidance further down the hierarchy. Soviet technical advisers supported every ministry and oversaw all aspects of the economy. Colonel Nikolai Vassiliev headed the group of advisers in the ministry of interior who trained and supported the police and border guard operations.

Thus, by the middle of 1949, Hoxha and Shehu found themselves with a renewed lease on life. Having fended off the Yugoslav attempts to take over the country, they had established direct lines of support with the Soviets, who began pumping material necessities in the country, including cereals and other food items, as well as farm and industrial equipment. Hoxha and Shehu controlled the country with an iron fist. The relentless pursuit of the anti-Communist elements who had remained in the country after the war had eliminated many and forced most to cross into Greece or Yugoslavia by 1949. There was still some active resistance in the countryside carried out by small bands whose activities were limited to harassing actions against the regime. None of them controlled any substantial area of the country.

* * *

By 1949, virtually the only surviving members of the opposition to the Albanian regime had settled in exile primarily in Italy, Greece, and Egypt, with smaller numbers in Turkey and Syria. Collaboration with the Italians and Germans during the war had tainted many of them to a greater or lesser extent. Although a good number came from the middle and upper classes of Albania's prewar society, all but a few were poverty-stricken, and living on international or local charity and in refugee camps in Greece and Italy. The émigrés gravitated into one of three political groups, two of which, the republican Balli Kombëtar (BK) and monarchist Legaliteti, were reincarnations abroad of the groupings that had existed in Albania during the war.

BK had most of its members in Italy and a scattering in Greece and the Near East. Mithat Frashëri, its founder, continued to lead the BK, which after the war had become firmly republican, anti-Italian, mildly leftist or reformist, and strongly anti-Communist. At the beginning of 1949, Frashëri was in Turkey attempting to form a united front of Albanian refugees that the Western powers would recognize. Abas Ermenji, another BK leader who had been a capable military figure during the war, was in Greece until the end of March 1949, when he moved to Italy under the auspices of the International Relief Organization (IRO). Ermenji led the left-leaning reformist current within the BK. He was educated and had the ear of Frashëri, who was himself an intellectual. Vasil Andoni was BK's Party secretary and Frashëri's principal lieutenant in Italy.

Legaliteti had at the front and center of its agenda King Zog, who had settled in Egypt in spring 1946 at the invitation of King Farouk, the tenth ruler of the Egyptian dynasty founded in 1805 by Muhammad Ali Pasha, an Albanian commander of the Ottoman Empire sent to Egypt to drive out Napoleon's forces. Zog had established close friendly relations with King Farouk and other royals in exile in Egypt, including the Italian and Bulgarian royal families.

Zog actively sought to build up his own prestige among his fellow countrymen in exile by arranging the settlement of prominent displaced Albanians in the Near East. Through his intervention, a number of former Albanian public officials settled in Egypt, including Abas Kupi, the wartime founder and nominal leader of Legaliteti; Musa Juka, minister of interior during Zog's regime; Mehdi Frashëri, formerly chief regent under the Germans; Mustafa Kruja, quisling prime minister until 1943; Xhafer Deva, minister of interior under the Germans; Koço Muka, quisling minster of education under the Germans; and Ali Klissura, the leader of the conservative current of the BK.

William (Bill) MacLean, one of the SOE operators attached to Abas Kupi during the war, painted an unflattering picture of Zog in early 1949:

> Very clever, the shrewdest and most cunning as well as the most capable and unscrupulous of Albanian politicians. He wants to run Albania as his private reserve and will use all means to that end. He has almost no following at all in Albania. His former supporters, the tribal chieftains, have either been liquidated or otherwise rendered powerless by the Communists. Among the younger, more active generation Zog is despised as an anachronistic Turkish pasha. His reputation is low because of the way he ruled the country when he was King, his precipitous flight in 1939, his political and military inactivity during the war, his amoral life abroad since 1939 (he is popularly supposed to maintain a harem) and because of more than 10 years of Fascist and Communist propaganda against him.[47]

In September 1947, Zog had sent emissaries to Washington and London with proposals to work together to overthrow the Communist regime in Albania. He requested official recognition and financial support of his entourage as the Albanian government in exile or, as an alternative, unofficial recognition through an American or British representative attached to the retinue under some sort of cover. He received no encouragement from the Department of State.[48] The British Foreign Office expressed sympathy but did not consider the moment at the time opportune for a move against Hoxha.[49]

Through the same channels, Zog approached the CIA offering the services of his followers for activities in propaganda, sabotage, and the collection of information in Albania and Yugoslavia, including the services of "twelve Albanian officers in Turkey trained as paratroopers which could be dropped into Albania."[50] Office of Special Operations staffers listened but decided not to pursue the matter further. In their assessment, Zog and his supporters offered no real intelligence value, their security was poor, and their ability questionable. They had no sources inside Albania, no facilities to cross the Greek-Albanian border, no knowledge of intelligence methods, and very little experience.[51]

The third grouping of Albanian émigrés, the Blloku Kombëtar Indipendent (BKI), or National Independent Bloc, existed since 1946 and included pro-Italian elements among anti-Communist exiles who had supported and participated in quisling governments during the Italian occupation. The leaders of the BKI were Ismail Vërlaci, a member of the Albanian Fascist Party and son of Albania's prime minister during the Italian occupation, and Gjon Markagjoni, the influential leader of Catholic tribes in the north-central mountains of Albania, courted by the Italians as the Prince of Mirdita. The spiritual and thought leader of the group was Ernest Koliqi, a noted scholar and one of the foremost poets writing in the Albanian language, as well as a leading authority on the language's origins. Influenced by his Catholic religion and long education in Italy, Koliqi had been a strong supporter of Albania's union with Italy and had held the post of Minister of Education during the Italian occupation.

The BKI was conservative and capitalistic in nature, and by virtue of its associations with Italian government and military officials of the war period, had the support of the Italian bureaucracy and intelligence services. Vërlaci was among the very few Albanian émigrés to have brought personal wealth out of Albania, which he used to move around refugee centers in Italy and recruit supporters.

The leaders of the three principal Albanian groups had been unable to find a lasting basis of agreement by themselves. What drew them together was only the hatred against their common enemies: the Communists who ruled their homeland and the Greek government who continued to press its claims on southern Albania. On pretty much everything else, they were continually at odds, divided by issues such as the form of government, economic and social reforms, and their position toward Kosovo, with some but not all advocating for its union with Albania under the boundaries of ethnic Albania that briefly existed during the war. These leaders could not forget that before the Communists came to power they had considered each other fierce political and personal rivals.[52] The clash of personalities among the leaders, in particular Zog, Frashëri, and Vërlaci, was probably the most important obstacle to the unification of the three groups.[53]

CHAPTER 3

Genesis of Operation Fiend

On December 23, 1948, Sotir T. Martini, minister of the Royal Court of Albania in Egypt submitted a letter to Colonel Norman E. Fiske, the US Military Attaché in Cairo, outlining a new proposal by King Zog to collaborate with the Americans in the overthrow of the Communist regime in Albania. Zog felt that an exceptional opportunity existed at the moment to reestablish in Albania a government friendly to the Western powers. According to Zog's letter, the people of Albania were thoroughly disillusioned with the regime and were ready to overthrow it at the earliest opportunity. Tito's difficulties with the Cominform could be exploited to ensure he wouldn't interfere with the action, and a friendly Albania would go far toward resolving the existing troublesome situation in Greece. The first crack in the ring of Soviet satellites would hearten other dominated peoples and be a definite influence against full-scale war.[1]

The letter couldn't have fallen into better hands. Fiske was an exceptionally bright army officer with firsthand experience in that area of the world. At a time when a quarter to a third of the officers in the army had no college education, Fiske had a bachelor's degree from the University of California and a master's degree from the University of Pennsylvania. He had also reached the highest levels of military schooling both in the US and abroad. He was a graduate of the United States Army Command and General Staff College at Fort Leavenworth, Kansas, and of the Italian Military Academy at Tor di

Quinto, Rome. He had been assistant military attaché in Rome in 1935 to 1940 and had spent some time in Albania during the Italo-Greek war in 1940.[2] Fiske understood immediately the importance of Zog's proposal. A few days later, he called on King Zog at his villa in Alexandria for a face-to-face conversation about the ideas Zog had outlined in his letter.

Zog said that he had based his analysis on information from his supporters in Albania, particularly leaders of mountain tribes, with whom he claimed to be in close touch. He felt that he could rally his supporters to supplant the Albanian regime with a relatively small amount of outside aid. Then, Zog went on to explain his plan for accomplishing the task, which was nearly identical to the plan he had devised in 1924 to orchestrate the overthrow of Noli's government and his return to power. Specifically, he proposed to organize an expeditionary force of some five hundred men recruited among Albanians abroad and possibly anti-Soviet Poles, Germans, and Hungarians, together with the requisite arms and equipment, primarily small arms, machine guns, mortars, light tanks, and transport. Zog would make available experienced Albanian officers for detailed planning, organization, training, and execution of the operation. However, he required outside financial and material assistance, and his first preference was to receive that assistance from the US. When Fiske asked for Zog's plans after the overthrow of the Albanian regime, Zog said he was prepared to have the ultimate form of government in Albania decided by popular referendum. "Being a King in the Balkans," he added somewhat ruefully, "is not always a happy career."[3]

On January 11, 1949, Fiske forwarded Martini's letter and a summary of his conversation with Zog to the US Army director of intelligence. Fiske's opinion was that, while the proposal seemed quite optimistic, the venture might succeed if actions from abroad were coordinated with internal preparations. The package eventually made its way onto Wisner's desk on March 21, 1949. That same day, Wisner received a detailed report on the Albanian situation by Burton Yost Berry, a State Department official[4] temporarily assigned to the Office of Policy Coordination, like many other Foreign Service officers who filled the ranks of the OPC in the first few months of its existence, until it had established its organizational structure on the ground.

* * *

Berry had spent his entire twenty years with the Foreign Service in diplomatic posts in the Balkans, Turkey, and Egypt. In 1944 he served as the head of the US diplomatic mission in Bucharest where he met Wisner, who at the time was running the OSS operations in Romania. In his OPC assignment, Berry toured the region in the first few months of 1949, contacting his connections and acquaintances and looking for opportunities Wisner could exploit for his operations.

Visiting Italy, Greece, Egypt, and Turkey, Berry realized that the CIA's regular intelligence gathering and reporting services had missed some important opportunities in Albania. As he got deeper into the investigation of the Albanian situation, he realized the urgency and importance of preparing an Albanian operation.

Because of Tito's split with the Soviet bloc, Albania was left physically isolated from the rest of the Soviet satellites, since it was surrounded by pro-Western Greece and Italy in addition to anti-Kremlin Yugoslavia. Experts in the region saw Enver Hoxha's regime in Tirana as very weak, given the bitter anti-Communist feelings in large regions of the country, especially in the northern and central areas. The trials of Koçi Xoxe and other Communist leaders closely affiliated with Tito and who had conspired with him against Hoxha, had just started in Tirana. Berry expected they would further divide Albania to the point where even a large swath of anti-Stalin and pro-Yugoslav Communists could support a revolt against the government. There were enough anti-Communist Albanians abroad to provide the initial thrust through the Greek border if they received logistics support, money, and munitions from supplies being given to Greece, advice from the American military mission in Greece, and help from Greek National Army troops. Some sources ventured as far as to suggest that "for peanuts the US could get a friendly government in Albania."[5]

The benefits of such a reversal would be significant and sensational. It would be the first open revolt behind the Iron Curtain and would encourage all anti-Communist elements in the Soviet satellite countries. It would knock out Kremlin's sense of security and show the Soviets that the West could match in kind their tactics for supporting guerrillas and subversive activities in their areas of influence.

It would save the situation in Greece by cutting off Albania as one of the remaining two sources of support for the Communist guerrillas; the other source, Bulgaria, would be intimidated into cutting off the flow of men and supplies through their borders for fear of risking a similar fate.

Berry argued that time was of the essence and they must launch the operation in Albania within the next few months in order to take advantage of the summer weather. If the fighting lasted longer than expected, the winter would force a cessation of hostilities, which would provide an opportunity to resupply the resistance forces through Greece and allow a political settlement of the conflict to take place.[6]

In his report of March 21, 1949, Berry recommended a series of actions in Greece and surrounding countries to prepare the groundwork for a successful campaign to replace the government in Albania. They included the victory of the Greek National Army against the remnants of the Communist opposition in the Epirus region; a government in Athens not bristling with hostility toward Albanians; cessation of factional fights among the various Albanian émigré groups and their unity in the fight against the Communist regime; a series of actions aimed at weakening the government in Tirana, primarily through propaganda means and increased infiltrations into the country from the Greek frontiers; and, finally, a clarification by the US policy-making establishment of the desired endgame in Albania, followed by the necessary actions to accomplish it.

Berry cautioned Wisner that the operation's success in Albania would not come easily, in spite of the low esteem in which the Albanians held the Hoxha government. He urged avoiding over-optimism and carefully preparing for success the hard way.

As an astute observer of the Balkans, Berry knew that the British considered the area to be in their sphere of influence and would learn quickly of any moves by the Office of Policy Coordination to organize Albanian refugees. Berry suggested that "the tentative plans be outlined to the British in Washington and that an effort be made to secure their passive cooperation—but no more."[7]

Berry's analysis of the situation and his outline of proposed actions in Albania served as catalysts for the young OPC, which had been formed just months earlier, in September 1948. Now that it had a

concrete target and a reasonable chance of success, its activities became
more focused and goal-oriented. In fact, through the end of 1949 and
beginning of 1950, the Albanian project was the major interest of the
OPC as a whole. Wisner himself and George Kennan, head of the
Policy Planning Staff at the State Department and the OPC's main
customer, regarded the activities against Albania as the most urgent
and sensitive operation being planned by the US at the time.[8]

* * *

After submitting his report to Wisner, Berry set out to unify the
different groups of Albanians in exile to fight the Communist regime.
His initial inclination was to build up the strength of one group to
the point where it could assume leadership of the émigré community,
then, push the other groups to support this lead group until the ouster
of the Communists from Albania, when they could hold a plebiscite
to determine the form of government that the Albanian people themselves desired. The choice of one group over the others meant in reality choosing between the heads of the three principal Albanian parties:
Frashëri, Zog, and Vërlaci.

Frashëri was the least objectionable choice, although given his
character and advanced age of seventy years, Berry considered him
a figurehead rather than an active leader of the day-to-day activities,
a role better suited for one of his subordinates. Frashëri and his close
followers shared the belief that Hoxha government couldn't be overthrown without a serious struggle. The Soviet authorities would resist
strongly any attempt to bring about a revolution in Albania. The Communist controls in the country were so strict that the resistance movement could not germinate inside Albania. In their opinion, the best
guarantee for success was a considerable supply of arms and ammunition in the hands of an expeditionary force of Albanian nationals
prepared and launched from abroad.

Zog reaffirmed ceaselessly that he wished to take an active part
in fighting the Communists in Albania and that he would be willing
to leave to the Albanian people the decision as to whether he should
rule the country again. Nevertheless, he had shown little willingness to
strike an agreement with his former political enemies and make good
on his fine words. In Berry's opinion: "Zog's friendship with King

Farouk, the prestige of his former position, his considerable personal wealth, plus his capacity for intrigue, made Zog, despite of the relatively small number of his followers, a power to be taken into consideration when weighing the sources of influence behind any Albanian revolutionary movement."[9]

Berry and others in the OPC briefly considered involving Vërlaci and his BKI followers but rejected the idea for two reasons. First, the State Department objected to their past involvement with quisling governments. Second, the Office of Special Operations (OSO) was already using Vërlaci and his people for intelligence-gathering purposes in joint operations with Italian Naval Intelligence. Although nominally part of the CIA, the OPC in its early day operated autonomously and considered the OSO more a competing organization than an ally.

* * *

On April 30, 1949, Berry and Robert G. Miner, political attaché in Athens, met with Mithat Frashëri in Piraeus, Greece, aboard the Turkish passenger ship *Istanbul*. Frashëri was en route to Italy from Turkey. After exchanging preliminary remarks regarding the situation in the Balkans and Albania, Berry informed Frashëri in confidence that the United States would look with favor on the formation of a united front of Albanian refugees headed by Frashëri himself. Such a front would include all anti-Communist refugee groups, irrespective of political opinions. Frashëri's Balli Kombëtar would provide the nucleus of the movement but accommodate all other Albanian patriots abroad in opposition to the Hoxha regime.

Berry urged Frashëri to follow the example of refugee leaders from other Soviet-dominated countries, like Bulgaria and Hungary who had achieved some success in creating a degree of unity among their followers and had thereby secured the moral right to be spokesmen of their people. He hoped a united front of Albanian refugees might achieve the same kind of success. Berry told Frashëri that he would convey similar views to Zog and his entourage in the immediate future. He believed that Zog would support a united front under the conditions outlined, given his public declarations during the war of his willingness to let the question of the regime lie dormant pending a plebiscite and his recent private declarations to the same effect.

Frashëri responded that he was entirely in agreement. He would undertake chairmanship of the united front and invite all non-Communist elements to come together, particularly certain personalities from the BKI and other independents. He desired that Zog and his entourage join, but Zog had to declare publicly and unequivocally that he considered his royal prerogatives suspended pending the free plebiscite in liberated Albania.

Concluding the conversation, Berry assured Frashëri that the United States was very interested in the plight of the Albanian people and that the proposed union of the refugee groups was an important first step toward improving their situation. But he repeatedly stressed to Frashëri the confidential nature of the views exchanged during their discussion, which he should not share with others. Frashëri should present the idea of the united front to his supporters as coming from himself and express his hope that the United States might look with favor upon the formation of such a united front of Albanian exiles.[10]

* * *

Encouraged by how quickly they had reached an understanding with Frashëri, Berry and Miner traveled from Athens to Egypt where, on May 5, 1949, they met with Zog at his villa in Alexandria. Queen Geraldine, who was half-American on her mother's side, was present in the meeting and served as an interpreter. Berry gave Zog the same outline he had provided Frashëri regarding the desire of the United States to see a united front of all anti-Communist Albanians abroad that would garner its leaders the moral right to be the spokesmen for their people. He informed Zog of Frashëri's position—that he favored such a united front and would work actively toward its formation—and encouraged Zog to adopt a similar attitude, conveying the American opinion that Mithat Frashëri should be the front's leader and that his group should form the nucleus of the movement.

The United States hoped for Zog's wholehearted support in endorsing the front and encouraging his followers to participate. He could make a significant contribution to the unity of Albanians abroad by stating in a public declaration that he welcomed a united front under the chairmanship of Mithat Frashëri, that the question of the future regime of Albania would be determined in a plebiscite by the free Albanian people, and that in the meantime he was suspending his royal prerogative.

Zog accepted most of what Berry asked for. He declared himself strongly in favor of the formation of the anti-Communist united front, agreed to leave the choice of the future regime to the Albanian people, accepted that Frashëri should be the front's leader, and stated that he would support the movement. He suggested that Frashëri should secure representatives from the Legaliteti and BKI parties and ensure that the committee would have two Muslims, one orthodox, and one Roman Catholic leader in order to represent the religious diversity of the Albanian population. He agreed to help on all of these points and to make a public declaration along the desired lines at the desired time.

With regard to the suspension of his royal prerogatives, however, Zog said that to do so would be unwise as well as disloyal to his pledge to the Albanian people. Such action, he said, would jeopardize the continued recognition of Albanian anti-Communist (royalist) diplomatic missions in Egypt, Turkey, and elsewhere. More fundamentally, he felt it would be equivalent to laying aside the duty that the Albanian National Assembly had placed on him before the Italian fascist occupation, which was to represent the nation abroad until its liberation.[11]

At the meetings with Frashëri and Zog, Berry brought a written statement that represented the American point of view, which he communicated verbally during the meeting. Miner, serving as note taker, summarized and added to this statement the words of the Albanian side. At the end of the meeting, Berry asked his Albanian interlocutor to read the consolidated statement in order to make sure there were no misunderstandings and that it represented accurately all essential points covered in the conversation. Frashëri signed the statement on the same day that the conversation took place. Zog on the other hand played for time and offered to sign the original when he had received a copy for his files.

Berry and Miner returned to Alexandria on June 14, 1949, bringing with them two copies of the minutes of the previous meeting, which Zog signed. Zog also provided a second statement with points to be included in a public declaration that would be released soon after the announcement of the united front. The draft declaration included all

MEMORANDUM OF CONVERSATION WITH KING ZOG I ON MAY 5 1949.

A meeting was held with King Zog I at Alexandria Egypt on May the 5th
1949. It was explained that the United States would look with favor
upon the formation of a united front of all anti Communist Albanians
abroad. It was pointed out that refugees from certain other Soviet-
dominated countries, such as Bulgaria and Hungary, had achieved a degree
of unity that enabled their leaders to be accorded the moral right to
be considered the spokesmaen for their peoples. It is hoped that the
Albanians abroad would be similarly successful.

Kir
favc
tows
simi
in t
foll
make
issu
unde
regi
by t
be c
King
shou
form
Gove
the
Alba

King
unit

Auth

leader of the united front and stated that he would support the movement
He felt that Frasheri should secure as associated a person of the
legitimist party as well as a person of merit from the Independant
party , so that the comitee should have 2 moslems, one orthodox and
one Roman catholic. King Zog stated that he could not declare his royal
prerogatives in suspense as this would be unwise as well as disloyal
to his pledge to the Albanian people. Such action, he said would jeopardize
the continued recognition of Albanian anti Communist / royalist/ diplo
matic missions in Egypt , Turkey and elsewhere. More fundametally, he felt
that such action would be equivalent to laying aside the duty which the
Albanian National Assembly had placed upon him before the italian faciste occupati
his flight. He stated
that the Assembly had upon that occasion charged him to represent the
nation abroad until its liberation. He recommends for the sake of the
movement that Frasheri should visit Egypt , Syria Turkey, Italy Greece
and whereever there were significant groups of Albanian exiles , talk to
them , secure from them written declarations of support, andthus become
recognised as the leader of the united front . King Zog volunteered
to help in the foregoing and to make a public declaration along the desired lines when it was considered useful.
King Zog expressed himself strongly on the importance that Midhat Frasheri
should come to Egypt and receive from His lips the assurance of His help.

the 14th June 1949

confidential

ZOG I ROI DES ALBANAIS

COPY 1 of 1 series

Minutes of meeting between Zog I, King of the Albanians, and Burton Y. Berry, on assignment for the CIA's Office of Policy Coordination, in Alexandria, Egypt, on May 5, 1949 the points that Zog and Berry had discussed and agreed upon in their previous meeting.

Berry and Miner returned to their hotel satisfied that the outcome of their discussions with Zog had been positive, although it had taken them six weeks to get from him what they had received from Frashëri in one afternoon. So they were surprised when Zog sent word the next day that he wanted to see them again. At his seaside villa, they found Zog much more noncommittal than in their previous meetings. After thinking things over, he said, he wanted to qualify the position documented in the statements he had signed just the day before. He now made his declaration of support conditional on three additional points, which were to be included in and considered part of the entire agreement that he had reached with the Americans.

First, given that constitutionally he represented the legitimacy and legality of Albanian power, Zog said he desired to be kept informed and consulted on all the key questions arising before the executive committee of the united Albanian front, through the mediation, if necessary, of competent American authorities. Second, in accordance with the same principles of legitimacy and legality, he took upon himself the responsibility of creating a provisional government completely neutral of any political bias that would organize the plebiscite following the liberation of Albania; this government would operate under the supervision of the Allies, if they considered it useful. Lastly, he said he had sanctioned the choice of Mithat Frashëri as president of the executive committee because of his full confidence in Frashëri's patriotism. However, if Frashëri resigned or was no longer able to function in this capacity for any other reason, Zog requested that he be consulted on the choice of his replacement or on any subsequent changes in the membership of the executive committee.[12] To keep the momentum going, Berry took these points under consideration without delving into their subtleties, which Zog would exploit in the months to come as he attempted to extend his control on the nascent anti-Communist movement.

* * *

While Berry and Minor laid the groundwork in Europe for uniting the Albanian émigré groups, James McCargar in Washington was busy preparing the overall plan for Albania, in collaboration with his boss, Franklin Lindsay. The plan called for three phases of operations. The first phase built upon the Berry's work and culminated with the formation of the Albanian committee. The target date for the announcement of the committee was set July 1, 1949. The committee would include members of Balli Kombëtar and Legaliteti, as well as independents. The leader would be Mithat Frashëri, and it would be headquartered in Paris.

The second phase included propaganda activities to soften up the Albanian regime and the training of a cadre of Albanians for infiltration inside Albania. Propaganda activities started with the announcement of the committee and included broadcasts of Albanian-language programs by Radio Athens, Radio Salonika, and possibly Radio Ankara. The committee would engage in propaganda efforts of its own, including the publication and dissemination inside and outside Albania of a newspaper and pamphlets. Black propaganda operations included fade-ins of Radio Tirana, and the establishment of a transmitter for the committee that would purport to operate from inside Albania. Training activities were set to begin on July 15 in a two step fashion. First, ten Albanians handpicked by Frashëri or his deputies would be trained directly by American instructors. Representatives from this first contingent would then serve as trainers for another forty Albanians selected by a subcommittee of the national committee. These forty trained agents would form the commandos to be infiltrated in Albania. The purpose for the two step approach to training was to hide American direct participation in the operation from the commandos who would eventually participate in it, thus satisfying the plausible deniability requirements of the operation.

The third phase would begin with the infiltration of the forty agents trained during phase two into Albania between August 15 and September 1 using various means, including airdrops, beach landings, and overland border crossings. The objective of the agents was to establish communication, supply lines, and liaisons with existing resistance groups inside Albania and to facilitate their preparations for an uprising against the government, which would be the final step of the operation. The plan assumed that Albanians already in the country would man and lead the uprising, with the support of the forty infiltrated commandos. Supplemental plans were required if it became desirable and feasible to train and equip an Albanian brigade outside the country to support the uprising.

The last step of the operation, open insurgency against the Tirana government, would be taken only if a series of conditions and requirements were met, including: the successful completion of the first two phases of the operation; the Greek national army had established control of its northern borders and had provided clear assurances that it would not move into southern Albania in the event of disturbances in Albania; Tito was still in control in Yugoslavia and his spat with the Cominform continued; and, finally, the National Security Council, the Joint Chiefs of Staff, and the Department of State concurred that the uprising in Albania would not conflict with overall American policy at the time.

During the three phases on the operation, the Office of Policy Coordination and the State Department would follow carefully the Greek attitude toward Albania and make efforts to influence it as necessary. In particular, they would bring strong pressure on the Greek government to cease its public utterances of claims against Albanian territory and to make a statement immediately following the formation of the committee renouncing any territory claims on an Albania with a freely elected democratic government that did not interfere in Greek internal affairs. Throughout the operation, the Office of Special Operations would be required to assist with intelligence gathering on Yugoslav actions inside Albania, Soviet and satellite arms shipments to Albania, and possible methods of interdiction.[13]

Carmel Offie, Wisner's special assistant, presented the plan to several State Department officials, including George Kennan, head of the Policy Planning Staff, Robert P. Joyce, liaison with the OPC, and Llewellyn Thompson, head of the East European branch. They found the plan acceptable provided that the department clear the initiation of each new phase of its implementation. Offie had some personal history with Albania in his background. After the war, he had been nominated as an attaché at the US mission in Tirana, but the Communist authorities denied him an entry visa in 1946, branding him as an "intelligence executive,"[14] although he was just a State Department employee at the time.

McCargar and Wisner presented the plan to the Joint Chiefs of Staff as well. Wisner explained that although the operation would start small, with reconnaissance activities, he hoped these activities would expand in order to reach the ultimate objective, the overthrow of the Hoxha government. The joint chiefs listened quietly. The only question came from the chief of naval operations, Admiral Louis E. Denfeld, who wanted to know about Soviet vessel traffic in Albania. McCargar said that they had identified nine Soviet ships going into Durrësi recently.

McCargar later recounted what happened next: "This admiral looked at me. He didn't say a word but he gave me a look that spoke volumes. I felt like such an ass because he had the whole bloody American Navy at his disposal. He didn't need some pipsqueak from over in the CIA or the State Department to tell him there were nine Soviet ships in Durrazzo during the last four months. I was embarrassed and mortified."[15] The joint chiefs raised no objections and approved the operation but asked Wisner to keep them informed.

On June 22, 1949, the OPC formally approved the Albanian operation and assigned it the code name BGFIEND. For simplicity, the operation will be referred to as Project Fiend or simply Fiend from now on. Fiend's ultimate objective was to overthrow the Hoxha regime in Albania and replace it with a government responsive to and supported by the Albanian people, oriented toward the Western powers and friendly to the United States. The CIA Office of Confidential Funds approved at least $900,000 (approximately $9 million in today's dollars) for the project through the end of June 1950. Of this amount, $130,000 was for personnel expenses, $100,000 for supplies, and $500,000 for equipment in the field. Five thousand gold sovereigns and five thousand gold napoleons were transferred to Rome in care of the OSO Custodian of Funds, to finance aspects of the operation where gold was the only medium of exchange, in particular for agents that would be infiltrated in hostile territory.[16]

* * *

On May 4, 1949, Wisner, Lindsey, McCargar, and Offie discussed and agreed upon the selection of Robert Low as operational chief for the Albanian plan. Low was a journalist by training and had been a *Time* reporter before World War II. When the war broke out, he joined the Office of Strategic Services and was stationed in Cairo. After the Normandy invasion, he was transferred to the First Army headquarters as an intelligence officer with the rank of captain. At the beginning of December 1944, Low was one of the few intelligence officers to have detected and reported the growing concentration of the Sixth Panzer Army commanded by the SS General Sepp Dietrich in the densely forested hills of the Ardennes. His warnings about a German counteroffensive fell on deaf ears, and the Battle of the Bulge, the bloodiest engagement of the American forces in Western Europe during World War II, ensued.[17] After the war, Low left the Army with the rank of colonel and returned to his journalistic life. He moved to Prague to become the East European correspondent for *Time-Life*.[18] Wisner had known Low since his Cairo days and took it upon himself to convince him to join the operation. To ensure there were no issues with Low's employer, Wisner went directly to Henry Luce, the magazine's publisher and editor-in-chief, and asked him "to obtain the services of Low on a basis of a loan for an indeterminate but limited period for a special assignment."[19]

Low received his clearance briefing on June 10, 1949, and immediately departed for Europe to begin his OPC assignment. He told his editor at *Time-Life* that he was on leave to write a book; while performing his duties as part of the Albanian project, Low maintained cover by regularly visiting *Time-Life* offices in Europe and occasionally furnishing special articles for the magazine.[20]

Low's first task was to travel to London, together with McCargar, to discuss joint efforts with British counterparts in arranging operational plans for Fiend. They soon discovered that the British had developed their own plan for an operation in Albania, code name Valuable. Their intention was to recruit a small contingent of agents among Balli Kombëtar members living at that time in refugee camps in Greece and Italy, organize them into four to six infiltration parties and send them during September and October of 1949 to areas in southern Albania where they would make contact with local BK sympathizers and convey them the following message: "We have been dispatched as emissaries of the British, who are willing to supply local bands of guerillas with money and arms if in return those guerillas will carry out attacks on the facilities and communications which the Communist Greeks enjoy in southern Albania."[21]

As evidence of the British good faith and intentions, the agents would bring gold to support their sympathizers in the initial stages and a token supply of arms, which they would carry with them or hide near their landing site. These agents and their sympathizers would engage in preliminary operations of a very limited scale. They would transmit immediately through the wireless transmitters (W/T) all available intelligence regarding Greek Communist activities and the support they received on Albanian territory. After two months, they would exfiltrate in order to report details to the British and receive further instructions and assignments.

The plan's assumption was that the anti-Greek nature of the initial assignment, as well as the supply of gold and arms the agents would convey, would be sufficient incentives for the local BK sympathizers to take action. BK leaders and sympathizers in Albania would ask inevitably about the British intentions concerning Albania. The plan suggested that "this bridge shall be crossed when it is reached,"[22] that is, after the activities in the initial stage had been completed successfully and the BK had grown in strength.

These activities were the fighting reconnaissance stage of the Valuable plan. From the six infiltrated parties, the British expected at best three or four to return, having accomplished some part of their mission. Using the knowledge gathered from these teams, the British would formulate plans for stage two, which consisted of increased infiltration of supplies and sabotage equipment and the direction of guerilla attacks against targets identified from intelligence gathered in stage one. These activities would be expanded gradually in scale and scope to a point where they would effectively supplement the actions of the Greek army against the Communist guerrillas and limit, if not deny, the refuge and facilities that the Greek Communists had enjoyed on Albanian soil up to that point.[23]

Upon his return from London, McCargar briefed Wisner on the British plan. Wisner felt the British had produced the plan in haste and had focused it narrowly on protecting their influence, positions, and ambitions in Greece. However, he saw advantages in coordinating the activities envisioned by their respective plans, especially in light of the fact that the British had thought out more details and had operational assets in Europe available to execute the plan. In conversations between the Office of Policy Coordination, Department of State, British Foreign Office, and Secret Intelligence Services representatives held in Washington on May 20 through 26, 1949, the OPC shared the details of the American plan. The consensus of the meeting was that Fiend was on a larger scale than the British Valuable and subject to wider external political influences and developments that were hard to foresee.[24]

But both parties saw the value of a joint operation, employing the British plan as part of Fiend's initial activities. On the American side, the decision to enter into the joint arrangement with the British was prompted both by policy considerations and by actual circumstances that developed as the OPC began to enter into the active phases of the operation. From the policy perspective, the overall guidance from the Department of State was: "The British Government should be approached, informally at first, with a view to ascertain British thinking in regard to Albania and reaching an early agreement on overall policy and program. Provisions should be made for close cooperation with respect to subsequent action."[25]

Members of the military establishment briefed on Project Fiend also encouraged cooperation with the British out of concern that the British might leverage the current situation in Albania in order to aggrandize British influence in the Balkans, Italy, and Eastern Mediterranean to the detriment of US interests and the general cause of halting Soviet expansion.

In addition to these policy considerations, there were numerous operational reasons in favor of a joint operation. It became clear from information coming in from the field that the British were prepared to proceed with their operation, with or without American consent. Separate British and American operations in Albania would create confusion among the Albanian exiles and would ultimately compromise security. A contest between American and British for control of Albanian personnel and geographical areas in Albania would jeopardize the success of the entire operation, since Albania was not large enough to accommodate the struggles of two major powers for control of its people and territory. Furthermore, the British were not concerned with hiding their support of Albanian resistance and were happy to take full credit for it. Thus, a joint effort would eliminate the strictly British influence and ensure that the British did not reap undeserved benefits from the operation.

There would still be an inevitable amount of jockeying for position between the British and Americans vis-à-vis Albania. To ensure that they could gradually assert American interests, the OPC pushed for the creation of a combined policy office in Washington to handle the broad coordination and control of the joint operation. A combined US-British team posted in Europe would manage the day-to-day activities, under the command of an American officer.[26]

The combined policy office included representatives from the OPC, SIS, Department of State, and Foreign Office. On the American side, Robert Joyce represented the Department of State and James McCargar the OPC. George Jellicoe from the British embassy in Washington represented the Foreign Office. Peter Dwyer, the SIS liaison in Washington, acted as the SIS representative until they found a person with more operational experience.

CHAPTER 4

The National Committee for Free Albania

After the official approval of Project Fiend, the OPC moved swiftly to implement the first phase of the operation, which consisted of forming a national committee or council that would include representatives of major Albanian groups in exile who were relatively untainted by collaboration with the Axis forces during the war. The committee's purpose was to provide cover for the covert activities that the US and UK would conduct jointly in the latter phases of the Albanian operation.

The committee would operate in the United States under the umbrella of the National Committee for Free Europe (NCFE), a private organization launched in New York on June 1, 1949, by a group of American businessmen, lawyers, and philanthropists, including Allen Dulles, who at the time was still in the private sector.[1] The NCFE's publicly announced goal was that of "assisting political and intellectual leaders who fled Communist tyranny in Eastern Europe." In reality, the NCFE was the OPC's cover for conducting coordinated psychological and political warfare against the Soviet bloc with plausible deniability for the United States government in the event that operations created embarrassing fallout.[2]

In July 1949, Low moved to Rome and conducted detailed and complicated negotiations "seated Turkish style in the Borghese Gardens, urging a number of Albanian elders toward agreement."[3] His efforts to announce the creation of the committee in July hit several obstacles and he had to postpone the original schedule.

While everyone accepted without any arguments Frashëri's position as president of the committee, an agreement for the handling of armed actions on behalf of the committee required considerable discussions. Abas Kupi, the leader of the monarchist Legaliteti party, felt that his qualifications and experience positioned him best to be in charge of military actions. Frashëri and Abas Ermenji, one of his most vocal lieutenants, advocated for the president of the committee to oversee all military questions.

As a compromise, all parties agreed to create a three-man military junta that would report to the executive committee and would be composed of Kupi, representing Legaliteti's Zog followers; Ermenji, representing Balli Kombëtar; and Said Kryeziu, representing nationalist leaders from northern Albania who were not affiliated with any of the three main Albanian political groups. They divided the country in three areas of responsibility, with a member of the junta assigned the lead for actions in each region. Ermenji and the BK were responsible for the south; Kupi and Legaliteti were responsible for the central part; Kryeziu and his followers were responsible for the northern part of the country.[4]

Another sticky issue became the involvement of Ismail Vërlaci and Gjon Markagjoni in the committee. The State Department had decided that their party, Blloku Kombëtar Indipendent, would not be included in the committee, given its leaders' history as collaborators during the war. However, they left open the possibility of including figureheads like Vërlaci and Markagjoni as individuals and not as representatives of their party. When Low broached the subject with other Albanian leaders, he encountered strong resistance from the BK. Abas Ermenji flatly refused to join the committee if the BKI, Vërlaci, or Markagjoni were included because they were "too tainted as traitors and collaborators to put in the Committee."[5] In the end, Low decided to leave them out.

Low developed particularly close ties with Abas Kupi, whom he sought to use as an intermediary to attract other Albanians in the committee. Recognizing the value that the chieftain placed on weapons,

Low asked McCargar to procure and mail via diplomatic pouch a sil-ver-handled Colt pistol, which he gave to Kupi as a sign of friend-ship. Low believed that developing the relationship with Kupi and promoting him in a position of importance in the committee would put pressure on Zog, who at the last meeting with Berry and Miner in Alexandria in mid-June 1949 had placed conditions for openly sup-porting the committee aiming to put him in control of the movement.

When Zog heard that Kupi was working with the Americans, he called him to Cairo and berated him for not putting Zog's interest in the forefront of the committee. Kupi stormed out, returned to Rome, and gave Low indications that he was prepared to sever his ties with Zog if the Americans would back him.[6] Low raised the issue with the headquarters and asked for advice. Offie provided guidance in a cable sent on July 6, 1949:

> We cannot expect to get very far by basing our action on a dou-ble-cross; Albanians are much more skilled at that than we are and they will certainly double-cross us first of all and most of all. It is of course possible that Abas Kupi is fooling us just as much as he fools Zog. He may be phoning Zog about our efforts to win him away, as Italian sleuths listen. The point here is that we should not base our action on a double-cross.[7]

Thus, Low worked to keep Kupi engaged as a representative of Legaliteti in the committee even though Zog himself did not come out to support it openly. To Low's aid in this task came Bill MacLean and Julian Amery, who had spent more than a year in Albania during the war as British liaison officers to Kupi's staff. After the war, MacLean had moved into politics—he ran as a Conservative candidate for the parliament and lost in the 1948 elections. Amery was an active-duty officer in the British army. In 1948 he published *Sons of the Eagle*, the account of his experience in Albania during the war, which became one of the rare sources of information on Albania and the émigré leaders for anyone interested in Albanian affairs at the time. At the request of the SIS, MacLean and Amery had played in the first half of 1949 the same role that Berry and Miner had played for OPC, traveling throughout Greece, Italy, and Egypt and meeting with Albanian leaders in exile on behalf of the British intelligence service.[8]

On July 14, Low, Amery, and MacLean met with Zog in Alexandria, with Geraldine serving as his interpreter. They informed him on the pending announcement of the committee under the leadership of Mithat Frashëri; Abas Kupi would serve as the leader of the military junta within the committee. Zog became very agitated and put up a show of indignation that the committee was taking the shape of a government in exile. Angrily, he said: "I left the country with the authority of the National Assembly and it is my duty to defend Albania. I cannot transfer this responsibility to anyone else other than my heir."[9]

To calm Zog's mood, Amery suggested they break for lunch. When the conversation resumed afterward, Amery explained patiently what Zog and Berry had agreed to in earlier meetings, namely that the committee was not a government in exile and supporting it did not mean that Zog was giving up his royal prerogatives. Amery also reiterated the joint British and American position that a plebiscite would decide the form of government in Albania after the liberation of the country. Low would later say about Amery: "He was like Talleyrand. I've never seen such diplomacy in my life."[10] Zog ended the meeting by promising not to work against the committee even though he could not openly support it at the moment. In a telephone conference with Washington ten days later, Low expressed his fear that Zog would walk away from his agreements with Berry, thus leaving the committee composed only of BK elements and a few independent members, with Zogist and BKI groups in opposition.[11]

Zog reiterated his wait-and-see approach in a letter handed to Colonel Fiske, the American military attaché in Cairo, on July 26. Zog wrote that the concept of the committee as presented to him by Low, Amery, and MacLean was in complete contradiction in form and in substance with the agreement that Zog and Berry had reached in May. Instead of representing national unity through the participation of all political parties outside the country, the proposed committee excluded significant émigré political groups and personalities.

Zog left out the fact that the excluded parties and individuals were former collaborators and chose to emphasize that the solidarity of all Albanians in exile was the most important factor to winning the struggle for liberation. Therefore, Zog wrote, he didn't consider it advisable to declare himself publicly in favor of the committee for the moment, but this shouldn't be taken as a sign of disapproval or opposition. He would continue to support any US action in favor of Albania and was ready to offer the moral and material support he had promised in his signed declarations to Berry.[12]

* * *

In early 1949, the Greek government was poised to end decisively the conflict with the Greek Communist guerrillas that had raged since 1946. General Papagos assumed command of the Greek National Army (GNA) and, with the support of American and British military missions in Greece, built up its strength to almost two hundred thousand men against the guerrillas, who counted slightly over thirty thousand fighters in their ranks. Within the first three months of taking command, Papagos conducted successful campaigns against the insurgents in Florina and Peloponnese, forcing them to rely on hit-and-run actions and retreat in the mountainous areas along the Albanian and Yugoslav borders.[13]

As the OPC was working to launch the Albanian committee, it began receiving reports about a rapidly mounting feeling in the Greek general staff, fueled by the fiercely nationalist Greek media, that when the GNA successfully advanced to the Albanian border, it should continue its pursuit of the guerrillas across the frontier in order to capture and annihilate them. On July 21, Wisner raised the alarm about potential dangers of a GNA incursion across the Albanian border. He sent a memo to Robert Joyce at the State Department's Policy Planning Staff stating that such actions would be very unfortunate from the point of view of the OPC's Albanian plan.

The invasion of Albanian territory by the US-supported Greek army, Wisner wrote, would rally popular support for the Hoxha regime, particularly in view of Albanians' long standing fears about Greek claims in Northern Epirus. Such military actions would also lend credence and support to both Soviet and Albanian Communist propaganda themes that US imperialism is threatening the "people's democracies" in the Balkans, particularly Albania. The greatest danger, however, was that the incursion might coincide with the last phase

of the Albanian plan, the open insurgency against the Tirana government. In that case, the public would link the two events and place the
onus for both operations on the US. This, Wisner warned, would give
Kremlin a pretext for direct military intervention into the situation.

Wisner urged that the pursuit of guerrilla fighters must not be policy, either official or unofficial, of the Greek government or its army
and asked the State Department and the US military mission in Greece
to exercise strong pressure on the Greek government to prevent this.[14]
On the same day, Wisner sent a cable to Berry in Athens asking him
to communicate these points to General James A. Van Fleet, the commander of the US military mission in Greece. Berry met with Van
Fleet on July 25, and obtained his commitment to work with General
Papagos to ensure that the GNA would not cross the Albanian frontier
on a large scale during the upcoming operations.[15]

At the same time, Berry and Miner worked with their network of
civilian Greek government officials to convey similar points. They met
with the Greek vice minister for foreign affairs, Panayiotis Pipinelis, on
July 26 to discuss concerns with editorials appearing in the Greek press
and radio broadcasts urging the GNA to conduct military operations in
Albania. Pipinelis provided assurances and stated categorically that the
Greek army would undertake no military adventures in Albania. However, Greece hoped and expected that the Western allies would take
measures to prevent Albania from continuing to serve as a refuge and
base for guerrilla activity against Greece.

Berry then informed Pipinelis that a group of prominent Albanian
exiles would soon announce the formation of a committee to work for
the liberation of their country from the Communist regime. Pipinelis
recognized this as a very important step that all the Balkan peoples
would consider as the first move in a campaign to roll back the Iron
Curtain. He urged that the committee not come under the domination
of either King Zog or the Italians. The former he characterized as the
most unreliable Albanian he had to deal with during his prewar mission in Albania. The ex-king had almost no influence in the country,
he felt, but he was a force to be reckoned with because of his financial
resources, political acumen, and ruthlessness. The Italians had already
begun to renew their efforts in Albania and were working through
the Independent Bloc, a group of former collaborationists headed by

Vërlaci. He urged the exclusion of all collaborationists from any position on the committee, especially any persons who had cooperated with the Italians.

Berry worked with Pipinelis to draft a brief statement that the Greek prime minster, Alexandros Diomedes, would issue soon after the announcement of the committee, calling it a source of hope for the improvement of Greece's relations with Albania. At the beginning of August, they took the statement to the prime minister, who approved it without altering a word.[16]

*　*　*

Mithat Frashëri announced the formation of the National Committee for Free Albania at a press conference in Paris on August 26, 1949. Frashëri issued the first proclamation of the committee describing its aims and responsibilities as follows:

A Committee for Free Albania is created to represent all those Albanians who wish to establish a government representative of the fundamental human rights in their country. The committee includes representatives of Albanian leaders in the social and political domain and will have its seat in New York. This committee is composed of two bodies. The Executive Committee includes:

Mithat Frashëri, Balli Kombëtar, Chairman
Abas Kupi, Legaliteti
Said Kryeziu, Independent
Zef Pali, Balli Kombëtar
Nuçi Kotta, Legaliteti

A General Committee that will assist the Executive Committee includes:

Halil Maçi, Balli Kombëtar
Abas Ermenji, Balli Kombëtar
Vasil Andoni, Balli Kombëtar
Gaqo Gogo, Legaliteti
Gani Tafili, Legaliteti
Asllan Zeineli, Legaliteti

Ihsan Toptani, Independent
Muharrem Bajraktari, Independent
Hysni Mulleti, Independent
Ekrem Telhai, Independent

The committee will pursue the following goals:

a) Guide and encourage our courageous people in their resistance against the cruel Communist tyranny and organize the Albanians abroad to aid effectively this resistance. Our people in Albania must know that the opposition to the Communist oppression is universal and that the power of the free and parliamentary nations is growing rapidly.

b) All activities of the committee aim at the restoration of the full independence, sovereignty and territorial integrity of the Albanian nation.

c) The committee for Free Albania, cognizant of the great responsibility it has undertaken, requests the assistance of all the free peoples and free and democratic countries.[17]

The news of committee's formation and supporting commentary were carried by the BBC (in their English- and Albanian-language programs) and by Voice of America in all broadcasts to Europe and the Near East. The Associated Press reported the pledge of the committee to the "complete restoration of independence, sovereignty and territorial integrity of the Albanian nation."[18] Radio Tirana reacted vigorously to the announcement with denunciations of the committee members as "fascists, collaborators and war criminals."[19] After the announcement, a selected group of NCFA leaders embarked on a visit to London and the United States.

* * *

In advance of the announcement of the NCFA, Wisner had drafted a dispatch that the State Department sent to diplomatic missions in key countries in Europe and the Balkans, with guidance on what they should and should not say concerning Albanian developments. The official line was to express the US government's satisfaction with formation of such an émigré Albanian committee but to point out that it did not regard the committee as a government-in-exile. It hoped that the committee might prove useful as a rallying point in event of collapse of the Hoxha regime. Wisner asked the diplomats to be careful to avoid any discussion beyond these lines, which might imply that the United States was more involved in the NCFA. For information only, he shared that the United States would give considerable moral support to the committee in the hope that these Albanians would be able to accomplish some constructive results.[20]

On August 29, the Greek prime minister made public his statement regarding the formation of the Albanian committee that Berry and Pipinelis had prepared for him. It was the culmination of a number of official and semi-official statements by the Greek government in favor of the committee.

> The Greek Government has taken cognizance of the setting up of a Committee for Free Albania, aiming at the establishment of representative government in that country.
>
> We are not surprised at these endeavors to accord liberty to the Albanian people, who are a proud people that have struggled for centuries to preserve their independence.
>
> The long history of our two neighboring countries has proved that an understanding with the Albanian people is perfectly possible.
>
> Having drawn from our history and from the present situation in the Balkans valuable lessons, we shall always be ready to seek the friendliest possible development of our relations with the Albanian people.
>
> If a regime truly representative of the Albanian people is brought into being, we shall be ready to cooperate with it earnestly and with the friendliest feelings. Our claims and differences would not be an obstacle. We will press any claims only by peaceful means and within the framework of the United Nations.[21]

McCargar wanted the members of the NCFA Executive Committee to issue a public statement expressing their gratitude for the statements of the Greek government, and welcoming the Greek prime minister's statement that Greece would press any claims against Albania only by peaceful means and within the framework of the United Nations.[22] He cabled the request to Joe Bryan, the OPC psychological warfare chief who was accompanying the NCFA leaders on their visit to London and assisting them with press releases for their public launching.[23] There is no record that Bryan was successful in convincing the NCFA leaders to issue such a press statement; rather, Bryan found ongoing arguments among the Albanians so acrimonious that he considered the trip wasted.[24]

The executive committee arrived in London on September 4 and stayed at the Berkeley Hotel. They visited the studios of the BBC World Service, where Mithat Frashëri recorded a fifteen-minute broadcast to Albania that went on the air at 4:00 p.m., Albanian time. Very few heard the message in the country, because the authorities in Albania did not switch the electricity on until six.[25]

* * *

On September 14, 1949, the NCFA Executive Committee members arrived in New York after a last-minute scramble by the US consulate in London to issue them visas. Only Mithat Frashëri and Abas Kupi carried valid passports issued by the Albanian royal legation in Cairo; Said Kryeziu and Zef Pali had Italian emergency identity certificates; Nuçi Kotta and Petrit Kupi had refugee passports. Petrit Kupi was Abas Kupi's son who served as his father's translator. He spoke quite good French having studied at a young age in the French lyceum at Korça, where, by a strange irony, Enver Hoxha had been his teacher.[26]

An operations officer received them at the airport, arranged for transportation in the city, and helped them settle in the hotel. Robert Low met them in the afternoon and gave a dinner for them that evening, which also included Harry T. Fultz and Reuben H. Markham. The OPC had asked Fultz to serve as a guide to the committee for the duration of the trip in the United States. Markham, the Balkans and Central European correspondent for the *Christian Science Monitor*, assisted with the interface between the committee and the National Committee for Free Europe. At the end of the dinner, Low gave each committee member five hundred dollars to cover any incidental expenses during their stay in the US.

The Americans wanted to impress the committee by assigning Fultz as an unofficial guide, certain that they would spread the word in the Albanian community of the great support they had received in the United States. Fultz enjoyed a special status among Albanians, due to his long history of involvement with Albania and Albanian affairs. He was the first director of the American Vocational School set up by the American Red Cross in Tirana during 1921 to 1933. Fultz had been forced to leave Albania in 1933 when Zog closed or nationalized all foreign and religious educational institutions that were, in the opinion of his minister of education, Mirash Ivanaj, sources of foreign political agitation and espionage. Subsequently, he became adviser on Balkan problems to the Department of State.[27] During World War II, he coordinated the Office of Strategic Services Albanian operations as head of the Albanian desk in Bari. After the war, he was second-in-command in the American mission sent to Albania in early 1945 and until its withdrawal in November 1946.

Fultz agreed to act as an escort to the committee but insisted on staying in the background and avoiding any publicity linking his name to it. He feared that if the government in Albania learned that he was associated in any way with the committee, they would clamp down on any persons who were American-educated, and particularly on his former students.[28]

Fultz took the members of the executive committee around New York and to Washington, covered their expenses for the trip out of OPC funds, and in general "played nursemaid for them during their stay in the US."[29] They attended meetings with officials in the Committee for Free Europe and the Department of State and exchanged views in multiple instances with representatives of the Albanian American community in the US. At the end of September, Frashëri and Kotta returned to New York City to establish the committee's headquarters; the other members of the delegation returned to Italy. Fultz observed the Albanian leaders closely during the visit and compiled a detailed report for Wisner and the Office of Special Operations that included his impressions about them and a detailed accounting of their interactions.[30]

* * *

In the early morning of October 3, Mithat Frashëri was found dead in his room at the Winthrop Hotel, 351 Lexington Avenue in New York,[31] where he had taken up residence since his arrival in the United States three weeks earlier with the other members of the NCFA Executive Committee. A medical doctor declared the cause of death a heart attack brought upon the seventy-year-old Frashëri by the hardships and the fatigue of the past few years. However, eyewitnesses who had met with Frashëri during his visit to the United States described him as a vivacious and energetic man.

While he may have simply succumbed to fatigue, there exists a possibility that Frashëri was poisoned by or at the behest of the Albanian secret police, the Drejtoria e Sigurimit të Shtetit (Directorate of State Security) or Sigurimi, as it was most commonly known. The Sigurimi had a direct interest in eliminating Frashëri, but at the time they most likely did not have the means and resources for a sophisticated hit such as this one in the heart of New York City. It isn't far-fetched to hypothesize that they requested and received assistance from their Soviet allies, who had carried out similar actions against other Communist opponents.

Frashëri's death brought to light a rift that had simmered for a while within the Balli Kombëtar, the organization he had founded and led since 1942. On one side were the conservative members led by Ali Klissura and Nuredin Vlora; on the other side were liberal members headed by Frashëri himself and including Hasan Dosti, Abas Ermenji, Vasil Andoni, Halil Maçi, and Zef Pali. Frashëri's age, wisdom, and stature had contributed to both sides maintaining an appearance of unity, which broke down on his death. Dosti, who had the majority of support among the BK rank and file, moved to claim the position of leader of the party and by implication, assume the position of president of the NCFA.

Dosti's selection as president of the NCFA encountered the strong resistance of Abas Kupi, a political and personal opponent of both the Balli Kombëtar and of Dosti himself. Kupi felt the post ought to go to him as the most senior member with highest standing in the executive committee. Zog weighed in from Egypt, strongly opposing the nomination of another member of BK as president. That would suggest that the BK ran everything, he said at a meeting on November 1 with American and British representatives. Once again, Zog advocated broadening of the executive committee to include Gjon Markagjoni and Ismail Vërlaci.[32]

The Joint Policy Committee, which provided overall guidance and coordinated the activities on Project Fiend, met in Washington on November 3 to discuss the issue and to prepare a set of directives for Low in Rome. In attendance were only the American members, including Robert Joyce of the State Department's Policy Planning Staff and liaison to the OPC, McCargar, and Kermit (Kim) Roosevelt, one of Wisner's key aides. They agreed that as a matter of principle the presidency of the NCFA would go to Balli Kombëtar, which was the only party in exile with a sizable following in Albania. "BK has the chairmanship as a right," said Roosevelt. Joyce added that they should not allow Kupi to think any other solution existed than a BK chairman. McCargar suggested they might have to cut Kupi out of the operation if he resisted, but everyone agreed that they ought to avoid splitting the committee. They directed Low to assess Kupi's objection to Dosti and, using a conciliatory tone, advise Kupi to accept Dosti if possible. If Kupi remained entrenched in his objections, then they should consider another BK member, in which case Low should work with Dosti and convince him to accept the alternative.[33]

On Saturday morning, November 12, George Jellicoe, third secretary of the British embassy in Washington and representative of the Foreign Office in the Joint Policy Committee, called Joyce for an urgent appointment to discuss Operation Fiend. Carmel Offie, Wisner's special assistant, Joyce, and Jellicoe met at noon. As an icebreaker, Jellicoe began the meeting with a brief exchange of views on the situation in Yugoslavia and the ongoing spat between Tito and the Cominform. Then Jellicoe quickly moved to the real reason why he had asked for the meeting, the question of the successor to Mithat Frashëri as head of the NCFA. He said that the British did not relish the prospect of Hasan Dosti as chairman of the committee and strongly favored the election of Abas Kupi.

Offie explained at length the official American view in the matter. He called the experience trying to create the committee earlier in 1949 as "not particularly inspiring or pleasant." When Frashëri died, the OPC had decided not to get involved in a "head-beating, gold-piece haggling, character assassination role" in connection with the election of Frashëri's successor. They had decided that the Albanians themselves should select their candidate without outside interference. Offie said he understood the British relationship and position vis-à-vis Abas Kupi and would have no objection to Kupi as the head of the Albanian committee, reiterating the US intention not to interfere in any way with negotiations. Offie noted that if the Albanians weren't able to agree on a chairman, then it might be appropriate to reconsider the position and agree to reenter the picture in an advisory role. Jellicoe stated he thought the American position was reasonable and that he would inform London.[34]

As the meeting broke up, Offie told Jellicoe that he didn't consider it necessary or desirable to antagonize a lot of people or stir up a battle over the matter. It was a subtle but clear message to the British to stop boosting their favorite candidate, Abas Kupi, for the presidency of the NCFA. Coupled with the firm guidance sent to Low in Rome to insist on the election of a BK leader, preferably Dosti, the American insistence seemed to have broken the impasse.

On November 16, Hasan Dosti proposed to Kupi that the executive committee should have two presidents, one for political affairs and one for military affairs. When the committee discussed political affairs, Dosti would be the president, and when it discussed military affairs, it would be under the presidency of Kupi. On November 17, the full executive committee met with Dosti present. Kupi put forward Dosti's suggestion but without specifically naming himself as military president. Pali, the BK representative, didn't turn down the proposal but requested a postponement of the meeting in order to discuss the proposal with the leadership of the BK party.

At that meeting, Ermenji strongly opposed the proposal because it gave Kupi too great a control on upcoming operations in Albania. When the meeting reconvened the next day, Pali announced to Kupi that BK had formally abandoned the principle that their party should hold the executive committee presidency. He put forward Dosti as the BK member on the committee in Frashëri's slot and requested that the committee proceed at that point to elect its own president. This concession surprised Kupi but at once he announced that he was willing to vote for Dosti provided BK agreed to his appointment as chief of staff for military affairs. Pali maintained that the committee's first job was to elect the president, and that they were not willing to discuss military affairs until they had resolved that issue. The committee adjourned and reconvened again on November 19. The announcement of Dosti as president of the executive committee of the NCFA came on Sunday, November 20, 1949.[35]

Ultimately, the driving force behind Dosti's selection seems to have been Carmel Offie. Although he represented to the British that the Albanians should decide on the next chairman of the NCFA, Offie pushed strongly in favor of Dosti. McCargar recalled in 1985 that Offie was absolutely insistent that Dosti be Frashëri's successor. McCargar's objections that Dosti had been minister of justice under the Italian occupation were brushed aside. "Over my dead body they made Hasan Dosti president of the Committee," McCargar said. "I didn't get anywhere. I lost the battle."[36]

The records available today do not show McCargar voicing any opposition to Dosti's selection at the time. His comments in 1985 may be an effort to distance himself from reports that had begun circulating in the press that the CIA in its early days had not shown any qualms about drafting former Axis collaborators in its operations against the Iron Curtain.[37] They had cited Hasan Dosti's choice as head of the NCFA as an example of such unscrupulous attitude.

Whatever the larger truth may be, using Dosti to support this claim shows a shallow understanding of facts and, worse, perpetuates character assassination campaigns that the Albanian Communists waged relentlessly against their exiled opponents over the years. Although Dosti held judicial posts under the Italian and German occupation, including serving for three months as minister of justice in 1942, he did so as part of Balli Kombëtar's strategy to infiltrate the government structures and organize the resistance from within.

After September 1944, when BK broke off all ties and moved to open action against the Germans, Dosti suffered the Wehrmacht wrath as much as anyone else did. German troops raided and set on fire the house where his family was staying. His brother and his wife were summarily shot, and his five children, between eight and sixteen years old, remained orphans and had to fend for themselves. The youngest of the children, an eight-year-old girl, was wounded by the same bullet that killed her mother, when it penetrated the wall behind which she was hiding.

Over the years, Dosti had established himself as a bridge builder among the different factions within the Albanian groups, which is what the NCFA badly needed at the time. Indeed, he had been instrumental in forging the short-lived Mukaj agreement of 1943 between the Communist-led LNÇ and the nationalist Balli Kombëtar. During the years of his exile in Italy, he had worked steadily to mitigate the traditional anti-Italian sentiment of the Balli Kombëtar. Dosti had gone to New York at the beginning of 1949 as a representative of Balli Kombëtar, charged, as one of his fellow émigrés put it, with the thankless task of "proselytizing among the notoriously pro-Communist Albanian colony in the United States."[38] Thus, the American backing of Dosti as the new head of the NCFA made a lot of sense given his education, background, and leadership style.

CHAPTER 5

Philby in Washington

As representatives of the Office of Policy Coordination and the Secret Intelligence Services on the Policy Coordination Group, James McCargar and Peter Dwyer met frequently during the summer of 1949 in order to harmonize activities between Fiend and Valuable. Frank Wisner became concerned that Dwyer's frequent movements in and out of the Lincoln Building near the Washington Reflecting Pool, where the OPC was located, exposed not only OPC but also OSO personnel to the British Secret Service and left them vulnerable to penetration efforts on its part. On September 21, he asked that trips of the British liaison officer to the OPC's offices be restricted to the absolute minimum. He requested his staff to meet with him outside the building until they could find separate quarters for the Policy Coordination Group that would supervise the Fiend-Valuable operation.[1]

The OPC found suitable quarters for conferences with the British in the Pentagon, room 2 C 869, in the area of the Munitions Board, near the Joint Chiefs of Staff. The cover for the room was "Liaison Section A" for State Department. At least one secretary remained on the premises during regular business hours, with instructions to direct any queries regarding the occupants or nature of their work there to Robert Joyce, the State Department representative in the Policy Coordination Group.[2]

The premises were set up in time to receive the new SIS liaison officer, Harold Adrian Russell "Kim" Philby, who arrived in Washington on October 10 to take over the post of first secretary at the British embassy. Philby's SIS assignment was to be the liaison with all the US intelligence agencies. London's guidance had been to move the focus of the US-British intelligence relations away from the FBI and toward the CIA. Within the CIA, Philby was most actively involved with the the OPC, whereas with regards to the OSO he focused primarily on "finding out what they were up to."[3]

Philby was very successful in establishing warm relations with everyone who mattered in the intelligence establishment. He found fertile ground for friendships among CIA officers, most of them OSS veterans who had worked closely with their British intelligence counterparts during the war, and had high regard for their skills and capabilities. Philby personally enjoyed very high repute for "having been the ringleader of a sort of revolt of younger officers in MI-6, who then showed his mettle by consigning to oblivion the man who had given him his chance in that organization."[4] Leveraging the superior British worldwide communication network, Philby was often able to provide information to his American counterparts well in advance of that information being available through their "often sparse, slow, and erratic"[5] communication channels.

Philby opened doors in Washington with his "undeniable charm" and the approachable down-to-earth character he portrayed. McCargar remembered him as follows: "Kim, when I knew him, was devoid of pretension. He was witty, courteous, and not lacking in engaging warmth. His smile, suggestive of complicity in a private joke, conveyed an unspoken understanding of the underlying ironies of our work. He was capable. Behind the modest, slightly rumpled exterior, there was no mistaking a quick mind and tenacious will."[6]

Philby also won friends over by welcoming them in his Washington, DC, house on 5228 Nebraska Avenue, where he and his wife, Aileen, threw parties that ". . . were very wet indeed; in their farther reaches, they were sometimes even uproarious. Luxury, chez Philby, was a full martini pitcher and several bottles of whiskey. It mattered not a whit who served them, or from what one drank."[7]

Philby would later reveal that the true reason behind the atmosphere of trust, warmth, and friendliness he created around him was so he could get his fingers into as many intelligence officers as possible.

"That, after all, was my aim in life,"[8] he wrote. Under the appearance of the brilliant SIS officer, who many expected would rise in the ranks of MI-6 to lead the service one day, hid a mole who had been an officer of the Soviet intelligence services for fifteen years by the time he arrived in Washington.

Born in India in 1912, Philby was the son of a high-ranking British official, who nicknamed him Kim after a spy character in a Rudyard Kipling story.[9] During his studies at the University of Cambridge in 1929 to 1933, he attracted the attention of Soviet intelligence spotters because of his socialist-leaning ideas and sympathy for the Soviet Union. In 1934, the Soviet intelligence recruited him and at least four other fellow students—Guy Burgess, Donald MacLean, Anthony Blunt, and John Cairncross—in what the public would later know as the Cambridge Five spy ring. The Soviets assigned the following codenames for their agents: Stanley to Philby, Hicks to Burgess, Homer or Gomer to MacLean, Johnson to Blunt, and Liszt to Cairncross.[10]

On orders from his Soviet handlers, Philby went to Spain to cover the Civil War as a reporter for the *London Times* embedded with General Franco's forces. Posing as a Fascist and receiving the Red Cross for Military Merit from Franco himself, Philby was able to build up solid rightwing credentials and disguise his affiliation with socialist activities during the college years. At the same time, he used the access granted to him by Franco to collect information about German and Italian weapons in Spain and pass it on to the Soviets.[11]

Upon returning to England, Philby joined the Secret Intelligence Service in the summer of 1940, without any inquiry into his past other than a routine check against MI-5 records that "came back with the laconic statement: Nothing Recorded Against."[12] His first direct supervisor at the SIS was Guy Burgess, his coconspirator. During the war, Philby's SIS responsibilities grew steadily to include running British intelligence in Spain, Portugal, North Africa, and Italy. Throughout the war, he provided important information to his Soviet contacts, which contributed to important strategic decisions Red Army generals made in key battles against the Germans. Philby's contributions to the Soviet war effort against the Germans remain the most significant achievements of his spying career.

In 1944, Philby assumed charge of a newly created section at the SIS headquarters in London designed to combat against Communism and the Soviet Union. In this capacity, he had access to all the plans of British intelligence against the Soviet Union, which he passed on to the Soviets. In 1946, he took a field assignment and became the SIS chief of station in Turkey under the cover of first secretary at the British embassy there.[13]

He held this post until August 1949, when he was offered the position of SIS liaison with all the US intelligence agencies in Washington. Realizing that this was an excellent opportunity for his spying career, Philby accepted the position immediately, without even consulting his Soviet intelligence handlers. He traveled to London for four weeks of briefings and then booked passage to New York on board of S.S. *Caronia*.

CHAPTER 6

First Infiltrations of 1949

The successful launch of the National Committee for Free Albania marked the completion of phase one of the Valuable Fiend operation. Next, the attention shifted to the execution of phase two activities, consisting initially of running sorties inside the country for reconnaissance purposes and to establish contacts with resistance leaders there. While the Americans had taken the lead on the execution of phase one, the British were in a better position to carry out the initial infiltrations, mostly because they had been planning for them since the spring of 1949 as part of their Valuable plan.

Another reason was that the British could count on the World War II experience of their SOE operators, who had actively roamed the country and engaged in warfare, whereas the OSS experience in Albania had been intelligence collection and reporting. According to McCargar, "The expertise was 99 percent British. They had so many people who had been there during the war, most of them young and intelligent. We only had American citizens of Albanian origin, none of them specialists in what we were trying to achieve."[1]

Finally, a more practical reason for the British taking the lead initially was that the Americans did not control any territory in the Mediterranean suitable as the base of operations, whereas the British had facilities available in Malta and Cyprus. As Wisner confided to Philby at the time, the British could always be counted on to have an island within easy reach of any place Americans wanted to subvert.[2]

The British put in charge of the operation David Smiley, a veteran of SOE operations in Albania who would be responsible for training the agents and the day-to-day conduct of the operations. In June 1949 Abas Ermenji and Vasil Andoni went to the International Relief Organization (IRO) camp in Bari, Italy, where they selected thirty Albanians to participate in the training program. In order to disguise the itinerary of the trainees, the British chartered a flight from Italy headed to Cyprus. The Albanians were offloaded at Malta clandestinely while the plane continued to Cyprus. The passenger manifest was written to indicate that the Albanians had actually arrived and been discharged in Cyprus. If any of the agents were picked up and interrogated in Albania, the British government could say that they had been taken to Cyprus for training for jobs in Mauritius but had been found unsatisfactory and discharged, and that it did not know what had become of them after that.[3]

The island of Malta, under British control at the time, was chosen to host the main base for the operation because it was the closest location to southern Albania, the intended target of the infiltrations. Other alternatives, including the US-controlled North African coast of Benghazi and the island of Cyprus, also under the British, were discarded due to their distance or security concerns.[4] The main operational base was located at Fort Bingemma in the northwest corner of Malta, about ten miles west of the capital, Valletta. A forward operating base and communication center was set up in Corfu, at Villa Boboli, with a staff of Albanian telephonists to exchange communications with the agents in the field, British wireless transmitter operators to exchange communications with the Malta center, and British officers to provide tactical guidance direct to the field and stay fully informed on the developments.[5]

For about a month a crew of six British SOE veterans led by Smiley instructed the Albanian recruits, whom they called affectionately "Pixies," probably because of their relatively small stature. Training covered the use of weapons, including rifles, Sten 9 mm submachine guns, pistols, grenades, and Bren light machine guns; handling explosives and setting up charges, mines, and booby traps; and other guerilla tactics that ranged from map reading and compass use to introductory and advanced demonstrations of silent killing, followed by practice.

Smiley didn't deem more extensive training necessary, on the assumption that the Albanians had a greater knowledge of guerilla warfare in their country than the British themselves. Two Albanians, Abdyl Sino and Jani Dilo, were put in charge of the trainees, although they weren't going to be part of the infiltration teams. They brought their knowledge of the Albanian terrain to the assignment and, in addition, served as interpreters between the trainees and the British instructors.[6]

In order to enhance their authority with the Albanians, Smiley gave Sino and Dilo the uniforms of British officers. Dilo, who spoke French and Italian but no English, passed for a French-Canadian officer from Quebec. At a polo match in November of that year, Smiley introduced him as such to a young woman, who went on to explain to Dilo the rules of the game in good French. She was Princess Elizabeth,[7] in Malta at the time visiting her husband, Philip, Duke of Edinburgh, posted to the first destroyer flotilla of the Mediterranean fleet in the autumn of 1949.[8]

Smiley's wife, Moy, who had spent the war years as a cipher clerk in Kenya, provided training in cryptography and handled the encryption of messages to and from London. Bill Collins, Smiley's radio operator during the SOE missions in Albania,[9] trained several recruits in operating the W/T equipment, which consisted of B.3 radio telephonic sets, new at the time and still undergoing user testing. The British hired a private boat, *Stormy Seas*, and a crew of former marines to transport the agents from Malta to the Albanian coast and land them at designated beaches and coves.

The radiophone sets allowed direct wireless telephonic speech between parties, a feature that shortened the mission preparation time by eliminating the need to train the Albanian radio operators in Morse code. Provided the agents could find a suitable location, these sets were supposed to allow communication over a range from ten to seventy miles, which was considered sufficient given that Corfu was only three miles away from the Albanian coast and most of the missions were expected to operate within range. For parties that would venture further inland, the plan was for them to communicate with other field teams closer to the coast, who would then relay their information to base. The British considered the sets "moderately handy sets with their own pedal generating plant which can be carried for short distances as a pack and for longer distances by ass or mule."[10]

After the training was completed, Dilo organized the recruits into operational groups and let them work out among themselves the details of the infiltration. Abas Ermenji went to Malta in August to assist with the planning and to provide a morale boost to the recruits. On the night of August 25–26, Smiley organized a dry run of the entire operation, codename RAKI, a name the Albanians had suggested after the national alcoholic drink they all enjoyed, whether Christian or Muslim. The purpose was to test the readiness of the captain and crew for embarkation and landing procedures, as well as to give them practice in landing at an unreconnoitered point, setting up and using the communications equipment, and performing in field conditions.[11]

The cost estimates for the initial six months of the operation were £70,000, about $200,000 at the time or $2 million today. One-third of the costs covered accommodation, equipment, salaries, W/T supplies, and transport at the advance base in Corfu; another third covered salaries, weapons for Albanians, training expenses, accommodations, etc. in Malta; and the final third covered gold for infiltration parties, payment for initial operational provisions, and costs for boat transport.[12]

* * *

The thirty agents, split in six groups, infiltrated in southern Albania within a span of six weeks starting in the first half of September 1949. All the agents wore British uniforms and carried Sten submachine guns, three hundred rounds of ammunition, and Parabellum pistols. Each man had an Albanian identity card and fifty gold sovereigns on him. Each team had a W/T set, power generator, and two pairs of binoculars assigned to it.

The first to go were a party of ten set ashore at the mouth of the Semani River, in the Lushnja-Fieri region of central Albania, in early September. One five-man team, led by Mustafa Kusa, had to travel east across the mid-section of the country for about seventy miles until they reached their operational area in near the city of Korça. The second five-man team, led by Ali Trebova, headed inland along the same route as the first team but stopped halfway in the Berati region in central

Albania. After completing its work in the Berati area, the Trebova group joined the Korça group, and together they entered Greece in mid-October in the Radovicka area. Both groups were able to make radio contact with the base at Corfu.[13]

A second party of nine Albanians attempted an initial infiltration in the Karaburun peninsula on the Ionian coast on September 9 but wasn't able to land due to poor weather. The second attempt, on September 16, was successful. The landing site, known as Seaview, was the same spot that the OSS and SOE had used during the war to infiltrate people and supplies for their missions in Albania and to evacuate wounded or sick personnel to Italy.

After landing onshore, the Albanians marched together in a northeasterly direction for about five miles over very rugged terrain until they reached the village of Dukati, where they split. A team of four led by Sami Lepenica and including his cousin Hysen Lepenica, Zogoll Sheno, and Safet Dani, headed north toward Vlora. Not far from Dukati, an Albanian pursuit detachment ambushed them; all four were killed after the firefight and pursuit ended on September 23.

The other five proceeded toward Kurveleshi and Gjirokastra about forty miles south-by-southeast; they were Ramiz Hataj, Turhan Aliko, Ahmet Kuka, Bido Kuka, and Hysen Isufi. They were able to send a radio message on the difficulties caused by the presence of pursuit detachments in the Dukati area, before hiding the wireless set and fleeing south to the Himara region on the Ionian coast. On October 4, this group fell into an ambush at Nivica, about halfway to their destination, and lost their leader, Ramiz Hataj. The remaining four headed separately toward Greece to confound their pursuers and increase their chances of escape. Hysen Isufi and Bido Kuka entered Greece on October 16. Upon questioning by Greek officials in Yanina, they claimed to be members of a resistance band from Vlore; the Greek regarded their story with suspicion and put them in prison.

On October 21, Turhan Aliko and Ahmet Kuka gave themselves up to the Greek gendarmerie post in Filates, where a representative of the Greek army intelligence questioned them thoroughly. They told the entire story of their recruitment and training by the British and infiltration into Albania. They also revealed the names of twenty-two other Albanians who had trained with them in Malta. The two men turned over their submachine guns, 174 sovereigns, and other personal items. On October 24, the Greek took all four men to Athens.[14]

The last sortie of eleven Albanians left Malta on September 15, 1949, for the Seaview cove where the Hataj and Lepenica groups had landed earlier. En route, they received the only W/T transmission the Hataj group had been able to send, which reported the heavy presence of government forces in the area. They turned back and tried again three weeks later, on the night of October 6, 1949, in an area north of Vlora near the mouth of the Viosa River.

The first team, under Xhemal Asllani, included Arif Xhaferri, Belul Senaj, Haki Gaba, Ago Dauti, and Bardhyl Gerveshi, all from villages in the Tepelena-Gjirokastra area, about sixty-five miles south-southeast, where they headed right after landing. They were able to reach their destination, but large-scale search operations there forced them to hide for five days. Fearing reprisals on local villagers who might help them, the team decided not to approach anyone for assistance but instead to make a run for Greece. On October 27, 1949, they surrendered to soldiers in the Greek army post in the Pogoni area, who sent them to the Yanina Aliens' Center.

The second team, under Sefer Luarasi, included Përparim Aliu, Petrit Butka, Sami Bardho, and Zihni Mançe. They headed toward Kolonja, one hundred miles southeast of their landing site, but by the time they reached the area heavy snowfalls began as an early winter set in. They had to move down from the mountains in the low-lying areas, which left them exposed and more vulnerable to pursuit. The team was able to contact the British by radio and report their precarious position. At the end of October, Dilo replied from Corfu with Smiley's permission for the team to cross into Greece.

By October 31, the Greek military authorities had transferred all the surviving members of the Albanian infiltration parties to Athens and handed them over to Smiley, who arranged to fly all the men to Italy on November 2, 1949.[15]

* * *

While the initial Valuable infiltrations were not a resounding success, the British and American planners didn't see them as a failure either. The loss of five out of thirty men was the cost of doing business.

Itineraries of the 1949 infiltration teams in southern Albania

After all, "twenty percent loss rate was deemed normal for these type of operations."[16] Even though the teams had been more or less on the run during their entire stay in Albania, they had brought back some useful snippets of first-hand intelligence for the SIS and OPC, considered valuable because both services up to that point relied mostly on second-source intelligence from other secret services, primarily Greek and Italian.

The operation had also provided a number of lessons regarding the suitability of equipment and material for operations in Albanian terrain. The heavy radiophone communication equipment proved too cumbersome and was abandoned by most of the teams; it didn't work as advertised and didn't allow teams operating in the Albanian mountain ranges to communicate with the Corfu base.

The British weapons and uniforms, while intended to impress the sympathizers in the field, ended up providing fodder for the Communist propaganda already trumpeting a coordinated assault against the Albanian government by the British, American, Greek, Italian, and Yugoslav intelligence services.

The propaganda claims were true but only to a certain extent. Each of the services was running operations in Albania, often with agents shared or jointly managed with another service. Yet the operations were not synchronized or coordinated, leading to redundant and overlapping missions, which often ended up exposing and compromising the agents. For example, within a period of three weeks in September 1949, the Italian, Greek, and British services attempted landings at the Seaview cove on the Karaburun peninsula. It seems likely that previous landings alerted the Albanian forces, which could explain why the British teams found themselves pursued almost immediately and suffered the heaviest losses.[17]

The most likely reason for the difficulties the teams encountered was the unexpected intensity with which the Tirana government pursued them. All the groups reported that the Communists were recruiting and arming local villagers as a force to operate against guerillas. Furthermore, the Communists were sending groups of provocateurs in British uniform into the mountains in order to mislead villagers and identify those among them who were against the government.[18]

There was certainly the possibility that a leak had compromised the operation from the outset. Nicholas Bethell, in his 1984 book *Betrayed*, wrote that the British "had no idea, of course, that Philby had told what he knew about the forthcoming landings to his Soviet contact in London in late September."[19] Bethell adds: "Everything he learned from British intelligence about the proposed operation had been communicated to the Soviet secret service and the Albanian police before he embarked on the S.S. *Caronia*."[20]

Bethell repeated and amplified this claim for the rest of his life, tying the fate of the Albanian operation to the treacherous actions of Philby. A number of books and articles written on the subject since picked up the claim as a fact and echoed it. Considering what we know today, it is very unlikely that it happened that way.

Philby was at his post in Istanbul until the end of August and couldn't have known about the selection, training, and targets of the agents or anything else related to the Albanian operation. He returned to London in September for briefings on his new position in Washington. By that time, Smiley had already infiltrated two-thirds of the agents, and the remainder went in early October. Even if the Albanian operation had been included in Philby's briefings, it is doubtful that he received operational details specific enough to compromise the action. If he received such details, the path they'd have to follow to reach the Albanian authorities on the ground is long and tortuous. Philby would have provided the information to his handler in London to forward it to Moscow center for evaluation and analysis. If deemed important, Moscow would have sent it to their staff in Tirana with instructions to share it with the Albanian authorities, which then had to react to the information and mount the pursuit efforts in the south of Albania. All these actions had to occur within a matter of days.

Even if the Communist intelligence networks had been able to work with such efficiency, the information was not sufficiently urgent or important to cause such a precipitous chain of events. Infiltration raids against the Soviet Union itself and its satellites, including Poland, the Baltic republics, Bulgaria, and Albania, were the norm rather than the exception at the time. Philby was rising to important positions and many insiders, including James Angleton, the CIA's chief of counter-intelligence, felt that Philby someday would head the British secret service.[21] It is not likely then that Moscow would have risked compromising Philby's cover over routine information like this.

During his month-long stay in London to prepare for the Washington mission, Philby focused mainly on trying to understand the extent to which the British and American cryptographers had been able to decipher a series of Soviet cables intercepted between Moscow and the Soviet missions in Washington and New York. He met once a week with his handler, "Max," to pass on the information he learned. The last time they met was a few days before Philby's departure. Philby reported everything that had happened over the week. Max summarized it for Moscow as "nothing substantial, no important news."[22]

* * *

If there was a leak, it came most likely from the Albanian community in Italy, which was infiltrated at many levels by the Albanian intelligence service, the Sigurimi, as well as elements from the Italian Communist Party, who reported directly to the Russians. Describing the atmosphere at the time, James McCargar recalled: "The leaks went in about 26 directions in Italy. Everybody was informing on everybody else, and the Russians were getting a lot of stuff out of there."[23]

A report that the OSO received in December 1949 from a source they considered of the highest reliability fingered Sotir Kosmo, an intellectual residing in Rome at the time, as Sigurimi's main source of information for the activities of the NCFA in Italy. Kosmo was a member of the Blloku Kombëtar Indipendent and was reported to have kept the Albanian Legation in Rome completely informed on the formation of the NCFA, the relations of the committee with the British and Americans, and the recruitment of Albanian elements by Abas Kupi and MacLean. Kosmo reportedly received a monthly salary of fifty thousand lire (eighty dollars at the time) from the Sigurimi.[24] Only a few months later, Kosmo was found in the Tiber River, shot and strangled.[25] Émigré circles in troubled times have no tolerance for people suspected of double-crossing their own brethren and waste little effort in finding out whether the suspicions are founded or not.

Yet another explanation for the demise of the Lepenica team, the only one that the Sigurimi completely annihilated, is that it fell victim to a control operation that the Sigurimi was running at the time. The British had instructed the team to establish contact with Ethem Çako, whom they assumed to be in their area of operations between Vlora and Dukati.[26] Çako had been recruited in early 1949 for an operation known as Plan Fontana, run jointly by the Italian Naval Intelligence and OSO.[27] On July 8, 1949, Çako and three others (Kasëm Zhupa, Llukman Lutfiu, and Zyber Lika) had been parachuted in southern Albania in the mountains of Kurveleshi 40 miles southeast of Vlora. Four days after their landing, the forces of the Sigurimi surrounded the group in an area called Buza e Bredhit, or Fir's Edge. In the ensuing firefight, they killed Lika and forced the other three to surrender.[28] Under the threat of execution, Çako agreed to work with the Sigurimi in order to lure more agents in the trap.

For almost a year, Çako exchanged over one hundred radio messages with his Italian handlers, providing fictitious information fed by Sigurimi and requesting drops of more agents, supplies, and arms— all of which the Albanian authorities promptly captured upon landing. The operation, code-named "Buza e Bredhit" by the Sigurimi, continued until May 24, 1950, when the Albanian media announced the trial in Tirana of Çako, Zhupa, and Lutfiu, who were accused of spying for Greek, Italian, and American services. At the end of the trial, on June 6, 1950, the court condemned all three defendants to death but the authorities commuted Çako's sentence later in light of his cooperation with the Sigurimi.[29]

The SIS and OSO had information to suggest that the Sigurimi controlled Çako as early as November 1949. Indeed, on November 1, 1949, when Colonel Smiley visited Captain Zotos, one of the intelligence officers in General Papagos's headquarters, Zotos volunteered the following information:

> [F]ive men including Ethem Chaku [sic] . . . were dropped by parachute in July. . . . This party was all captured by Communists and four of them were executed. Ethem Chaku, after being in custody for some time was allowed to escape. He is moving in the mountains receiving supply drops (he received two drops of 28 containers on October 17th and October 18th). The Communists helped him to collect supplies!![30]

A summary of Smiley's meeting with Captain Zotos, including his suspicions about Çako, was in the OSO's hands within a few days and then forwarded to the OPC. No one noticed any worrisome signs in the report or connected Çako with the fate of the Lepenica team. It would be a harbinger of worse things to come.

* * *

Bob Low, the American commander of Fiend in Rome, had planned to follow the preliminary infiltrations of the British agents with fifty agents he would select among supporters of Abas Kupi and Said Kryeziu, train in Malta, and infiltrate into central and northern Albania.[31] By the end of October 1949, neither Kupi nor Kryeziu had identified any candidates. The British had planned all along to close the Malta training base by December 1 as part of their cover story—in case its existence became publicly known, they could deny it had ever existed. Thus, Low and McCargar found themselves with no agents readily available for continued infiltrations and no location where to train future agents.

By that time, the Greek National Army had put an end to the Communist guerrillas in Greece by capturing and dispersing most of them and pushing the few remaining hardcore fighters completely out of Greece and into Albania. Hence, one of the major objectives of the Fiend operation no longer applied and proceeding with the infiltration schedule was less urgent. As a result, McCargar instructed Low to temporarily suspend all activity toward infiltration operations and focus his efforts on resolving the NCFA leadership crisis that had developed after Frashëri's death.[32]

CHAPTER 7

Reevaluation of Project Fiend

I n its original version, Project Fiend had as a minimum objective to develop internal conflict within Albania so as to impair the government's ability to support the Greek guerrillas. The maximum objective was the overthrow of the Hoxha regime in order to eliminate Albania as a base for the Greek guerrillas, to deny the Soviet military air and naval bases in the Mediterranean, and to boost the morale of other Eastern European nations by demonstrating that it was possible to remove a securely entrenched Communist dictatorship. As 1949 was coming to a close, two major changes occurred that pushed the Office of Policy Coordination to reexamine the status, objectives, and conduct of Fiend. The first was the cessation of guerrilla warfare in Greece, and the second was the intensification of pressure by the Cominform on the Tito regime, which led the US-British policy to shift toward maintaining that regime as an obstacle against the Soviet Union.

In addition, the existence of the operation and the fact that the British and Americans were behind it had become widely known to the intelligence services of all the countries that had an interest in the nature of the regime in Albania, particularly Greece and Italy, and to some extent France and Yugoslavia. OPC and State Department officials overseeing the operation feared that considerable conflict might develop among these countries as they tried to take advantage of an unstable situation in Albania, particularly since the National

Committee for Free Albania was not equally acceptable to all these players as an alternative to the Hoxha regime.

On November 15, 1949, Frank Wisner convened a meeting at the Policy Coordination Group offices in the Pentagon to discuss the operation. Attendees included Wisner, Kermit Roosevelt, and James McCargar from the OPC and Kim Philby representing the SIS. Wisner opened the meeting by stating that time had come to reexamine the Albanian operation and determine whether they should continue on the original course or adjust their plans to account for a number of difficulties they had encountered, including the poor quality of recruits obtained thus far, the lack of a training base, and the serious security leaks.

"An operation that was supposed to be kept under the wraps of secrecy was known in all relevant details by anyone in the region that had an interest in Albania," Wisner said. By November 4, 1949, the Office of Special Operations had received a thorough accounting of the status of the Albanian infiltration parties from their sources inside the Greek army intelligence, which had been able to extract the details from British agents as they exfiltrated to Greece.[1] The Italians had just as much if not more information. Just a few days after the first landing, McCargar had received a visit from James Angleton, who brought with him a report he had obtained from an OSO source within Italian Naval Intelligence. McCargar recalled that Angleton read to him passages from the report providing a fully detailed description of the landing, including accurate details about the boat, its passengers, their equipment, and the purpose of their mission.[2]

Wisner brought up concerns the Department of State had expressed, that their activities could start a chain reaction that might involve the US in the hostilities or at the very least seriously affect the precarious position of the Yugoslav government. He then proposed that the OPC and SIS explore the possibility of utilizing other means, such as psychological or economic warfare to accomplish the objectives in Albania, while deemphasizing paramilitary operations. "I have been thinking," Wisner said, "of the idea of giving the Albanians the impression that our interest does not lie in any attempt to overthrow the Hoxha Government."[3]

Philby replied that the British shared fundamentally the same concerns with the operation and that the onset of winter was an opportunity to review the plans. The British were similarly worried about the security of the operation, since it was clear that the French, Italian, and Greek intelligence services were obviously well informed. Philby stated that one of the chief sources of the leaks was the conversations and correspondence between the Albanians themselves. Given that it was impossible to get them to maintain silence, Philby suggested carefully developing a formula under which the political leaders in the NCFA were generally informed but had no access to details of paramilitary operations. "It might be possible," he added, "to keep the political leaders so busy with other activities that they could not take a hand in, or have full knowledge of the operations." Wisner agreed with this suggestion.[4]

Philby didn't think it was necessary to abandon clandestine operations. Given the lack of sufficient information on which to make future decisions about Albania, London would be very reluctant to stop the reconnaissance. Philby felt they should continue to acquire additional recruits and devise new methods for their use, including the possibility of "hit and run" operations, that is, the infiltration of agents followed by their rapid exfiltration to Greece. On their way out, they could bring additional personnel with them. Combined with skillful interrogation, such operations might produce good intelligence results, Philby said.

McCargar brought up the need to analyze how much information the Soviets had on the Albanian operations. "I have a feeling that our British friends don't care as much as we do about how much the Soviets know," he suggested. To which Philby replied that there was no difference in opinion between the two sides on the seriousness of Soviet knowledge; the Foreign Office probably felt the same in this respect as the State Department. He pointed out, however, that the satellite states had plenty of proof of British SIS operations, but none of the espionage trials to date had brought to light any genuine cases.

Wisner supported McCargar's assertion that the British were always less concerned about the security implications of the Albanian operation. He brought up the example of the Valuable plan, which made no efforts to camouflage the involvement of the British in agent training and conduct of the operation. Philby replied with a smile that the Foreign Office was always happier when there was no British mission in Albania.[5]

The discussion then moved to the effects of psychological and economic warfare on the stability of the regime in Albania. Wisner considered these methods as benign ways for accomplishing the collapse of the regime without eliciting Soviet intervention against Albania or Yugoslavia that armed operations might provoke. He asked openly whether the British really favored the overthrow of the Albanian government. After some contemplation, Philby said he would ask London for a firm answer, adding however that "in the entire history of British foreign policy, this question has never been answered." With regard to Soviet intervention, he said that the Soviets would act against Yugoslavia if they wished, regardless of Albania, which was not important enough to sway them one way or the other. In conclusion, Wisner invited SIS officials to travel from London in order to present and discuss concrete proposals, views, and recommendations on alternative methods on the operation.[6]

* * *

During the meetings held in early December in Washington, the British and American services reevaluated the objectives and future conduct of Operation Valuable Fiend. The major change was to deemphasize the active pursuit of regime change in Albania. From that point forward, the activities would focus on creating and maintaining, both inside and outside of Albania, capabilities that would allow the British and Americans to exploit to their advantage any developments that might arise in Yugoslavia or Albania. Actions taken toward Albania would aim to weaken or eliminate the usefulness of Albania as a base of operations against Yugoslavia. At the same time, they wouldn't be aggressive to the point of triggering repercussion against Yugoslavia by the Soviet bloc.

In order to accomplish these objectives, the OPC and SIS agreed to move the emphasis away from challenging the Albanian regime through paramilitary means and toward propaganda and other destabilizing activities, including agent infiltrations, clandestine broadcasts in the name of the NCFA, leaflet drops, deception rumors, overt press activities, and measures to exacerbate the already difficult economic situation in Albania. Over time, a handful of subprojects sprung up to make it easier to manage these activities and keep them compartmentalized for increased security.

Neither the British nor the Americans shared the reevaluation of Fiend objectives with members of the NCFA who continued to embrace the concept of a force of a thousand armed Albanians, known as the follow-up force, that would start the insurgency after the initial infiltration teams had laid the groundwork. The case officers began to draw the attention of the Albanian leaders to the fact that it would be financially difficult to maintain a large number of refugees when the International Relief Organization camps closed down. They began carefully to feed the idea of emigration to other countries, without raising suspicions that they had abandoned the idea of the follow-up force.

Future agents that would participate in infiltration activities would remain in the country as long as possible. At a joint meeting between OPC and SIS officers, they decided that "All agents exfiltrated should be treated as couriers coming out to report and should be reinfiltrated with the minimum delay. This procedure to be prosecuted ad nauseam in the hope that ultimately the agents might think it safer to stay in Pixieland [cryptonym for Albania]."[7] The disposal of agents who for physical or psychological reasons could not be reinfiltrated and were rejected for future operations remained an open problem.

* * *

As the OPC began the planning and execution of the rescoped Albanian plan, they discovered that running the effort jointly with the British was proving to be a frustrating experience. While the Americans had shown some deference to the British on the planning and execution of the initial infiltrations, they intended to assert themselves and take the lead as the operation progressed, especially since, according to their estimates, the Americans were probably carrying 90 percent of the total cost of British-American operations in Albania.[8] The British on their end dragged their feet on a number of cases and resisted American efforts to seek cooperation of the French, Greek, and Italian Services.[9]

The leaks about the operation continued and became more widespread. On March 27, 1950, the *New York Times* carried an article by Cyrus L. Sulzberger datelined Istanbul, reporting on US-British policy and activities on Albania. The OPC identified certain statements in the article that could have come only from official sources with insider knowledge of their plans. Sulzberger wrote that Washington and London had coordinated their positions in the last few months and moved away from their desire to overthrow the puppet government of Hoxha. At the moment they were content to see the Communist regime remain in power for fear that Moscow could use any move to upset the Albanian regime as an excuse to take violent action against Yugoslavia, which would "serve as the traditional Balkan ignition of the powder keg—inherent in that area."[10]

The State Department became very concerned over this apparent leak and began querying diplomats in Rome, Belgrade, Athens, and Istanbul for clues on the source of information for Sulzberger. The OPC put forth the theory that the article was a deliberate leak from the British. It informed Philby of the concern and requested that he ask the SIS to investigate, since Sulzberger had excellent sources among both British and US government officials.[11]

McCargar was acquainted with Sulzberger and met him in an attempt to understand whether he had received the information from American or British sources. McCargar wrote about the encounter: "I gave him the usual bureaucratic reproach for irresponsible journalism. His answer was quick. 'Look, friend,' he said. 'That story did not come from any confidential briefing. If I could put it together, so could the Russians and a lot of other people. Take it as a measure of how well your arrangements are working.' I found the logic irrefutable."[12]

Wisner convened a meeting on February 27, 1950, with Carmel Offie, his special assistant, Merritt K. Ruddock, the OPC liaison to the SIS in London, and James McCargar to review the status of US-British relationship in Fiend. Wisner began by counting all the ways in which the British had failed to play their part in the operation. The list was long: the British had not provided bases and propaganda boat facilities; had seriously hurt the security of the operation by the conduct of their agents in Italy; had conducted Valuable in an unprofessional fashion; had sabotaged the concept of a general policy headquarters in Washington; had generally slowed down the operations; and had perhaps established some sort of covert unilateral relationship with Tito.

The OPC for its part had shown a lack of clarity in executing the operation and had not made sufficient real operational contributions. Reaching back for language from his days as a lawyer, Wisner observed, however, that "the weight of errors and omissions was against the British" and that this was the main reason the OPC should go ahead on a more independent basis. "We should approach the British on a friendly and conciliatory, non-recriminatory basis," Wisner said, "but we should definitely get a firm and clear agreement that we intend to give ourselves more flexibility in the future."

They decided that the OPC and the British would continue to run the operation jointly at the policy level and on certain economic and propaganda activities, but on operational matters connected with infiltration activities the OPC would disengage itself and handle them on a unilateral basis. Either service was entitled to make separate approaches to other national services for assistance or collaboration on certain specific phases of the operation.

The second major decision that Wisner and his team made at the meeting was to reprioritize the OPC activities in the Balkans. While the Albanian operation had been their top priority in the second half of 1949, in early 1950 the OPC had launched an operation against Bulgaria under the code name QKSTAIR, structured in the mold of Fiend. Given the opportunities that a target like Bulgaria presented, there was consensus that Fiend should have a lower priority than in the past and its size should be cut back. Nevertheless, Wisner urged his team to push the smaller operation with all possible vigor.[13]

* * *

The OPC's efforts to establish relations directly with other services encountered strong resistance by the Office of Special Operations, who felt that this was an encroachment in their jurisdiction. The OSO saw the Valuable phase of Fiend as nothing more than an intelligence operation, and asserted that the Office of Policy Coordination had no jurisdiction to conduct intelligence operations. The OSO's position was that they could provide the OPC with assets, liaison functions, and support as needed in countries like Greece, Italy, and France where the OSO had operated for years. There was no reason for the OPC to establish redundant and parallel structures that would only confuse the other services. The OPC's position was that the OSO was trying to tell them how to do their job.[14]

The OSO was also upset that the OPC had chosen to turn to the British to execute the first infiltrations in Albania without taking into consideration the agents that the OSO already had inserted in the country as part of Project Charity, jointly run with Italian Naval Intelligence. Project Charity had been the brainchild of James Angleton, the OSO station chief in Italy during 1947 to 1948. Its purpose was to mount joint operations to parachute teams of agents into Albania to collect and report intelligence for use by both the Italians and the Americans.

The OSO had provided a C-47 aircraft in October 1948 for use in airdrops of personnel, as well as supplies and funds for the operation. The Italians provided the case officers to handle the teams and the housing and training of the agents in Italy. The immediate objective of the plan was the infiltration of two-agent teams by air, equipped with W/T sets tied into a base station in Italy, to make contact with established resistance groups, collect intelligence, survey the local situation, establish a communication base, and arrange for the continued reception of operational supplies and personnel as required. Washington assigned specific intelligence targets, including collecting information on resistance groups, internal political situation, various defense installations, and the order of battle of the Albanian armed forces.

Ismail Vërlaci worked with the Italian intelligence and the OSO to recruit team members from displaced persons (DP) camps in Italy and Greece. He selected them based on their family connections and familiarity with the Elbasani and Mirdita areas of Albania where resistance groups were still operating. The plan entered the operational phase on February 15, 1949, when four agents forming two teams each with separate W/T communications parachuted in the Serishti district of Mirdita in the north-central part of the country. Alush Leshanaku and Xhevdet Bloshmi formed one team that planned to operate in the Elbasani region about forty miles south of the drop zone. They lost the W/T equipment and couldn't communicate with the center in Italy, so they made their way to Greece. By April 28, they had arrived in Athens, where Greek army intelligence debriefed them.[15] Leshanaku returned to Italy, where he helped train additional agents for the operation. He was parachuted again in early 1950. After several months of operations in Albania, the Sigurimi caught up with him and killed him.[16]

Ndue Pjeter Gjonmarkaj and Ndue Mëlyshi formed a second team destined for the Mirdita region. They were able to establish a base of operations there, where they created an organization called Komiteti i Maleve, or the Mountains' Committee. On behalf of the committee, they roamed the area harassing officials of the regime and their supporters. The most spectacular action of the Mountains' Committee was the ambush and assassination of Bardhok Biba, a relative of Gjon Markagjoni who had turned against the tribal system to become the ranking Communist official for Mirdita and a deputy in the National Assembly. On the morning of August 7, 1949, Biba was leading a group of villagers drafted to work as volunteers in labor brigades. As he entered a narrow mountain path between the villages of Kaçinarri and Shupali, two shots rang out and Biba fell dead on the spot. The villagers searching the area after the ambush found a document signed by Ndue Pjeter Gjonmarkaj with the decision by the Mountains' Committee to assassinate Biba.

Biba was among the most fervent supporters of Hoxha in the traditionally anti-Communist north-central part of Albania, and his assassination jolted the Communist regime into action. The First Division of the army and the Special Pursuit Brigade of the ministry of interior were dispatched to Mirdita immediately to comb the area villages for anyone remotely suspected of opposing the regime. The minister of interior, Mehmet Shehu, personally supervised the efforts to clear the area and capture the assassins. "Don't fret, because starting from today the Party and Comrade Enver [Hoxha] will be like your son," he told Bib Marka Kola, the eighty-year-old father of Bardhok Biba, at the funeral. When Shehu vowed to avenge many times over the murder of his son, Kola said: "My son is gone and nothing will bring him back. If you find the man who pulled the trigger, do with him what you wish, but don't make the people of Mirdita pay for my son's sake."[17]

Despite this plea for moderation, Shehu's reprisals were swift and merciless. On August 17, 1949, four villagers were hanged;[18] ten more were shot and dumped in a common grave, some of them still alive.[19] Mehmet Shehu gathered two thousand villagers from the area at the execution site and in a fiery speech vowed not to leave the area until he had shot one hundred and one men to revenge Bardhok Biba. After the massacre, Shehu ordered the indiscriminate imprisonment of three hundred men and the deportation of four hundred families, including women, children, and the elderly, to Tepelena and Lushnja internment camps in the south of Albania. Luckily, the terror campaign was cut short at the end of August when the government units were withdrawn hastily and sent south to counter Greek national army units, which were pushing the remnant forces of the Greek Communist guerrillas across the frontier.[20]

CHAPTER 8

Labor Services Company 4000

Spring 1950 brought two significant changes in personnel for Project Fiend. Colonel Gratian M. Yatsevitch replaced James McCargar as the overall operation commander in Washington, while E. Michael Burke took over for Robert Low in Rome as commander in the field.

Yatsevitch was an active duty US Army officer with a considerable knowledge of Russia, Eastern Europe, and the Balkans, although not of Albania specifically. He was born in Kiev, Ukraine, in 1911 into a family of old Polish nobility, which was shattered by the Bolshevik Revolution in ways that left permanent marks on Yatsevitch. His father, an official in the Russian imperial government, was in London when the October Revolution started, and remained stranded there while the family struggled to survive the chaos of the revolution and the civil war that followed. His mother, the daughter of the British consul in St. Petersburg, died in 1919 during the influenza pandemic. Helped by an aunt, Gratian and his younger brother made a harrowing journey through the war-ravaged countryside to join their father. Years later, scenes from *Doctor Zhivago* would bring tears to his eyes, for they reminded him of his own travel west in cattle cars packed with terrified people and trains rushing through ghost villages where women and children were starving to death.[1]

After spending his youth in England, Yatsevitch went to the US, where he studied mining and mineralogy at Harvard. Upon graduation, he spent five years between 1935 and 1940 in Yugoslavia, where he managed a small gold mine and was the engineer in charge of prospecting for a group of British mining companies.[2] Once World War II started, certain that the Germans were going to take over Yugoslavia, Yatsevitch blew up the mine works and returned to the United States.

He spent the war years in the army, in the Office of the Chief of Ordnance in Washington, DC, where he was in charge of the development and procurement of all artillery shells from twenty millimeters on up to sixteen inches in caliber. Due to this experience, he attended later as an observer the test firing of one of the early atomic cannons, nicknamed Atomic Annie, developed in the late 1940s and fielded in the early 1950s. In 1945, he joined Army Intelligence, G-2, and served as military attaché in Moscow and then, from 1946 to the end of 1949, as military attaché in Bulgaria.[3]

Yatsevitch was fluent in Russian and Serbo-Croatian and spoke good French, German, and a number of other languages—skills that came handy in his military and intelligence career. From his years in England, he retained a noticeable English accent, which complemented his striking appearance and led women who met him at the time to describe him as "devastatingly handsome and charming beyond belief!"[4]

As the newly appointed head of OPC's Southeast European branch, Yatsevitch brought to the job the discipline and rigor of his military career. While McCargar routinely arrived ten minutes late at meetings, he "made it a point of being five minutes early."[5] He began his assignment with a thorough review of the Albanian plan, the assumptions upon which it rested, and the progress up to that point. In a memo on May 17, 1950, Yatsevitch asked:

> Do we now believe that the reasons for which the "ultimate objective" of the original BGFIEND Project was cancelled are still valid? Or have new factors entered the picture and/or new developments taken place which make the time more propitious and, in general, make it desirable to attempt the accomplishment of that "ultimate objective?" A paper covering present thinking on a re-evaluation of BGFIEND is now under preparation.[6]

Yatsevitch established a good rapport with Philby, who continued to serve as the British joint commander of the Albanian operations. Philby spent a few days at the Yatsevitch's summer place on an island in Maine. It was a rather Spartan arrangement, because the house at that time was "devoid of any urban entertainment and with no telephone, electricity or running water." But there was plenty of time to sit around and talk, sail out on the water, or just read, thus a great opportunity to know someone without competition from others. Yatsevitch was not a drinker, but he kept a well-supplied bar. He described Philby as never "spilling the beans," regardless of how much alcohol he consumed.[7]

* * *

Michael Burke had spent the war years with the OSS, which he had joined at the invitation of William J. Donovan in 1942. Donovan had first noticed Burke when he was an all-American halfback at the University of Pennsylvania before his graduation in 1939. In addition to his athletic prowess, Burke possessed other qualifications that fitted perfectly the type of man Donovan was interested in for dangerous OSS assignments. He had spent his early life in Europe, spoke French fluently, and knew the country well.

Burke was assigned to the Mediterranean Theater of Operations six months before the Salerno invasion, with the task of infiltrating OSS men into Italy. During this time and following the Salerno invasion, Burke worked on several daring OSS assignments contacting Italian naval leaders and scientists working on advanced torpedo systems and spiriting them to the United States.

Burke was in England just before the Normandy invasion. At that time OSS teams of three were being parachuted into France. Called Jedburgh teams, they usually consisted of either two Americans and a Frenchman or two British and a Frenchman. Each team carried a radio, and one of the members was a qualified radio operator. In constant radio communication with these "Jed" units scattered throughout France, the Allied High Command was able to coordinate and integrate their underground activities with overall military operations.

Burke prepared and dropped forty-six agent teams, eighty-six people in total,[8] behind German lines. In July 1944 he led his own team parachuting into the Haute-Saône province in the northeastern section of France for intelligence gathering and sabotage purposes. He also organized and trained members of the French resistance and led them in repeated skirmishes with the Germans. For his exploits during the war, Burke earned the Silver Star medal and the Navy Cross.

Burke left active duty in October 1945, returned to the United States, and worked in Hollywood as a technical adviser to the script-writers for *Cloak and Dagger*, a tribute to the OSS directed by Fritz Lang and starring Gary Cooper.[9] Then he moved to New York, scraping by, living in a "dim railroad flat in Greenwich Village,"[10] borrowing from his father to make ends meet and keep his wife and infant daughter from going hungry.[11]

When the CIA called, offering him a contract staff position at fifteen thousand dollars a year for "an exploratory mission, a clinical case" that suited his experience overseas,[12] Burke jumped at the opportunity. In March 1950 he moved to Rome to take over from Low the Project Fiend activities in the field. On the way, he stopped in London for meetings with his SIS counterparts, including Philby, who was there at the time and invited him to dinner.

Burke's description of Philby echoes those of others who knew him. He was pleasantly surprised and flattered that a man of Philby's rank would invite him to a private dinner. He found Philby "entirely likable and very much at home in and on top of his profession." Burke expected Philby to know about his assignment, but he was surprised with his familiarity with operational matters. Burke later wrote that Philby "was a heavy, indiscriminate drinker, but his protective mechanisms were so deeply rooted that no amount of drink betrayed him."[13]

Burke's assignment in Rome was to maintain the relationship with the National Committee for Free Albania leaders and to coordinate the first paramilitary actions of Fiend, which meant selecting agents among the NCFA supporters, training and inserting them in Albania in order to connect with any resistance elements that still survived, and creating an underground movement. He saw the NCFA leaders as people with "disparate political philosophies and personal interests; a modest but regular allotment of US dollars was the glue." They were "political activists—agrarians, socialists, royalists. In exile, like all refugees, they were a threadbare lot, drawn loosely together in common cause against a Communist dictatorship and by a longing to go home."[14]

Burke realized that he was in a position of power over the Albanian leaders. He commanded their attention as the representative of a rich and young country, but as an individual he had to earn their respect. In dealing with them, he tried to convey his "human sympathy for their plight and a sense of shared equality with them as individuals."[15] He was particularly fond of Abas Kupi, the Legaliteti leader: "I liked him from the start and grew fond of him as our enterprise progressed, though apart from smiles, embraces, and other body language our communication was through the interpreter, inasmuch he spoke no language but his own, and could write nothing but his name."[16]

* * *

As the OPC began to energize efforts across all the components of the Fiend project, one of the first achievements was the creation in Germany of a holding area for Albanians that would be involved in these activities.

After World War II, the US Army created a number of guard and labor service units composed of displaced persons from Eastern and Central European countries. They were responsible for guarding railways, bridges, military depots, and roadblocks in postwar Germany, thus freeing up US personnel from such duties. Carmel Offie, who had spent time dealing with issues of displaced persons in Germany and maintained very close connections with the army, came up with the idea of using the Labor Service as cover to assemble a company of 220 to 250 Albanian refugees who had potential for agent training and operational activity in Albania. He traveled to Germany in January 1950 to work out the details with the US Army European Command (EUCOM).

According to the agreement, the OPC provided funds to pay the individuals who would join the Albanian Labor Service Company—on average about 250 marks ($60 at the time or $600 today) per month per man. In order to maintain secrecy over the source of these payments, the OPC deposited the funds in the Army Intelligence (G-2) confidential accounts, and G-2 transferred them to Army Logistics (G-4) accounts through the comptroller. G-4 used its own funds to cover rationing, housing, and administration of the company without OPC assistance and without causing comment among German civilians.[17]

Labor Services Company 4000 was officially launched on June 7, 1950,[18] in the Pulaski Barracks in Kaiserslautern,[19] in the US zone of Germany. Members of the NCFA military junta Abas Ermenji, Abas Kupi, and Said Kryeziu selected the members of the company mostly from IRO camps in Italy and then from similar camps in Greece. The company structure was along party affiliations with strict proportions in personnel: 40 percent from Balli Kombëtar, 40 percent from Legaliteti, and the remainder from Said Kryeziu's followers. Members of a political party were assigned in the same unit, slept in the same barracks, took their meals together, and performed guard duties together. This structure deepened the existing divisions between the groups and led from the beginning to quarrels, fights, and even murders among members of different factions.

The Albanian commander of the company was Major Çaush Basho, a member of the Ermenji's left wing of the BK. Basho ran the company with an iron fist, forcing his will on BK followers within the company and treating harshly members of other parties. Excerpts from a letter that Hatip Reka, a soldier in the company, wrote to a friend in Greece paint a clear picture of the atmosphere:

> The situation of the company here is something like it is in Russia. We have been civilized so much that they are bringing us pork meat three times a week. They are trying to destroy our religion. The officers who belong to Balli . . . have said that whoever does not eat pork is not a Ballist. Due to this one hundred persons are staying without food . . . We would have been better off if we had collaborated with Hoxha because these guys are worse.[20]

Overseeing the entire camp was a captain of the US Army, Thomas Mangelli, who came from an Albanian-American family in Boston, Massachusetts, affiliated with left-leaning Zog opponents in the United States. Mangelli favored the BK elements of the Guard Company, although in general he did not hold any of the Albanians stationed there in high esteem. He said: "As far as I am concerned, they could all be turned over to Enver Hoxha; but I have to carry out orders of the American Government which desires to train them for action against the present regime."[21] Initially, Mangelli was also responsible for working with the NCFA military junta in selecting members from the company's personnel for infiltration training. To cover the trainees' disappearance from the barracks, the officials announced that they had been transferred to another camp or had emigrated to another country. In reality, CIA staff had transported the men to a covert site they had set up to train Albanian and Bulgarian agents.

* * *

The covert training site was located at the Loeb estate in Murnau, about seventy kilometers south of Munich. The estate consisted of approximately sixty acres of rolling wooded terrain fronting on a lake. The terrain offered good visual cover and concealment from surrounding points, and the entire exterior line of the property was fenced. The estate accommodated two farmhouses, a gatehouse, a guesthouse, and the main mansion. The OPC signed a lease for the estate on the first week in October 1950 and promptly evicted the occupants of the gatehouse and renters of the second floors in the two farmhouses.

They allowed two families occupying ground floors in the farmhouses to remain, because they were located in a depression at one edge of the estate, away from and out of sight of the main mansion. OPC personnel warned the two families to stay away from the mansion, threatening to evict and thus deprive them of their means of livelihood if they failed to heed the warning. The OPC staffers retained an elderly man and his wife as servants in the mansion where they'd conduct the training. The couple received the same threats of firing and eviction if they ever disclosed what they saw at the mansion. All roads leading up to the estate had posted signs warning intruders to stay out and the gates remained locked at all times. The parachute instructors built a training rig on an old tennis court located in a depression and surrounded by trees. The only facility the trainees ever utilized off the estate was the army range located approximately seven miles from Murnau.[22]

OPC trainers found issues with the process used to select candidates for training. They felt that Mangelli and Basho had chosen most of the trainees among men they had blacklisted as undesirables and wanted to remove from the company. Often the prospective agents didn't know the true purpose of their mission, which created grievances and unhappiness once they found out during training what they were getting into.[23]

The physical and mental state of the agents created problems as well. A lot of them had physical handicaps or were emotionally and mentally unstable, which led to their elimination from the training program. Medical exams of the contingent of eleven agents in training in the summer of 1951 found "five who had active syphilis, three acute anxiety reactions, one man with apparently chronic ulcerative colitis, and one man with possible active tuberculosis." The medical officer in charge of the screening wrote: "No attempt is being made to demand that these men be of the caliber of Army Profile A, but I believe it is important that we do not find ourselves saddled with men who are either psycho-neurotic, actively syphilitic or actively tubercular, because these men are liable at any moment to present severe security problems and subsequently disposal problems."[24]

* * *

Under the auspices of the US Army, personnel in labor service companies throughout the American-occupied zone of Germany engaged in guard duties and reconstruction activities. The Albanians assigned to Company 4000 were responsible for guarding depots and other installations around their camp, which is why the unit is also known as the Albanian Guard Company. Their activities were public knowledge, and there was no real security around the facility or the movement of personnel inside and out. This had been the intent from the beginning in order to provide official cover for the use of agents selected from the company in the OPC Albanian operation. However, even supposedly covert activities, such as the selection of agents for training and their transfer from the main camp to the training site, were secrets poorly kept.

The covert training site had security issues of its own due to its location in a residential area, only two miles from Murnau. The rumor that it was an intelligence center spread among the local population, "accustomed to intrigue and of a highly suspicious nature," as one of the OPC training officers described them. The German housekeeping personnel who worked at the site never received a security clearance.[25]

There is evidence that the Albanian secret service had infiltrated the company and knew fully well what was going on there. One reported story is that of Dalip Cena, who escaped from Albania in 1949 and settled in the IRO camp of Cinecittà in Rome. There he joined the BK organization and in 1950 was selected in the BK contingent that joined the Labor Services Company. In 1951 he was among a handful of candidates that received training at the covert site. At the end of the training course, he escaped to the Soviet zone of Germany. The authorities there handed him over to Czechoslovak service agents, who transferred him by plane to Tirana.[26]

Due to the security issues around it and the low of quality of personnel there, by the end of 1951 the OPC had given up recruiting potential agents from the Albanian Labor Services company. Apparently, the issues were not unique to the Albanian company. By the end of 1952, the CIA terminated all of its connections with the Albanian, Bulgarian, and Czech guard companies and turned them over completely to the US Army. In a cable to headquarters on December 13, 1952, the OPC Frankfurt station chief reported that the CIA was "no longer in Guard Company Business."[27] The US Army continued to use Company 4000 through the end of 1955 for auxiliary guard duty.

The Sigurimi conducted intelligence activities against the Albanian Labor Services company for as long as it lasted, years after the CIA had stopped recruiting agents from it for activities in Albania. As late as the end of 1954, CIA case officers in Rome, using information obtained from a double agent they were running against the

Sigurimi in Italy, proposed to headquarters a deception operation: "to throw a bit more dust in the Sigurimi's eyes by arranging body movements and periodically getting a creditable rumor or two started in the right places. . . . It would seem to be a deception activity which would confuse the opposition and draw his attention to a cold scent and would not be an expensive undertaking."[28]

CHAPTER 9

Odyssey of the First CIA
Paramilitary Team

In August 1950, Yatsevitch and Burke accelerated the efforts to infiltrate the first group of OPC agents in Albania. Yatsevitch defined the agents' mission as laying the foundation for and forming the nucleus of resistance groups in their area of operations, establishing safehouses, and preparing facilities for eventual covert air supply of limited guerrilla groups.[1] Burke shuttled between Germany, Rome, and Greece, occupied with selecting and training the agents, and developing infiltration plans, supply plans, communication plans, and other operational tasks required for the execution of the mission.

The Office of Special Operations, which had its own agents in Albania jointly run with the Italian Naval Intelligence as part of Project Charity, followed the progress with interest initially. The interest turned into concern when the OPC decided that the first group of agents would parachute into the northeastern part of the country, where the OSO teams were operating. There was clearly the potential for overlapping activities and a great deal of confusion that might ensue.

James Angleton took the lead on behalf of the OSO to work out some sort of arrangement with the OPC to avoid the issues. The Charity agents were members of the Blloku Kombëtar Indipendent, BKI, which the OPC had decided to leave out of the National Committee for Free Albania in 1949.[2] Angleton argued that they needed to review that decision now that OPC activities in Albania had matured to the point where they were considering operations on the ground.

In his view, the BKI was one of the strongest, if not the strongest, Albanian opposition group, who, unlike the NCFA, had proven that they had a following in Albania. The OPC couldn't ignore their intelligence and operational capabilities. Including them in the NCFA would keep them from aligning with the Italians, French, or Greeks. It would also give the Italians, the BKI's main supporters, an incentive to support the NCFA, which they barely tolerated only as a favor to the Americans. Ultimately, Angleton argued, whether the NCFA liked it or not, they could not keep the BKI out of operations in Albania or out of the government if the revolution was successful.[3]

Angleton believed that the OPC and OSO should collaborate and staff officers from both organizations at headquarters and in the field should have frank discussions about running Charity and Fiend jointly and leveraging the respective agents they were parachuting in Albania for the benefit of both organizations. He proposed an operational arrangement between the OPC and OSO in which Charity agents operated under joint OPC-OSO jurisdiction in the zone where they already were in contact with resistance personalities. The OSO also proposed to arrange some type of alliance between the BKI and NCFA, in which the BKI took a lead role in a specific area of the country and in turn supported the NCFA as an organization outside the committee.[4]

The OPC would have none of the OSO suggestions. OPC officers had little regard for the work of their OSO counterparts or the quality of intelligence they were producing. They would often ridicule the OSO reports for their F-6 ratings,[5] indicating that the authors couldn't vouch for the reliability of sources and had no way of judging the veracity of the reports' content. OPC officers relished in taking potshots at their OSO counterparts. For example, the OPC had anxiously requested an assessment of the Albanian Air Force capabilities to intercept covert flights they planned to start toward the end of 1950. The OSO duly delivered a package containing forty intelligence items on Albania, or Pixieland as they referred to it at the time. After reading it, Michael Burke sent the following scathing comments:

The data first appeared as an excellent compilation of undisputed information by subject, probably a granite foundation for all future intelligence. There was one glaring exception: none of it had been evaluated. For example, Item #14 ('Air Force') was a startling pearl of news. Until this pouch, Pixieland had been pictured nude of air power, with the possible exception of three Junkers in unknown but probable moth-eaten condition and an equal number of discarded [crop] dusters perhaps unserviceable but surely not moth-eaten. Suddenly we are confronted by a phantom, 300-plane force, without any evidence of aircraft shipments, accelerated training programs, or increase in operating personnel. And our subsequent query of ZRMETAL [code name for Washington, DC] only confessed that the Pixie Air Force so mightily described was F-6. As you are aware, air power within Pixieland is a touchy matter with us. The damage of all this was the complete disenchantment of the other 39 items.[6]

The failure of the OSO to establish a good working relationship with the OPC was perhaps the last in a string of reasons that pushed the OSO to downsize significantly its efforts on intelligence collection activities in Albania at the beginning of 1951. Starting in mid-1947 and for two and one-half years, OSO had made a concerted effort to obtain intelligence about Albania. These efforts had been expensive in the loss of agents, consumption of staff officer time, and expenditure of funds. The hostilities on the Korean peninsula compelled the OSO to reprioritize its resources, and Albania was now deemed a low priority from the intelligence perspective. As a result, the OSO cut down infiltration of agents from abroad in favor of efforts to develop legal resident agents inside the country who could provide sufficient information to reasonably service customers' intelligence requests, including OPC requirements growing out of their Fiend operation.[7]

* * *

While Colonel Yatsevitch ran interference in Washington and navigated the political issues between the OPC and OSO, Burke kept busy in Europe with the myriad of tasks required to make a successful infiltration in Albania. Building on his war experience, his preferred infiltration method for Fiend was to parachute the agents from low-flying aircraft, leaving landings by boat along the coastline to the British. There was one complication, however, created by the need to provide the operation full deniability in case things went wrong: neither the aircraft flying over Albania nor the crew operating it could be linked in any way to the United States. Burke worked with Major General Truman H. Landon, the director of the Air Force Office of Plans and Operations and chief of staff for the US Air Forces in Europe to secure the necessary aircraft. On June 9, 1950, Landon approved the OPC request for aircraft and made available two C-47 aircraft for communication flights. They would not fly in hostile air space; therefore they retained the air force markings and were operated by air force crews. A third C-47, which would be used for flights over denied areas, was stripped of any air force insignia and was transferred to the OPC for operations.

Having secured the aircraft from the US Air Force, Burke turned to the British for help with the crew that would fly the covert plane. The SIS recruited a crew of Polish Air Force veterans who had fought with the Western allies during World War II and had chosen to stay in Britain rather than serve under the Communist regime the Soviets established in Poland after the war.[8] The leader of the crew was Roman Rudkowski, an ex-colonel with the Polish Air Force who had commanded a bomber squadron that had completed thirty operational bombing missions during the war.[9] It included the pilot Zbigniew Wysiekierski, the navigator Stanisław Król, the engineer Władimir Brundel, the dispatcher and radio operator Janusz Barcz, and the jumpmaster Władysław Buryn. The Polish crew received operational clearance at the end of August, and arrived in Frankfurt in early September 1950 to take delivery of the covert aircraft.[10]

The plans were for the crew to fly out of Frankfurt at midnight on September 13 and arrive in the early morning hours of September 14 at the Eleusis airstrip, near Athens, which was to be its permanent location. The OPC arranged for a Greek Air Force officer to receive the plane and to keep its presence under cover from the rest of the personnel at the airfield. However, the US Air Force headquarters in Frankfurt sent the plane ahead of schedule. When the plane arrived in Greece prematurely at 1900 hours on September 13, the Greek officer was not at the Eleusis airfield. His subordinate, faced with an unmarked plane that had just made an unscheduled landing on his tarmac, arrested the crew, searched the plane, and summoned Major Harold A. Tidmarsh, the American military attaché, to identify the crew. Fortunately, before the Greeks had blown the cover completely, the briefed officer returned to Eleusis, immediately placed the plane under physical security of the Greek service, and took the necessary steps to avoid further interest on the matter. Tidmarsh received a cable from his commanding officer ordering him to drop further investigation of the incident and classify all discussions of the plane as "Top Secret."[11]

Having secured the covert plane and the crew, Burke focused next on the agents. Captain Mangelli, the American commander of the Albanian Labor Service Company in Germany, selected sixteen members of the company from Balli Kombëtar, Legaliteti, and Kryeziu followers, grouped in teams based on their region of origin, which would also be their operations area.

On the night of October 12, US Army personnel transported the sixteen future agents from the Labor Services Company to a rendezvous point near Munich, where staff from the covert school transferred them to a blacked-out truck and drove to the training site in Murnau, Germany. Burke had set November 3, 1950, as the target date for the drop into Albania, so time was of the essence and training started the following morning, October 13. Thirteen intensive days of training from 0615 until 1700 included calisthenics, close combat, weapons handling and firing, communications, and parachute training. The training officers maintained a semi-military discipline, not allowing themselves to become familiar with the trainees, in order to emphasize the seriousness of the mission in which they were about to embark. At the same time, they did their best to maintain the morale of the trainees, including providing good food in sufficient quantities, in contrast to the conditions that existed at the Labor Services Company and that the agents had experienced for the past several years. The agents had access to free candy, tobacco, chewing gum, and beer, as well as a radio, playing cards, and chess and checker sets for use during the little time they had available for recreation.[12]

On October 26, the last day of training, the staff officers helped the agents prepare their personal packs and issued the equipment, weapons and ammunition. The agents would carry with them personal clothing and weapons, together with a small quantity of ammunition, food, and other supplies. The plan was to resupply them from the air as soon as they had established a base in Albania and could communicate back the coordinates of a good drop zone.

The training was rushed because of the approaching winter, which could be unforgiving, especially in the mountainous parts of Albania where the teams were going to operate. Burke had just received information from the OSO that many members of the Albanian resistance movement felt they could no longer endure the suffering and they planned to flee to Yugoslavia at the first opportunity. They were unwilling to spend another winter in the mountains, since life there was so difficult that it drove men mad.[13]

Yet, hurrying through the training and preparations for the mission didn't set the teams on a strong footing for their work on the ground. Here is how Halil Nerguti, the leader of one of the teams, described their experience: "The preparations and training done so hurriedly, in thirteen days, were not at all sufficient to fulfill a special mission. The ammunitions for the machine guns and revolvers were few. On account of the hurried time they did not even give us maps we would have used if the radio did not work."[14]

Late in the evening of October 26, the training staff loaded the agents and their equipment in the blacked-out truck and drove the entire night to Frankfurt, about three hundred miles north of the covert school location. There, the agents boarded a covert flight to Athens and arrived at the Eleusis airfield the next day. Burke traveled from Rome to personally see the agents off on their flight, scheduled for the night of November 3. Upon arrival, he found that several of the agents had developed pneumonia or felt so stressed out physically and mentally that they were no longer fit for the mission.

Burke allowed only nine of the sixteen agents to proceed. Halil Nerguti, Myftar Planeja, Ramadan Cenaj, and Rexh Berisha would operate in the Kukësi area in the northeastern part of the country, along the border with Yugoslavia. Adem Gjurra, Zetan Daci, and Sali Dalliu were destined for the Dibra region, fifty miles south of the

Kukësi team. Iliaz Toptani and Selim Daci would operate in the mountains of Kruja in central Albania only twenty miles north of Tirana.

The covert aircraft flew out on the night of November 3 but had to return without completing the drop because the weather had been rough over the target area. A second attempt just a few days later failed because the navigator had not been able to find the drop zone. They made a third attempt on the night of November 11–12, 1950. The crew reported upon return that they had successfully dropped nine agents and six bundles of equipment into the two preselected drop zones in Albania. But reading between the lines, Burke could see that it had not been a perfect operation.

The drops were performed on a moonless night and in mountainous areas. The aircrew, unfamiliar with the terrain, had guessed the location of drop zones on the ground, having spent more than an hour circling the area, unable to find the precise DZ. The arrangements were for the crew to drop the men first, then, after receiving their recognition signals from the ground, to drop the supply bundles. However, the plane had remained over the targets two or three minutes at the most, hardly enough time for the jumpers to descend, recover, and signal as agreed upon in the briefings.[15] Information received later from Nerguti would confirm Burke's concerns. Nerguti wrote:

Instead of dropping us at the pre-agreed point Fusha e Degës near Tropoja, the pilot by mistake dropped us ten kilometers further from this point, in the forest of the village Zarish–Qarr. We had received instructions that as soon as we landed we had to signal to the pilot in order for him to throw the material. But the pilot did not wait for the signal and threw the material in the darkness, without us knowing where it had fallen. The ammunition fell in the middle of the village Zarish. We looked for it in vain. The next day, the material was caught by the forces of Sigurimi and the frontier guards.[16]

Under any circumstance, the poor quality of the drops would have compromised the success of the agents' mission. In this particular case, it seems to have saved their lives. Both parachuted groups reported that the authorities had set up reception parties on the ground, clearly on the alert and expecting their arrival. Nerguti described the narrow escape of the Kukësi team on the night of the drop as follows: "All the people of the village were mobilized and with the forces of Sigurimi at their head, entered the forest searching for us. . . . We remained encircled for three days. Our rescuer was a young boy of seventeen, who we did not know, Islam Limani from the village of Nikolic, whose brother was shot three months later."[17]

Adem Gjurra and the rest of the agents in the second drop had a similar but less fortunate experience. Villagers in the area told Gjurra that the police had warned them of his arrival from the skies and were waiting. They evaded capture on the first night only because they had landed several miles away from the prearranged drop zone. After landing, the two groups split and headed for their separate areas of operations. Almost immediately, they encountered pursuit detachments. Gjurra's team spent several days on the run, then, with Gjurra wounded on the leg, crossed into Yugoslavia, where the authorities arrested them. After several month's detention, they were set free but kept under surveillance. Gjurra was able to emigrate to the United States after seventeen years. Forty of his family members and relatives in Albania were not so lucky—the Sigurimi shot his brother and cousin outright. The authorities sent the rest to prison, where a number of them, including three of Gjurra's children, died of disease and malnutrition.[18]

The pursuit forces captured Iliaz Toptani and Selim Daci the day after they parachuted. Under torture, they confessed of their activities in the Labor Service Company and at the Murnau training facility. These confessions were broadcast publicly at their 1951 show trial in Tirana and included in a report that the Albanian government submitted to the president of the General Assembly of the United Nations at the time.[19] Both Toptani and Daci received life sentences of hard labor. Selim Daci managed to get out alive in 1990, forty years after his capture.[20]

* * *

Burke's misgivings about the status of his teams increased when efforts to establish communications with them failed. Each team had radiophones and receivers operating on VHF frequencies, which they were to use at prearranged time slots to contact the base. A communications aircraft, often referred to by staff as the commo plane, flew in international airspace along the Albanian coastline during these time slots. A radio specialist on board monitored the frequencies and attempted to raise each team on the radio—without success.

The commo flights were long, and the crew onboard found them unnecessarily demanding, uncomfortable, and risky. After one of the first flights, they reported:

> News of a blacked-out aircraft floating over the narrow confines of Western Adriatic for six of more hours could not be hidden for long. This was anything but a clever show of deception.
>
> The elongated duration of the mission violated all JBALERT [Cryptonym for US Air Force] regulations for flying safely. With less than an hour's supply of fuel remaining when the flight was completed, there was no margin of safety at all. Had any weather developed in the LCDRINK [Cryptonym for Greece] area, one aircraft and everything aboard would have been ditched. The ensuing furor of such an incident is fearfully obvious.[21]

After a few tries, Burke and Yatsevitch considered the communication plan operationally impossible and abandoned it. The search continued for better wireless transmitter equipment and a more successful method of communication.

* * *

Left to fend for themselves, Nerguti and his team resorted to communicating by letters hand-carried across the border to Yugoslavia and then mailed to their NCFA contacts in Rome or Athens. Because of lack of training and an undeveloped sense of security, they wrote letters in the clear referring to people and places by their real names. Attempts by OPC staff to explain to the "prolific letter writers" the dangers of a complete disregard of security did not go anywhere. Upon receiving a letter that Nerguti had sent to his NCFA contacts in January 1952, in which he mentioned a number of local contacts by name, an exasperated Athens station chief commented: "The tragic part is that Nerguti mentions the names of people within KMWAHOO [Cryptonym for Albania] who befriended him, which is tantamount to signing their death warrants if the information has fallen into the wrong hands."[22]

The letters often contained intelligence information, such as description of Albanian military units, or the names of sympathizers and opponents of the regime in the areas where they operated. However, this information lost its value in the eyes of the OPC because Yugoslav, Italian, or Greek services had read it by the time it arrived in OPC hands.

With the help of local villagers, Nerguti and his three teammates were able to evade capture for a few weeks. At the end of December 1950, they heard news broadcast by Radio Tirana of the capture of Selim Daci and Iliaz Toptani, their fellow parachutists slated to operate in the Kruja area north of Tirana. With pursuit forces closing in, they crossed the border into Yugoslavia. In the area of Prizreni, they recruited sixteen men among friends and family, equipped them with weapons and ammunition purchased with the gold sovereigns they had brought with them, and headed back to Albania.

Yugoslav authorities did not tolerate armed men roaming the countryside any more than the Albanians did. On the way to the Albanian border, Nerguti's group fought through seven skirmishes with the Yugoslav police. On the other side of the border, two battalions of Albanian security and border police, alerted of the shooting, were waiting for them. The band of twenty fought until the evening and in the cover of darkness was able to evade encirclement and cross into the mountains of Mirdita in central Albania.

For the next several months, they roamed the countryside under constant pursuit, often betrayed by former friends who felt no longer safe to offer them refuge. Recapping the situation in his letter of January 1952, Nerguti wrote: "After long months of activity without means, without any signs from the center, not even a bullet, the friends to whom we went were very demoralized because they saw no signs of help. We had fourteen killed and another winter came. In spite of this we are expecting spring and will go on with our fight, hoping that this time you will give us some sign of life."[23]

A cynical Athens station chief had a different reading of Nerguti's activities:

> In reading Nerguti's report, we are struck with the utter stupidity of the team leader's actions, which seem to be in complete disregard of our instructions. It is difficult to understand what Nerguti thought he could accomplish by leading an army of twenty men into KMWAHOO after having taken refuge on the TPROACH [Cryptonym for Yugoslavia] border. Nevertheless, he did it and, as the reader can well realize, he is now a hero in the hearts of his HTNEIGH [Cryptonym for NCFA] compatriots.[24]

Nerguti continued his correspondence with anyone who would listen to him. Writing to Said Kryeziu in Rome, he urged that future groups sent to Albania should be much better equipped than they had been. "They ought to be dressed with a regular uniform, and not with a jacket made of blanket cloth and German trousers made of tent [material]. This is a thing that catches the eyes of the population, brings a demoralization both with the people and the groups, and this is the main thing that damages our propaganda."[25]

The unorthodox communications remained a nuisance for the Athens station chief, who failed to notice in Nerguti's letters red flags and helpful suggestions that would improve the quality of operations for future teams. He wrote to Washington that they were sending aid to the team, but:

> We cannot see how this team can be of great assistance since its leader seems bent on conducting an international correspondence club. An effort is being made, however, to persuade subject to confine his writing to one individual within HTNEIGH's Military Junta. HTNEIGH leaders are also asked to respect this procedure. Knowing the KMWAHOO flair for letter writing, we are of the opinion that mashing potatoes with a needle might be an easier accomplishment.[26]

* * *

Aid to the stranded agents came in the form of a relief team of two, Tahir Vata and Liman Peposhi, code name Pine Tree, who were parachuted in the Luma region in central Albania on May 18, 1951. A few months later, this team was augmented with two other parachutists, Dalip Kaiku and Dule Koçi, who was the first W/T operator fully trained in Morse code and cryptography and equipped with a RS-1 radio set able to communicate directly with the base in Athens.

This team was the first one in the Albanian operation to use one-time pads (OTPs) to encrypt and decrypt communications with the center. OTPs offered a virtually unbreakable encryption, which, at the same time, was simple to explain and very suitable for use by agents in the field—all they needed to secure their messages was a pencil and paper. OTPs worked in matching sets of two: the agent in the field kept one pad of sheets and the case officer in Athens kept the matching pad. No two sets and no two sheets within a set were alike. Each sheet contained a random key in the form of five-digit groups, which the radiomen used to encrypt the messages. After using the sheet, the communication agent tore it off the pad and physically destroyed it to prevent the enemy from breaking the cipher should it have intercepted the message.[27]

The improvements in communication enabled the base for the first time to coordinate supply missions with agents in the ground and drop provisions in reception areas they prepared. Pine Tree team received seventy-one containers of supplies and arms that enabled them to survive in the mountains through the spring and summer of 1951.[28]

However, their activities compromised a number of friends and relatives that the Sigurimi kept under surveillance. The authorities had rounded up and imprisoned over twenty of them by the end of 1951. With the onset of winter and unwilling to risk their local friends further, the relief team exfiltrated to Yugoslavia, where the authorities tried to recruit them for their own missions to Albania. Pine Tree refused to cooperate. In June 1952, Yugoslav soldiers led them to the border and, on the morning of June 9, 1952, ushered them into Albania.

The team recrossed into Yugoslavia that night and proceeded toward the Greek border, traveling by night to avoid detection by the Yugoslav authorities. Pine Tree crossed the Greek frontier eighteen days after they had begun their journey. OPC personnel picked up and debriefed them in Athens and sent them to the Labor Services Company in Germany.[29] The achievements of Pine Tree were modest. Despite their efforts, they had not been able to connect with or assist in any way Nerguti, Gjurra, or any of the other agents parachuted in November 1950. They provided only scant information of limited intelligence value upon their return to Athens. However, compared to the experience of the agents that preceded and followed them, Pine Tree would go on record as one of the most successful and luckiest teams that the CIA sent to Albania as part of Operation Fiend.

* * *

From the Pine Tree debriefing and other sources, OPC staff learned that all the surviving members of the November 1950 drops had crossed definitely in Yugoslavia by 1952. Some reports indicated that the Yugoslavs were holding them in prison and tortured them. On April 1953, word came that the Yugoslav minister of interior had pardoned two Kosovar members of the team, Rexh Berisha and Myftar Planeja, and had given them all the privileges and rights of Yugoslav citizens. Berisha was living with relatives in Peja, and Planeja was residing with friends in Prizreni.

The CIA liaison with the NCFA in Rome informed the military junta that, if the information were true, he would consider both Berisha and Planeja to have defected; the pay being accumulated for them would cease immediately and no further funds would be sent to their accounts.[30]

The other surviving members of the team, Halil Nerguti, Adem Gjurra, Ramadan Cenaj, and Sali Dalliu, remained in a Yugoslav concentration camp.[31] At the time, the CIA had just established a cooperation agreement with the Yugoslav secret service, the UDB, and one of the staff officers raised the question whether they should use the opportunity to request the return of the agents to US control. On May 3, 1953, headquarters requested Athens station's reaction to the possibility of reviving the team. In HQ's opinion, reestablishing connection with the team simply for debriefing purposes would not be useful because it brought to the forefront the need to dispose of the agents afterward. HQ asked Athens to determine whether the agents would be willing to resume activities for the US before accepting them back. HQ also cautioned against possible Yugoslav efforts to exploit the returning agents for their own benefit.[32] Four days later, Athens cabled the following response: "Negative to reaction in view low caliber team, performance on operations and subsequent activities in Yugo."[33]

Fiend personnel wanted to bring finality to the status of the team members who had taken refuge in Yugoslavia, even though they were not willing to intercede with the Yugoslavs on their behalf. In June 1953, the CIA liaison with the NCFA in Rome informed the military junta that the agents had until November 1, 1953, to report at the Greek frontier if they wished to continue to be associated with the NCFA and enjoy the benefits of the US support. If they failed to get to Greece by the deadline, the agency would assume that they no longer wished to represent the NCFA, in which case any remuneration accumulated in the accounts of these agents would stop.[34]

It is not known whether the agents received the message or whether they could leave Yugoslavia if they wished to. None of them reported to the Greek border by the deadline of November 1, 1953.

CHAPTER 10

Philby's Exit

The first team of OPC agents infiltrated into Albania experienced misfortune and setbacks from the beginning. In later years, after Philby's role as a Soviet mole inside the British Secret Intelligence Services was uncovered, it became convenient to ascribe their difficulties to his betrayal. The survivors of the operation, in particular Nerguti, Gjurra, and Berisha, went to the grave believing this version of events. But did Philby really betray their operation?

The review of the facts presented earlier and below raises doubts about whether he had access to sufficient information to compromise their mission, even if he were motivated to do so. Since the beginning of 1950, the CIA and SIS had agreed on a separation of Fiend and Valuable at the operational level, although the overall plans continued to be coordinated at the policy level.

Policy integration and coordination included a joint understanding of the end results desired in Albania and the general methods for accomplishing these results; the composition and general character of activities of the National Committee for Free Albanian; the propaganda lines to be pursued against Albania and with respect to Albania's neighbors; and economic measures taken against Albania.

Operationally, Fiend and Valuable were entirely separate, although field activities were coordinated in general terms to prevent operations of one service from interfering with those of the other service. Key personnel of Fiend and Valuable in the field met quarterly to exchange information regarding areas of operation and approximate timing of activities. They exchanged freely operational intelligence as well as certain general intelligence and occasional estimates.[1]

In his memoir, *My Silent War*, Philby said that when there was an overlap of operations between the British and Americans, they exchanged precise information about the timing and coordinates of the drops. There was no need for an exchange of this kind in the case of the Albanian operation. The British area of operations had always been in the southern Albania, whereas Burke sent his teams in the northeast. The British mode of infiltration was by boat landings, quite different from the parachute drops employed by the Americans.

So it's reasonable to think that, while Philby was aware of the overall Albanian plan, he was not supposed to have access to the specifics of the operation, including drop zones and times. An intelligence officer as good as Philby certainly could try to get the information from his CIA contacts. But was intelligence on the Albanian operation worth the risk of him drawing attention to himself?

Philby described his involvement in the Albanian operation at some length in his memoir, but he did not indicate having reported it to his Soviet handlers. He was not shy describing other instances where he provided information to the Soviets, such as the case of three teams the British parachuted in Ukraine in May 1951. "I do not know what happened to the parties concerned," Philby wrote coyly. "But I can make an informed guess."[2] It's worth noting that Philby wrote his memoir in Moscow under the close supervision of the KGB in the mid-1960s, when the Soviet Union and Albania had completely broken off all relations due to Albania's siding with Maoist China in its conflict with Moscow. If Philby and the KGB had played a significant role in sabotaging the Valuable Fiend agents, it is hard to believe they did not use the opportunity to credit themselves for it and take a swipe at Hoxha's regime in Tirana.

Philby himself outlined several reasons the operation was futile from the beginning. The infiltrators were not able to penetrate the towns, which were firmly under Communist control. Forced to stay in the mountains in order to survive, they could have made a difference only if the anti-Communist sentiment in the country had reached a boiling point. Philby wrote: "That, perhaps, was the unspoken assumption behind the whole venture, just as it was assumed more recently (when people should have known better) that a landing in the Bay of Pigs would set Cuba on fire."[3]

Ultimately, Philby wrote, the political contradictions between the British and Americans bedeviled their plans in Albania and elsewhere more than anything else.

* * *

There is a simpler explanation for the difficulties that Burke's teams encountered from the first moment they parachuted into Albania. The Communist regime received detailed information about everything that was happening at the Labor Service Company 4000 in Germany. When the nine members of the first infiltration teams were removed from the company in October 1950, their names and the purpose of their mission would have been passed on to the Sigurimi, who then mobilized the pursuit forces in the areas where the agents hailed from, where they were expected to be parachuted.

As luck had it, most of the agents, except for Toptani and Daci, managed to evade the trap that the Sigurimi had laid for them. What made their mission impossible to succeed afterward was the inadequate training they received and Burke's failure to put in place working communication and support plans. Burke's own memoir, *Outrageous Good Fortune*, describes his sympathies for the plight of the Albanian agents, but leaves the clear impression that Burke was fully immersed in the luxuries of his life in Europe, a sheer heaven after the hardships he and his family had endured in New York City. It's hard to believe Burke fully focused on the success and survival of his team in those months of 1950, while he enjoyed: "A very attractive villa, a cook, a maid, a nurse for [his daughter], the beauty of the ancient city itself, a beach cabana a half-hour away, October holidays on the Mediterranean, summer visits to Austria, marvelous journeys on the Scandinavian Express through the spectacular Italian and Swiss Alps and out into the beautiful forests and lakes of Bavaria."[4]

Just a few weeks after the team was parachuted into Albania, Burke returned to Washington in December 1950 to accept the position of head of OPC operations in Germany, this time as a full-time CIA employee. He assumed the new post in March

1951, not before attending a number of warm and hospitable parties thrown by members of the intelligence community in Washington, the largest, jolliest, and wettest of which was given by the Philbys on February 24, 1951 at their home in Nebraska Avenue.[5]

Philby's two-year assignment to Washington was coming to an end, as well. In September, he was supposed to return to London for his next assignment. Unforeseen circumstances forced his early exit from Washington and the SIS in July 1951.

* * *

Since 1940, the Army's Signal Security Agency, the precursor of the National Security Agency, had been collecting encrypted messages sent to and from Soviet Union's diplomatic missions in the United States. They recorded and filed the messages away until February 1, 1943, when a small and very secretive project began to decrypt and read their content. The project would later receive the code name Venona. Decrypting the messages was an impossible task at first. While the American cryptanalysts had been successful in breaking the encryption of the German and the Japanese, breaking the Soviet codes proved extremely difficult.

The Russians used two levels of encryption for their communications. First, they converted the clear text messages to numeric representation by using a codebook, a sort of dictionary that mapped words and phrases to numbers. Then, they padded the numbers with random sequences of digits from one-time pads. In order to attack the underlying codebook at the heart of the encryption challenge, the American cryptanalysts had to first strip away these added numerals.

One way to recognize these numbers was to possess the OTP page used to encrypt the message. Another way was to know the Russian algorithm that generated the random sequences of the OTPs and try to guess the numbers used to encrypt a particular message. The small team of cryptanalysts working on the problem devised brilliant analytical techniques trying to break the code using "brute force" methods, but for a number of years the efforts yielded disappointing results.

A third possibility was that the Russians could misuse or reuse the numbers in the pads, which could leave them vulnerable to attack. As it happened, the flaw in the Soviet messages resulted from the duplication

of OTP pages during the printing process, rather than from a malfunc-
tioning random-number generator or extensive reuse of pages by code
clerks. For a few months in early 1942, for reasons that remain unknown,
the cryptographic material manufacturing center in the Soviet Union
printed some thirty-five thousand pages with the same sequence of
numbers on them, which then were assembled and bound in thousands
of OTP codebooks.[6]

This misstep gave the Venona cryptanalysts the break they needed
to solve the problem. The number of messages that were eventually
decrypted was directly tied to the number of defective OTP pages used
to encipher the messages. The analysts could decrypt very few of the
1942 messages because there was very little duplication of OTP pages
used in those messages. The number of duplicate pages apparently
increased in 1943 and then even more in 1944, and the success rate of
deciphering messages from these years improved accordingly.[7]

In his role as SIS liaison with US intelligence agencies, Philby had
participated in several discussions on Venona with the American cryptanalysts working on the project. He also received regular reports with
summaries of the Soviet messages that the American analysts were
decoding.[8] A number of messages from 1944–1945 showed that Soviet
intelligence was receiving regular updates on exchanges between the
US and British governments at the time, and in particular exchanges
between Roosevelt and Churchill. They indicated that the information
was coming from a highly placed source, which the Soviets variably
referred to as G, G., GOMER, GOMMER, and HOMER.

Philby knew that all these codes referred to Donald MacLean, his
fellow Soviet intelligence conspirator, who had been first secretary at
the British embassy in Washington between 1944 and 1948. MacLean's
codename had been Homer, which the Soviet cables writers routinely
spelled by replacing *H* with its Cyrillic equivalent, *G* since the Cyrillic alphabet has no letter representing the sound "H" of the Roman
alphabet.

Philby and his Soviet contact in the US agreed that the FBI and
MI-5 would eventually zero in on MacLean by a process of elimination as content from more and more cables was becoming readable.
With MacLean's exposure a certainty, they decided to cause his defection on their own terms rather than allow the British to capture and

interrogate him. In spring 1951, the British had indeed narrowed the list of possible suspects to six individuals and MacLean was on it. In his autobiography, Philby says that he wrote a memo to London providing the hints that led MI-5 to MacLean's trail.[9] It was part of the plan put in motion by the Soviets in order to provide Philby with a credible cover against accusations of being an associate of MacLean. They expected the British to raise these issues because it was widely known that Philby and MacLean were old associates since their Cambridge years.

As soon as the British received Philby's letter, they revoked MacLean's access to highly sensitive documents and placed him under surveillance while MI-5 began to gather evidence of his culpability. At this point, Philby and his Soviet handlers took the second step in the orchestrated defection of MacLean. Guy Burgess, the third Soviet spy inside British government structures, who at the time was working at the British embassy in Washington and living in Philby's house, engaged in a series of flagrant acts that caused the US authorities to label him persona non grata and ask for his return to the UK.

It was an act put on by Burgess to give him a reason to return to London, where he would make contact with MacLean and the Russian handlers there and arrange MacLean's defection to the Soviet Union. Given his own close association with Burgess, Philby knew that he was the Achilles' heel in the plan. His last words to Burgess at Union Station in Washington were, only half-jokingly, "Don't you go too."[10] However, upon his return to London, Moscow ordered that Burgess flee together with MacLean for reasons that are not entirely clear, perhaps because the Russians found Burgess too unstable to face the MI-5 inquiries that would inevitably follow MacLean's disappearance.

On Sunday, March 25, 1951, three days before he was due to appear in front of an inquiry commission to respond to evidence from MI-5 and the FBI, MacLean celebrated his thirty-eighth birthday at home with his eight-month pregnant wife and two young children. Then Burgess arrived and picked him up in his car for what was supposed to be a short ride in the countryside. They drove to Southampton, took a ferry across the Channel to France, and then traveled by train to Paris and Moscow in one of the most spectacular spy escapes of the Cold War.

By virtue of his association with Burgess, Philby fell immediately under suspicion and was recalled to London. The CIA performed a counterespionage assessment of Philby's career and contacts that concluded he was a Soviet agent. Upon receiving the report, the director of Central Intelligence, Walter B. Smith, forwarded it to his British counterpart, the head of the SIS, Stewart Menzies, commonly referred to as "C," with a forceful demand that "C" fire Philby or Smith would sever all links between the SIS and the CIA.[11] In July 1951, Philby, facing almost certain dismissal, resigned from MI-6. He had to forgo his pension, but "C" agreed to give him a lump sum of two thousand pounds and four installments of five hundred pounds every six months as a severance package.[12]

* * *

Philby's hasty exit from Washington under a cloud of suspicion led the CIA to review the access that the SIS had to its operations. Henceforward, CIA director Smith pushed to restrict access to OPC offices in Washington by SIS representatives. Project Fiend came to the forefront of scrutiny, given its unique character among OPC projects in the close liaison with the British and the fact that certain phases of the operation had depended to some degree on British good will.

On August 28, 1951, Yatsevitch wrote a memo summarizing the nature of the relationship with the British on Project Fiend, which was operational independence in the field but close cooperation with respect to policy and sharing of intelligence garnered from the operation. Then, Yatsevitch described the arrangements that existed between the British and American liaison officers in the operation. In Washington, the OPC commander—McCargar until April 1950 followed by Yatsevitch—and Philby as SIS representative had established a system for prompt action on all matters of mutual concern to Fiend and Valuable. They met in the Joint Policy Committee office at the Pentagon that had been established from the beginning to minimize SIS access to the CIA work environments.

In London, the OPC liaison officer handling Fiend-Valuable relations held an SIS pass, which gave him free access to SIS headquarters at all times and allowed him to come and go as he pleased. SIS headquarters personnel dealing with Fiend met him in their regular offices and gave him ready access at their environment as well as operational and other information relating to Valuable activities in Albania. He also dealt directly with the British on certain matters outside the scope of Fiend itself, such as the recruiting of Polish crews and personnel for miscellaneous OPC needs in the Balkan area and in Germany. Because of the close personal relationship he had established, he had been able to receive numerous favors and assistance that was extremely useful to OPC.

Therefore, Yatsevitch warned, if the agency was planning to restrict SIS access to OPC offices in Washington as a reaction to the doubts about Philby, they should do this carefully to avoid retaliatory treatment in London that could interfere with the smooth course of Fiend-Valuable relations and affect the work of the Fiend liaison officer there.[13]

CHAPTER II

Propaganda and Psychological and Economic Warfare

In April 1950, when Michael Burke was appointed to a full-time position with the CIA and assigned to run the German section in Frankfurt, the NCFA leaders in Rome threw a farewell lunch party for him. An eight-course meal was served, complete with Valpolicella, burgundy, and cognac. At the end, they gave him as a souvenir the lunch menu in a specially designed and bound folder, in which the Albanian eagle was prominently displayed and the following message from the Sons of the Eagle, as Albanians often refer to themselves, was inscribed in red and black—the colors of Albania's flag:

> To our dear friend Michael Burke,
>
> Parting is not merely an occasion for sad rituals.
>
> For us this temporary parting is also an occasion for recalling your many acts of kindness and your devotion to our cause and your continuing efforts in our behalf.
>
> In return for your priceless gift of friendship, we extend our heartfelt gratitude to you and yours.
>
> Our wish is that your lives may be brightest in the days ahead as you have brightened the lives of those you have left behind.[1]

It was a touching gesture that must have left an impression on Burke, because he saved the folder for the rest of his life in a collection of personal memorabilia still preserved today. In return, he wrote a brief note of appreciation to his "dear friend Abas Kupi" that said:

> It is with deep regret that I relinquish my place beside you in our common fight, but I remain emotionally bound and constantly devoted to the cause to which we dedicated ourselves and so long worked for together in basic harmony.
>
> As we separate momentarily, I carry with me something of the splendid spirit of the Sons of the Eagle and an indelible memory of each one whom I have grown to know so well and love; I hope in turn that some small part of me rests with them.
>
> My dear Abas Aga, I salute you as a great soldier of Albania and look for the day when we will be joined again in final victory.[2]

Joseph C. Lieb took Burke's place as the Fiend field commander and Rome OPC station chief. Lieb came from a public relations and advertising background—he had been a Madison Avenue executive in New York City before World War II. During the war, Lieb served as a US Army major in the Pacific theater, where he conducted propaganda operations against the Japanese and later served in the Combined Chiefs of Staff, the precursor of the Joint Chiefs of Staff. Lieb returned to New York City after the war and went back to his advertising career until 1950, when OPC officers familiar with his work in propaganda during the war reached out and recruited him to conduct similar operations against the Iron Curtain.

Like Burke, Lieb worked as a contract officer for the CIA. He traveled to Germany in September 1950, where he met Burke at the Schwarzer Bock Hotel in Wiesbaden for a thorough debriefing on the Albanian operation and the NCFA. Then he traveled to Rome, where he settled under the cover of a *Parade* magazine reporter. While much of Lieb's work in Rome focused on the Albanian operation, he was also involved in other OPC and CIA projects, working closely with the Italians and the Vatican.[3]

Building upon his experience in advertising and public relations, Lieb pushed forward a number of operational activities in the areas of propaganda and psychological warfare. He expanded the circulation of *Shqipëria* (Albania), the semi-monthly NCFA newspaper in the Albanian language, and pushed to disseminate it in major cities in Europe and the United States. Lieb encouraged all the members of the NCFA to support the newspaper, to improve its content, and in general to make it a worthy representative journal of the committee.

In Rome, he established a subcommittee of the NCFA to expand on the work that NCFA members in New York had done in preparing propaganda material. For several months in 1950, they had drafted propaganda leaflets under the guidance of E. Howard Hunt, who at the time worked in the Paramilitary and Propaganda Warfare division of the OPC, in his first assignment as a CIA officer.[4] The covert OPC aircraft and British Royal Air Force planes dropped about five hundred thousand leaflets approximately once a month over the principal population centers of Albania. The timing of leaflet drops coincided with important dates, such as Enver Hoxha's birthday, the anniversary of the

CIA leaflet about Soviet aid to Albania: "The conductor [USSR] promises the donkey [the Albanian people] more food because he is weak and slow." Leading the donkey is the Albanian government.

In this CIA leaflet, Nastradini, the sage in Albanian folklore, says to the villager on the right: "This beast may look like a donkey but he is not one because he has not joined the Communist Party."

October Revolution, or Albania's Independence Day. The design and content of the leaflets conveyed messages related to those historical markers. Because a majority of the Albanian population was illiterate, most of the leaflets were nothing more than humorous cartoons with brief captions.

As a further means of implementing the psychological warfare phase, OPC staff installed camouflaged short-wave and medium-wave radio transmitters aboard a yacht, called *Juanita*, which they operated under a Panamanian flag in the Mediterranean. The cover for the boat was a scientific expedition in the field of marine biology. The transmitter was scheduled to begin beaming covert propaganda into Albania by spring 1951.[5] However, a series of operational tests throughout spring and summer showed that it was impossible to broadcast radio transmissions from a moving yacht in the middle of the sea. The OPC

National Archives and Records Administration (NARA)

Rear Admiral Roscoe H. Hillenkoetter, US Navy, first director of the Central Intelligence Agency, 1947–1950.

NARA

General Walter B. Smith, US Army, director of Central Intelligence, 1950–1953.

NARA

Allen W. Dulles, DCI, 1953–1961.

NARA

The CIA's first headquarters in Washington, DC, across the street from the State Department.

CIA officers reviewing cables in the communications room.

NARA

Xhevdet Shehu

Albanian armed forces general staff in 1952. Starting from left, Mehmet Shehu is fifth, Enver Hoxha is sixth, and Kadri Hazbiu is last.

Albert Lalushi

Enver Hoxha giving his first speech as head of the Albanian government on November, 28, 1944. With an ominous demeanor and tone, he threatened to pursue all those who had not joined his side in the war.

Xhevdet Shehu

Hoxha in an official 1954 photo. Hoxha always presented an immaculate image that inspired his followers.

Xhevdet Shehu

Mehmet Shehu (left), minister of Interior between 1949 and 1954, and Kadri Hazbiu, his deputy and head of the Sigurimi, the Albanian security and intelligence service.

Frank G. Wisner headed the CIA's Office of Policy Coordination and then the Directorate of Plans.

James McCargar, the OPC's chief of Foreign Branch B, Section I (FB-I), was the first commander of Project Fiend.

Julian Amery, a veteran of British SOE missions to Albania during World War II, coordinated the Operation Valuable actions in Europe.

Colonel Gratian M. Yatsevitch II, the CIA's Southeast Europe branch chief, replaced McCargar and commanded Project Fiend between 1950 and 1953.

Albert Lulushi

Xhevdet Shehu

Top Left: Zog I, King of the Albanians, "the shrewdest, most cunning, as well as the most capable and unscrupulous of Albanian politicians."

Top Right: Mithat Frashëri (left), leader of the republican Balli Kombëtar (National Front), and Abas Kupi, leader of the royalist Legaliteti (Legitimacy), had very little in common other than being against Hoxha's regime.

Center Right: Hasan Dosti, leader of the BK after Frashëri's death in 1949.

Bottom Right: Ismail Vërlaci, leader of the Blloku Kombëtar Indipendent (National Independent Bloc).

Bottom Left: Gjon Markagjoni (right), Prince of Mirdita, and son Ndue, who was parachuted in Albania as part of CIA-sponsored and Italian-run operations.

Dosti family

Albert Lulushi

Albert Lulushi

Albert Lalushi

Albanian émigrés announced the creation of the National Committee for Free Albania in Paris on August 26, 1949. In the front row starting from left are Said Kryeziu, Mithat Frashëri (in white suit), and Abas Kupi.

Albert Lalushi

NCFA Executive Committee members during their September 1949 visit in London. From left to right are Nuçi Kota, Zef Pali, Mithat Frashëri, Abaz Kupi, and Said Kryeziu.

Albert Lalushi

NCFA Executive Committee members at the BBC World Service studios. Seated from the left are Nuçi Kota, Abaz Kupi, Mithat Frashëri, and Said Kryeziu.

Mithat Frashëri recording his BBC broadcast to Albania. Not many people in the country heard it due to the lack of radio sets and electricity.

Xhevdet Shehu

Albert Lulushi

Albanian trainees and their British instructors in
Malta in August 1949. In front row starting from
left are Abdyl Sino, Moy Smiley, and David Smiley.

Albert Lulushi

ABOVE RIGHT Jani Dilo organized
the trainees in operational groups
for infiltration.

RIGHT Albanian trainees in Malta.

Albert Lulushi

Participants in Exercise Raki, the
dress rehearsal for the infiltrations.
The small stature of the recruits
earned them the moniker "Pixies."

Albert Lulushi

Stormy Seas ferried agents from Malta to the Albanian coast.

Albert Lulushi

Agents aboard *Stormy Seas*.

Albert Lulushi

Albert Lulushi

Members of the second infiltration party that landed at Seaview cove. Starting from the second on the left are Sami Lepenica, Zogoll Sheno, and Hysni Lepenica, who were ambushed and killed by Albanian pursuit detachments. Most likely, they fell victim not to Kim Philby's betrayal but to an early Sigurimi playback operation using Ethem Çako.

Kim Philby in Washington, DC, circa 1950.

Philby at an improvised October 1955 press conference at his London flat after being cleared of suspicion of being the "third man" of the KGB in the ranks of the British secret services.

Philby in his Moscow apartment in the 1980s.

E. Michael Burke in his World War II Jedburgh parachutist uniform.

Rear Admiral E. M. Pace, Jr., US Navy, awards the Navy Cross to Burke in September 1946. Warner Brothers staged the ceremony at its offices in Hollywood as a publicity stunt for the release of *Cloak and Dagger*, a tribute to OSS directed by Fritz Lang and starring Gary Cooper. Burke had served as technical adviser to the scriptwriters.

Burke's diary entry for November 3, 1950, outlining preparations for the first drop of the CIA-trained agents. The last item is a reminder to order "L" tablets—poison pills the agents could use if captured.

Colonel F. E. Dun, US Army, inspects personnel of the Albanian Labor Services Company 4000.

NARA

Albert Lulushi

Company 4000 service badge.

Albert Lulushi

Company 4000 service patch.

Top Close combat train-
ing of agents in Murnau,
Germany, in 1951.

Right Learning to keep a
safe distance from
the enemy.

Bottom Pistol practice at
the range.

Top Practicing jumping from a mock aircraft door.

Right Practicing the manipulation of parachute raisers on descent.

Bottom Practicing landing.

NARA

Top Practicing the assembly of wireless transmitter radios.

Right Practicing sending in Morse code.

Bottom Practicing receiving messages.

NARA

NARA

Jon Lieb

Top Members of the National Committee for Free
Albania with their US and British liaisons in Rome.
Seated from second on the left are Archibald Lyall,
British liaison, Mildred Lieb, Abas Kupi, and Joseph
C. Lieb. Standing behind Lieb is Gaqo Gogo, his
translator, who may have been one of several
Sigurimi sources within the NCFA complex.

Right Joseph C. Lieb, CIA case officer in Rome.

Bottom Right Alfred C. Ulmer, CIA station chief
in Athens.

Bottom Left There was not much chemistry left
between Lieb and Kupi (right) in spring 1954 as a
result of the significant cuts in the CIA's funds for
the NCFA. Lieb and Lyall left Rome simulta-
neously in June 1954 and were not replaced.

Jon Lieb

Jon Lieb

Marguerite Ulmer-Power

Anton Ashta

Anton Ashta

Anton Ashta

REPUBLIKA POPULLORE E SHQIPËR.SË

Nr. 364525 Ser' G.

z. *Xunus Thar*

Nenëshkrimi i mbajtësit

Kryetar' Zyrës *Fim?*

Anton Ashta

TOP Sigurimi photo of Ethem Çako, with bandaged head, crouching on the right and sending messages to his case officers in Italy in 1949. The Sigurimi repeated a similar playback operation against the CIA Apple team in 1952–53.

ABOVE LEFT Staged Sigurimi photo of Zenel Shehi.

ABOVE RIGHT Staged Sigurimi photo of Hamit Matiani.

RIGHT CIA-produced Albanian identity card for Ahmet Kabashi.

At the April 1954 trial of the Apple agents, the Sigurimi displayed weapons, money, radio transmitters, crypto pads, and other items that the CIA parachuted into their hands.

Anton Ashta

Zenel Shehi testifies. A CIA counterespionage review of the trial suspected "psychological preconditioning of the defendants by hypnosis, brainwashing, drugs, or other means." The court sentenced all six surviving CIA agents to death. Shehi was shot.

Anton Ashta

Top Right Hamit Matiani was hanged.

Second Right Halil Branica was shot.

Third Right Ahmet Kabashi was shot.

Fourth Right Naum Sula was shot.

Bottom Right Gani Malushi was shot.

Anton Ashta

abandoned the plan to use *Juanita* in August 1951 and transferred the operations and support staff to a broadcasting facility in Athens. The yacht, purchased for $80,000 in August 1950, was sold in May 1953 for $10,037.50.[6]

The clandestine radio Voice of Free Albania began regular short-wave broadcasts from Athens at 10:00 p.m. on September 18, 1951, on the 43-meter band. The programs reached various European cities and were praised by NCFA committee members who heard them. The station received considerable publicity from VOA, BBC, Radio Free Europe, and the *New York Times*.[7]

A powerful radio transmitter in Salonika established by the Americans and jointly run with the Greeks amplified the anti-Communist propaganda broadcasts beamed to Greece, Albania, Bulgaria, and Yugoslavia. The operation, with the code name Dora, had some hiccups before it finally got off the ground. When the Americans shipped the first packing cases of equipment marked with "Dora," the Greek authorities refused to allow them through. A short time before their arrival a new clerk with the name Dora had arrived at the US consulate in Salonika. She brought some things with her and said some more personal things were to follow. When a few weeks later, steel towers and dynamos for Dora arrived, the customs officials opened their eyes wide. They said they would have to know more about Dora before allowing the shipment. Only after some delay did they agree to release the cases, once they had received an official, signed, sealed, and certified statement stating that Dora was a code name for a government project and that the cases marked "Dora" had no relation whatsoever with the personal effects of the recently arrived American clerk at the consulate.[8]

Another psychological warfare program at this time used letters and messages to arouse suspicions within the ranks of government officials against one another and to frame Communist personalities by accusing them of corruption or secret relations with the West. Knowing that all mail from abroad was opened and inspected, CIA case officers in Rome and Athens prepared and sent gift packages, fake bank statements, and confirmation of deposit transactions into foreign accounts to prominent Communists and their family members, including Enver Hoxha, whose CIA pseudonym was Nelson J.

Murat. At the end of June 1951, Lieb informed headquarters that "two such gift packages had been sent to Mrs. Nelson J. Murat," referring to Hoxha's wife, Nexhmije. They also prepared character assassination and denunciation letters against other party, military, and government officials that were carried across the border by agents infiltrated from Greece, who mailed them to the authorities from inside Albania to create the appearance that they were coming from concerned and vigilant citizens.[9]

* * *

On September 13, 1951, Hasan Dosti, president of the NCFA, sent the following commercial cable to Enver Hoxha offering aid to oppressed Albanians in the form of food, clothing, and medicine:

> As you well know, the National Committee for Free Albania has long been dedicated to the overthrow of your regime and the re-establishment of a free and independent Albania. While we are making every effort to hasten the day of your demise, which is not far off, we want to help our people and to ease their suffering in the meantime. In view of the widespread poverty and lack of foodstuffs, medicines, and other household necessities, we, the National Committee for Free Albania, therefore make the following offer to your Government:
>
> Starting immediately, this Committee will supply aid to our people on a continuing basis each and every month if your Government will agree to distribute such aid equitably and impartially to our needy brothers and sisters regardless of their political affiliations. Will you agree to accept foodstuffs, medicines, and household necessities not now available to our people, and will you agree to distribute them?
>
> May we have your early reply to this offer by commercial cable?
> (Signed) The National Committee for Free Albania[10]

The telegram marked the opening of the propaganda program to supply token aid to Albania. The text of this telegram, together with the fact that Hoxha didn't even have the decency to reply to the offer, was incorporated in leaflets and other NCFA propaganda materials addressed to the Albanian people. CIA and State Department officials discussed preparations to drop thirty thousand one-pound bags of white flour over Albania by the end of the year[11] but eventually abandoned the idea for fear they might hurt someone on the ground or that the Communists might poison them. Instead, they opted for lightweight envelopes and tin cans filled with NCFA propaganda materials together with badly needed supplies to provide a token relief to the impoverished Albanian population, such as thread, needles, cloth, socks, scarves, soap, and razor blades. According to its records, between 1950 and 1955 the agency dropped 33 million propaganda leaflets and over thirty thousand care packets over Albania.[12]

* * *

As Lieb and Yatsevitch began considering economic warfare activities against Albania, they saw mercantile shipping as one of its greatest vulnerabilities. Other economic warfare actions, such as devaluation of currency, black market activities, and encouraging hoarding, were useful but had limited, if not questionable effect against Albania. It was a small country where there was not much to be hoarded, where trading was done by barter rather than with money, and whose primitive form of economy would not be greatly affected by black market activities.

Lieb raised the possibility of burning on the high seas two Albanian vessels sailing between the ports of Durrësi and Trieste. To a small country like Albania, with very limited resources, a successful action of this character would constitute a significant psychological and economic blow. It would also have far-reaching psychological effect on the Albanians who were involved in other Fiend activities—it would provide concrete proof that the Americans were conducting tangible actions with concrete results. Even if the operation failed, the loss would be small and it would be worth the effort if only for the experience it provided.[13]

Although the OPC had responsibility over Trieste, it didn't have any presence there, so it asked the OSO to help evaluate the plan's feasibility. Richard Stolz, a young OSO operative on his first assignment in Trieste at the time, received the assignment and described it as follows:

> The Office of Policy Coordination (OPC), the euphemistic name of the then covert action arm of the Agency, heard that an Albanian "ship," the *Queen Teuta* out of Durrësi, regularly stopped at Trieste. We were instructed to check this out and examine the possibility of using limpet mines to put it out of action. Another case officer and I soon discovered that this ship was a small, wooden-hulled tub that was hauling sand up and down the Adriatic. We had some difficulty in persuading OPC that their idea was not a good one.[14]

* * *

A campaign of terror began in Albania in February 1951, triggered by the explosion of a pack of dynamite thrown in the courtyard of the Soviet embassy in Tirana on February 19, 1951. The explosion occurred in the evening when very few people were on the premises, and the damage was limited to a broken door and shattered glass of a few windows. It is not clear to this date whether this was a spontaneous act of individuals opposed to the regime, an act sponsored by the Yugoslav secret service, or a provocation by the Sigurimi. The Albanian authorities used the explosion as a pretext to arrest hundreds of individuals in the capital immediately afterward. On February 27, they executed extrajudicially twenty-two of them, mostly intellectuals unaffiliated with the Communists, and sentenced to long prison terms another eighty.

The terror spread to the rest of the country. Radio Tirana announced that the trial of four Greek agents took place on March 19 in the village of Zemblaku in the Korça prefecture. Two of the accused, Abdul Kalaja and Fuad Kulla, were sentenced to be hanged and the other two to a term of twenty years' imprisonment. According to Radio Tirana, all four confessed to have collaborated with the Balli Kombëtar during the war and that, on the orders of the Greek security service, they set fire to a Zemblaku collective farm building.[15]

American newspapers began reporting in a series of sensational articles in March that the situation in Albania was about to explode in open revolt against the government and that the Soviets had sent reinforcements, including ten or more MiG fighter jets to Tirana. The OPC was concerned that the events in Albania were accelerating beyond their control, despite the OSO's assurances that news of an uprising against the Hoxha government was a gross exaggeration by misinformed journalists. The OSO discounted press reports that the bomb episode was the result of a wide-scale plot to overthrow the government or that the Soviets had sent military reinforcements.[16]

The Yugoslav government had always considered the activities of the British and Americans in Albania as trespassing in their own backyard and took the opportunity to link these activities with the escalation of tensions in Albania. Leveraging the goodwill that their opposition to the Soviet Union had created among Western allies, Yugoslav officials pointed out to the US and British ambassadors in Belgrade that the activities of the NCFA and other groups in Albania were likely to cause the Soviets to intervene and thus endanger the peace in the Balkans.[17]

At a meeting at the State Department in early April, Frank Wisner and officials of the Policy Planning Staff, including Robert Joyce, liaison with the OPC, John C. Campbell, in charge of Balkan affairs, and Randolph H. Higgs, covering Yugoslavia and Trieste issues, agreed that "matters in Albania should be allowed to cool off a bit for the present." They would suspend all propaganda leaflet drops for a period of two months, at the end of which the situation would be reconsidered. The OPC could proceed quietly to build an internal network in Albania with occasional secret parachute drops of agents and small supplies for their support. But until further notice, the OPC would avoid measures designed to create violent outbursts, or provocative activities that could attract notice.[18]

The State Department's ban on leaflet drops continued for several months. At the end of June, the CIA decided to cancel all leaflet-dropping flights over Albania and end the entire program of preparing leaflet texts. They would continue to drop existing leaflets and miniature copies of the NCFA newspaper *Shqipëria* only as a diversion during flights to parachute agents or supplies.[19]

CIA director Walter B. Smith involved himself personally in ensuring that the OPC followed the guidance. At a meeting on April 18, he told Wisner to make certain that the covert aircraft used for the drops would not go close to the Yugoslav frontier or take a roundabout route over Albania and risk being shot down. "The plane goes straight to the dropping point, makes the drop and comes straight out," said Smith.[20] Strict directives like this are an example of the degree to which Wisner and the OPC had lost their autonomy of the early days and come under the direct control of the director of Central Intelligence.

A plainspoken Midwesterner who never earned a college degree, General Walter B. Smith rose through the ranks to become a key aide to General George C. Marshall early in World War II and then Eisenhower's chief of staff in Europe. After the war, President Harry S. Truman named Smith as ambassador to Moscow, where he served until 1949.[21]

Smith took over as DCI on October 7, 1950, and quickly moved to reorganize the CIA into a cohesive and integrated intelligence organization, which to this day remains structured according to the blueprint that Smith put in place in the early 1950s. One of his first changes at the CIA was to put an end to the autonomous status that the Office of Policy Coordination had enjoyed since its creation in 1948. In early January 1951 Smith ordered the merger of the OPC and the Office of Special Operations under one organization, the Directorate of Plans, and assigned Allen Dulles to be the first deputy director for plans—DD/P. Frank Wisner succeeded Dulles as DD/P in August 1951. It took until August 1952 to fully merge the OSO and OPC—each with its own culture, methods, and pay scales—into an effective, single directorate of intelligence, with Wisner at its helm as the CIA's first deputy director for intelligence.[22]

* * *

In early June 1951, OPC began receiving reports about the proceedings of a Congress of the Albanian League of Political Refugees held in May in Prizreni, a town in Kosovo, only ten miles east of the Albanian border. The Congress had been an idea of Dushan Mugosha, a member of the Yugoslav Communist Party Central Committee, who ten years earlier had been instrumental in creating the Albanian Communist Party and controlling its actions during World War II. The league took the line that "democratic" Albanians in Yugoslavia rather than "reactionary" émigrés in Italy, Greece, and elsewhere should oust the Hoxha regime.[23] The Congress claimed to represent four thousand Albanians and passed a resolution calling for the mobilization of eighty thousand Albanians to form a force to overthrow the Hoxha government. They would proclaim a republic for which the Yugoslavs gave guarantees of independence and inviolability of borders.[24]

The league's president was Apostol Tenefi, a former member of the Albanian Communist Party and professor of Mathematics in Tirana until 1948, when he escaped to Yugoslavia. Tenefi was an ardent Titoist and a close follower of Koçi Xoxe, the former Albanian minister of interior executed in 1949 for being pro-Tito.[25]

The announcement of the creation of this group caused considerable agitation within the National Committee for Free Albania and in Albanian émigré circles in the West. Yugoslav diplomats and league representatives approached prominent Albanian refugees in Italy and outlined the militant nature of the new organization, clearly aimed at overthrowing the Hoxha regime. It was becoming clear to the Albanian emigration that the Yugoslavs were prepared to support a much more vigorous program against Hoxha than the relatively mild one that the Americans and British had undertaken in the name of the NCFA. There was a serious danger that the Yugoslav cause would lure Albanians away from the NCFA and erode its support among the Albanian public outside and inside the country.[26]

To maintain the situation under control, Lieb instructed the NCFA to adopt an attitude of skepticism toward the Prizreni proclamation calling for a "Free, Independent and Republican Albania," without launching into an exchange of polemics with the Yugoslav league.[27] In the meantime, Wisner insisted through his contacts in the Policy Planning Staff that the State Department take action at the diplomatic level in order to clarify Yugoslav intentions and factor them into the formulation of the US policy toward Albania and the OPC plans for immediate action in that area.[28]

The US ambassador in Belgrade met with Yugoslav officials to point out the inconsistency of their positions. On one hand, they complained that Western-sponsored resistance groups such as the NCFA could bring about Soviet intervention in Albania and Yugoslavia; on the other hand, the Yugoslavs themselves had permitted the creation of a far more militant organization that was openly announcing its intention to recruit a large armed force to overthrow the Albanian government. General Omar Bradley of the Joint Chiefs of Staff also brought up the subject up with General Koća Popović, the Yugoslav minister of defense, during the course of conversations between the US and Yugoslav military representatives that were taking place in Washington at the time.[29]

* * *

The creation of the League of Albanian Refugees by the Yugoslavs was part of a plan they had set in motion to replace the Hoxha regime with one friendly to Tito. Another step in the plan was the preparation by Generals Peko Dapćević, Svetozar Vukmanović Tempo, and Kosta Nadj of a military program for the invasion of Albania. Known as Plan R-7, it envisioned a preparatory period during which diversionary and propaganda actions would arouse the Albanian public against Hoxha and the Soviets. Then, armed units of the League of Refugees in Yugoslavia, interspersed with a division of the Yugoslav regular army made up of Kosovar elements, would enter Albania and converge on Tirana from several different approaches. The ranks of the strike force would grow to approximately 50,000 during its march to Tirana from internal supporters and deserters of the Albanian army. The operation was expected to accomplish its mission within a very short time.[30]

As they prepared the plan, the Yugoslavs approached the Greek government in June 1951 with a proposal for cooperation in case hostilities broke out in Albania. They said that if the Albanian regime collapsed or if Soviet Union or its satellites attacked Yugoslavia, the Yugoslav army would immediately invade Albania. Since they expected the Greeks to follow suit, the Yugoslavs wanted to prearrange zones of influence and demarcation lines in order to avoid confrontation between the Greek and Yugoslav armies when hostilities started.

The Greek Foreign Office sought the advice of the US State Department on responding to the Yugoslav proposal, which in turn invited the British to voice their opinion in the matter. The British Foreign Office sent a memorandum to Washington on June 20, 1951, in which it summarized the British position in one sentence: "If the

US and UK wish to see Albania remain independent they should extract assurances from Greece and Yugoslavia that the occupation will be temporary; if Albanian independence is no longer vital, they should restrict efforts to merely averting a clash between Greece and Yugoslavia."[31]

The memo went on to explain that the British preferred an independent Albania friendly to the West, but not at the cost of weakening Yugoslavia or Greece, and they wanted to see a line of demarcation agreed upon, just in case. In favor of the continued independence of Albania, the British memo listed factors such as ethnic and historical considerations, the existence of the NCFA, and the difficulty of implementing an alternative solution without conflict between the interested powers. Factors against Albania's independence were its size and instability as state, which, the British argued, might position it better as a Yugoslav Federative Republic, with or without the Northern Epirus region claimed by Greece. This alternative might be acceptable to Yugoslavia, Greece, and even Albanians, but might alienate Italy. However, the British memo concluded, "since the Yugoslavs were orienting towards the West and in view of the large Albanian population already there [within Yugoslav borders], this might not be a wholly unacceptable solution."[32]

The ambiguity of the British position concerning the future status of Albania caused concern and agitation among State Department officials. In a forcefully worded response, the State Department emphasized the US government's objective that Albania become an independent state friendly to the West. The United States would not support any policy aimed at the extinction of Albanian independence, such as partition between Yugoslavia and Greece.

Reasons for this position included the fact that the Albanian people had a definite national character and strong patriotic sentiments. Furthermore, their right to independence had been recognized and supported in various public statements by the US and British governments and there had been a nominally independent Albanian state in existence since 1912.

The State Department emphasized that "without an independent Albania there seemed no way to reconcile the conflicting interests of Yugoslavia, Greece and Italy in this strategic area which affected the security of all three."[33] None of these states would willingly accept a special position of either of the others; any partition arrangement would be inherently unstable and would only sow seeds of long-term minority problems, which would undermine the security of the whole area.

Finally, recanting Albania's right to independence was morally indefensible before public opinion and would provide the Soviet government and its Albanian puppets with a powerful propaganda weapon.

The US position was that they should continue diplomatic and other efforts toward the transition from a Soviet-dominated Albania to a free and independent Albania not dominated by neighboring states and supported by Western countries. They could keep in mind the possibility of Albania's inclusion in a larger federal unit at some future time. However, such a federation would have to be at least Balkan in scope and not limited to some special federal arrangement with Yugoslavia or Greece. The Western powers should encourage no federal arrangement with Yugoslavia until and unless that country's regime showed closer affinity with Western ideals.

The main obstacle to achieving the Albanian objective was the tangle of conflicting interests that Yugoslavia, Greece, and Italy had in their neighbor. Each of them feared and suspected the designs of the others in Albania. The State Department proposed that the US and UK initiate diplomatic efforts to get the three countries to state openly that they had no claims to a privileged position in Albania and recognized the right of the Albanian people to independence and institutions of their choosing. Ideally, their statements would renounce all territorial claims on Albania, although Greece would have difficulties accepting this. Such pledges by the three neighboring countries, with the backing of the US, UK, and possibly France, would prove most helpful to the efforts to liberate Albania from the Soviet-Communist domination and to future efforts to reestablish an independent Albania after the elimination of the Hoxha regime.

The memo concluded with a clear indication to the British that the American side would not allow them to drag their feet on this issue. The State Department suggested clearly that the moves they proposed might be accomplished easier on a broader basis than action by the US and UK alone. It might be more efficacious to deal with these aspects of the Albanian problem in the context of NATO and its considerations and planning of the defense of the North Atlantic area.[34]

CHAPTER 12

Adverse Developments in the Infiltration Program

T he increased pace of Operation Fiend activities in the areas of propaganda and psychological and economic warfare was matched by an equally accelerated tempo in preparing for the 1951 infiltrations in Albania. There was one significant change in the planning of infiltrations compared to the previous season. The leadership of National Committee for Free Albania pressed for a more active role in the selection of agents and operational areas in Albania. They blamed the unimpressive outcome of the November 1950 drops on the fact that the Americans had selected the agents and the drop zones. In endless arguments with Lieb in Rome, the members of the military junta, Abas Kupi, Said Kryeziu, and Abas Ermenji insisted on assuming this responsibility and even threatened to withdraw from the NCFA if the Americans didn't grant them the privilege. Reluctantly, Lieb agreed and Yatsevitch seconded his decision from Washington.

The operational activities for 1951 began with the physical and psychological assessment of all Albanian personnel in the Labor Services Company 4000 in Germany, which the OPC had set up in June 1950 as cover for maintaining a pool of potential infiltration agents. An OPC screening team evaluated the medical and mental conditions of everyone there. From 220 personnel, only sixty-six of them were fit for infiltration purposes. The finding caused considerable aggravation among the NCFA leaders, who considered all the Company 4000 members "first-class fierce fighters." The assessment team reported that at the insistence of the NCFA military junta, they had included in the selection men with physical illnesses, among them a man with one kidney, a man prone to diabetes, and one with spots on his lungs. The junta agreed to scratch from the list one man with rheumatism, who they felt might not be able to run fast enough in an emergency.[1]

The plans for 1951 were to infiltrate ten teams of four men each plus several smaller teams for special missions. Four of these teams began training in late May at the Loeb country estate in Murnau for infiltration in the coastal plain area during the June moonless period.[2] A typical day of training included physical conditioning, radio-telephone usage, knife use, wrestling, boxing, and weapons training. In the afternoon, there were lessons on geography, map reading, and two hours of parachute training. In the evening, the agents saw army training movies.[3]

At the same time, sixteen agents began training as wireless transmitter operators. They would be part of the teams that would go in the autumn—three teams in late September and three teams in October. While regular team members received six weeks' training, the W/T operators required approximately four months of training.[4] The schedule of infiltrations in 1951, as in 1950, did not take into account the realities of the weather in Albania, where winter set in early, especially in the mountains where most of the teams were headed.

The pace of infiltrations planned for 1951 upset the members of the NCFA military junta. Abas Ermenji was particularly vocal in expressing his discontent with the American operatives who had turned a deaf ear for the past two years to his suggestions to train a large force and send it to drive the Communists from Albania. Ermenji also favored infiltrations by sea rather than airdrops and threatened to refuse to allow members of the Balli Kombëtar to participate in parachute drops. He argued that Albania was their country and they knew it like the palm of their hand, and that sufficiently large dropping areas did not exist in its mountainous terrain to stage airdrop operations.[5]

Lieb had to walk a fine line in explaining to the junta the reasons for the disappointing number of infiltrations without revealing that the CIA had abandoned the concept of actively training and equipping a larger force with the ultimate objective of overthrowing the Hoxha government. To deflect their attention, he sent them to visit the covert training school on July 3 and 4. They found the morale of the trainees high and complimented the staff on the training program.[6]

The first class of fourteen agents completed training in mid-July and were transferred from Germany to Athens on July 20. The ferrying plane returned to Germany with forty-six Albanians from the Lavrion IRO camp, who joined the reservoir of Albanian personnel in the Labor Services Company.[7]

The first three operational teams for 1951 were parachuted into Albania between July 22 and 24. One of the teams, code name Olive, was dropped in Delvina, near the Greek border in southern Albania; a second team, code name Cypress, in the center of the country between Berati and Elbasani; and the third team, code name Oak, in the Puka district in the north.

* * *

After the drop of the four-man Olive team near Delvina, the OPC station in Athens had no news of them for weeks. Then, reports began arriving indicating the annihilation of the team. The first report came from a British team, code name Tiger, which entered southern Albania by sea on July 10 and came out to Greece on the night of August 7–8. The Tiger team had spent a hectic month on the run, suffering four ambushes by special pursuit detachments, police, armed civilians, and soldiers. One of these attacks, which lasted twenty-four hours, depleted the team's ammunition supply and ended with an escape so miraculous that the members did not know themselves how it happened. Informers and Communist followers had replaced shepherds who had been sympathetic to their cause in the past, probably because of the nationalization of the flocks and subsequent removal of the original owners. En route to Greece, the team followed the higher flats of the Drino River valley, away from roads, which were swarming with troops.

They seized civilian hostages all along the escape route, a practice commonly used by infiltration teams to discourage local villagers from betraying them. The fate of these hostages was often tragic, as shown by the case of Servet Pupe, seized by the Tiger team near the village of Nepravishta only a few miles from the Greek border. Caught in the crossfire between the Tiger team and local Communists pursuing them, Pupe was wounded and unable to move. The team left him behind as they continued their escape toward Greece. The leader of the Communist posse found Pupe bleeding to death and saw an opportunity to earn the government's good graces. He finished Pupe off, dragged his body in the village, and branded him as a collaborator of the "diversionist" agents. The local Communist leader received rewards for his deed and for the next forty years he and his children enjoyed the favors of the Communist government. Pupe's children, branded as offspring of a traitor, languished in menial jobs digging trenches and laboring in a collective farm.

The members of the British Tiger team learned the fate of the OPC Olive team from a local man from the village of Lazarati, just south of Gjirokastra. Initially, he had provided the Olive agents with food and shelter. Later, he was forced to participate in their roundup, together with all civilians and troops in the area nearby. This was a new development, because up to that point only trusted Communists were armed and pressed into posse duty. The search party also included unarmed civilians, some of them women, who preceded the armed hunters with pleas to surrender, obviously in the belief that the hunted would not fire on unarmed searchers and might give up more easily.[8]

Nijaz Rrapushi, a former corporal of the 7th Regiment of Gjirokastra, who had escaped to Greece, recounted that the Sigurimi had asked for aid from his regiment to pursue "reactionaries" in the area. He recounted that the Sigurimi, police, and army troops had surrounded the members of the Olive team and exchanged fire in a battle that lasted five hours. When they overran Olive's position, they found Riza Zyberi and Fido Veliu dead. They had agreed to a double suicide with a grenade; one died when the grenade exploded, but the other lived to kill himself with his pistol. The pursuit forces captured Kasem Shehu, who was wounded. Muhamet Hoxha, the fourth member of the team, had also been wounded but was not in position with the other three men. When he spent his ammo and it became obvious that the Communist forces would overrun their position, Hoxha had decided to head for the border, but he passed out from loss of blood and was captured some distance from the position.[9] Both Hoxha and Shehu, no relation to the top two Communist leaders of the country, faced trial in October 1951 and received a sentenced of twenty years hard labor each.[10] Hoxha was the only one who lived long enough to see the fall of the Communist regime. He died at an old people's home in Gjiro-kastra in the 1990s.[11]

* * *

The second team, Cypress, was dropped in the central Devolli River region between Berati and Elbasani and included five men. This team exfiltrated over the Greek border on August 15 due to lack of food. They had lost all their supply containers during the drop. They had been able to receive communications from the commo plane, but the plane was unable to receive the team's communications, another example showing that the Motorola voice radios were totally inade-quate for communications and they needed to be replaced with W/T sets.[12] Upon their return to Greece, the team reported utterly deplor-able living conditions in the country. They described the growing uselessness of gold and other foreign currencies and the increasing value of barter items. Measures against infiltrations, including random unannounced searches, had intensified.

The team members reported a general lack of confidence in the NCFA. They pointed out that, although the Albanians they met received them well, the team had not been able to accomplish its goals without the services of an educated, respected NCFA officer. People in Albania were looking for deeds rather than words and longed for genuine liberation that involved neither the Yugoslavs nor the Greeks.

The most disconcerting fact from the debriefing was that the team confirmed counterintelligence reports received earlier, indicating that the Sigurimi knew of their July infiltration before its actual staging. Two team members reported that government officials had visited their families with news of the arrival in Albania of their relatives three days before they actually appeared.

A Communist reception party awaited their drop at the designated landing area. Luckily, the team dropped a few miles from the prese-lected DZ into a village; dogs barked, the aircraft roared overhead, and the villagers awoke. A patrol was organized and the intruders hastened their exit, leaving their equipment behind.

The suspicion for the source of the leak immediately fell on members of the NCFA. The military junta had selected the drop zones and picked the team members. The only vital information kept from them was the exact drop date. From all the parachute drops that Fiend had completed up to that point, either for the OPC or the OSO, this was the first one in which the NCFA was allowed this much operational latitude; this was also the first of these operations where the security breach was confirmed. Was it a coincidence?

The CIA considered polygraph tests for members of the executive committee of the NCFA and the military junta who were familiar with Fiend operational details.[13] It is not known whether they were carried out, although polygraph tests became standard practice for agents before they were sent on missions and after they returned for debriefing.

Lieb and the rest of the Fiend staff saw this NCFA-inspired debacle as the final proof that they should no longer accept the junta's operational proposals. They felt that the premium placed on the junta's intelligence was too high, and that their criteria for forming the teams were primarily political and partisan rather than serving the needs of the operation. Lieb proposed to Yatsevitch the elimination of the NCFA's executive committee as a body and the complete removal of NCFA from any operational aspects of the endeavor.[14]

There was certainly no love lost between Lieb and the NCFA leaders, in particular Abas Ermenji. In an interview more than thirty years later, Ermenji laid the blame for the security compromise on the Americans in general and Lieb in particular. He blamed Lieb for putting too much trust on the Legaliteti followers, whom he described as a group without order, discipline, or sophistication thoroughly penetrated by the Communists. Ermenji said that Gaqo Gogo, the NCFA's secretary and Lieb's translator, learned all the details of the drops from Lieb and gossiped about them in cafés. As a result, the Albanian embassy in Rome was well aware of all the operations coordinated with the NCFA, according to Ermenji.[15]

* * *

There is one significant piece of evidence that adds credence to the hypothesis that NCFA members compromised the 1951 drops.

During that same time, Fiend staff oversaw two successful infiltrations of agents that were not affiliated with NCFA—one by parachute drop and another one overland from Greece—by Hamit Matiani and his followers.

Hamit Matiani first came to the attention of the OPC in spring of 1951. He had been used since 1949 in an operation sponsored by the OSO and fronted by the Greek intelligence, which consisted of leading teams into Albania to collect intelligence and distribute propaganda materials. Matiani had established a very good track record. He knew his way inside the country, accomplished the tasks assigned, and made it out with minimal losses.[16] He had a considerable following in Albania and was well respected by the Albanian émigrés in Greece. The OPC planned to use him to form several teams that would enter Albania via Greece for resistance activities and "special tasks," such as mailing derogatory letters about Communist leaders, distributing targeted propaganda materials inside the country, performing acts of sabotage, and carrying out coups-de-main actions.[17]

On the night of June 23–24, 1951, the OPC covert plane dropped a seven-man team led by Matiani a few miles southeast of Peqini in central Albania on an intelligence-gathering mission for the OSO.[18] Takeoff from Athens occurred at 2310 hours on June 23. Climbing to six thousand feet, the aircraft proceeded on course through the Gulf of Corinth, then west of Corfu, turned north, and cruised along the Albanian coast. The aircraft crew reported that all team members behaved very well during the flight. All men sat upright and remained awake. The air was notably smooth and no one became ill. There was some singing and a considerable amount of smoking.

At 0129 hours, the aircraft headed in a northeasterly direction and began a descent to 1,500 feet. Five minutes before the Albanian coast was crossed, the dispatchers unfastened the door and readied the static lines. All but two of the men took a drink of cognac. They penetrated the Albanian coast at the mouth of the Shkumbini River at 0203 hours at 1,500 feet altitude. The aircraft crossed the village of Divjaka and the northern quarter of Lake Tërbufi and turning east flew directly to the drop area. Steady moonlight outlined vividly the streams, roads, fields, woods, lakes, and land shapes. Matiani, recognizing his whereabouts, pointed out known landmarks to others, as the terrain unfolded below.

At 0210 hours, the pilot gave the jump signal, at which point the dispatchers tossed two bundles. The team leader followed by three men jumped headfirst almost atop the containers. No. 5 quickly sat on the floor, legs on the doorway, and pushed himself into the air. No. 6 immediately dived out, and the last man followed in the same manner after a fraction of a second of hesitation. The seven men had left the plane in under twenty seconds with no prompting from either dispatcher. The dispatchers judged the group unusually good and deemed their manner and rate of jumping exceptional—there were no noticeable worries, mainly noticeable confidence. The aircraft proceeded to fly around Elbasani then set on the outbound course, dropping fifty thousand leaflets along the way as a deceptive measure.

At about one and one-half miles west of Lushnja, the aircrew observed a large, rectangular pattern of strong, evenly spaced lights. They had seen and reported this pattern on other Albanian missions. From the air, it looked to them like a special area similar to the concentration camps they had often observed in Germany during the war. It was Gradishta, an infamous Albanian gulag built in the middle of nowhere and reserved for special enemies of the government and their families. The plane crossed the coast just north of the Viosa River mouth at 0233 hours and the aircraft flew homeward to Athens, where it landed at 0505 hours. Total time of flight was 5 hours 55 minutes; time over Albania was 34 minutes.[19]

This was Matiani's last mission for the OSO. At the end of June, the OPC and OSO reached an understanding to jointly handle and control the Matiani group. The group would have an operational mission aligned with OPC objectives but would also include personnel specifically trained and briefed by the OSO for intelligence reporting. The OPC and OSO would share the expenses to maintain the group, with the OPC carrying 40 percent of the costs.[20]

Upon Matiani's return from his mission, the Fiend field chief in Athens met with him in late July and made plans for an infiltration into the Kolonja area in southern Albania across the Greek border on or about August 10. The team would split up then meet at a prearranged spot on August 22, when the OPC covert plane would drop supplies to them together with a W/T operator.[21]

On the night of August 9–10, 1951, a six-man team, code name Pear, walked across the Greek border south of Korça under the leadership of Matiani.[22] The team exfiltrated intact from Albania on September 3. Upon their return, they reported that they had been involved in a battle with Albanian Communists between Gramshi and Voskopoja and killed two without loss, including Thoma Prifti, secretary of the Communist Party for the district of Gramshi. The team was very successful in obtaining assets for future operations—a considerable number of Communist identity documents in current use. In addition, they compiled a list of hundreds of potential safehouses.[23]

However, the team disobeyed instructions by operating outside their assigned area and becoming involved with the enemy before becoming properly established. In addition, they failed to display fires for the supply drop to the team. The British case officer in Athens was annoyed, because the activities of the Pear team took place in one of the British operating areas and had forced his own team to abandon its operation and retreat to Greece. The Fiend Athens chief recommended disbanding the Pear team but requested they retain its two top members, Hamit Matiani and Xheladin Sakollari, for future hit-and-run operations.[24]

Matiani was his own man in the field and allowed only his own instincts to guide his actions. They had helped him survive while being constantly on the run in the years since the Communists had taken over Albania. Matiani knew his way around the countryside and over the years had developed a network of trusted people who helped him scout the terrain and find the paths in and out the country that best avoided pursuit forces. He distrusted resupply drops by aircraft, which he felt alerted the security forces and weighed down the team. His cunning sense of survival had turned Matiani into a legend, hated and vilified by the Communists but admired and respected by opponents of the regime.

* * *

A joint Fiend-Valuable meeting was held in Rome on October 22–24, 1951. Yatsevitch, Lieb, and other field officers of Project Fiend attended from the American side; their Valuable counterparts Harold Perkins and Anthony Northrop represented the British side.[25] The meeting began with a discussion of external political factors that influenced the activities of both projects. The British believed that 1952 was the last year that their operation could continue at its current pace. Following that year's activities, the operation either had to be sharply curtailed or expanded into a full-fledged effort to overthrow the Hoxha regime. Both sides agreed that failure to develop an active resistance movement in the near future would result in disillusionment and apathy within the ranks of the opposition inside and outside Albania. They discussed overt and covert propaganda efforts that were necessary to sustain the will to resist among the Albanian people but, at the same time, avoid raising morale prematurely.

The meeting then focused on Yugoslav intentions, particularly in light of the activities of the Yugoslav-sponsored League of Albanian Refugees against the National Committee for Free Albania. Both the Office of Policy Coordination and Secret Intelligence Services agreed that the Yugoslav government desired only enough of a change in the Albanian regime to break away from the Soviet Union and become again friendly toward Belgrade. An Albania oriented toward the West was only a second choice for Tito, and a non-Communist Albania would be contrary to Yugoslavia's basic desires.

Next, the discussion moved to the internal political structure of the NCFA. Both sides felt that the original NCFA structure composed of an executive committee and a general committee had outlived its initial usefulness. The British saw a need to reconstruct the committee in order to increase its power and appeal, prevent it from becoming a two-party organ of Balli Kombëtar and Legaliteti, and to make it a real, capable committee, not merely a grouping of people. The Americans agreed and suggested that the process of broadening the committee would provide an opportunity to include outside elements that would be of value as potential assets in the event of armed insurrection.

The reorganized committee would function as a cover, a source of propaganda, and a body of Albanians interested in the welfare of their nation. Under no circumstances would the new NCFA meddle in operational matters. The new committee would include functional subcommittees appointed from time to time and as situations arose to oversee propaganda, welfare, and other activities. The Americans suggested additional subcommittees to deal with future problems of Albania, but the British considered such sponsorship tantamount to unofficial recognition of the NCFA as a government in exile, which they would not countenance. Although the military junta would continue to exist as a clandestine and unpublicized offshoot of the NCFA, its members would be stripped of access to operational matters.

The discussion then moved to the operational and security aspects of the effort. Fiend's summary of actions in 1951 included thirty-nine agents infiltrated, five leaflet drop missions, thirty-one covert flights totaling forty-six hours over Albanian territory, resupply drops totaling 8,200 pounds of arms and supplies, and twenty-three covert commo flights. Thirty-three of the thirty-nine agents infiltrated went by air. At the time of the meeting, twelve agents remained in Albania, organized in three teams, code names Pine, Chestnut, and Walnut, with at least one W/T operator in each team. Seventeen agents had exfiltrated successfully and seven had defected to Tito. The Sigurimi had captured four agents and put them on a public trial, which Radio Tirana had announced only a few days before the meeting, on October 10, 1951. They were Iliaz Toptani and Selim Daci from the November 1950 drop and Muhamet Hoxha and Kasem Shehu from the July 1951 drop. By way of buttressing the Albanian government's claim that it was facing a coordinated international conspiracy, the list of the apprehended spies on trial also included two agents sent by the British, one by the Italians, four by the Yugoslavs, and three by the Greek.[26]

The British on their end had infiltrated nineteen agents, all by sea, between July and September, of which four were killed, one was wounded and captured, and fourteen made it out to Greece. One four-man team, code name Barley, remained twenty-four days in the Vlora-Gjirokastra area in the south and then exfiltrated to Greece after they were surrounded by Communist forces and lost their equipment. Two teams of four men each, Slipper and Ebony, destined for the central Kruja–Mati areas, were surprised by the pursuit forces five days after infiltration, lost their equipment, and made their way to Yugoslavia first and then Greece. They lost two members in Albania and one in Yugoslavia. Another five-man team had operated in Gramshi for thirteen days. They were in a position to prolong their stay but were ambushed by security forces on alert after the murder of Communist officials in their district by Matiani's team. The team broke up, and only three surviving members were able to exfiltrate to Greece.[27] When describing the experience of this last team, the British case officers said that it underscored the fact that Albania was a small country; a closer integration of Fiend and Valuable operations was necessary to preclude mission overlap and keep their respective agents from running into each other.

Both Fiend and Valuable officers felt that the amount of information brought back by the teams was minimal and the intelligence yield low. Everyone wholeheartedly agreed that the use of low-level agents in teams had been more harmful than useful and that most of the inadequacies of the 1951 teams stemmed almost directly from the low-quality agents the NCFA provided.

For 1952, Fiend intentions were to train eight to ten W/T operators by June 1, 1952, launch short-term missions only to contact known personalities in the Albanian government and army, establish permanent W/T stations, and effect special assignments such as defections, intelligence gathering, propaganda, and sabotage. Resupply and leaflet raids would continue. Yatsevitch said that he hoped to make 1952 operations decidedly covert. He considered the Labor Services Company in Germany and other sources of agents they had used thus far as thoroughly penetrated by the Sigurimi. They would cease immediately to recruit agents from these pools and focus efforts on identifying high-level assets for high payoff missions in Albania. When the British wondered where the Americans would find these high-level assets, Yatsevitch remained reticent, only indicating that they had something in the works but were not ready to share details at that point.

That gave the British an opening to press for closer and more detailed coordination of their respective operations. Perkins and Northrop argued that such coordination was essential in order to avoid situations where both the British and Americans tried to contact the same Albanian target or, worse, where the British might be trying to compromise a man whom the Americans were seeking to cultivate and vice versa. OPC representatives agreed that the exchange of operational information was highly desirable. They viewed the degree of coordination in the past as inadequate for the future, but at the same time felt that the policy of "operational disengagement" that governed the Valuable-Fiend relationship precluded closer coordination.

Both sides agreed that information leaks on operational activities had occurred because of poor security within the NCFA and because of the Albanian propensity for letter writing. The exchange of letters among members of the committee, Labor Services Company members selected by the committee for operational use, and agents undergoing training had resulted in security violations and the transmission of information to Greek, Italian, Yugoslav, and possibly German services through the interception of correspondence. As a corrective measure, they agreed to keep all operational intelligence from the NCFA and to cut the NCFA out of operations completely.

The training of agents required some adjustment as well. The meeting participants expressed concern at the ease with which the Sigurimi ambushed their field parties. There was a general feeling that they had overestimated the Albanian's ability to move in his own country without capture.

The meeting concluded with an exchange of views on handling the disposal of agents. The SIS considered all their operators "blown" and intended to discharge every Albanian with whom they had worked in the past. The CIA wouldn't go that far, but they also needed to dispose of agents who dropped out of training or were no longer needed operationally. Up until then, they had sent these agents to International Relief Organization refugee camps in Greece, Italy, and other countries, but these camps were going to close in 1952 because the IRO favored resettling and integrating refugees in the society and economy of host countries.[28] Americans planned to send the agents who were not suitable for clandestine work to the Labor Service Company in Germany. The British were making good use of a similar service in the UK, which located displaced people as tenants on British farms that needed labor.

Someone brought up the idea of purchasing a plantation or some colonial property in a remote part of the world where agents "could be put out to pasture." The arrangement required an initial outlay of capital but would allow the Albanians to contribute to their support or even become self-supporting. Some discussion ensued, at the end of which all parties agreed that the idea was worth investigating further,[29] although no trace exists in the record to indicate that anyone followed up to develop the scheme any further.

* * *

On October 24, the same day that the case officers of Fiend and Valuable wrapped up their meeting in Rome, Radio Tirana reported the "annihilation of thirteen spies dropped by parachute on Albanian territory by United States Espionage Services." Of the eight agents mentioned by name, the broadcast identified seven members of OPC teams. They were the leader of the Chestnut team, Hysen Sallku, dropped in the Peshkopi area; two members of the Olive team dropped in Delvina, Fido Veliu and Riza Zyberi; and the entire Oak team dropped east of Shkoder, Rifat Zyberi, Ded Hila, Azis Rusta, and Hamid Toshi.[30]

The Oak team had come under fire immediately upon landing. Zyberi was gravely wounded and committed suicide in order not to be taken alive. The other three team members were able to escape the initial ambush and head east toward the highlands of Dukagjini. They managed to reach the house of Ded Hila only to be betrayed by a local villager who alerted the Sigurimi forces. Rusta, Toshi, and Hila died after exchanging fire for eight hours with their pursuers on August 16, 1951. When Hila's family asked for the bodies, the Communist commander consented upon condition that they be buried anonymously. Rusta, Toshi, and Hila remained in unmarked graves until 1991, when family members exhumed their remains and reburied them not far from where they died.[31]

The next day, October 25, Radio Tirana reported the elimination of "seven spies and diversionists parachuted into Albania by the British Intelligence Services. They had been specially trained in espionage by the British Intelligence services in Greece and Malta, and taken to Albania by sea and by air to carry out espionage and diversionary activities for the British Intelligence Service."[32]

The Radio Tirana radio broadcast and testimony at the Tirana trials of the captured agents that they had trained at the "Munich United States

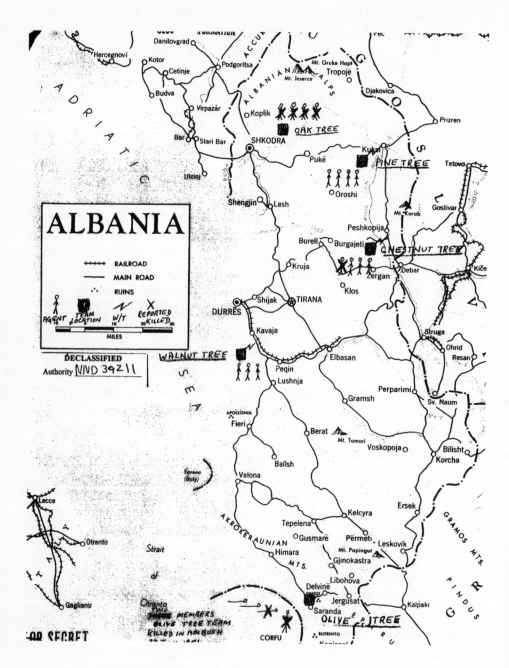

CIA map indicating the status of teams in Albania by the end of October 1951

Espionage Center" suggested that the Communists had pinpointed the Murnau estate covert training site for Albanian and Bulgarian agents. The OPC moved immediately to abandon the training site as a security precaution. The Loeb estate, which the CIA had considered purchasing outright only a few months before, was turned over to the owner and the lease was terminated in May 1952.[33]

By the end of October, it was clear that the Albanian security forces had effectively countered the OPC's increased tempo of operations in the summer and fall of 1951. Out of forty-nine Fiend agents infiltrated in Albania since November 1950, only two were still alive in Albania and in communication with the Athens control center. Seven agents were confirmed dead and one was presumed dead; four were captured, tried, and convicted as spies; another nine were of status unknown but very much suspected of having perished, given Radio Tirana reports of additional unidentified agents killed; six agents had defected to Yugoslavia. From the ten agents who had been able to survive and exfiltrate to Greece, one four-man team, Cypress, had been practically on the run the whole time and, for lack of food, was forced to leave without accomplishing any of their mission objectives. Only Hamit Matiani at the head of his six-man team had shown the ability to move inside Albania and produce operational results.

The Office of Special Operations had experienced similar disappointing results with their teams and had decided to curtail their operations in 1952. As the head of the OSO Albanian project explained at the time: "No service could expect to any longer receive the outright support and cooperation of the Albanian people in the face of the reprisal measures adopted by the Sigurimi."[34]

These disastrous results, described benignly as "adverse developments in the infiltration program" in the Fiend status report for October 1951,[35] nevertheless triggered a complete review of the infiltration methods and objectives. The OPC dismissed all agents already trained but not infiltrated as a security precaution. They decided to build a new training center in Greece for future agents, located under the cover of a radar station on the Kalanisia Islands, just a few miles from Corinth.[36]

Other security measures discussed at the joint Fiend-Valuable meeting in Rome on October 22–24 went into effect immediately, including the complete separation of the project's operational planning from NCFA influence and assistance. Moving forward, the CIA would rely principally on agents supplied from a new source that Yatsevitch had cultivated over the past few months, King Zog of Albania.

CHAPTER 13

A Bucket of Diamonds and Rubies

After the lukewarm support that King Zog had provided to the National Committee for Free Albania in its early days, the CIA case officers had more or less sidelined him from the Fiend operation. That had not stopped Zog from staying current with the developments and receiving regular updates from his supporters inside the NCFA. He was aware of the unfortunate outcome of the initial infiltrations into Albania and the frictions that had developed between the Americans and the NCFA leaders. He judged the summer of 1951 an opportune time to offer the Americans an alternative. While in the past he had offered his services via letters delivered to US diplomats in Cairo, this time Zog decided to travel to the United States and deliver his pitch in person. He felt the trip was urgent enough to warrant a transatlantic flight, a novelty in those days when ocean liners were still the default mode of travel between Europe and the United States.

On July 26, 1951, King Zog arrived by plane from Paris at New York International Airport, known as Idlewild Airport at the time and until 1963, when it was renamed after John F. Kennedy. To the waiting journalists, he declared: "I come from a country that has had six thousand years of civilization to this country to see modern civilization. My trip is strictly private and is only to see the United States."[1]

While in New York, Zog stayed at the Ritz Tower in Manhattan. He hired Baron William Frary von Blomberg, a public relations man from Boston who specialized in catering to European and Middle East royalty, to help him buy property in the United States and "to aid in meeting State Department officials and others who might be 'helpful' to the monarch in exile."[2] According to a registration that von Blomberg filed later with the Justice Department, Zog paid six hundred dollars for his services.[3] As he began calling officials in Washington on behalf of his client, von Blomberg expressed Zog's preference that as head of the Albanian state he should first present his card to President Truman and then to Secretary of State Acheson. Any officials of lower rank who wished to meet with him should call upon him. However, the State Department made it clear that the United States government did not recognize Zog in any official capacity. In the end, Zog had to settle for a meeting with officials from the European division at the State Department on August 8, 1951.[4]

Von Blomberg reached out to his contacts in the CIA to arrange a meeting between Zog and the director. Both the Office of Policy Coordination and the Office of Special Operations were interested in understanding Zog's potential to contribute to their operational and intelligence gathering efforts in Albania. On August 15, 1951, Colonel Yatsevitch of the OPC and his OSO counterpart met with King Zog at his suite at the Mayflower Hotel in Washington. Zog received them very cordially and spoke with what both of them perceived to be complete candor. The conversation lasted approximately an hour and a half.

Zog began by saying that his main reason for visiting the United States was to find a suitable preparatory school somewhere in the general area of Washington and New York for his son, who was then twelve and a half years of age and whom he wished to bring up in the United States. Then the conversation moved to Queen Geraldine, who hadn't accompanied him because she was visiting the Levant, the eastern Mediterranean coastal region that comprises today's Syria, Lebanon, Israel, Jordan and Palestine. Zog reminisced about his boyhood in Istanbul and trips he had taken himself in the Levant to see numerous historical ruins of interest.

After this social conversation, Yatsevitch conveyed Director Smith's compliments to the king and his regrets that he was unable to see him. "General Smith has instructed me to talk about any matters that Your Majesty might wish to bring up," Yatsevitch said.

Zog began by expressing uneasiness with regard to the political position of Yugoslavia, which, in his opinion, hadn't taken decisive steps to commit itself to a partnership with the West. "Something needs to be done," he said, "to force Yugoslavia to take a stand on one side or the other." Early action in Albania to overthrow the Hoxha regime would serve such a purpose, Zog believed. An added advantage of destroying the Communist regime in Albania would be the encouragement it would give to other satellite countries to revolt against Soviet domination.

With regard to Albania, the king made four points that he considered of particular importance from the American and Western perspective and indicated the necessity for early action in Albania. "Please bring these points directly to General Smith's attention," Zog said.

First, a Soviet-controlled Albania constituted a potential threat of 100,000 armed men behind Yugoslavia's back, and second, the Soviets were enlarging and improving several airfields and other air facilities in Albania clearly directed toward the Mediterranean and the US bases being established in the region. His third and fourth points concerned the Bay of Vlora and the Island of Sazani, which provided facilities for a naval and submarine base that the Soviets could use to paralyze shipping in the Mediterranean and the Adriatic.

"The first step in any plan of action against Albania," Zog continued, "is a declaration from the US in the immediate future that it stand firmly for the preservation of the territorial integrity of Albania." The US should also induce Greece, Yugoslavia, and Italy to declare that they wouldn't seek any Albanian territory by force of arms and they would pursue any territorial claims they might have through the United Nations. These two steps, Zog said, would hearten and strengthen the position of the anti-Communist Albanians and make it difficult for the Albanian regime to pose as the sole champion of Albanian territorial integrity.

With regards to actual operations in Albania, the king saw three possible courses of action. The first one, an invasion of Albania by the United States, he dismissed as unrealistic and impractical. The second option was the invasion of Albania by an Albanian force assembled and led by the king. He could bring together up to ten thousand men, recruited from among the various Albanian groups scattered around the world. However, the countries that would support the assembly, equipment, and training of the invasion elements wouldn't be able to hide their support and would be vulnerable to Soviet retaliations. The most feasible and desirable option was to overthrow the Communist regime by an insurrection developed within the country under the king's leadership. Because the action would have all the earmarks of a spontaneous Albanian activity, it would be harder for the Soviets to frame it as an act of foreign intervention or aggression.

Up to that point, Zog hadn't said anything the CIA didn't know. What followed next was a careful attempt on his part to offer the agency an alternative to the National Committee for Free Albania as the leading force behind the insurgency. Despite the strength of the Albanian armed forces and their support by Soviet specialists in the country, Zog stated that a considerable proportion of officers were still loyal to him and would defect and turn against the regime in the event of an uprising. "Scattered throughout the country," he said, "there are some two thousand former reserve officers with war experience who are loyal to me and would provide local leadership in operations against the Government." He also asserted that a number of nonmilitary people in the Hoxha administration remained loyal to him and would turn against the regime when called to do so.

Having made the case for why the Americans should support him, Zog then addressed what had always been his greatest weakness in the eyes of the Western allies, the legitimacy of his claim to the Albanian throne. Fully aware that doubts about his intentions lingered in the minds of the Americans, the king emphasized that his interest in action in Albania was not based on a desire to be restored to the throne but was purely an expression of his interest as a patriotic Albanian who wished to help his country. As proof of his lack of self-interest, he committed to inviting a UN-sponsored group to supervise the establishment of any postinsurrection system of government that the people of Albania might choose in free elections.

Zog concluded the meeting by reiterating again that he was in the best position to lead the resistance movement and make a real contribution in Albania due to the loyal following he still had in the country. He stood ready to do anything that the Americans needed of him in the future and was at their disposal.[5]

* * *

The conversation with Zog must have struck a chord with Yatsevitch. He clearly saw potential in developing him as a source for ideas and tapping into his followers for operations in Albania in addition to the pool already available to the CIA in the Labor Services Company in Germany. Two days after their first meeting, on August 17, Yatsevitch met again with Zog at his suite at the Mayflower Hotel. As usual, Zog began the conversation in a lighthearted mode by reminiscing about his activities in World War I and his detention by the emperor of Austria in Vienna; then, both he and Yatsevitch discussed their mutual interest in fencing. After this initial exchange of pleasantries, Yatsevitch said that the CIA was very interested in having more information on Zog's ideas concerning the best way of creating a revolution in his country.

"I have given the matter a lot of thought," Zog said and went on to reiterate his earlier statement that it would be most desirable to conduct the action as though it were a spontaneous revolution breaking out within Albania. He outlined the ideal sequence of activities in order to carry out a successful operation.

To start with, it was necessary to create the political conditions for the success of the effort. They included a declaration from the United States expressing firm support of Albania's territorial integrity and declarations from Yugoslavia, Greece, and Italy committing not to attack Albania and to use UN mechanisms for pursuing any territorial claims they might have. He thought that the United States could exert sufficient economic pressure to force the Greeks, Italians, and Yugoslavs to make these declarations. "I raise this issue again," Zog said, "because I am afraid that the British have a secret deal with the Greeks to allow them to occupy Northern Epirus in exchange for abandoning their claims on Cyprus."

Next, a US staff, working jointly with Zog's staff, would prepare the operational plans, including training and stockpiling arms and ammunition for ten thousand men. Four or five of King Zog's officers would make reconnaissance trips throughout Albania to assess the situation and prepare the ground for local support. Small forces would move clandestinely into Greece and other staging areas from which they would enter Albania.

The open revolt operations would begin with a few carefully chosen assassinations carried out by persons within the Albanian government who were still loyal to King Zog. At the same time, small Albanian forces would be introduced by air and land, with King Zog and his staff in the lead, followed by the members of the NCFA and any other Albanian groups who would be willing to participate in the revolution. Arms would be dropped by air to supply guerrilla units in advance. Defections from regular ground forces would increase the revolutionary army to the strength required to overcome any forces that remained loyal to the regime.

Upon termination of the military phase, the NCFA and other political groups would begin their activities. "At this point," Zog said, "I will invite the UN to send representatives to ensure that formation of the new Albanian government is in accordance with democratic principles."

Zog emphasized that, if the Americans desired, he would undertake to plan, organize, and execute the operation. Otherwise, the United States could conduct the entire operation, and he would be willing to perform whatever functions the Americans considered most useful.[6]

* * *

Zog's plan was far grander than what the agency was prepared to try at the time in Albania. However, Yatsevitch saw useful elements in what Zog proposed that he could weave into the ongoing activities of operation Fiend. On August 30, 1951, Yatsevitch returned for a third and final meeting with Zog at Hotel Delmonico in New York on the eve of his departure from the United States. "My agency has given serious thought to our recent conversations on the subject of Albanian operations," Yatsevitch said. If Zog considered it a useful thing to do, they would provide all possible material assistance in infiltrating a small party of high-grade agents provided by Zog, complemented by a good wireless transmitter operator trained by the Americans. They would perform reconnaissance in Albania and establish contact with people who were friendly to Zog within the Albanian armed forces and government. They would also establish relations with any resistance groups they would be able to reach.

Zog said he would willingly place his men at the agency's disposal. He would select officers from his retinue in Egypt who would need to move clandestinely to Greece through another European country in order to maintain the secrecy of the operation. Colonel Hysen Selmani, his aide-de-camp, would assist the Americans in screening a list of Zog supporters among refugees in the Lavrion camp in Greece and selecting a few guides to assist these officers in moving through critical areas in Albania. Zog warned Yatsevitch that he would probably not have any information on the W/T operator the Americans would select to be part of the team. He assumed they would vet the person thoroughly and would be responsible for his trustworthiness and reliability. "I also hope," Zog said, "that you use cryptographic material that could not be broken by the Russians, who are very good at breaking codes and ciphers."[7]

After they covered the topic of operations in Albania, Zog and Yatsevitch continued the conversation for another hour or so, during which Yatsevitch wanted to hear about Zog's impressions of the United States and his views on other world issues. Zog emphasized the importance of finding a resolution soon to the Jewish-Arab problem and the need for vigorous action against Communists in China. He also described the meetings von Blomberg had arranged for him with Generals Douglas MacArthur and Lucius Clay and said that he was impressed by their grasp of the matters he had brought up in the conversation with them.[8]

* * *

One of the last items of business Zog conducted before leaving the United States was the purchase of property in the Muttontown section of Nassau County, in what is known as the Gold Coast of Long Island, NY. The Knollwood Estate was one of the most impressive country estates in the area, built between 1906 and 1920 by Charles Hudson, a prosperous stockbroker. A fabulous sixty-room mansion stood on a hill overlooking rolling meadows of landscaping and gardens by Ferruccio Vitale.[9] The house had "wide terraces, high Roman columns and massive stone steps leading to the gardens." The interior was equally impressive, with the main winding staircase made of Caen marble and a white marble fountain in the center of one of the entertainment rooms.[10]

One additional feature that attracted Zog to the property was that it included a dairy farm complex with stables, a poultry plant capable of housing one thousand chickens, and several farmhouses that could accommodate multiple families of tenants. By Zog's calculations, the property could support an entourage of 115 persons, including servants and farmers, in addition to his family.

Shortly after the transaction was concluded, a front-page article in the *New York Times* reported that Zog had paid for the property with a "bucket of diamonds and rubies," requiring the services of jewel experts to close the deal, in addition to the usual assortment of real estate agents, appraisers, and lawyers. The romantic image of an exiled Muslim monarch married to a young half-American countess emptying a bucket of jewels on the table like the Count of Monte Cristo struck the imagination of the public. Sightseers began appearing in the neighborhood, although the handwrought iron gates of the property remained locked.

A little more than a year later, King Zog and his estate were in the news again. Citing as a precedent his favorable tax treatment in Europe due to his kingly status, Zog claimed "sovereign immunity from the imposition of local taxes" and refused to pay the Long Island annual property tax assessment. The Nassau County Treasurer H. Bogart Seaman was not impressed. He imposed a $2,654 tax lien on the estate, and scheduled it for sale at auction on December 1, 1952, at the opening of the Nassau County annual tax sale.[11] Through his lawyer, Zog paid almost three thousand dollars in back taxes and penalties but not before the property was put on the tax list and inspected by a number of people.[12]

Most of the visitors were attracted by rumors that Zog had buried a treasure somewhere in the property. For a while, the presence of the caretaker, a White Russian former Cossack officer who lived on the property, deterred the treasure hunters. The Nassau County Police Department also leased one of the buildings on the property as the headquarters for its Second Precinct. But by the end of March 1953, Zog had evicted both the caretaker and the police, leaving the ninety-five-acre property locked but completely empty.[13]

* * *

At the beginning of September 1951, Yatsevitch was in Europe, reviewing the final preparations for the infiltration operations that were planned for the season. He took a detour to Egypt and on September 12, 1951, called on King Zog in Alexandria, in order to complete the arrangements for the team of officers he was going to supply for infiltration into Albania. Yatsevitch provided Zog with a set of cryptonyms and pseudonyms to use in their correspondence. The CIA cryptonym for Zog himself was RNCASTING. His pseudonym was Mr. Yarborough. Yatsevitch would write to Colonel Selmani, care of the Albanian legation in Cairo, using the agreed-upon cryptonyms and pseudonyms, and the letters would be delivered to Egypt through a secure CIA channel. Zog would have his letters delivered to Yatsevitch through the American military attaché in Cairo who had secure means for forwarding them to Washington.

The king stated that he would prefer to have this particular operation handled exclusively as an American undertaking, without British participation, although he had no objection to the sharing of intelligence results with the British. He also agreed with Yatsevitch that the matter must be handled without the knowledge of the NCFA.[14]

From his meeting with Zog in Alexandria, Yatsevitch proceeded to visits in Germany and Greece and finally in Rome for the joint Fiend-Valuable on October 22–24. There he received news of the disastrous outcome of the 1951 infiltrations broadcast by Radio Tirana, which served as the final push for activating Zog's agents.

At Yatsevitch's request, the OPC station chief in Cairo met with Zog at his villa in Alexandria on October 26 and 27 to further discuss the selection of the intelligence team that he had agreed to furnish for the mission in Albania. The team would attempt to establish contact with and determine the whereabouts and status of various officers in the armed forces and other individuals in the Albanian government who might be willing to participate in operations to overthrow the Hoxha regime.

The king agreed that at all times the team would make favorable reference to the National Committee for Free Albania. The king again repeated his earlier assurances that he favored the committee and was exerting his influence to maintain unity within it.

Concerning the timing of the operation, Zog indicated that a spring infiltration of the team would substantially improve their chances of survival and the success of the mission. Although the men were ready to go if asked, it was best to postpone the mission until spring 1952, with the end of March as the target date. In the meanwhile, Zog would keep his officers on hand in Egypt and would await instructions from the Americans as to when to send them to Germany.[15]

CHAPTER 14

A Rich Harvest of Bitter Fruit

The preparations for the infiltration of the first Zog team into Albania began in March 1952. Zog selected three officers from his retinue in Egypt, members of the former Royal Guard that had followed him in exile and had served as bodyguards for him and his family. He chose Halil Branica for his contacts in the Burgajeti village of Mati from which Zog himself hailed; Zenel Shehi for his connections in the Burreli area; and Haxhi Gjyla for his acquaintances in the Martaneshi area.

Colonel Hysen Selmani, Zog's aide-de-camp, accompanied Branica, Shehi, and Gjyla as they traveled by ship from Cairo to Marseille, using their royal Albanian passports and under the cover of escorting Zog's sisters visiting Europe. They then continued to Paris, where a CIA officer met them and arranged transport by car to the German border. There they changed in US military uniforms, crossed covertly into the American zone, and then traveled to a safehouse in Bad Tölz, fifty kilometers south of Munich, where they met Tahir Premçi, the team W/T operator. On March 26, CIA staff drove them to the airport in Fürstenfeldbruck, thirty kilometers west of Munich, and put them on board a covert aircraft for their flight to Athens. Alfred C. Ulmer, CIA Athens station chief, and Gordon Mason, chief of external operations in charge of running agents into Albania and Bulgaria, met them at the airport.

Ulmer was born in Jacksonville, Florida, in 1916 and spent the early years of his life there, including two years as a reporter for the

Jaksonville Journal, before going to Princeton, where he graduated with honors in 1939. He worked for two years in public relations for Bentown and Bowles in New York City before joining the Navy in 1941. He served with distinction in Europe and the Middle East, received a Bronze Star and the Medal of Merit, and reached the rank of lieutenant commander by the end of the war. Ulmer joined the State Department in 1945 and served as attaché in Vienna and Madrid until 1950. After a brief stint in 1951 working for a real estate development company in Florida, Ulmer joined the CIA and was posted as chief of station in Athens, under the cover of first secretary of the embassy and special assistant to the ambassador.[1]

Gordon Mason, who would be the case officer for the team, took them to a safehouse on the outskirts of Athens, which the CIA staff called "the farm"—not to be confused with "The Farm," the CIA Camp Peary training facility in the United States, outside Williamsburg, Virginia. Hamit Matiani and Xheladin Sakollari, who would be the team guides into Albania, were already waiting for them at the safehouse. The farm consisted of two main houses where the Albanians and the CIA staff lived, plus the caretaker's cottage. A big garden surrounded the buildings and offered privacy from the outside. Nevertheless, because the CIA had used the farm since 1950 to stage Albanian teams and a considerable number of Bulgarian agents, the locals knew that Americans held refugees there. Eventually, security compromises with the caretakers forced the CIA to abandon this safehouse and take a second safe house, a fenced building situated on a backstreet in the Kifisia neighborhood in North Athens.[2]

Gordon Mason chose the code name Apple for the team. Its mission was to conduct reconnaissance and determine conditions within Albania; to attempt to locate and establish contacts with friends in government and military circles; and to send out intelligence reports by W/T or runners who could act as guides for future infiltration operations. Unlike other Fiend teams, which generally were instructed to exfiltrate after six to eight weeks in the terrain, Apple would remain within its area of operations as long as conditions permitted.

The CIA staff led the team through one month of training and conditioning in the hilly area northeast of the farm. Training included: survival problems; night compass orientation; firing of Mauser rifles,

Schmeisser automatics, and Walther P38 pistols; daily marches in mountainous areas carrying field equipment; map reading and familiarization with the coordinate system; first aid and field hygiene; use of concentrated rations; setting up and operating the radio set in the field and establishing contact with base in order to transmit mock intelligence and observation reports. The CIA staff instructed the team on the type of intelligence they were particularly interest in receiving.

The staff officers maintained absolute security and allowed none of the team members to leave the safehouse unless accompanied by members of Fiend staff. Colonel Selmani was a headache from the start and constantly interfered with the training program and communication exercises, although he took no part in them himself. In the end the team members and Fiend staff ignored him completely in the interest of getting the show on the road. In a progress report sent to Washington, Ulmer commented about Selmani: "In the future it is recommended that he confine his activities to Yarborough's [Zog's] court in BGBRAWL [cryptonym for Egypt] where it is felt they will be more appreciated and useful."

The team was equipped with rifles, Schmeisser submachine guns, Walther P38 9-mm semiautomatic pistols, hand grenades, knives, and ammunition. They also carried food supplies for several days, cigarettes, medical kits, flashlights, one SR-5 radio with extra batteries, and the everpresent L-pill filled with liquid potassium cyanide. The team received 225 gold pounds and $260 in one-dollar bills. Detailed accounting records kept by the Fiend staff showed that clothing and nonmilitary supplies for the team cost seven million drachmas or about $230, since one million drachmas was worth around thirty-three dollars at the time; food supplies for the team in March and April cost twelve million drachmas or slightly over $400.[3]

On April 28, the team was flown to Kastoria, a small Greek town about ten miles from the Albanian border that served as the forward staging area for infiltration teams. The infiltration was scheduled for the first of May in order to take advantage of the May Day atmosphere, when the Communist security patrols would be celebrating and perhaps paying less attention to their duties. The team received the final mission briefing, covering security forces and mined areas in the border region, safe houses and friendly contacts along the route. The team code name in Albanian, *Mollë*, would serve as the password in the event any team members recrossed into Greece. Any runners sent out by the team would use the code words, *Mollë Speciale*, to iden- tify themselves to the Greek border guards. Team members received Albanian identity cards with false biographic information on them.

The CIA case officers who had worked to prepare the team of agents for the mission had a very good feeling about them. Ulmer wrote to Washington: "Apple is by far the best team we have ever dispatched. Its members are way above the caliber of the Wahoos [Albanians] we have had to deal with in the past and every effort should be made to recruit more of this type from the same source if possible. They were a pleasure to work with and gave no trouble whatsoever, which is a far cry from the teams we have dealt with in the past."[4]

On May first, Gordon Mason turned the team over to the Greek services that were responsible for escorting the agents to the border. CIA officers never went closer than a few miles of the Albanian bor- der for fear that they might be caught in the skirmishes that regularly occurred between Albanian and Greek border guards or even worse snatched by the Albanians and transferred across the border. Two Albanian guides, Sherif Pleshti and Hysen Kapllani, would take the team to the Albanian border.

The team began its trek toward the border in the evening. After walking for three and a half hours, and just before crossing into Albania, Branica began suffering from pains in the chest. The team conferred on the condition of its ailing member and decided that he should remain behind because he would probably delay their prog- ress. Upon his return to Kastoria, Branica was sent to the holding area in Athens where he was examined and found to have a serious coro- nary condition that could prove fatal with overexertion. Because of his age—he was forty-eight years old—his poor physical condition, and his heart problem, the Americans didn't want to permit him to par- ticipate further in the operation, even though his loss was considered substantial, for he was said to be well known in the Mati area and was supposed to have made all the contacts there.[5] Nevertheless, Branica was anxious to rejoin the team, and he asked to be parachuted in with the first supply drop.[6]

The team infiltrated between the towns of Bozhigradi and Erseka and proceeded toward the operational area, traveling only at night. During the day they remained in hiding in secluded areas or with friends. According to prearranged plans, the covert plane flew on the night of May 8, one week later, and dropped one container with supplies in the area between Elbasani and Gramshi. At the reception field, the plane crew saw light signals from powerful flashlights of a type not furnished to Apple. Repeated attempts to contact the team by radio were not successful, and Athens staff feared the Communist security forces had captured them.[7]

On May 27, the team finally established wireless contact and informed the base that they had arrived at the operations area and all was well; further, the team acknowledged receipt of the May 8 supply drop.[8] The base immediately radioed the case officer challenge phrase: "How many rifles have you?" The purpose of the challenge was to determine whether the opposition controlled the team. At their next W/T communication on June 3, Apple replied with the prearranged answer indicating they were not controlled: "We want blankets." Although not again rechallenged, the team for some reason repeated this safety phrase on June 12, 15 (on this date they sent it in English, contrary to instructions), 18 (again in English), 24, and 27.[9]

The news of Apple's safe arrival in their operational area after the ominous silence of the first few weeks generated relief in Washington. The fact that the team had continued on its mission in accordance with prearranged instructions—despite being handicapped by the loss of an important team member at the very outset, and despite their inability to make wireless contact or resupply on the scheduled nights in May—was seen as indicative not only of the high morale and competence of the team but also of the thoroughness and efficacy of the Fiend staff in Athens that had prepared them.

In a congratulatory message sent in June, CIA headquarters praised the field for the attention given to all the ingredients of success in the preparation and activation of the mission. Yatsevitch wrote: "The care and minuteness in planning is evident from the May-Day entry to capitalize on BGGYPSY [cryptonym for Communist] celebrations, to the immediate reaction to a possibly controlled team. Now with the W/T contact established and a body and supply drop on the way, there is a basis of hope that this Apple Tree will bear a rich harvest of bitter fruit for BGGYPSY palates."[10]

* * *

On May 28, Shehi, the team leader, ordered three members of the team, Matiani, Gjyla, and Sakollari, to return to Greece because of the difficulties in obtaining food supplies in the operating area sufficient to support a large team. The three men separated from Shehi and Premçi on the same day and exfiltrated to Greece on June 15.[11] The debriefing of the returned agents offered some eye-opening information about the situation in Albania.

The many infiltration teams with different sponsors confused the population, who felt that unless the various groups united, they were doing more harm than good to their country. The Albanian government generated effective propaganda from the situation by claiming that the National Committee for Free Albania, working out of Greece and Italy, wanted to turn Northern Epirus over to the Greeks and bring the rest of the country under Italian control again. Agents captured in the past had been forced to reveal the names of local sympathizers who had aided and sheltered them. These sympathizers had suffered draconian punishments, which included the imprisonment or deportation to forced labor camps of their entire family circle. As a consequence, many people were predisposed to report to the authorities any infiltrators who contacted them. The government had also drafted local villagers into civil protection units to guard against infiltration or agents and to pick up any leaflets or supplies dropped.[12]

On the other hand, the team also reported that the majority of the Communists were disappointed with the Hoxha regime and were ready to work with any organization that planned to overthrow the government. Less than one fourth of the police force was loyal to the government, they said. Ninety people out of a hundred were ready to act if there were some serious attempt to overthrow the government, but they wanted reassurance that there would be no territorial concession to Greece, Italy, or Yugoslavia.[13] These encouraging assessments by the team were certainly exaggerated, given the realities that existed on the ground. It seems probable the agents made up the information in order to tell their debriefers what they wanted to hear.

While all along the plan had been for Matiani and Sakollari to return, Ulmer and Mason in Athens were surprised that Gjyla returned as well. They assumed that Shehi had sent him back in order to report progress to Zog directly, without the Americans as intermediaries. Later, Sakollari recalled that Gjyla had little or no sense of security and, furthermore, had an inflated sense of his own importance. He explained that Shehi, while being a more able person, lacked the strength to control Gjyla effectively and that was the primary reason for returning him to Greece with Matiani and Sakollari. Another reason was Gjyla's inability to make the contacts he had claimed he was able to make before he infiltrated. Even his own relatives in the Martaneshi area had been too scared to help when he approached them.[14]

With regards to Shehi, Sakollari remembered that he, too, had shown little awareness of the security precautions needed to safeguard his mission in Albania. On at least one occasion, it was the direct intervention of Matiani and Sakollari that saved the team from capture when Shehi was attempting to make contact with a friend. Sakollari explained that Shehi did not fully realize the vast changes that had taken place in Albania since he had left in 1939. Thus, the departure of Matiani and Sakollari left Shehi without any experienced men who could ensure the safety of his team.[15]

Two examples of Shehi's carelessness after Matiani's departure are the noticeable increase in the volume of radio communication and the excessive number of contacts with local people. When Matiani was with the team, over a period of twenty-eight days they sent only three W/T messages with a total of sixteen words. In twenty-eight days following Matiani's departure, the team sent nine messages ranging in length from eighteen to sixty words each. During that same period, on June 12, the team reported "We have found five friends who are now working for us." On June 18, they sent "Twelve persons are working for us."[16]

The Sigurimi exploited both these weaknesses to draw the team into a trap on the night of June 28–29 in what would be the opening gambit of a sixteen-month long playback operation they conducted against the CIA.

* * *

The Sigurimi had first been alerted of the presence of the team by the covert aircraft flight on the night of May 8. They searched the area and determined that it had been a supply drop rather than a body drop. Shortly after, they received reports of footprints at the border, indicating that a group of five to six men had infiltrated from Greece at the beginning of May. On May 15, a shepherd reported seeing men in military clothes and armed with German automatic guns in a forest in the Martaneshi area.

The Sigurimi tied these three events together and concluded that a team had infiltrated at the beginning of May, had been supplied from air on May 8, and was making its way to the north-central part of Albania. They alerted their agents in the area to report any suspicious activities. Using equipment and guidance from a team of Soviet advisers led by Lieutenant General Dimitri Kurbatov, chief counselor to the minister of interior,[17] the Sigurimi was able to detect radio transmissions coming out of the region and triangulate their source in the area between the mine of Bulqiza and Lake Vajkali. Shehi was a native of this area and had moved there with Premçi after Matiani and the rest of the team had departed for Greece.[18]

On June 4, Myslim Shehi, a Communist from the area and informer of the Sigurimi known by the pseudonym Mexhi, reported that his distant relative, Zenel Shehi, had contacted him on behalf of King Zog and wished to use him in an important mission assigned to him by the King himself. The report garnered immediate attention and was elevated to the highest levels in the Sigurimi hierarchy who understood that this group was unlike other groups that Sigurimi dealt with on a regular basis.

Shehi was not tainted by collaboration with the Italians or Germans during the war, as most of the infiltrated agents were; he claimed to speak for the king; and he had been sent to agitate in the region where the king hailed from and where he still had a considerable influence. Further information from Mexhi revealed that the Americans were behind Shehi's group and that Hamit Matiani had escorted him personally from Greece. The Sigurimi decided to mount an operation to capture the group and to turn it against their control center. They gave the operation the code name *Liqeni i Vajkalit* after the nearby lake where the team was located.[19]

Kadri Hazbiu, vice–minister of interior and head of the Sigurimi, personally directed the planning and the execution of the operation. Born in 1922, Hazbiu became a Communist at an early age and participated actively in partisan formations during the war. In 1945, only twenty-three years old, he became chief of intelligence in the Albanian army and in 1947 went to the Soviet Union for specialized training by Soviet intelligence. In 1950, he was appointed deputy to Mehmet Shehu, minister of interior at the time, and was put in charge of the Sigurimi.

Since 1949, the Sigurimi had maintained a special task force focused on locating and eliminating anti-government resistance groups throughout the country. It was composed of a handful of selected operatives who typically passed for resistance fighters, penetrated the bands and embedded with them for months, collecting intelligence on their movements, safe havens, and supporters. They placed the information in prearranged secret locations, or dead drops, which the Sigurimi checked frequently; or they passed it through a network of couriers, also known as cutouts—trusted intermediaries whose knowledge of the links in the communication chain was purposefully kept to a minimum in order to maintain secrecy.[20]

Hazbiu selected a team of five members from the task force and assigned them the mission to capture Shehi and Premçi alive, taking special care not to hurt arms or hands; and they should do this in complete secrecy without alerting the population at large or any contacts Shehi may have established about their capture. In this operation, they would present themselves not as opponents of the regime but as disgruntled Communists, members of Mexhi's organization, who had remained loyal to King Zog and were dissatisfied with the Hoxha government.[21]

Once Hazbiu's group was in place, Mexhi got back in touch with Shehi to inform him that he had several friends who were dissatisfied with the regime—potentially more could be convinced. Shehi asked Mexhi to arrange a meeting and relayed the information to the CIA case officers in Athens in his messages of June 12 and 18, together with a request for clothing and food for seven people for three months. The meeting occurred on the night of June 28–29 in a remote uninhabited house in the mountains near Bulqiza. Many years later, Mark Dodani, one of the members of the Sigurimi task force, told the story of how he and four other Sigurimi officers, the informer Mexhi, Shehi, and Premçi spent several hours into the night conversing and raising toasts to the health of Zog. Toward dawn, as Shehi and Premçi loaded themselves with their equipment and prepared to take leave, the Sigurimi men jumped on them and after a brief scuffle immobilized them.[22]

King Zog later provided a different version of Zenel Shehi's betrayal and capture. In a letter to the CIA on May 1, 1954, Colonel Selmani, writing for Zog, said that Shehi's mission had been to contact three Communists whom Zog believed had remained his sympathizers: Haxhi Lleshi, his uncle Aqif Lleshi, and Myslim Peza, their influential friend. Aqif Lleshi and Myslim Peza came to a complete understanding with Shehi and promised to help him contact Haxhi Lleshi and ensure his adherence as well. Unfortunately, Haxhi Lleshi seized this as a chance of ingratiating himself to the Communist regime. A cousin of Zenel Shehi, Myslim Shehi, lured Zenel to the house of another cousin by marriage, Muharrem Gjurra, under the guise of making contact with Haxhi Lleshi there. That's where the Sigurimi forces caught him. For this action, the Communists rewarded Haxhi Lleshi by making him chairman of the Presidium of the National Assembly in Tirana.[23]

Zog did not provide any further details to substantiate his story, so it is hard to determine how much of this account was speculation on his part. But it is a fact that Haxhi Lleshi was indeed appointed chairman of the Presidium of the National Assembly on August 1, 1953. He kept this position, equivalent to the Albania's head of state, until 1982. Whatever the true story of the betrayal may have been, the fact remains that on June 29, the Sigurimi had in their hands not only Shehi and Premçi but all their equipment, radio set, crypto pads, and notebooks.

* * *

Hazbiu moved swiftly to the next stage of the operation, which was to debrief thoroughly the two captured agents and convince them to collaborate in his playback scheme. Sigurimi histories say that both

Shehi and Premçi agreed to cooperate relatively quickly. So quickly, in fact, that they aroused the suspicion of their captors, who feared that Premçi would send a signal to his control officer in Athens as soon as he had access to the radio. They pressured Premçi to reveal the danger codes agreed upon with the control, but he told them there weren't any. The Sigurimi assigned a radio operator to become familiar with Premçi's style of transmitting Morse code and to monitor the encryption and transmission of all his messages. They exchanged several trial messages, which they recorded and played back to Premçi. The Sigurimi made it clear that all future exchanges with the control center in Athens would be similarly monitored and that he would suffer severe consequences if he didn't send exactly what was prescribed by his handlers.

The Sigurimi gave a lot of thought to how they were going to phrase their messages. Despite the information they had extracted from Shehu and Premçi, they could not be sure of the context of the previous messages and could easily say something that would trigger the Americans' suspicions. Hazbiu assigned a senior officer by the name of Pilo Shanto with the sole responsibility of crafting the messages and feeding them to Premçi for transmission. Shanto later wrote a memoir describing the details of the operation from the Sigurimi point of view.

Figuring out what to say in the first couple of messages was particularly agonizing, because a false step could blow up the entire operation from the outset. After lengthy discussions, Hazbiu ordered that the first messages provide some generic information about the area, including some language to explain why the team had not been in contact for the past several days.

On July 3, the Sigurimi sent the first two messages to the Athens control center. They took Premçi and his radio set on location in Bulqiza just in case the Americans were tracking the origin of the signal. They paid attention even to details, such as Shehi's style of speech and his northern Albanian dialect, to ensure that the messages were as authentic as possible.

The content of the first messages sent by the Sigurimi are below, together with the messages that Athens received on its end:

Message Sent by the Sigurimi[24]	Message Received by Athens Center[25]
13. A plane circled on the 25th. Police forces and population are moving. It is not yet known when they will leave. Cancel DZ until second notice.	13. Date 5. Circulating the plan. They are put in forced movement (garble) population. It is not yet known when they will depart. Begin 7 until the second understanding.
14. In Mat, they are working to build a hydroelectric power station. More than 300 people work there volunteers and with pay, most are from Burreli.	15. In Mat they are working to fix the center. About 3,000 workers volunteers but with pay. Most of them are from the North (garble of four letters).

There are significant discrepancies between what was sent and what was received: the first message to arrive in Athens contained an unusual extent of garbling and the request to cancel the upcoming supply drop was missing altogether; the second message was miss-numbered, going from 13 to 15, skipping 14. Perhaps these variances and omissions can be explained by taking into account the unavoidable information loss in the process of enciphering and transmitting messages from the field and receiving, deciphering, and translating them at the center. However, another very plausible explanation is that Premçi was risking his life by intentionally distorting the messages dictated by the Sigurimi captors in order to attract his control officer's attention to their situation.

* * *

Two days later, Athens replied, informing Apple to expect eight parachutes at the prearranged DZ between July 7 and 10. The Sigurimi team was elated to receive the reply—it showed that their first communications hadn't aroused suspicions. But after the initial jubilation, puzzling questions began to surface. How did the Americans expect only two men to haul a load of eight parachutes? Were they so naïve as to think the team could wait for four days at a DZ without being detected—especially after it had asked to cancel the

DZ because police forces were in the area and it wasn't known when they would leave.

The reason the Sigurimi had requested cancellation was that the DZ location was close to villages where Shehi had tried to establish contact before his capture. When the villagers saw the supplies fall from the sky with Shehi nowhere around to collect them, they might suspect he had been captured, and the Sigurimi wanted to avoid spreading that rumor at all costs.

After weighing all the pros and cons, they decided not to set up a reception for the drop, supposing the plane would go back if the pilot didn't see the signals from the ground. They were astonished when the plane showed up on the night of July 6–7 and, after circling several times, dropped the parachutes over the mine of Bulqiza, apparently confusing its lights with reception signals from the team. The local forces in the area collected a wealth of supplies, including a radio set, arms, food, and ammunition.[26]

Sigurimi decided to turn their adversary's somewhat perplexing behavior to their advantage by taking the upper hand in the exchanges with the control center. The first message after the drop, on July 12, stated that the plane had circled for one hour over Bulqiza, the pilots had made the drop without seeing their signals, the police had found the material, and the team had been forced to hide in wooded areas. A second message on the same date took a harder stance: "We know the situation here. That is why each drop should be made as we like and where our signals are."[27]

Next, Sigurimi trained their sights on Halil Branica and decided to lure him into parachuting into Albania. From questioning Shehi and reviewing notes they had found on him, they knew Branica had been part of the original team and had been forced to turn back. They assumed the Americans were waiting for the right opportunity to send him in. In several messages sent on July 15 and 18, they fed center information about the situation on the ground that included military unit locations and the coordinates of a DZ they had found in Mati. Then, on July 25, the team urgently requested the dispatch of Branica to develop contacts in the Mati area:[28] "We are in a situation to await Halil. Good DZ. The situation is quiet. Halil is very necessary because he will give us first hand authority for a larger zone of action and more bases especially in Mat. Being three of us movement will be safer."[29]

Athens replied right away, telling them to wait for Branica on August 4. The Sigurimi wanted to capture Branica alive and unhurt, so they could proceed immediately with debriefing him for information and instructions he was expected to bring with him. They set up the trap so that he wouldn't suspect foul play immediately on landing or have an opportunity to react against capture, either by opening fire or by poisoning himself. On August 3, Apple sent reception information for Branica: "Friends of ours will be at the DZ to hide the supplies. If he is not found immediately, Halil is to give the password Berat; the counter password is Burrel."[30]

Branica was parachuted on August 4, along with fourteen thousand pounds of supplies, including an RS-1 radio set. Apple contacted center on August 6 to confirm Branica's safe arrival. To inject a dose of realism, the Sigurimi wrote that the team had received only three of the five containers dropped by the plane and that security forces were searching the area. Later, they reported that the radio was missing the transmitting unit. The case officers in Athens reviewing the messages assumed that the communications staff had mistakenly packed a power supply unit instead of the transmitter. On September 6, Apple received another complete RS-1 with spare parts.[31]

* * *

After receiving the report of Branica's safe arrival, Athens radioed, "Good job, Halil and Apple." Not knowing that Apple was the code name of the team, Sigurimi took it for a hidden code word meant for Branica. They tried to get him to reveal its meaning, but Branica steadfastly rejected their inducements to cooperate, even after the Sigurimi told him that Shehi and Premçi had been collaborating. To make the story more convincing, Sigurimi arranged for Branica to encounter Shehi smartly dressed in a fancy suit, conferring amicably with a uniformed officer of the Sigurimi in Tirana.[32] Nevertheless, Branica refused to cooperate until the end.

In later analysis after the fiasco became clear, the CIA counterespionage staff at headquarters recognized that the officers in Athens should have raised the case officer challenge before parachuting

Branica, especially in light of the fact that all the reception details, including the DZ and passwords had been set up by Apple.[33] But they didn't pay attention. It was only on August 12 that Athens issued the challenge question, "How many rifles have you?" Sigurimi scrambled trying to figure out how to respond to the challenge. Shehi and Premçi, although fairly cooperative up to that point, refused to reveal the right answer to the challenge. Left with no options, Sigurimi ignored the challenge in exchanges on August 13, 15, 16, 18, and 24.

The base rechallenged Apple on August 24 and 27. On August 28, Sigurimi replied with a direct answer to the question by reporting the number of arms on hand: "We have one rifle, two automatic guns, three pistols on us plus three pistols and three automatic guns for spares. The rest, we gave to friends."[34]

Rather than take this answer to be a signal of control, meaning that the operator was under duress and the mission likely compromised, Athens reissued the challenge on August 28, only to receive a similar reply on September 3. Gordon Mason, the CIA case officer for the team, explained this situation by commenting that, "it is improbable that the team had forgotten its instructions on this signal, but due to the impending resupply drop, it may have been interpreted as a straight question."[35] To support his belief that the team was not controlled, he pointed out that other control signals embedded in the radio communications continued to be negative.

However, in June when a similar resupply drop was impending, Apple had not confused the control challenge from the case officer. The constant reiteration of the question by Athens this time would have easily called their attention to the fact that center was raising the control question, making Mason's explanation hard to credit. Also, why the long delay in responding if the team was uncontrolled but misconstrued the questions?

The later counterespionage review of the Apple operations concluded that CIA staff had failed to recognize the possibility that Premçi could have yielded the radio communication control signals to his captors to demonstrate that he was cooperating with them without revealing the second layer of security, which was the case officer control question and expected answer. Such redundant challenge/response exchanges were included in communication plans with agents with precisely such an eventuality in mind.[36] The chief of CIA's Communications Security Division wrote: "One general feature which seems to be common to many instances of controlled operations is the unconscious effort on the part of all concerned to rationalize the appearance of security checks when used to indicate control. Such a reaction is natural when considered in terms of the case officer's identification with the Agent. Obviously, however, . . . such a rationalization negates the entire purpose of such checks."[37]

After the resupply mission was completed successfully on the night of September 6–7, Athens reported to headquarters: "As this station has implied, a possibility existed that Apple may have been under control, due to their failure to answer the case officer's danger signal. We now feel that failure to answer properly may have resulted from Apple's desire to receive certain items on this resupply attempt."[38]

It would have been reasonable for Athens at this point to raise the case officer control challenge, if for no other reason than to test the validity of their hypothesis that the team had misconstrued the challenge because of the impeding supply drop. But they did not raise it. As a means of testing the bona fides of Apple, center asked for "friends" to exfiltrate in messages on September 5 and 16 and October 6. The Sigurimi ignored these requests in their replies, without raising any suspicions.[39]

Instead, during the month of October, Sigurimi sent several bits of information in an effort to inject realism, build up the team's potential, and mislead the Americans. On October 3, they requested that "for many reasons" there be no drops in October. On October 10, they asked that King Zog be informed that his influence was great in Tirana, Kruja, Mati, Martaneshi, and Peshkopi; they also requested the dispatch of new agents. On October 27, they reported an indirect contact with a sergeant major of the police in Peshkopi.[40]

Sigurimi's efforts to divert base's attention seem clearly to have been successful. In October, Fiend staff in Athens reviewed the communication traffic and reported to headquarters that they were "impressed and gratified" by the successful utilization of the team's radio equipment and time schedule. The team had made contact every three days—as allowed by communications security regulations. Seventy-five percent of the radio traffic had been related to Apple's support and primary mission, with the remaining traffic strictly of an intelligence nature. Apple had reported to have extended their network with contacts in Peshkopi and Burrel and was working to obtain contacts in other areas. They stated that they could do a better job if other teams were sent to these areas.[41]

* * *

Things were going very well for the Sigurimi until October 29, when Premçi managed to escape from his holding cell in Tirana with the assistance of the police officer assigned to guard him. A pursuit party was formed immediately to attempt to recapture him at any cost. Premçi and his friend fell into an ambush in the mountains northeast of Tirana but managed to evade capture. At that point, Mehmet Shehu ordered the Sigurimi to capture Premçi if possible but to find ways to continue the operation without Premçi.

On November 3, pursuit forces killed Premçi in the forests of Martaneshi. On the same day, Athens received a message from Apple stating that Premçi was sending with his left hand because he had fallen and broken his operating hand. The CIA communications staff in Athens analyzed the new "fist," the term used to describe the unique pattern of dots and dashes that distinguishes every Morse wireless operator. Upon receiving their analysis, Ulmer immediately informed Yatsevitch at headquarters that, although the message had negative radio communication control signals, it had been sent by a new fist operating at a speed far below normal, giving credence of the left-hand explanation they had received. Yet the sharp dots in the transmission indicated that, on the contrary, a trained fist was sending the messages. This was suspicious, for Premçi, like the rest of the wireless operators trained by the CIA at the time, had received training on only one hand. The communications officer who had instructed Premçi added that he highly doubted Premçi was capable of using his other hand, although in theory it was possible.

The base immediately (on November 3) raised the case officer control challenge, "How many rifles have you?" Apple didn't respond to the challenge in contacts on November 6, 12, 15, and 18. On November 15, Apple radioed, "Tahir is very ill." Then, on November 24: "Tahir is no longer able to work. His hand is very bad. We ask to return or else send us another radio man." Asking to return was a calculated risk on the part of the Sigurimi—they knew Athens would consider it practically impossible for the team to exfiltrate at that time because of deep snows, mountainous terrain, and general winter weather conditions.

On November 18, Athens, in response to headquarters' instructions, asked for specific positive intelligence, in order to assess the possibility of control: "How many friends do you have ready to receive our arms? Who is known to oppose the regime in the areas where you are?" The Sigurimi crafted the response to reflect the reality on the ground, which they suspected the CIA was able to cross-check with other sources. "If hostilities broke, dozens are ready to take up arms, mainly in the area of Bulqiza," they radioed. Then, they send the names of six people in the area they knew the CIA would recognize as regime opponents. Indeed, the names were cross-checked against registries and did not raise any suspicions in Athens or at the headquarters.

The Americans issued the challenge again on November 24 and 27. On November 29, Apple responded by giving the number of arms on hand, which should have been taken as an indication that the team was controlled. Gordon Mason, the case officer for the team, discounted that possibility, again advancing as a reasonable explanation that his challenge had been misunderstood as an inquiry for purposes of resupply. Given that Apple continued to provide uncontrolled replies to radio communication danger signals, Al Ulmer, the Athens station chief, wrote to Yatsevitch in Washington that the "case officers who trained and dispatched the team consider it of the highest caliber and feel confident the team would have found some clear way of showing control if it existed."

On December 3, Apple claimed to have forgotten the content of the base's challenge message and asked it be repeated. To add more evidence of Premçi's "forgetfulness," the Sigurimi omitted from the radio message the standard cryptographic control signal that was supposed to be added at the end of all messages to indicate positive or negative control. Athens hypothesized that since the other radio communication danger signals were regular and since this was the first time confirmation crypto signals were omitted, Premçi had forgotten to include them when he was recopying the message.[42]

In their next message, the Sigurimi decided to put some pressure on Athens. They radioed: "Broken hand not set right. Wound infected. Tahir is very weak. He cannot function as planned. We demand you notify King Zog about the situation. Hasten a decision or we'll be forced to make a decision ourselves."

* * *

On November 26, CIA officers visited King Zog to inform him of the situation. They asked him for possible questions they could ask the radio operator to determine whether he was actually in touch with the team leader and sending for him. On December 8, Zog replied with two questions to be passed to the team:

Are you in good condition?
Do you remember in whose hands you left your silver cuff links before your departure?

Zog had discussed the first question with Shehi and Branica prior to their departure from Cairo. It was to be their code word, to which they would respond in one of three ways: "Good condition" meant "The people believe in us and help us by putting themselves at the king's disposal." "Very good condition" meant "We are in contact with government officials and army officers in our favor." "Situation in our favor" meant "People are ready to take up arms; there are armed actions against the government and officials are participating in them." From the responses Zog expected to receive from his officers on the ground, it's obvious how disconnected he was from the real situation in Albania at the time.

Only Shehi, Zog, and the queen knew the subject of the second question. Before his departure from Cairo, Shehi, who had been Geraldine's bodyguard since 1939, entrusted to her a box of precious items, among which were a pair of silver cuff links. So the answer to the question posed was expected to be something like "To the Queen (or Mistress) of the house."

Athens radioed both questions on December 12. Although Sig-urimi had found the first question and the three expected answers in a notebook captured on Shehi, they either overlooked this question or didn't bother to answer it. Instead, they focused on the cuff link question. Their assumption was that the Americans had been digging into Shehi's and Branica's belongings in Athens for something recognizable and yet simple they could query them on. Branica and Shehi, upon questioning confirmed that they indeed had left cuff links in their luggage in Athens. So, on December 13, Apple radioed the following message: "The silver cuff links are in our suitcases. Zenel's and Halil's. Don't bother us unnecessarily."

Athens overlooked the fact that the first question was unanswered. Fiend staff in Athens searched Shehi's suitcases left in the safehouse and indeed found the cuff links as stated. When Zog learned of the radio reply, he said that he felt that the team's answer, while not as expected, was accurate and genuine since they had no prearranged control signals and the leader probably had more than one set of cuff links.

As a result, Athens shelved the suspicions about the team's status and the suggestions to deny it further support. The team was considered safe and uncontrolled; preparations began to provide another W/T operator equipped with enough medical supplies to attempt to save the operator's injured arm.

* * *

On December 12, the Sigurimi increased the pressure to get the Americans to send the replacement radio operator. They radioed that Premçi was very weak from his infected hand. The transmissions indeed were very slow. Then, they failed to make contact at scheduled times on December 15, 18, 21, and 24. On December 27, Athens center radioed: "Matter discussed with King. Sending radio operator and two parachutes at DZ G-1531 January 3–7. Confirm DZ and date."

On December 31, Apple informed center that there would be some friends at the DZ to await for the radioman and that the password and counter-password would be "Kruja" and "Korabi" respectively.

Athens chose Ahmet Kabashi as the replacement W/T operator. Between 1949 and 1951, Kabashi had carried out several infiltrations into Albania from Italy and Greece in missions sponsored by the Office of Special Operations. He had proven to be mature, courageous, dedicated, reliable, and security conscious in the accomplishment of these missions. When the OSO curtailed its involvement in Albania, Kabashi had been transferred into the rolls of the Office of Policy Coordination. They held him for future use at an Athens safehouse, where he received W/T training. Kabashi consistently received commendatory evaluations on his progress and no derogatory information was uncovered during this period.[43]

Fiend staff in Athens saw Kabashi's drop as an opportunity to rectify a number of security shortcomings that had plagued the Apple operation up to that point. Kabashi received specific instructions to answer control questions properly and to respond to the case officer's danger signals immediately. A number of redundant danger signals were put in place as a fail-safe way to clarify once and for all whether or not Apple was under the control of the Sigurimi.

If the team was not under control, Kabashi would encipher the word *Gur*, which meant "rock" in Albanian, immediately after the message number, followed by the message text. If the team was under control, Kabashi wouldn't encipher this keyword. In addition, if the team was not under control, Kabashi was instructed to incorporate the phrase "The snows have arrived" in his very first message upon parachuting in.

Gordon Mason chose two case officer control questions rather than the customary one, and he selected questions that were unlikely to confuse the team in the field into believing that they were legitimate questions. The first control question was, "Is your *Letër Njoftim* in order?" The *Letër Njoftim* was the identity card that every citizen in Albania was required to carry at all times. The negative control answer was: "My *Letër Njoftim* is no good." The positive control answer was: "Yes, my *Letër Njoftim* is in order." The second control question was, "Do you need any *lek*?" referring to the Albanian currency. The negative control answer was "Send us maps." Mason chose the nonsense answer to the question on purpose, to avoid a lucky guess by the opposition or confusion by the agents in the field, similar to the "rifles" question that had been used earlier. Indeed, a direct answer to the question would indicate positive control.[44]

After delays due to the weather conditions, Kabashi was parachuted on the night of January 29–30, 1953. He radioed his first message to center in the morning of January 31: "66-1 Gur-Gur [pause]

The snows have arrived. Radio operator arrived well. Received two parachutes. Thank the pilots for good drop."[45]

Thus, in less than thirty-six hours, the Sigurimi had been able to extract all the security codes from Kabashi and convince him to participate in their deception. To fully debrief Kabashi in such a short amount of time, it's possible the Sigurimi used a cooperative Zenel Shehi. Kabashi's instructions in Athens prior to departure had been: "Upon making contact with Apple team you will come under the command of Captain Zenel. He has been fully instructed of your responsibilities and will make all decisions pertaining to the security and operations for your team."[46]

Regardless of what methods the Sigurimi used to turn him, Kabashi remained fully cooperative until the end of the operation. While Premçi seems to have found several opportunities to send indications that the team was under control, Kabashi consistently sent negative control responses to all challenge signals received from center.

Between February and April, Apple sent a number of messages indicating contacts with Communist forces and reporting the names of supporters in order to add the appearance of realism to the communications and entice more supply drops from the base. For example, on February 4, Apple reported their location to be in the Dibra area near the Yugoslav border, where they had been forced to move after Communist forces, alerted by the January 29 drop, had begun operations in their old location. On the way, the team said they had encountered armed civilians and engaged them in a firefight. No one on the team was lost, and one Communist civilian was killed. Premçi's poor physical condition and the snow were hampering the progress of the team, they said. Based on this information, on February 8 Athens carried out a diversionary drop to aid the team in eluding the security forces.[47]

* * *

When he was parachuted to the team at the end of January, Kabashi had carried a letter with the following instructions:

> We feel that your captain [Zenel Shehi] should return to the base
> to report to us and to his King in the springtime. After this he will

return to you. We propose two methods for his reaching the base. First, we could send Hamit [Matiani] to meet him at a prearranged time at the rendezvous point which you would send us. Secondly, we could arrange for Hamit to meet him at the point where you received your first food supplies on your route last year. However, the final decision as to time and place must be left to the captain and we would do our best to have Hamit meet him and act as his escort back to the base.[48]

Hamit Matiani had eluded Communist forces for years. His ability to evade traps and escape unharmed had become a legend. The Sigurimi recognized a golden opportunity to have Matiani delivered to their hands. On February 13, they radioed that Shehi agreed to exfiltrate, but he required the assistance of Matiani as guide. On April 16, to sweeten the deal, they said that Shehi was ready to return with Premçi and "one friend who pretends to be a Communist."

On the night of May 1–2, Matiani was parachuted at a DZ site in the Biza Plateau approximately ten miles northeast of Tirana.[49] With him dropped Naum Sula and Gani Malushi—longtime followers of Matiani and veterans of OSO operations in Albania since 1949. Matiani was equipped with one RS-5 radio set and a special signal plan calling for contacts every other day once they had started the journey to Greece. Matiani himself carried the signal plan, cipher pads, and danger signals. The password to be used on the night of the drop was "Puka," with counter-password "Përmeti." The supply containers dispatched with Matiani carried food, clothing, arms, ammo, and numerous other operational items that the Sigurimi had requested. Matiani carried gold on him that he was to turn over to Branica, who would be in charge during Shehi's absence.[50]

Upon their return to Athens, the covert plane crew reported that they had to make three passes over the DZ, consuming eight minutes time. This extraordinary procedure was dictated by the hesitation of Matiani, who was supposed to be the first agent to jump.[51] Matiani had completed parachute jumps before and was praised by the aircrew for his swift and decisive jumps. Was his hesitation caused by a premonition that this drop would be his last? We'll never know. What we do know is that he was promptly captured upon landing and that very night was taken to Hazbiu, who supervised his interrogation and debriefing.

* * *

On May 4, Apple acknowledged receiving three agents and four containers and announced that Sula had injured his legs and ribs falling in a wooded area "because of a poor drop by the pilot." The news of Sula's injury was not a surprise for Athens, since it was his first jump and he was considered the least capable of the three men on Matiani's team.

At this point, the Sigurimi played out the communications so as to prolong the benefits of control as much and to the widest extent possible. Athens had ordered Shehi's exfiltration, so on May 12 Apple radioed that the exfiltration group composed of Matiani, Sula, Malushi, Shehi, Premçi, and an unidentified friend had separated from Branica and Kabashi who remained behind.

The next day, Matiani's group established W/T contact with the base according to the communication signals and plan Matiani had received from Athens before his departure. Thus, it had taken Sigurimi twelve days to extract from Matiani all the danger signals and any other control signs that the Athens base expected in his messages.

On May 15, Matiani's group radioed that they would have to change the planned exfiltration route, which was the same one Matiani had used the previous year. Sula and two other members of the group, the message said, were too weak to walk the mountains. Sigurimi knew that unless they changed the original plan, the base would be able to cross-reference their progress reports against known checkpoints along the route. By controlling the exfiltration route, Sigurimi was clearly in position to make more realistic reports and respond to queries they might receive from Athens. The route they proposed was sensible because it went very close to Matiani's home region, where the team could receive aid in the event of trouble.[52]

Other communications described a slow exfiltration progress hampered by the poor physical condition of three of the six-member team: Shehi had dysentery, Sula was injured from the drop, and Premçi was weakened due to illness following the breaking of his hand in November 1952.[53] They requested food and medicine but at the same time stated they were unable to receive a drop. The Sigurimi had a good opportunity to receive supplies and still keep the operation active, but they chose not to exploit it. Painting a realistic scenario for the center helped them in the long run by removing any potential doubts that the team was controlled. Indeed, after Ulmer performed a thorough review of this team's radio messages, he cabled headquarters on August 18, 1953: "The writer finds it extremely difficult to believe that if the group were controlled the opposition would play them back for the short period that they did without fully exploiting the potential before closing this circuit down."[54]

On June 5, the team reported that they had run into an ambush near Vithkuqi, twelve miles from the Greek border, in which Matiani was wounded. They stated that their difficulty was caused by center's attempt to infiltrate additional teams in the area through which they were attempting to exfiltrate. Athens saw a trace of Matiani's hand in this message. In past operations he had always been adamant that other groups be kept out of the border area during his exfiltration attempts.[55] It's clear that by this time the Sigurimi had been able to debrief Matiani on even the smallest nuances of his way of working and was able to weave the information into their messages to the Americans.

On June 10, the team radioed that they were unable to move because of Matiani's condition and requested: "Send us a guide to cross the border and withdraw Matiani from us or else chances are we will have to put him in a base here."

Creating the illusion that the team was within reach of the Greek border, Sigurimi was attempting to discover and neutralize additional American assets in the area, such as internal supporters who could be called upon to serve as guides or houses where teams could find refuge. Ulmer would later write: "I personally discount the belief that the opposition would be willing to settle for so little gain as one guide, when so much was available to them for the asking."[56]

Athens saw the request for a guide as suspicious and a good indication the team was controlled. Center radioed a suggested exfiltration route, which they had planned after long discussions with the Greek border guard units. Greek patrols would be placed in positions to fire upon pursuit forces and clear the exfiltration route for the team. Then, on June 13, Athens requested that, "If Hamit is unable to travel then Zenel and one man should exfiltrate to receive medicine, help and further instructions."[57]

The response two days later said that Matiani refused to stay behind and that the team would follow base's instructions. They made their last contact on June 18, reporting their position to be approximately twelve miles from the border. The base's outgoing message on the same day cautioned the team move carefully, instructed them to attempt to cross in the next two nights, and informed them that the recommended border crossing area had been quiet for one week.[58]

The Sigurimi staged a firefight to give the impression of an ambush in the area and spread rumors about the killing of the agents, which they knew would not fail to reach the base. Indeed, a team that exfiltrated from Albania on July 26 reported learning of a gun battle against a group fitting the description of Matiani's team about June 20, in which all members were killed, with the exception of Matiani who poisoned himself after expending his ammunition.

Athens would not hear any more news about the members of this team until December 1953.

* * *

While tracking the progress of Matiani's team, Athens had maintained contact with Branica and Kabashi, who they thought had stayed behind. In the last two weeks of May, communications with them centered on coordinating the drop of additional agents and supplies. On May 18, the team suggested the use of the same DZ that Matiani and his team had used on May 1. To add a dose of realism in the communications, when the base set the drop window between May 29 and June 4, the Sigurimi sent a message complaining about the security involved in a six-day waiting period at the DZ.

On the night of June 4–5, a three-man team composed of Haxhi Gjyla, Zenun Gjolena, and Nuri Plaka, as well as the leader of a second team, Pal Nikolla, were dispatched. The two remaining men of Nikolla's team missed the five-second safe jump window when one of them froze at the door of the aircraft for a few seconds and blocked the other. The aircrew reported they made an accurate drop at seven hundred feet over the DZ.[59]

The mission of the new teams was to remain with Branica and Kabashi until they became familiar with the conditions within the country and then move to their respective areas of operation—Elbasani in central Albania for Gjyla's team and Mirdita in the north-central part of the country for Nikolla's team.[60]

The morning after the drop, on June 5, the team radioed that the airplane had made the drop from high altitude and they were surprised that not all the members of Nikolla's team had parachuted. They asked whether there would be another drop later that night. The base replied that there would not be another drop and that Nikolla should remain with Branica and Kabashi until he received further instructions. On June 10, the base informed Branica that it would drop arms during the period of June 17–20 and asked that Nikolla be informed that his radio operators would be sent later. They also asked for news of Gjyla's team, since they had failed to enter in radio contact with the base according to their communications plan.

The Sigurimi sent a reply on the same day, which contradicted the message they had sent on June 5. It stated that the drop had been made away from the DZ and they had no contact with the persons dropped. They reported they had to leave after dawn because Communist forces had appeared in the DZ zone. They had heard rifle fire in the DZ area but did not know what had happened.

It is hard to explain this contradiction on the Sigurimi's part. It is clear that they first sought to entice Athens in sending in the remainder of Nikolla's team, and failing to do so immediately, they tried to provide a reasonable explanation for the disposal of the four agents parachuted on the night of June 5. If the agents were not killed on the night of the drop, it is possible they died under torture without revealing their W/T signal plan; or they could have been eliminated because the Sigurimi didn't have sufficient resources to exploit several playback operations concurrently. Athens would hear nothing further about the fate of the four agents parachuted on the night of June 5 until December 1953.

* * *

On June 12, Athens notified headquarters that, as a result of the contradictory exchanges of June 5 and 10, it was handling the Branica and Matiani teams as probably controlled by the opposition. On June 19 Branica's team radioed a list of required supplies. They further stated that their local contacts were losing confidence in the team due to the failure of the June 4 resupply mission and subsequent delays in sending needed supplies. For the first time, the base raised one of two case officer control challenges given Kabashi, "Do you need *lek?*" He replied the next day "We want maps," which was interpreted by Athens to indicate negative control, although the actual prearranged response was "Send us maps."

Alerted by the challenge and to put center's doubts at rest, the Sigurimi sent a message on June 25 with some information about the four missing agents from the June 5 drop. The message stated that Pali Lushi (interpreted by the base to mean Pal Nikolla) had sent one of his people to Branica's relatives to say that they were in the Mirdita zone. The message said that Branica would attempt to make contact and requested a drop as soon as possible.

The ruse worked. Athens reported to headquarters on June 26 that it continued to recognize the possibility of control of the team but felt warranted in taking a calculated risk to maintain the operation, particularly in view of the latest report of and indirect contact with Nikolla. Headquarters concurred with the plans. When Athens proposed to determine independently the fate of the missing agents, headquarters turned them down, citing as one of the reasons the belief that Branica who was "operative and apparently not controlled," could provide them that information.

After repeated exchanges to set up the time and DZ, the supply drop was completed on July 22. On the 26th, Apple advised that the airplane had made a bad drop and they had received only three of the five bundles, apparently an attempt by the Sigurimi to push Athens to make another drop.

After this, the team missed five consecutive contacts, not reappearing until August 13 when they said that they had distributed the arms and were awaiting the return of Shehi. Athens replied that unforeseen circumstances were complicating Zenel's return at that time. Then, on September 1, Athens asked if the team was able to exfiltrate to Greece.

On September 14, Apple parried the base's request: "We are waiting for Shehi and you tell us to return to Greece. This, and no answer on the information promised about Shehi has us greatly worried. We await information tomorrow."

The base informed Apple on September 15 that Shehi could not return that season and that the team must make plans to come out. Apple replied on September 17 that it could not stay without Shehi and agreed to exfiltrate after a supply drop, specifically requesting food and clothing for their return trip and gold to pay off their local contacts. The supplies were dropped on September 19. The Sigurimi sent a message on September 22 acknowledging receipt of the two containers and thanked the crew for the drop.

On September 26, Apple reported on the preparations they were making for their departure. Athens advised them to get started before the onset of winter weather. On September 29, Apple announced they planned to begin the trek to Greece on October 15, after making appropriate explanations to their friends and contacts. On the October 4 transmission, the team announced that its departure was causing despair among friends but that all was under control. They said they were bringing out some friends who would guide them and asked for another drop of food and clothing for these friends. On the 17th of October, base asked Apple to await a drop during the period of October 21–25.

At the next scheduled communication, on October 22, Apple confirmed the resupply plan and reported that it had been waiting at the drop zone since October 19. Athens told them to await the drop that same night of October 22–23. A radio communication control challenge was issued with the message. Later that same day, Apple made an unscheduled contact stating that they had not arrived at the DZ yet and would not be able to receive the drop that night, but would be ready the following night. Kabashi provided a negative control response to the latest challenge, as he had done throughout his exchanges with Athens.

On October 23 Athens received this message from the team: "In 212. Tonight we will await the drop at DZ I-1531 between the hours of 21 until 23 local time. The zone is quiet."

The response that went out was: "Out 140. Await drop tonight 23 October."[61]

* * *

Red flags should have been raised in Athens by the fact that Apple had chosen the DZ and had reported on October 22 that they had been on location since October 19, only to contradict themselves later that same day by indicating that they had not arrived at the DZ and were unable to receive the drop that night. Even though Athens suspected the team to be controlled, it went along with the sudden change in plans.

On the night of October 23–24, the C-47 covert aircraft approached the designated DZ at three hundred feet altitude with an airspeed of 105 mph. While the plane was crossing the illuminated "T," which was the ground signal pointing at the precise location of the drop point, two anti-aircraft batteries opened fire. The pilot applied take-off power immediately and began a right turn. A few instants after starting the turn, the aircraft was hit by one 20 mm shell and oil pressure on the left engine dropped to zero. The pilot cut off power to the engine to prevent fire, feathered the propeller to reduce drag to a minimum, and flew the aircraft on one engine. As the plane escaped from the valley, another five anti-aircraft positions opened fire. The plane was forced to make an emergency landing at Brindisi, Italy. According to the flight navigator, only the pilot's exceptional skill made escape possible.[62]

The firing on the aircraft left no doubts that Sigurimi had been controlling the Apple team. The Athens Fiend staff and headquarters began dissecting the operational records to determine how big the damage was, how long the team had been under control, and what were the possible sources of compromise. E. Howard Hunt, based in Rome at the time as head of covert operations for the CIA's Southeast European Branch, began to search for a possible double agent in the midst of the Albanians who had knowledge of the operations. Doubts first fell on Colonel Selmani, who had escorted the four agents parachuted on June 5 and on his way back to Cairo had talked about them to Abas Kupi in Rome. Then Hunt scrutinized sympathizers of Zog in

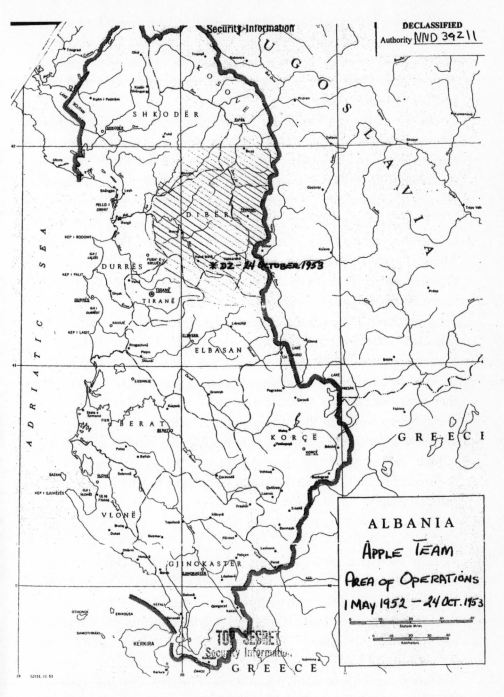

CIA map indicating the area of operations of Apple team and the spot where the covert plane was hit by antiaircraft fire on October 24, 1953

the Albanian Labor Services Company 4000 in Germany. Hunt would later say that he asked the head of a branch within the CIA in charge of "wet jobs" whether they had the capability to liquidate the double agent if found, but because his query had not been specific enough it had been brushed aside.[63]

In November and December, information began to trickle in from sources in Yugoslavia that Zenel Shehi and several of his comrades had been captured by the Sigurimi. Reports indicated that Shehi had been separated from the other prisoners and Mehmet Shehu, the minister of interior, was personally conducting his interrogation.

Then, on December 29, Radio Tirana announced the capture of six members of the group, Zenel Shehi, Halil Branica, Hamit Matiani, Ahmet Kabashi, Gani Malushi, and Naum Sula. Three men were reported killed, Nuri Plaka, Zenun Gjolena, and Haxhi Gjyla. No mention was made of Tahir Premçi and Pal Nikolla.

The news caused a great deal of distress and sorrow in the Albanian émigré circles. There was disbelief particularly with Matiani's capture. All of those who knew or had worked with Matiani believed he must have been drugged or so surprised that he could neither fight nor take his own life to avoid capture. Operational teams spending the winter in the Athens area indicated that this whole incident had given them even more motivation for activity against the regime. However, the morale of Albanians at large, in refugee camps in Greece, in Italy, and at the Labor Service Company in Germany, suffered deeply.[64]

* * *

The show trial of the six captured Apple agents and two of their internal contacts began on April 5, 1954, in Tirana. The trial was aimed at the United States in a propaganda attempt to show that it was the main organizer of all clandestine activities against the Communist government in Albania. The trial disclosed the close collaboration between the United States and King Zog in the recruitment of agents and mounting of agent teams into Albania. The close working relationship between Greece and the United States was discussed at length, with special emphasis on the subordinate position held by Greece and other Western nations to the United States and the relative ease with which undocumented American agents were able to cross borders and operate in these countries.[65]

During their testimony, the defendants gave the true names of over forty men with whom they had worked in the past as fellow agents or with whom they had had some operational contact within the country during earlier missions. With regard to CIA staff personnel, no true full names were disclosed during the trial except that of a contract agent who had left service in the fall of 1951. The true first names of only two staff personnel were disclosed. Some information was disclosed concerning the methods of training and physical location of holding and training areas for agents in Greece. The CIA moved swiftly to abandon the locations that were still in use at the time of the trials. All of Apple's supplies and equipment, including weapons, clothing, documentation, poisons, radio equipment, gold coins, and dollar bills that were captured had been subjected to detailed examination and were exhibited and reported on at the trial.[66]

Though during the trial the prosecutor mentioned that Tahir Premçi and Pal Nikolla had been arrested, he provided no indication of their disposition. Haxhi Gjyla, Zenun Gjolena, and Nuri Plaka were also mentioned as having been arrested, although the Radio Tirana broadcast of December 29 had reported them killed upon landing. The true fate of these men was never learned, although the Sigurimi later displayed pictures of their bloodied corpses for propaganda purposes. If they had indeed been arrested, they could have died during interrogations or been summarily executed for refusing to cooperate at the proceedings.

The trial ended on April 12 with the conviction of all defendants. The prosecution asked for the death sentence for all but one of the defendants in the trial. These sentences were harsh even by Tirana's standards. Captured agents tried and convicted in similar trials in the past had received sentences ranging from ten years to life in prison but very rarely had been sentenced to death.

Many years later, after the fall of Communism, reports surfaced that Kadri Hazbiu had advocated for sparing the life of some of the agents, especially Zenel Shehi, in light of their cooperation during the playback operation against the CIA and their testimonies during the trials. At a meeting of the Albanian leaders, Mehmet Shehu strongly opposed any pardon and was very critical of Hazbiu for considering only the operational aspects of the matter and not its political and ideological implications. Shehu forcefully argued that handing out tough sentences would serve as a lesson to the Americans, King Zog, and any Albanians abroad who might still consider coming in the country with the intent to disrupt the regime. Enver Hoxha agreed and added that if Shehi and others had cooperated it was because they had been afraid and not because they had wanted to help. Mehmet Shehu was also the main proponent for hanging Matiani at a public execution and keeping his body on public display for several hours. Hoxha himself favored execution by firing squad for fear that a public display of the hanged man might cause unrest and backfire.[67]

In the end, Shehu's argument prevailed. Hamit Matiani was sentenced to die by hanging. The following were sentenced to death by shooting: Zenel Shehi, Halil Branica, Naum Sula, Ahmet Kabashi, Gani Malushi, and Rrapush Agolli, a principal agent recruited by Apple inside Albania. Ibrahim Lamçe, a minor contact of the team, was sentenced to ten years' imprisonment.[68] Radio Tirana announced the sentences on the evening of April 13. That very night, over two hundred thousand leaflets were dropped over Tirana in a single pass by the covert aircraft flying at top speed. The leaflets had the following message in front:

> Albanian People,
> A group of nationalist heroes have been condemned by the Communist masters for fighting to liberate Albania. They are the true heroes of the Albanian people and they deserve revenge. Honor them as our legendary heroes and as valiant offspring of the Albanian hearth.
> Long Live Free Albania!
> Long Live the Martyrs of the Resistance!
> They Will Never Be Forgotten![69]

The back the leaflet read:

> Despite the evil tricks and bloody methods of the Communist clique, the heroic will for the liberation of Albania will never be extinguished. Other patriots will take the places of the fallen and together

will continue to act until the puppets of the Kremlin are driven once and forever from the blessed soil of Albania.

Long Live Free Albania!

Long Live Albanian Martyrs![70]

The CIA considered countering the Communist propaganda coup of the Apple trial with additional leaflets but in the end decided not to pursue the idea. By that time printing leaflets regularly and dropping them at pre-agreed times had become difficult due to limitation of resources available for the operation. In addition, the CIA staff in Athens felt that the Apple agents, including Matiani, had offered weak testimonies at the trial, mostly repeating scripted lines that the Sigurimi had wanted them to say. Furthermore, the circumstances surrounding the control of Apple by the Communists were still unclear, and there was a general feeling that letting the story be forgotten might be the best thing to do after all.[71]

The last episode in the Apple agents' tragedy occurred almost one year after their demise. Three staff officers in Athens conducted a thorough examination of the possessions that the deceased agents had left behind. These were generally items the agents were wearing or carrying at the time the CIA staff picked them up for staging. The practice then was that each agent left any worthwhile possessions with friends or relatives prior to undertaking a mission, so the bulk of the effects were clothes. Items issued by the case officers while the agents resided at the safehouse were returned to the Supply Section of the Athens station for proper disposal; the rest were sent to refugee camps for distribution. In addition to the clothing, there were personal possessions, including small change, papers, letters, photos, pocketknives, and sunglasses. The examining officers found that none of these items had any significant monetary value or sufficient sentimental importance to warrant forwarding to headquarters. They segregated them into separate envelopes for each former owner and held them for distribution to former friends or relatives who might request them.[72] There is no record of anyone ever coming forward to claim them or when they were finally disposed of.

CHAPTER 15

King Zog Overstays His Time in Egypt

The news of the demise of all the agents he had sent to Albania could not have come at a worse time for King Zog. His situation in Egypt had become extremely precarious after the overthrow of his host and protector, King Farouk, who had recognized Zog as an exiled monarch and granted him and his entourage diplomatic immunities. On July 1952, a coup d'état by a group of Egyptian officers led by Muhammad Naguib and Gamal Abdel Nasser toppled the king from power and forced him to abdicate in favor of his infant son, then flee into exile. Less than a year later, on June 18, 1953, the revolutionaries abolished the monarchy and declared Egypt a republic. For Zog, this meant the loss of an important supporter and the beginning of a period of tribulation and harassment.

On August 5, 1953, the Egyptian government informed Zog that it considered the Royal Albanian Legation closed and that it would stop recognizing Albanian diplomatic passports. However, they would issue Zog Egyptian laissez-passer and would be glad to have him and his family remain in Egypt as honored guests as long as they wished to stay. Press reports at the same time stated that Zog was to be arrested any day and tried for "arms trafficking during the Palestine war" of 1948. On September 5, *Al Ahram* ran a story accusing Albanian Legation officials of helping Farouk smuggle money out of Egypt and stating that an investigation of Zog's entourage showed activities "contrary to the interests of Egypt." This article was the first salvo in a press campaign against Zog that would be conducted over the next several months with the full blessing of the Egyptian authorities.

At this time, the CIA had accelerated its efforts to bring Zog and his entourage to the United States. Since he purchased his estate in Long Island, Zog had expressed the desire to live in the United States. Working arrangements established initially by Yatsevitch had been fruitful and Zog had become a good asset for the agency in Egypt. In September 1952, he presented an unsolicited offer through his case officer in Cairo to help the CIA penetrate the Muslim Brotherhood in Egypt by leveraging the connections that Zog had formed with its leaders. A review of the proposal in Washington concluded that this was an opportunity to be capitalized upon and that the agency should make every effort to do so.[1]

Throughout 1952 and until fall 1953, when the fiasco of Zog's emissaries in Albania became known, the king had been the main source of infiltration agents for the Albanian operations. The agency hoped that his continued cooperation in clandestine activity would increase in value if Zog resettled to the United States, which would also resolve difficulties the agency had in communicating with him on sensitive matters over long distances. However, Zog did not wish to enter the US under a refugee or immigrant visa. Doing so, he felt, would impair his prestige, prejudice his political status in Albania, and detract from his claim to the throne of Albania. The agency's general counsel worked with the Department of Justice to waive normal entry requirements in the interest of national security. In a letter to the attorney general of the United States on July 24, 1953, the director of Central Intelligence Allen Dulles wrote:

> The entry of King Zog and his family through the exercise of discretionary powers pertaining to the Office of the Attorney General would be substantially less likely to arouse speculation regarding the nature of the interest of this Government in his entry.
>
> It is requested, therefore, that you review the question of entry of King Zog and his family and, in so doing, that you consider the national interests in continuing the cooperation of King Zog on important clandestine activities of this Agency.[2]

The attorney general waived the statutory requirements for Zog and nine members of his immediate family. On September 22, 1953, the State Department notified the Alexandria consulate that Zog and his party would be allowed into the US even though no visas were to be issued. Zog then booked passage on a French ship to leave Egypt for France on October 18.

* * *

Apparently alerted of Zog's imminent departure, the Egyptian police under the direction of the lieutenant governor and prosecutor of Alexandria raided his villa on September 26. They seized certain of his personal papers, but Zog resisted a body search of himself and Queen Geraldine. On September 30, Zog notified his CIA contact in Egypt that his bank accounts were frozen and that although the Ministry of Foreign Affairs had granted exit permits to him and his entourage, he was not allowed to carry with him the gold and jewels in his possession, and, therefore, he had refused the exit permits. On October 3, the Foreign Ministry informed Jefferson Caffery, the US ambassador in Cairo, that Egypt would not confiscate Zog's gold but they would not allow the gold to be exported either. On the same day, the Department of State, at the request of the CIA, asked that Ambassador Caffery communicate informally to appropriate Egyptian officials that: "The US Government feels Zog represents a real asset in the struggle against Communism and hoped the Egyptian Government, acting in the general interest, will be able to permit Zog to leave Egypt with such property as remains to him and without exposing him to further actions which will tend to diminish his prestige as a top Albanian leader and important figure in the anti-Communist struggle."[3]

On October 8, all the Egyptian newspapers carried a story that the Ministry of Interior had refused exit visas to King Zog and his suite pending settlement of a tax claim and a decision regarding gold found in his villa. A detailed estimate valued Zog's gold at twenty thousand Egyptian pounds, approximately sixty thousand dollars at the time,[4] or about nine times that much in today's dollars.[5] The story stated that Zog had failed to submit a currency declaration upon his entry into Egypt. The director of the General Income Tax Section in the Ministry of Finance was quoted as saying that Zog could be considered a tax evader and liable from one month to three years' imprisonment and/or a maximum fine of one thousand Egyptian pounds. Ambassador Caffery, commenting upon the incident, called it "the latest in a series of maneuvers to scare Zog into parting with some of his gold."

On October 16, an embassy officer met with the Egyptian vice premier Nasser and asked why Zog was not allowed to pay a tax settlement and leave Egypt. Nasser replied that his government had attempted to collect taxes from Zog, but he had denied tax liability. And, because Zog had not made a proper customs declaration when he brought in his gold, the Egyptian government legally could confiscate it. The embassy officer pointed out that because Zog had entered Egypt as a guest of the then reigning monarch, confiscation of Zog's gold would seem neither just nor ethical; he added that Zog had been helpful to the West in opposing Communist domination of Albania, which had gained him friends in the US, where he owned property. The embassy official added that anything resembling persecution of Zog by the Egyptian government would probably be unpopular in the US and adversely impact Egyptian prestige there.

Then Nasser, seemingly improvising, proposed a complicated scheme for resolving the impasse: if the US were to buy Zog's gold in Egypt, paying him in dollars in the US, the US could sell the gold to Egyptian banks for Egyptian pounds, which then could be used to pay for US government expenses in Egypt. When informed of Nasser's suggestion, Ambassador Caffery commented that he hoped the CIA would be able to accomplish the proposed transaction discretely. After studying the proposal, the State Department eventually decided not to pursue it because it was a complicated transaction without precedent, and, from a diplomatic viewpoint, it was insulting to the US government. It also had the potential to hurt US prestige and could be used by hostile press to paint the State Department as supporting a villain.

On October 21, at the request of the CIA, Ambassador Caffery again asked the foreign minister about Zog and urged restraint and moderation on the part of the Egyptian government. At the same time, Caffery advised the CIA station chief in Cairo that he could go no further on Zog's behalf. As he put it:

Zog's present plight would seem to be, to a considerable extent, of his own making, particularly since, despite the obvious turn of events, he chose to overstay his time in Egypt. If he had left some time ago before the Egyptian Government withdrew its diplomatic recognition of Albania, he would undoubtedly have been spared his present troubles. The Embassy will continue its informal efforts to resolve the present difficulties but there is obviously a limit to the intervention which can be profitably undertaken on his behalf.[6]

Caffery explained that on several occasions he had made the point with the Egyptian authorities that any discrediting of Zog would be against the Free World's interests and he had requested the Egyptian government to permit Zog to leave Egypt with his property and his dignity unimpaired. However, Caffery was reluctant to use more pressure, because he felt that the US influence ought to be reserved for paramount policy objectives, such as finding a settlement to the Egyptian-British-Israel issues. After intervening five times without success on Zog's behalf, Ambassador Caffery wrote that, short of physical coercion or threats "inappropriate to the importance of the Zog affair relative to other area issues,"[7] there was not much else the US government could do to influence the manner in which the Egyptians were handling the matter.

* * *

Negative stories continued to appear in the press almost daily. On October 30, *Agence France-Presse* claimed that Zog, Queen Geraldine, and ten members of their suite who had allegedly "participated actively in the clandestine commercial operations of the former King" had been placed under police surveillance until they appeared before a Cairo court. The *Alexandria Reformer* of November 2 reported that Zog's residence had been raided the day before by the police, who seized arms, including three revolvers that were licensed and two machine-guns, four shotguns, and eight pistols that were unlicensed.

At the same time, the CIA station in Cairo received a report from a reliable source indicating that the minister of state, Fathi Radwan, and Revolutionary Commanding Council member Anwar Sadat were working under guidance from the Soviet legation in Cairo to discredit

King Zog to the point where he could no longer be a threat to the Hoxha regime.[8]

Other reports indicated the possibility that the Communists, fully aware of Zog's engagement against the Tirana regime, were making a concerted and deliberate effort to discredit and intimidate Zog. A friend of Queen Geraldine in the US wrote to Ambassador Caffery stating that Zog's Long Island estate had been damaged by Communists. Then, on November 5, a Franciscan priest who visited Queen Geraldine regularly reported that at their last meeting she had expressed fear for the life of her son, stating that Zog had learned that Communist agents had recently arrived in Alexandria and that they might attempt to kidnap the boy.[9]

The moves of the Egyptian government against Zog furnished the Albanian Communist press good material in its propaganda against the king and the Albanian emigrant community in general. In its broadcasts of November 9, Radio Tirana quoted *Zëri i Popullit* (*People's Voice*), the newspaper of the Albanian Communist Party, as stating that Zog's "frauds" are nothing new to the Albanian people who know him as a "bandit, adventurer, and a traitor." *Bashkimi* (*Union*), the newspaper of the Democratic Front of Albania, stated that "Zog, an individual without principles and morals," has had as his sole aim his own enrichment and that of the "clique" surrounding him. As a leader of Albanian "traitors and criminals" abroad, the paper continued, he and his followers constitute reserves for the American-British espionage. It is not accidental that their next place of residence will be the United States, stated *Bashkimi*.[10]

* * *

King Zog's situation continued to deteriorate. On December 22, he was ordered to appear for trial on January 4, 1954, where he would be charged with tax evasion and with evasion of customs duties at the time of his entry into Egypt in 1946. CIA officers involved in the case felt that the agency needed to take further actions to dissuade the Egyptian government from proceeding with Zog's public trial and probable conviction, which would seriously reduce his prestige as an anti-Communist leader and strengthen the propaganda of the Albanian Communist regime and other Communist countries. Having exhausted all other possibilities, the CIA decided to make a high-level liaison approach to Vice Premier Nasser in the hope of dissuading the Egyptian government from further public humiliation of the former monarch.

Miles Copeland, the CIA chief of station in Cairo, met with Nasser on the morning of January 4 and pointed out to him, in the name of the director of Central Intelligence, the potential damage to the Free World that would come from the discrediting of Zog by a continuation of the Egyptian proceedings. He did not argue the merits of the case or reveal the CIA's clandestine relationship with Zog. Instead, he stressed that the mutual US and Egyptian interests required denying "further grist to the worldwide Communist propaganda mill." During the discussion, Copeland was careful not to commit the prestige of the DCI to the release of Zog; he indicated that US interest was not in Zog the man but in Zog the symbol of resistance to Communist domination of Albania.[11] Nasser explained apologetically that it was too late to cease entirely the action against Zog, but he promised that he would do all he could to minimize such action.[12]

The Zog hearing before the Egyptian customs court was held later that afternoon as scheduled. Zog personally was not required to appear. His lawyers protested that the customs claim of ten thousand pounds Egyptian was "outrageous" and requested the court to overrule the customs administration. The court took the matter under advisement and set a new hearing for May 1. Zog was free to post a deposit of ten thousand Egyptian pounds against the final judgment and depart, obtaining a refund if the subsequent ruling was favorable. Copeland urged Zog to settle his customs case either by payment or deposit, apply for exit visas and permission to export his gold and jewelry, and leave Egypt without delay.[13]

But only a few days later the Egyptian authorities ordered the dissolution of the Muslim Brotherhood and the mass arrest of its leaders, blaming them for an assassination attempt on Nasser. The newspaper *Le Progrès Egyptien* on January 15 reported that Zog and his entourage were on the Ministry of Interior's blacklist and were prohibited from leaving Egypt. The CIA station, concerned over the possible closeness of Zog's relationship with the Muslim Brotherhood, believed that if the Egyptians had or could obtain concrete evidence of his involvement with the brotherhood, Zog's chances of leaving Egypt would be considerably lessened. Horace W. Fuller, a retired US Marine Reserve brigadier general who had taken over from Gordon Mason as the CIA's chief of external operations in Athens, traveled to Egypt and met with Zog on February 3 to discuss the entire situation with him.[14]

According to Zog, the tax officials' inquiry of January 28 to 30 had discovered no irregularities and, as a result, his lawyers as well as the Egyptian officials expected full tax clearance papers within fifteen days, which would enable him to depart from the country. Zog estimated he would have approximately eight thousand Egyptian pounds' worth of gold coins remaining after the payment of debts, taxes, and customs. Apart from this sum and his family jewels, he had no other means of support. Regarding his alleged involvement with the Muslim Brotherhood and other anti-regime personalities, Zog asserted that his contacts had been infrequent and purely social, denying any interference with Egyptian internal or external affairs.

Fuller told Zog that the Americans were making every possible effort to assist him and facilitate his early departure to the US. He advised Zog that the special entry arrangements made by the CIA covered only himself and nine members of his family; the balance of his entourage had to go through normal entry and immigration procedures. Zog agreed to avoid publicity and press conferences en route to the US and to make no derogatory statements concerning the Egyptian government and its treatment of his case. Fuller also asked Zog to destroy, burn, or return to him every paper describing any of Zog's interactions with CIA up to that point.[15] At the end of the meeting, Fuller obtained Zog's signed statement covering the points of their discussion.[16]

Despite the assurances given Zog in January 1954 that he could expect clearance to depart Egypt within fifteen days, at the end of February Zog reported that his passport was still at the Ministry of Interior and his gold and jewels still impounded. Now the Finance Ministry required proof that he had not purchased his Long Island estate with money exported from Egypt. Zog was sure this was yet another excuse to hold him and expressed anxiety about the real reason for the latest move by the Egyptian authorities.[17]

The Egyptian customs administration held another hearing of Zog's case on March 4. The tax officials stated that Zog's bank balance in Egypt was insufficient to cover the claim against him of ten thousand Egyptian pounds and requested permission to seize other properties. The court granted a postponement of the case to March 22.[18]

After other postponements, on May 20, the Egyptian court ordered the release of all Zog's assets in fifteen Egyptian banks.[19] It took several more months until Zog finally received the exit visas for himself and his entourage. He booked passage to France and left Egypt immediately afterward.

CHAPTER 16

Planning the Fondest Dream

In December 1951, a small group of analysts led by Rear Admiral Leslie C. Stevens, the Joint Chiefs of Staff liaison with the CIA, had begun drafting a strategic plan for cold war operations for the Psychological Strategy Board (PSB). The PSB was a committee set up by presidential directive on April 4, 1951, to coordinate national psychological warfare objectives, policies, and programs across agencies in the US government.[1] Board members included the undersecretary of state, the deputy secretary of defense, and the director of Central Intelligence, or their designated representatives.[2] DCI Walter B. Smith, intent on curtailing the autonomy that the Office of Policy Coordination had enjoyed up to that point, had insisted that the PSB assume the responsibility of providing the CIA with guidance on the conduct of covert operations and become the approval body for covert action.[3]

In May 1952, the group considered including in the strategic plan the goal of detaching Albania from the Soviet orbit. Everyone remembered that the OPC had considered this action since the first months of its existence, in an effort to disrupt and deny the use of Albania by the Communist side as an operating base of guerrilla warfare against Greece and possibly Yugoslavia. The priority of attention and effort with respect to Albania had dropped sharply with the end of Greek guerrilla hostilities in 1949. Nevertheless, since the CIA was still active in the area, the PSB asked it to submit an analysis of pros and cons for such an action. Wisner and his team prepared the analysis, and Allen Dulles, the CIA's deputy director for plans at the time, presented it to the board on June 4, 1952.

In the event of a general Soviet attack, Wisner wrote, Albania had to be cleaned up in order to remove the threat to the Adriatic and to eliminate the dagger at Tito's back. The resources required to accomplish this objective were not that significant. Admiral Robert Carney, commander in chief of NATO forces in Southern Europe, believed that he could knock out Albania in fairly short order by aerial bombardment. Tito had consistently taken the position that his forces could overrun and clean up Albania within two weeks. But such resources, no matter how small, would need to be diverted at the moment when everything might be required to fend off Soviet assaults elsewhere. Not having to face this trade-off in a war situation, Wisner emphasized, was the most significant argument for a cold war effort to detach Albania from the Soviet orbit.

The list of arguments against the coup included the fact that providing for the economic requirements of Albania after its liberation would place an additional strain on the US resources. Wisner wrote:

> From a purely cold-blooded point of view, it might be better for us to concentrate all efforts to further disorganize and hamstring the tottering Albanian economy, thus leaving the Russians with the unhappy alternative of pouring in resources of their own or allowing the fate of a rotting and desperate Albania to appear before all the world as further evidence of what happens to countries and peoples within the Soviet orbit.[4]

As a final, but considerably significant point against an Albanian coup, Wisner pointed at the amount of effort that such a program would involve and the extent to which it would reduce CIA's capabilities of attacking other and perhaps more useful targets.[5]

On November 26, 1952, the PSB finalized its paper, entitled "A Strategic Concept for a National Psychological Program with Particular Reference to Cold War Operations under NSC 10/5," which outlined a number of useful ways to erode Soviet power and influence.

Regarding covert operations, the PSB recommended placing the greatest emphasis in three broad areas:

First, weakening of Kremlin control over the internal assets of the Soviet-controlled bloc, and increasingly occupying the Kremlin with problems within this area.

Next, direct action to reduce subversive Soviet influence in those areas of the free world that were most immediately threatened by it.

Last, covert manipulation of key elements in unstable countries of the free world to increase the stability and utility to the objectives of US foreign policy of those countries.

Within these three broad fields of activity, the PSB highlighted several actions that should receive greater emphasis. One of them was the detachment of Albania from the Soviet orbit, considered feasible because of Albania's unique geographical position and desirable to demonstrate that the Soviet influence in the world could be held in check and even diminished. The principal advantage to be gained from this would be its psychological effects both in subjugated countries and in areas under intense Soviet pressure; secondary benefits included military advantages from the removal of Soviet forward operating bases in the Mediterranean and improved security of Albania's neighbors, especially Yugoslavia and Greece.

The PSB cited preliminary estimates indicating that Albanian personnel could accomplish the detachment without the overt participation of Western military forces. Ignoring the most recent analysis of the CIA, which clearly leaned against intervening in Albania, the PSB directed the agency to make a detailed plan specifying each step such an action would require up to its successful completion, including time phasing, logistics, estimates of personnel and material requirements, together with plans for meeting them.[6]

* * *

The task for preparing the plan fell to the Paramilitary Operations branch of the CIA's new Directorate of Plans, created by the merger of the OPC with the OSO in August 1952. Under the direction of Brigadier General John Weckerling, former chief of US Army Intelligence, staff officers worked in "crash" mode to prepare the plan at a level of detail sufficient to satisfy the PSB requirements.

On February 6, 1953, Weckerling provided a detailed paramilitary plan for a coup d'état in Albania supported multilaterally by the US, UK, and Yugoslavia. The plan called for a bare minimum of fifteen months of preparations before reaching sufficient readiness to launch the coup; Weckerling suggested eighteen months to two years as a far more desirable time to prepare.

During this period, the State Department would negotiate agreements to incorporate the Yugoslav-sponsored League of Albanian Refugees into the National Committee for Free Albania under joint US-UK-Yugoslav control and turn NCFA into an instrument for the creation of a new provisional government in Albania. Yugoslavia and Greece would agree to allow paramilitary operations to be launched and supported from bases in their territories, including assembling, equipping, and training over ten thousand Albanian personnel who would carry out the initial phase of the coup. The Yugoslav and Greek armed forces would prevent land and aerial reinforcement of Albanian opposition forces by Soviet or satellite nations moving through or flying over their territories during the coup; in return, the US and UK would give military support to Yugoslavia and Greece in the event of invasion of these countries by Soviet or satellite forces. In addition, US naval forces would conduct maneuvers near the mouth of the Adriatic when the coup started in order to discourage Soviet or satellite forces from sending reinforcements by sea.

The strike force would be organized in three commands. The Central Field Command included Task Force A and had 5,000 men, half of whom would be staged in Yugoslavia and the other half in Greece. They would be inserted by air and sea to capture and hold the Tirana, Durrësi, and Elbasani areas. The Northern Field Command, 1,300 strong, would be staged in Yugoslavia and included Task Force C responsible for Shkodra and Task Force D responsible for Kukësi. The Southern Field Command, 2,150 strong, would be staged in Greece and included Task Force B, responsible for Vlora, Task Force E, responsible for Korça, and Task Force F, responsible for Gjirokastra. Approximately 2,000 men would be kept in reserve as part of Task Force G.

Another 1,000 men would provide complete logistical support to the forces infiltrated into Albania and their supporters throughout the coup. They were divided into two major support commands with the North Support Command being a Yugoslav effort and the South Support Command a combined US-UK activity. Their responsibilities included transporting over 10,000 infiltrated troops in the country and provisioning these troops and their supporters during the operations with almost 1,000 tons of arms, ammunition, food rations, and other supplies. Using 180 C-47 aircraft, 80 landing craft assault (LCA) boats and six landing craft utility (LCU) boats, the support commands would move field forces from staging areas in Yugoslavia and Greece to objective areas in Albania on D-Day, then move reserves and additional supply shipments as required.

The weather conditions in Albania were such that the coup would have to be executed during the period of June 1 to September 30. Target D-Day was set for July 1, 1954. By simultaneous night attack beginning at 0100 (H hour) on D-Day, field forces would attack, seize, secure, and establish control of their assigned objective areas. Assault elements would overpower sentries, seize and replace officers, seize key supply dumps and installations, cut communications, and cause the defection or isolation of opposition armed forces and security personnel. They would secure all airfields, aircraft, key transportation centers, and headquarters of the Communist government. They would also seize and hold key government leaders opposed to the coup. Special units would be responsible for the security and protection of thousands of Soviet advisers and their families in the country at the time, in order to avoid giving the Soviet Union a pretext to intervene.

The NCFA leaders would set up a provisional government, present it to the world as the free independent government of Albania, and force leaders of Hoxha regime to publicly announce their resignations and to urge support of the provisional government. The US, UK, Yugoslavia, Greece, Italy, France, and Turkey would recognize the provisional Albanian government as soon as it was established. The allies would take whatever overt measures were necessary to preserve the complete independence of liberated Albania.

Anti-Communist sympathizers inside the country would take up arms and assist the task forces in carrying out the coup. The planners estimated that the number of armed elements from internal supporters who would join the fight was one thousand on D-Day, five thousand

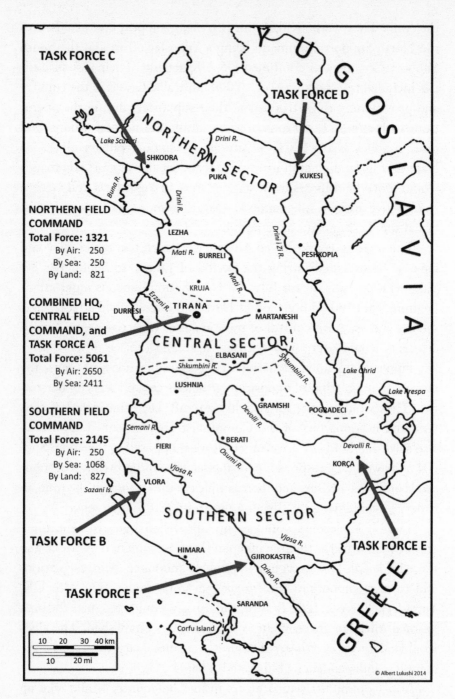

Operational map showing the movement of forces during the planned coup d'état in Albania

within the next three days, and ten thousand within thirty days. They also expected the majority of the eighty thousand armed forces that the Hoxha government had at its disposals to defect and join the coup or else throw down their weapons and return to their homes. The combined forces were expected to accomplish most of the objectives of the coup, overthrow the Hoxha regime, and establish a free and independent government in Albania within thirty days from D-Day.[7]

* * *

Weckerling submitted the plan with major caveats, or, as he called it, as a "static plan," because the fundamental assumptions upon which the plan was based did not exist and the required resources were not available. He wrote: "I gravely doubt the advisability of undertaking an Albanian coup in accordance with the attached plan in view of the extremely sensitive political factors involved and the bigger issues that might be touched off by an inopportune disclosure of the US preparations as compared to the relatively meager gains to the West."[8]

Yatsevitch added weight to this opinion as chief of CIA's Southeast European branch with direct responsibility over Albania. Yatsevitch wrote at the beginning of February 1953 that although detaching Albania from the Soviet orbit was in the realm of possibility, doing so under the circumstances at the time would be unwise. It would entail diplomatic exposure of US intentions and clandestine operations to an undesirable extent and would require a much closer collaboration with the Tito regime than was possible or even advisable at the time. If successful, it would impose an economic burden (albeit a relatively small one) on the US, disturb the delicate power balances in the Balkans, reopen the question of Greek territorial claims on Northern Epirus, and lead to additional frictions between Italy and Yugoslavia. It could invite unpredictable retaliatory aggression on Yugoslavia, Albania, and elsewhere (e.g., Berlin, Iran, Indochina) and even possibly risk starting World War III inadvertently, by placing the Soviets in a position they couldn't accept and forcing them to react. If unsuccessful, the failure would produce a major psychological victory for the Kremlin and severely strain the relationships of Western Allies.

On the other hand, Yatsevitch argued, it would be equally unwise for the United States to abandon or substantially reduce its ongoing program of covert and clandestine action toward Albania. Over the past four years, the US had built a respectable store of assets in the form of tested agents, political influences, followers both inside and outside the country, operational material, and know-how. While not sufficient to detach Albania from the Soviet orbit, these assets had value and would provide a useful contribution to a broadened effort at a proper time. At the least, Yatsevitch pointed out, they dampened the ambitions of other powers, Yugoslavia first among them, to attempt unilateral action. At the most, they frustrated the Kremlin's efforts to develop Albania into a useful political and strategic instrument.

The reasonable course of action, Yatsevitch said, was to continue ongoing efforts to maintain the spirit of resistance by carefully crafted propaganda, retain and strengthen the Albanian political assets, preserve the US bargaining power, achieve a broadening area of agreement with Yugoslavia, and "play for breaks," which for Yatsevitch meant taking more drastic action if circumstances allowed or the national policy required.

The only argument against this course was that it would be impossible to maintain internal resistance much longer. The resistance spirit would be broken unless decisive actions were taken with the clear goal of overthrowing the Communist government. A gradual erosion of Albanian morale would have far less serious consequences than a premature and unsuccessful coup, Yatsevitch wrote. However, available information indicated no approaching breaking point but rather hardened and more durable resistance against the government.[9] The information Yatsevitch referenced in his analysis came from intelligence reports being received from the Apple team, which, unbeknownst to Yatsevitch, were fed to them by the Sigurimi in their efforts to entice the CIA to send additional agents and resources to Albania.

* * *

The mood in Washington in the first half of 1953 called for more action rather than caution. The new Eisenhower administration, inaugurated at the beginning of the year, wanted to differentiate itself from the Truman administration, which the Republicans had branded during the presidential campaign as timid against the Soviets and focused on a policy of passive containment rather than aggressive rollback actions. In fulfilling this new direction, the administration expected the CIA to put into play the paramilitary capabilities of its recently created Directorate of Plans. With his characteristic enthusiasm, Frank Wisner, the newly named Deputy Director for Plans (DDP), steered the organization toward maximum development of covert action in preference to clandestine collection of intelligence.

On June 25, 1953, Wisner sent a memo to all area division chiefs requesting their input on aggressive actions that could be taken in their areas of responsibility. Responding to Wisner's memo became one of the first tasks for John "Jocko" Richardson in his new assignment as chief of the Southeast European branch at the Directorate of Plans, when he took over the responsibilities of Yatsevitch.

Richardson was born in Burma, where his father, a geologist, was prospecting for oil. He grew up in Whittier, California, a Quaker town surrounded by orange and lemon groves. Richard Nixon was one class ahead of him all through high school and college.[10] Richardson began his intelligence career during World War II in the US Army's Counter Intelligence Corps. He was instrumental in tracking down and capturing German spies in Italy during 1944–1945. After the war, he switched to the Central Intelligence Group, the precursor to the CIA, and worked on a number of assignments in Italy and Austria, where he earned praise for his integrity and professionalism. His assignment as chief of the Southeast European branch, in fact, had been a promotion for a successful operation he had run in Vienna turning and handling a Russian military intelligence officer.[11]

Richardson prepared his response to Wisner's request with the collaboration of one of his deputies, E. Howard Hunt, recently transferred to Washington after having served as Mexico City's OPC chief of station for the past two and a half years. Hunt later described his assignment to the Southeast European branch as follows: "True to what must be unpublished government specifications to hire the worst person for a job, I found out that my new position was as chief of covert operations for an area of the world that I knew absolutely nothing about—the Balkans."[12]

On June 30, 1953, Richardson wrote to Wisner that it was the "fondest dream" of his branch to overthrow the Hoxha regime in Albania by fall of 1954. The plan that Richardson presented was not as detailed or substantiated as the one that Weckerling and Yatsevitch had prepared earlier, which had been full of organizational diagrams, estimates of force strength, and activity descriptions for the strike force. Both plans had in common the need to broaden the NCFA and give it the traits of a provisional government in exile as a prerequisite to preparing the ground for the coup d'état.

The Weckerling plan had proposed a strike force of over 10,000 men from the outside complemented by another 10,000 insurgents within the country within the first thirty days. Richardson's plan required only 1,000 to 1,500 Albanians entering Albania overland from Greece and Yugoslavia and from the sea by amphibious landings at the time of the coup d'état. This much smaller force would be backed up by 4,000 men that the Yugoslavs claimed to have organized under the Prizreni League of Albanian Refugees, as well as units of the Yugoslav and Greek armies, standing by to intimidate the Communist government in Tirana and to assist if called upon. If Yugoslav and Greek forces were involved, they would retire beyond their Albanian frontiers immediately upon the successful conclusion of the revolution. The American Sixth Fleet would engage in maneuvers in the Adriatic and Ionian Seas during the revolution to cover the amphibious landings and to assist the revolutionaries in the name of the United Nations if called upon to do so. The fleet would remain in the area for some weeks to discourage any retaliatory action by the Soviet Union or any of its satellites.

Another difference between the Richardson plan and earlier plans is that for the first time it envisioned the direct involvement of Americans in the operations on the ground, brushing aside the "plausible deniability" constraints that had been in place up to that point. In one instance, American experts would be recruited and infiltrated as soon as weather permitted in order to direct resistance activities and establish a dependable trained nucleus around which the population would rally on signal. These experts would operate primarily in the north, where Richardson assumed a skeleton resistance organization already existed, based on reports he had been receiving from the Apple team. They would be supplied by airdrops with food, arms, and ammunition for the revolt. In the second instance, in the weeks leading up to the coup, the CIA would infiltrate into Albania a high-level American agent with authority to contact Enver Hoxha and Mehmet Shehu and offer up to $500,000 and future safety for their defection in place, which would include issuing orders to the army and the Sigurimi to lay down their arms at the appropriate moment.

What makes the Richardson plan striking, though, is the bold and brazen disregard for the legality of some of the other actions it recommended. It proposed that the CIA print sufficient counterfeited Albanian *lek* banknotes to finance the agent operations. Fiend staff officers, frustrated by their inability to procure genuine *leks* despite extensive efforts to do so, had been advocating this action for some time. As early as October 1951, Wisner had presented a request to the director of Central Intelligence, Walter B. Smith, to authorize the reproduction of at least one million Albanian leks, approximately $26,000 at the artificial exchange rate of that time, to sustain CIA agent teams in Albania during the six-month period beginning May 1, 1952.

Next, the agency would procure five submarines to effect a complete blockade of all shipping into and out of Albania. The submarines, Richardson wrote, would not be identifiable as American but would be pirate vessels operating under no flag out of Greece and Italy and would be manned by "volunteers" without papers. Both countries would be required to assist in enforcing the blockade by stopping all commerce between themselves and Albania. Right before the launch date of the coup, the CIA would kidnap the Albanian ministers in both Rome and Paris. Clandestine radio, leaflet drops, and the NCFA newspaper would announce that the ministers had defected.

Other psychological warfare activities would be stepped up and take an increasingly inflammatory line as the day of revolt approached. All émigré leaders would broadcast appeals urging their followers to join the resistance movement. By August 1954, the members of the military junta would be dropped into Albania to lead the insurrection. Simultaneous action by the resistance forces from within and the striking force from the outside would end in the successful overthrow of the Communist regime and the establishment of an acceptable interim government under UN auspices, to be replaced as soon as possible by a freely elected democratic government.[13]

It was a highly optimistic plan that surely provided what the CIA customers had asked, aggressive actions against the Communist opponents. At the same time, it was infused with a bravado that shaded into arrogance, especially when one takes into account that the plan contained no analysis of risks or even a minimal attempt to identify where things could go wrong, let alone to develop mitigation actions or contingencies to counter the enemy's moves. Unfortunately for the agency, it was not an aberration, but rather a byproduct of the atmosphere, attitude, and mindset that existed at the time, which gave birth to similar plans for action around the world, whose outcomes would shape the legacy of the CIA for years to come.

* * *

Dulles submitted the plan for the Albanian coup d'état to the Psychological Strategy Board on July 29, 1953,[14] where it was discussed at several meetings throughout the summer of 1953, "with continued enthusiasm for a program of action both broad enough and strong enough to accomplish the objective of detaching Albania from the Iron Curtain bloc if possible."[15] As these discussions were occurring, news began coming out of Iran about the coup d'état that had overthrown the Mossadegh government and brought to power Mohammad Reza Pahlavi, the new shah. Kim Roosevelt, one of the early planners of Project Fiend, had moved on to lead the OPC's Middle East division in 1950 and was the principal planner of the Iran operation, code name TPAJAX, which, like the Albanian project, was a joint venture between the CIA and SIS.

The coup was successful, thanks to a large extent to the energetic efforts of Roosevelt in Teheran, who during the critical phase of the operation cut off all communications with London and Washington and took complete operational control. At a meeting with SIS chief John A. Sinclair afterward, Roosevelt gave as his reason for acting this way that: "if they had simply reported what they were doing, London and Washington would have thought they were crazy and told them to stop immediately; if they had reported the reasons why they felt justified in taking such action, they would have had no time to take action; accordingly, they followed the third course which was to act, and report practically nothing."[16]

On August 26, Winston Churchill, bedridden and in bad shape physically, received Roosevelt at 10 Downing Street and heard a firsthand account of how the operation had been executed. Churchill expressed envy of Roosevelt's role and wished he had been a few years younger to serve under his command. "If the success of this operation could be maintained," Churchill said, "it would be the finest operation since the end of the war."[17]

That same day, on the other side of the Atlantic, the Psychological Strategy Board met in Washington and decided that the situation in Iran needed to settle and the victory there had to be consolidated before other actions were attempted that could aggravate the Soviet Union. Two weeks earlier, on August 12, the National Security Council had authorized covert action in Guatemala to overthrow President Jacobo Arbenz, leading to the expectation of further turmoil. As a result, the PSB decided that "the question of a covert operation in Albania be put on ice for the moment being." At the same time, it requested that preparations be made to put the US in a position to act quickly and decisively when such a covert operation might become feasible and desirable. At the end of August 1953, the PSB established a working group with representatives from the Department of Defense, CIA, and State Department to explore the problem thoroughly and to recommend actions that the appropriate departments and agencies could take to prepare for such an operation.[18]

Ray Thurston, deputy chief of the East European division at the State Department, chaired the working group, which over the next several months developed serious reservations about the feasibility of detaching Albania from the Soviet orbit in the immediately foreseeable future. Thurston himself had a very dim view of the subject. The chief aim of American policy in Southeastern Europe at the moment was to bring about some sort of working agreement between Yugoslavia and Italy on the matter of Trieste. He feared that exacerbation of the Albanian problem would increase tensions between those two countries, while at the same time reviving Greek irredentism with respect to Northern Epirus. He doubted that the balance of forces in the Balkans at that time was stable enough to permit success.[19]

CHAPTER 17

The American Backers Are Obliged to Withdraw

The US operations in Albania in 1953 were dominated by the loss of the Apple team, which was a huge blow to the CIA plans. Apple was comprised of the highest caliber agents ever fielded by the CIA. Matiani was probably the best of their Albanian field agents because of his fame, experience, and influence. Zenel Shehi, too, was considered an unusually intelligent and experienced leader.

Two more teams of five men each, code names Willow and Fig, had been able to complete one overland infiltration mission each. On a second mission, Fig was betrayed by a contact and forced to fight its way to Greece through two ambushes of Communist pursuers. A third team of two men had infiltrated and exfiltrated intact, but they had yielded so little intelligence that the mission didn't justify the cost and effort expanded in mounting it. During 1953, the operation suffered a 50 percent loss rate, including the agents killed, captured, and missing. The CIA had no agents operational inside Albania by the end of the year. Summarizing the situation at the end of 1953, the CIA's chief of the Southeast European branch, Jocko Richardson, wrote: "Although the casualties and disappointments of this operational season have been considerable, they are not out of line with the overall statistics of past OBOPUS [CIA's cryptonym for the Albanian operation since 1953] operations. We have attempted to counter the increasing effectiveness of Albanian security forces with the infiltration of higher caliber and more thoroughly trained agents. Although we will continue to attempt to improve our assets we must accept the fact that the price of a so-called simmering pot in Albania is high."[1]

The failure of 1953 activities triggered a critical review of past operations and the capabilities of the Albanian security forces, which served as a guide in planning future operations. Richardson reached the conclusion that:

> the main effort should no longer be directed at mounting of groups whose purpose is a) to enter an area and organize resistance nets, and b) to remain in the area as long as possible while maintaining W/T contact with the base and being resupplied from the air. The three and half operational seasons which have been devoted largely to this type of activity have produced few permanent assets and have brought heavy losses in men and equipment.[2]

The new guidance was to focus operational activities toward keeping groups as small as possible and reducing the time they spent in hostile territory to the minimum required to perform their new missions. The scope of the missions was redefined to include initially only contacting specific individuals who had prospects for developing positive intelligence or recruit officials in the political, security, and police apparatus. When contact had been established, attempts would be made to recruit these individuals as resident agents. Permanent communication links in the form of dead letter drops near the southern border would be established to enable these agents to send information out of the country. Such a scheme would allow CIA runners from Greece to be infiltrated for brief duration, no more than a day or two, in order to service the drops and maintain contacts with the resident agents.

The problem was that there were very few trained and experienced agents left. As a security precaution after the Sigurimi had folded the Apple operation, the CIA had discharged dozens of agents who had been named in the trials or were known by members of the Apple team. With the few remaining agents left in spring 1954, the CIA could cover only one out of ten areas of the country for which it had received intelligence requirements from its customers in the

State Department, NATO, and US Army European Command.[3] The pools of potential agents had dried out in Rome, Athens, and at the Labor Service Company in Germany. Trieste and Istanbul had a handful of Albanian refugees who were screened but did not yield any suitable candidates for agent material. That left Zog and his entourage, but given the wholesale neutralization of all his agents in the previous operations and his entanglements with the Egyptian government at the time, it was decided to leave him alone "until the dust had settled."[4]

For all these reasons, by the end of summer 1954, the CIA virtually abandoned all infiltration operations in Albania and dismissed the handful of Albanian agents still on its rolls in Greece. Those agents who wished to emigrate to other countries were given assistance and letters of recommendations. At the exit interview, an agent received six million Greek drachmas, approximately two hundred dollars, as severance pay after signing the following quitclaim form:

> I, [Name of Agent], do hereby release the United States of America, its agents and representatives from all manner of money, claims and demands which I now have or which my heirs, executors, and administrators could, would or might have against the United States of America, its agents or representatives for any reason whatsoever up to the date of this statement.
>
> I further agree never to tell anyone, orally or in writing, about the work I have done or the work it was planned that I do, nor will I tell anyone about the activities of the people for/and with whom I have worked.
>
> I fully understand that any violation of the foregoing agreement about the preservation of full secrecy will subject me to judgment and punishment according to applicable espionage law.[5]

* * *

The retreat was not just at the operational level but also on the policy and strategic levels. The Psychological Strategy Board formally rejected the plan to detach Albania from the Soviet orbit on August 25, 1954, almost a year after the CIA had submitted it for a decision. The reason for the rejection was that the ongoing negotiations over

Trieste were the primary concern of US foreign policy in the region at the time. Actions for the liberation of Albania could interfere with these negotiations and should be postponed until the Trieste problem was satisfactorily resolved. In the future the State Department would broker an agreement covering the future status of Albania among the neighboring states of Yugoslavia, Greece, and Italy before any action for liberation would be undertaken.[6] The policy guidance for the CIA was to keep the situation in Albania under continuing surveillance, "with a view to the possibility of detachment of that country from the Soviet bloc at such time as its detachment might be judged to serve the overall US interest."[7]

The defunding for the Albanian program between 1953 and 1955 tells the story of its rapid disintegration. In fiscal year (FY) 1953 (July 1, 1952–June 30, 1953) the funds approved included $402,000 for personnel requirements, $30,000 of which was for the upkeep of thirty Albanian agents and the balance for thirty-six CIA staff employees, agents, and contractors.[8] In FY 1954 funding for personnel requirements dropped to $258,000 causing a sharp reduction in staff resources to only twenty-two staff employees, agents, and contractors.[9] The CIA diverted its resources to projects that promised higher returns for their investment, in places like Iran and Guatemala.

FY 1955 operations involved only twelve CIA staff employees, agents, and contractors; spending for the administration of the program and for the psychological warfare components of the program was cut to half the size of the previous year's spending ($69,000 for administration, $40,000 for radio Voice of Free Albania operations, $61,000 for NCFA support, and $62,600 for propaganda drops).[12] Completely eliminated in the FY 1955 budget were $300,000 that were spent in FY 1954 for agent land and air infiltration operations based out of Greece.

* * *

The budget cuts reduced significantly the money available to support the National Committee for Free Albania, which, despite its political infighting and acrimonious relations with its US and British sponsors, had provided adequate cover for CIA's clandestine operations over the years. Reprioritizing the NCFA efforts to fit the new budget realities offered an opportunity to restructure the NCFA itself to reflect better the new CIA priorities. The restructuring effort resulted in the expansion of the NCFA to include right-of-center political groupings and individuals who until then had been unable to participate in the organization. As a byproduct of this expansion, left-of-center elements of the NCFA broke away.

At the time of its formation, the NCFA was regarded by the Albanian refugee circles as a representative, democratic body that would further the interests of all anti-Communist Albanians. By November 1950, Balli Kombëtar, one of the major political parties represented in the NCFA, had split apart, with the conservative elements led by Ali Klissura forming the Balli Kombëtar Organization (BKO), while Hasan Dosti's followers and left-leaning elements led by Abas Ermenji and Zef Pali regrouped under the name of Balli Kombëtar Agrarian (BKA). After the split, Ermenji and Pali expelled two supporters of Klissura from the NCFA Executive Committee and replaced them with their own followers, which increased their majority to a dominating role within the committee.

Ermenji, a member of the NCFA's military junta together with Kupi and Kryeziu, had strong opinions on how the agent selection, training, and infiltration operations should be run. He constantly clashed with Joseph Lieb, the CIA station officer in Rome and liaison with the NCFA, while trying to play up to his advantage the support he was receiving from the British. At the end of 1951, after the Americans decided to stop recruiting agents from NCFA supporters and to cut the military junta out of the field operations, Ermenji became more vocal in expressing his disagreements with the conduct of activities.[9]

He steadfastly refused to accept American proposals to expand the NCFA in 1952 with representatives from the Blloku Kombëtar Indipendent and the BKO and threatened to withdraw altogether from the committee, which the CIA feared would lead to the breakup of the entire NCFA. Klissura's BKO faction retaliated by, among other things, threating to appeal to Senator Joseph McCarthy's Senate Permanent Subcommittee on Investigations to look into the left-leaning elements of the NCFA, which would have had potentially serious consequences for all the CIA-controlled émigré operations at the time, not just the Albanian one.[12]

At the end of 1953 an exasperated Lieb summarized his two years' experience dealing with the NCFA in Rome as follows:

> At times the writer is stunned by the cross currents, or forces of discord, which pervade HTNEIGH [cryptonym for NCFA]. It seems that, no matter what the magnitude of any given problem (or activity), some pressure group, impelled by some unworthy purpose, invariably arises. Almost without exception, these groups are seeking (1) individual gain for themselves, or (2) to improve the political fortunes of their political party, or (3) to block what they believe to be a personal (or political) gain for certain of their associates.[13]

Reserving his toughest words for the members of the Balli Kombëtar Agrarian, Lieb added:

> More often, however, XNMALEDICT [cryptonym for BKA] represents the opposition to any solution which would benefit HTNEIGH as a whole. Theirs is a program designed to wear down the opposition while strengthening their own party position a bit at a time as a result of the failure manifested by their brothers-in-arms.
>
> Such a policy may well sweep all concerned down the drain, but such a possibility appears to be of little concern to the XNMALEDICTS. The XNMALEDICTS realize they have only one chance of attaining their goal—that they must ride into office under the auspices of an HTNEIGH so demoralized as a body that out of its embers only XNMALEDICT can arise quickly to seek control of the country.[14]

This ongoing bickering among the different factions and the self-interest displayed by the different members of the NCFA lowered its prestige and reduced its appeal to Albanians both abroad and within the country. In December 1953, Lieb pushed through the reorganization of the NCFA, which now included the overwhelming majority of the Albanian exile groupings: Dosti's faction of the BKA, Klissura's BKO, Kupi's Legaliteti, Vërlaci's Blloku Kombetar Indipendent, Kryeziu's followers, and other independents. The new NCFA elected Dosti president and Abas Kupi vice president of the Executive Committee.

Ermenji, Pali, and their followers of the left wing of the BKA refused to join the reorganized NCFA.

The restructured NCFA continued to support psychological and propaganda tasks for another couple of years, including the publication of the newspaper *Shqipëria* and its continued distribution among the exile community in Italy, Greece, Germany, and the United States. They also prepared propaganda leaflets and scripts for clandestine radio broadcasts. In September 1954, sixteen members of the NCFA led by Dosti were included in the executive board of the Assembly of Captive European Nations (ACEN)—a coalition of representatives from nine nations who found themselves under the yoke of Soviet domination after World War II. Funded by the Free Europe Committee (FEC), which itself was funded covertly by the CIA, the ACEN worked to become the authorized source of information about conditions behind the Iron Curtain, educate public opinion on the actual situation in their countries, and enlist the cooperation and assistance of governmental and nongovernmental institutions.[15] The ACEN and the FEC marked a shift in the CIA's strategy for propaganda against the Soviet Union and its satellites. Although supported by CIA funds, the activities of these organizations were not covert in nature. Instead, their work was public and in the open.

* * *

The incorporation of the Blloku Kombëtar Indipendent in the NCFA placed all the Albanian anti-Communist groups that the CIA wanted to control under one umbrella, thus simplifying the agency's efforts to influence them. The CIA-BKI relationship had begun in 1949 with Plan Charity, the joint operation between the Office of Special Operations and Italian Naval Intelligence that had parachuted into Albania several followers of Ismail Vërlaci and Gjon Markagjoni. After years spent in the mountains of northern Albania, nine surviving Charity agents had crossed the border to Yugoslavia in 1952, thus significantly reducing the operational and intelligence value of the BKI.

Nevertheless, the agency continued to support the BKI under a new plan, code name Obstacle, which replaced Charity between 1952 and 1954. A CIA review of its operations with the BKI since 1950 found that "the principal agents were consumed by Albanian émigré politics, were marked by intrigues implicating Americans, Britains [sic], and Italians, and schemes to enhance personal prestige. . . . OSO and OPC entanglements . . . in retrospect, acted more favorably to the Albanians than to either US organization."[16]

As a result of the analysis, the agency replaced Obstacle in August 1954 with a much smaller project, code name Obdurate, focused only on foreign intelligence and counterespionage targets. The new project kept on the payroll as principal agents Gjon Markagjoni, the tribal chieftain of the Catholic regions, and Ernest Koliqi, the scholar, poet, and spiritual guide of the BKI. Through them the CIA continued to maintain control on the BKI and to strengthen relations with the Italian intelligence services, which remained the strongest supporters of the BKI. An additional goal of the plan was to use the nine agents in Yugoslavia who corresponded regularly with their leaders in Rome as a source of information about Yugoslavia's intentions toward Albania.[17]

Obdurate paid Ernest Koliqi $400 per month for operating his net and for providing informational reports on Albanian émigré circles; another $40 per month was used for gifts and care packages sent to the former Charity agents in Yugoslavia. Gjon Markagjoni received $320 per month, mostly to maintain his good will and for any intelligence he might provide on Albania and Yugoslavia.[18]

The third principal agent under Obdurate was Iliaz Kraja, a BKI member who had been approached by Sigurimi officers attached to the Albanian legation in Rome looking for information on agent infiltrations into Albania and the Labor Services Company in Germany. CIA officers in Rome decided to use Kraja as a double agent in a counterespionage play aimed primarily at discovering the Sigurimi's personalities, functions, policies, and modus operandi in Italy. They placed a payment of $100 per month in an escrow account for Kraja for as long as he continued to meet with his Sigurimi handlers and report on their interactions.[19]

In August 1955, Obdurate was further reduced in scope to reflect the course of actions over the past fourteen months. Markagjoni's payments were cut in half to $160 per month because there had been no substantial direct contribution on his part to intelligence production. Careful review of Koliqi's reports at headquarters raised pointed questions about the quality and reliability of his information, such as:

"Does [he] represent a small, private 'papermill'? Is the information we gain from this source simply fabrication available to any purchaser?"[20] Koliqi himself told his control officer that his teaching at the University of Rome, his writing, and other duties, such as being secretary of the Association of Refugee Intellectuals in Italy, did not leave him as much time as before to support intelligence collection and reporting. The CIA changed Koliqi's status from principal agent to informant and reduced his compensation from $400 to $80 per month.[21]

Iliaz Kraja's double agent effort throughout 1954 had yielded 63 counterintelligence reports on Sigurimi activities in Rome. Skënder Konica, Aleko Shyti, and Jonuz Mersini, Sigurimi's legal residents in Italy working under the cover of the Albanian legation, had approached Vërlaci, leader of the BKI, and other Albanian refugees with offers to cooperate or to repatriate to Albania. Various techniques they used against targets included pressure on family members in Albania, appeal to their patriotism, instilling confidence in the Sigurimi's abilities as evidenced by its success against the Apple team, and meager payments offered to those in dire need. The contacts confirmed that the Sigurimi was consumed with the idea that agents were being recruited and trained at the Albanian company in Germany and continued to pump Kraja for information on agent operations in Albania. They also provided indications that the Sigurimi had a number of informants in the NCFA complex, possibly including Gaqo Gogo, Ibrahim Kodra, Kadri Myftiu, and Rrapo Bineri.[22] But at the beginning of 1955, the trail went cold. The CIA had decided to take more control of the exchange and attempt to defect Mersini. Mersini most certainly reported the approach to his bosses in Tirana, who decided to fold the entire operation. At the end of 1955, Mersini reappeared in New York, having been sent there by the Sigurimi as a legal resident, with cover as an adviser to the newly opened Albanian mission at the UN.

Around the same time, the last character of note appeared on the list of CIA-controlled Albanian assets. It was Xhafer Deva, a fervently anti-Slav Albanian leader from Kosovo, who embraced the dream of Ethnic Albania offered by the Italians and Germans during World War II and threw in his lot with them in open collaboration. Deva served as minister of interior for a short period during the German occupation, when he gained notoriety for allowing the February 4,

1944, massacre in Tirana of eighty-four civilians suspected of being Communist sympathizers. Deva fled with the German troops in 1944 and lived in Vienna, Turkey, and Egypt until 1948, when he moved to Italy. Deva was on intimate terms with Italian intelligence personnel and collaborated with them in recruiting Kosovars who were later parachuted into Albania under Project Lawbook, another US-Italian joint venture cosponsored by the CIA. Under the cryptonym DECADAL, Deva's CIA assignment in 1955 was to report on Albanian émigré matters as well as on his dealings with the Italian intelligence services. In the past, Deva had been reluctant to accept compensation for what he considered "advisory services" in order to avoid being under any obligation to his benefactors. His CIA contact convinced him to accept $80 per month to cover the rental of his apartment in Rome, which the control officer insisted was necessary for debriefings.[23]

* * *

By 1956 the National Committee for Free Albania had outlived its usefulness and no longer served the purposes for which the Americans had created it in 1949. The geopolitical situation had changed as well. Nikita Khrushchev, the new leader of the Soviet Union, was signaling a desire to improve relations with the West. At the twentieth Congress of the Communist Party of the Soviet Union, he delivered a secret speech, leaked almost immediately to Western media, denouncing the purges and atrocities of Stalin. The other theses advanced at the Congress—"peaceful coexistence" between Communist and capitalist countries—marked the beginning of a thaw in the Soviet relations with the United States.

On April 28, 1956, the CIA representative in Rome requested a meeting with all the members of the executive committee of the NCFA[24] where he read a statement that included the following:

> It is with deep regret that I must announce that the American backers are obliged to withdraw from active sponsorship of the NCFA, effective immediately. However, since the backers realize that they have a moral obligation to honor their financial commitment to the NCFA, contained in the current budget in the hands of the Committee, the

final checks to be mailed from New York upon return of Mr. Dosti will include payments due the Committee through the month of June 1956. With these payments, the funds committed to the current NCFA budget will be completely exhausted and financial support by the backers terminated.

Termination of active support and the existing relationship with the NCFA by the backers had been found necessary for budgetary reasons and because of the relative ineffectiveness for political purposes of the existing agreement.

I wish to reemphasize that the backers' termination of the existing relationship with the NCFA does not mean that the Americans are abandoning Albanians. It is only the backers who now are obliged to curtail their activities. The American government and private organizations . . . will continue to render moral and other support wherever possible to Albanians everywhere and in the fight against Communism. . . .

Finally, the backers have instructed me to speak with each member of the Executive Committee and staff present to extend, on behalf of the backers, their personal and warm appreciation for the cooperation rendered by one and all during the many years of collaboration. The backers, gentlemen, will never forget the sacrifices made by the leaders and loyal followers of the Committee for the welfare of the Albanian people and in the fight against Communism.[25]

A short informal discussion followed the reading of the statement, in which the CIA representative recognized the agency's obligation to the NCFA agents stranded in Yugoslavia when and if they came out. He asked Dosti to prepare as soon as possible the list of commitments beyond that fiscal year and problems, including emergency hardship cases. Then, he had brief private meetings with each of the members where he thanked them personally on behalf of the backers.

The reaction of the NCFA members was confined largely to expressing concerns about their personal status and pleas for aid in expediting resettlement. The members had expected that the Americans would make changes given the ineffectiveness of their work, but most were shocked at the drastic nature of the action. Some NCFA leaders expressed concern that the opposition would exploit the American withdrawal for their own propaganda benefits.[26]

* * *

One of the last agreements negotiated between the CIA and NCFA covered the compensation of five surviving agents from the very first infiltration team sent to Albania in November 1950, who were stranded in Yugoslavia. Halil Nerguti, who had been able to get out of Yugoslavia in 1955, had received a lump sum settlement of $1,750. The NCFA took the position that this sum was the minimum acceptable for the remainder of the agents (Adem Gjurra, Rexh Berisha, Myftar Maloku, Ramadan Cenaj, and Sali Dalliu).

However, the CIA case officer handling the negotiation argued that it was quite possible that the other agents might not receive as large a settlement as Nerguti, because it was not clear whether they were truly stranded or had defected to Yugoslavia. In the case of Rexh Berisha and Myftar Maloku, the CIA had received reports that Yugoslavia had bestowed all the privileges and rights of Yugoslav citizens on them and that they were residing with friends or relatives there.

As its starting point in the negotiations, the CIA offered a one-time payment of $500 to each of the five agents involved, but kept open the option to determine the sum of each settlement on the merit of each individual, provided that "a thorough debriefing is conducted for the purpose among other things to ascertain if (a) subjects performed their mission and remained loyal to HTNEIGH [NCFA]; and (b) there was any willingness on their part to remain in Yugoslavia as long as they have."[27]

The final agreement on the matter reached at the end of June 1956 was the last transaction between the NCFA and the CIA. The NCFA ceased to exist officially on June 28, 1956, when their New York office was closed permanently and all contacts with the CIA were terminated.[28]

There is evidence that the CIA honored its side of the agreement to get the money to its agents even when it took many years to find them. A ninety-one-year-old Rexh Berisha, perhaps the last surviving agent covered by the June 1956 agreement, surfaced in 2004 in Kosovo. In an interview he gave to Albanian newspapers, he told of a visit he had received from two Kosovar leaders, Hashim Thaçi and Agim Çeku, accompanied by seven Americans representing the CIA. Berisha said the Americans had given him a medal and $35,000—his back pay for the time he had spent in service of the CIA. It had been enough, Berisha said at the time, to help him rebuild the house that had been burned down by the Serb paramilitary forces as they swept through Kosovo in 1999.[29]

* * *

Once the CIA severed the link with the NCFA, it eliminated the remaining operational threads one by one. The NCFA newspaper *Shqipëria* ceased publication in 1956. The clandestine radio, Voice of Free Albania, went off the air in 1957. It was replaced for a short period of time by a much smaller broadcasting facility, Radio Socialist Albania, which directed its content against mid-level Communist officials. After 1954, infiltration activities had been reduced to only a couple of incursions a year, in which one or two agents ventured no more than a few miles into Albania and exfiltrated overnight. These missions were completely terminated effective January 31, 1958.[30]

The last remnant of the projects that had been started under Fiend, code name OBTUSE, continued into 1959 and consisted of mailing anti-Communist newspapers and revisionist letters to select Albanian government and Communist officials. Because there was no evidence that the mail was getting past the Albanian censorship, and in view of the low priority that Albania presented as a target, the Eastern European Division moved to terminate the project effective December 31, 1959. In the routing sheet that accompanied the request, the approving officer wrote: "Delighted to terminate."[31]

CHAPTER 18

Lessons and Legacy
of Project Fiend

Project Fiend was the first paramilitary operation planned and executed by the CIA in its early days. As such, it left an imprint on the planning and execution of other Cold War paramilitary actions that followed, including CIA's coups in Iran and Guatemala, and the Bay of Pigs invasion in Cuba. A number of procedures, methods, and techniques first introduced in this operation would become standard issue for covert operations by the agency in the ensuing years. CIA officers who participated in the operation took with them the experience and lessons learned, both good and bad, as they moved on to other projects.

For example, the radio communication issues experienced by the first teams infiltrated in 1949 to 1950 showed that radio-telephones operating on VHF frequencies, which relied on ground-to-ground or ground-to-air radio exchanges, were not suitable for the operational tempo of paramilitary forces. The agents were always on the move across rugged terrain and often hiding in caves and forests, with limited access to exposed areas for clear communication. Such requirements led to the development of the RS-1 radio sets, which were introduced in the field in 1950 with the first Albanian team using an RS-1 radio in May 1951. The RS-1 spy set became a staple of CIA operations throughout the 1950s and well into the 1960s. The Albanian infiltration teams were also among the first paramilitary CIA teams to test and use advanced spycraft techniques, such as invisible ink and the coding and decoding of messages using one-time pad keys.

The agency used the experience of the Apple team in 1952 to 1953 to draw a number of lessons that would enhance the chances of success for future operations and increase the survival rate of its agents. On November 17, 1952, Yatsevitch, while facing the dilemma of Premçi's broken arm, had suggested that a regular procedure be established to make periodic tape recordings of both the right- and left-hand sending patterns of all W/T operators. Such recordings could then be used to determine whether a set was being operated by the correct person, if doubts arose.[1]

On April 20, 1954, the CIA Office of Training requested the permission of the Southeast European Division to use the case of the Apple team as a training exercise in their counterespionage courses.[2] On May 18, 1954, a counterespionage review of the proceedings of the trial of Apple agents in Tirana recommended a study of the trial to determine the extent of psychological preconditioning of the defendants by hypnosis, brainwashing, drugs, or other means. The testimonies of Zenel Shehi and Hamit Matiani were especially interesting in this respect, because the men had obviously been rehearsed. Zenel Shehi at times was an exceptionally reluctant witness, responding initially with "I beg your pardon" to queries that may have been particularly repugnant, in order to gain time and allow himself to compose an answer.[3]

* * *

However, what makes Project Fiend impressive from today's perspective is not necessarily what the agency learned from it but what it failed to learn: the opportunities missed to pause, reflect on successes and failures both, and adjust the course of future plans and operations based on the experience gained.

As early as August 1949, only a few weeks after BGFIEND had been officially launched, a CIA officer concerned with the progress of events wrote: "I am very strongly of the opinion that the lessons which are daily being borne in upon us by the development of this Project are to a considerable extent being neglected in favor of rapidly growing vested interests, and that as a result we stand a very good chance of being faced with a failure the nature and causes of which will be confused in an exchange of recriminations."[4] It was a warning that was not heeded and a premonition that proved true in a number of cases.

First, the experience of the Apple team is perhaps the earliest example in the history of US intelligence of asymmetrical warfare as the means by which a small but very focused and determined adversary, like the Sigurimi at the time, can even the odds against a much larger enemy. It was a small, isolated episode for the CIA, certainly a blip on the radar compared with the hundreds of operations and thousands of agents it was running at the time around the world. But the failure to analyze properly and learn from that experience led the agency throughout the Cold War to emphasize spying against and defending from the Soviet Union alone as its primary task. In the late 1980s, as the Iron Curtain began to fall, secrets of intelligence activities from the Soviet satellites began coming to light, showing that the agency had ignored them at its own peril. The significant deception and playback operations that these smaller adversaries had executed successfully and over an extended period of time make the Albanian experience of the early 1950s look like child's play.

In 1987, Florentino Aspillaga Lombard was the chief of station for the Cuban Directorate of General Intelligence in Bratislava in what was then Communist Czechoslovakia. From the city on the banks of the Danube, he ran the network of agents spying on Austria and kept under surveillance over four thousands Cubans working in Czechoslovakia in lieu of payments for the economic aid it was giving Cuba at the time. On Saturday, June 7, Aspillaga put his girlfriend, one of the Cuban guest workers, in the trunk of his car, crossed the border into Austria and drove to the US embassy in Vienna fifty miles away, where he turned himself in to the CIA hands. Whisked away to a Virginia safehouse, Aspillaga revealed everything he knew about the Cuban intelligence operations against the United States. His most shocking revelation was that all the Cuban agents that the agency was handling at the time, about fifty of them, had been double agents run by Cuban intelligence in what is probably the longest-running deception operation known in the history of modern spycraft. Overnight, the US intelligence capabilities in Cuba had become nil and everything had to be rebuilt from scratch.[5]

Equally damaging and embarrassing, albeit on a smaller scale, were the revelations of deception operations run by the East German Ministry of State Security, Ministerium für Staatssicherheit in German, or Stasi, as it became commonly known after the fall of the Berlin Wall. Markus Wolf, the head of Stasi's foreign intelligence department and the mastermind of most of these operations, wrote contentedly in his memoir: "By the late 1980s, we were in the enviable position of knowing that not a single CIA agent had worked in East Germany without having been turned into a double agent or working for us from the start." There had been only a handful of them, six or seven in total, but they had all been Stasi plants who had delivered handpicked information and disinformation to their CIA case officers over the years.[6]

* * *

In 1975, the Congressional investigations looking into government abuses after the Watergate scandal revealed that the agency had on several occasions considered assassinations of foreign leaders as part of its covert operations. The Senate Select Committee to Study Governmental Operations with Respect to Intelligence Activities, known as the Church Committee after its chairman Frank Church, discovered that in the early days of the CIA, a "special operations" unit known as Program Branch 7 (PB/7) was assigned the responsibility "for assassinations, kidnapping, and such other functions as from time to time may be given it . . . by higher authority."[7]

E. Howard Hunt testified to the committee that in 1954, when he was chief of political and psychological warfare for Southeast Europe, he had suspected the presence of a double agent, a penetration by the Sigurimi, into the ranks of the Albanian Labor Services Company in Germany. Hunt recalled approaching the head of PB/7, Colonel Boris Pash, in "a search mission to determine whether the alleged capability of Colonel Pash in 'wet affairs,' . . . that is, liquidations, would have any relevance to our particular problem of the Albanian disappointments."[8]

Hunt's inquiry was on a hypothetical basis, and he "didn't get any satisfaction from Pash," who was startled at the subject and told Hunt that such a move would have to be approved by a higher authority.[9] Hunt understood the higher authority to be Wisner and did not pursue the matter further, since his suspicions had not yet focused on a particular agent and he didn't have the name of the suspected individual. Other people within PB/7 at the time testified that "higher authority" included "State Department, Defense Department, National Security Council, the President of the United States."[10] All the witnesses who appeared before the Church Committee on this matter, including Hunt himself, testified that no actual assassination operation or planning was ever undertaken by PB/7 or its successor organization when all program branches were merged in the Directorate of Plans in late 1952.

Reminiscing in 1985 on his activities in the early days of Project Fiend, James McCargar said that he was astounded to hear that the CIA had gotten involved in assassinations. The question of assassinations had come up once in the early days of the Office of Policy Coordination, but the decision had been not to get into that because the Albanians "were so much better at it than we were." McCargar said that Albanian agents were not authorized to carry out any assassinations inside Albania.[11]

The opposition certainly did not have any qualms about engaging in such actions. The Russians had a unit at the time, known as Spets Byuro #1 (Special Office #1), assigned to carry out such tasks as sabotage, political murders, and kidnappings. A KGB[12] assassin, Bogdan Stashinsky, who defected to the West in 1961, described two hits during the previous few years, against Lev Rebet, a Ukrainian émigré writer, and Stepan Bandera, a leader of the Ukrainian Nationalist movement. In both cases, he had used a gun that fired vaporized poison, which killed almost instantly upon being inhaled. The properties of the killing agent were such that, until the defection of the assassin, both victims were officially believed to have died from heart attacks.[13] It is conceivable that Soviet intelligence may have used a similar technique in October 1949 to eliminate Mithat Frashëri, the first president of the NCFA, who was found dead in his hotel room New York of an apparent heart attack.

While the Albanian Sigurimi may not have had the means to act in the United States at the time, they certainly were active in planning and carrying out assassinations and kidnappings in European countries, particularly in Italy and France. A memo to Wisner on December 2, 1949, reported that the Albanian intelligence service had assigned an agent in Italy the task of assassinating Hasan Dosti and Abas Kupi. This agent had also received the mission to assassinate Ismail Vërlaci, leader of the BKI. An attempt had already been made on Vërlaci's life on November 25, 1949, when he was shot at in front of his house from a passing car but managed to escape the bullets by throwing himself to the ground.[14] Two years later, another report described a four-man assassination team that was in Rome to kill important Albanians on the NCFA. In both cases, measures were taken to foil the plots, including "authorizing the Italian Service to handle these Hoxha hirelings."[15]

In 1953, Joseph Lieb's sister received a postcard from Rome saying that her brother had been in the hospital recovering from an appendectomy. The story did not jibe for her because Lieb's appendix had been removed years before. She traveled to Rome to find her brother recovering from a gunshot wound he had received during an assassination attempt, which he had survived thanks to the quick reaction of his Italian bodyguard.[16]

Despite the astonishment that McCargar expressed in 1985, there is evidence that the CIA considered, planned, and even carried out "special operations," including assassinations, with a varied degree of finality during the height of its activities against the Albanian Communist regime. The first example is the assassination in August 1949 of Bardhok Biba, party secretary and deputy for Mirdita, by agents sent to Albania under Plan Fontana, run jointly by the Office of Special Operations and Italian Naval Intelligence. It is possible that the agents acted on their own initiative, although for such a high visibility action they would have consulted their case officers in Italy.

Hamit Matiani and his team carried out a similar action in September 1952 when they killed the party secretary for Gramshi and another senior government official. The CIA station in Athens reported to headquarters that the Communist officials were killed during a firefight with their agents.[17] The Albanian government version of the story was that Matiani and his followers executed the two officials in cold blood. At his trial in April 1954, Matiani recounted the events to support this claim, which, of course, could have been because he was under duress or had been brainwashed, as was suspected later.

Another thread of evidence can be found in Michal Burke's diary entries between December 1950 and January 1951, which contain cryptic notes about special operations targeting Hysni Kapo and Haxhi Lleshi, high-ranking Communist and government leaders at the time. Finally, after a field visit to Athens in June 1951, a Fiend staff officer reported among other things: "Tewfik Kuka will be glad to assassinate anyone if asked to do so, but at the moment the Greeks are using him and don't want to let us have him for the next couple of months. He is in Albania now and considers himself too old to be brought out, so he will be glad to perform any little assignments that may be thrown his way. . . ."[18]

All of the examples above are certainly not conclusive and are open to interpretation. But the following case shows unequivocally that assassinations were part of the operations in Project Fiend, and the threshold of approval apparently was even lower than Wisner's level.

On January 3, 1952, the Albanian Telegraphic Agency broadcast the story of Hamdi Bodgani, a peasant from the Pogradeci district who persuaded three "diversionary agents who had been sent from Italy to Albania" for espionage purposes to come to his house. While the agents slept, he withdrew his family and cattle and summoned the Security Police who burned the house with the agents inside. "Today, a new house is being built for this patriot," the broadcast concluded.

Officers in the Southeast European branch decided to mount an operation to eliminate Bodgani. They selected an initial team in Greece to carry out the action, but the agents lost enthusiasm for the job. In July 1952, the Athens station sent to headquarters an operational plan and clearance request for a new team of "two enthusiastic volunteers" to serve as the "Coup-de-Main liquidation team." The team, code name Lightning, was composed of Vangjel Vangjellari, the proposed assassin, and Pavlo Kostandinos, who would serve as his guide and offer any assistance necessary. The team would be infiltrated from Greece and, after traveling to the operational area, observe Bogdani's daily habits "with a view towards terminating his career." The cable from Athens continued:

It is proposed that they attempt to ambush him killing him out-right rather than to do away with him by employing poison or other less violent means. It is felt that the publicity and propaganda thus gained will be of far greater value. If the mission is successfully completed, its propaganda value will be exploited by HTGRUBBY [cryptonym for the clandestine radio Voice of Free Albania], QKPALING [cryptonym for the NCFA newspaper *Shqipëria*], as well as by leaflets.[19]

It isn't clear whether or not the Lightning team was activated. In a memo to Yatsevitch in December 1952, the Athens staff indicated that a third team, code name Obsession, had been assembled to go after Bodgani but their mission was cancelled when they received reli-able reports that the subject had been eliminated, which Athens was endeavoring to verify.[20]

* * *

E. Howard Hunt's 1953 assignment in the Southeast European branch was short-lived. In 1954, he was summoned to Washington by C. Tracy Barnes, a former law firm colleague of Wisner who had joined the CIA in 1951, and by the end of 1953 was serving as a special assis-tant for paramilitary and psychological operations to DCI Dulles. Hunt was read into "the most important clandestine project in the world"[21] at the time—the overthrow of Guatemala's Communist-leaning regime of President Jacobo Arbenz Guzman. He took over the propaganda and political action side of the project, code name PBSUCCESS.

Hunt was a perfect fit for this operation. During his earlier assign-ment as station chief in Mexico City, he had followed developments in Guatemala closely. He had run agents across the Mexican border into Guatemala to assess the situation and collect intelligence inde-pendently from the CIA station in that country. Based on the informa-tion gathered, he had forwarded to headquarters a number of reports with urgent calls for action. In an effort to further collect evidence of Arbenz's slow drifting to the left, Hunt organized a clandestine break-in at the Guatemalan embassy in Mexico City, during which a team of agents copied all the Guatemalan documents and code books they could find in the ambassador's safe.[22]

In many aspects, project PBSUCCESS was a miniature replica of the activities that had been conducted in Project Fiend since 1949 and of the proposed Albanian coup d'état that had been presented to the Psychological Strategy Board in the summer of 1953. The CIA screened Guatemalan anti-Communist leaders in exile and decided to back Colonel Castillo Armas and his group of supporters as the nucleus of the movement against the Arbenz government, which would be known as El Ejército de Liberación, or the Army of Liberation. The agency trained approximately eighty-five Castillo supporters in sabotage and paramilitary activities in Honduras and Nicaragua. They would serve as team leaders for a cadre of 260 shock troops located in Honduras and El Salvador. Another thirteen radio operators were trained in radio communications and cryptography in Nicaragua between March and June 1954. Approximately eighty-nine tons of equipment were positioned in forward operating bases by black flights along Guatemala's borders in Honduras and Nicaragua.[23]

Even more striking are the similarities between the Guatemala and Albanian operations in the area of propaganda and psychological warfare. A political pamphlet, *El Combate* (*The Fight*), was published under the direction of CIA officers and distributed weekly. Unmarked aircraft flew over Guatemala City regularly dropping leaflets with calls to the army to turn against Arbenz and support Castillo Armas. The CIA established a clandestine radio broadcasting station, called La Voz de la Liberación (the Voice of Liberation), in Nicaragua and broadcast daily programs dramatizing examples of Communist tyranny and promoting the Liberation movement's ideologies and aims.[24]

One of the propaganda ploys was to fabricate reports of Soviet arms shipments to Guatemala. The CIA planned to hide Soviet arms in the jungle that, when "discovered," would substantiate these reports. In the end, there was no need to take this action because Arbenz decided on his own to purchase five million dollars' worth of arms from Czechoslovakia.[25] A ship carrying two thousand tons of Czech weapons and ammunitions arrived at the Guatemalan Atlantic port of Puerto Barrios on May 20, 1954. It provided substantiation for the CIA propaganda claim that Guatemala under Arbenz had become a Soviet satellite.[26]

On the same day, the US Navy established air-sea patrols in the Gulf of Honduras with the declared purpose of protecting Honduras from invasion and controlling arms shipments to Guatemala. A formal Navy operation, code-named HARDROCK BAKER, began on May 24 to establish a sea blockade of Guatemala. Submarines and warships patrolled the coast and stopped all ships headed to Guatemala, including British and French ones, in search of arms. The blatant illegality of the blockade made it a powerful weapon of intimidation against the Arbenz government.[27] On June 3, the United States airlifted arms to Honduras. Four days later, a contingency evacuation force was ordered to the area. It included an anti-submarine warfare vessel and five amphibious ships with a US Marine battalion landing team aboard.[28]

The moves were aimed at ratcheting up the psychological pressure on key Guatemalan army officers and causing them to defect to Castillo's side. However, before abandoning Arbenz, they demanded either official assurance of US government support or an overt military incident that would demonstrate Castillo's strength. The first option was a nonstarter. Operating under the principle of plausible deniability, the CIA had tried to hide the involvement of the US government from the beginning of the operation. CIA case officers always dealt with Castillo's group as representatives of a group of rich American investors in the United Fruit Company interested in eliminating Communism from South America.[29] A similar cover had been provided by the National Committee for Free Europe and the National Committee for Free Albania, the political front of the Albanian operation.

The overt military action that the Guatemalan army officers had demanded came on the night of June 18, 1954. Four hundred and eighty men trained by the agency and organized in five task forces crossed into Guatemala from Honduras and El Salvador. From the beginning, they ran into more resistance and difficulties than they had planned. The largest task force attacking Porto Barrios suffered a disastrous defeat on June 21. Agency files indicate that at least twenty-seven agents were killed there.[30] The turning point for Castillo's forces came as a result of the intense psychological warfare waged by the clandestine broadcasts and leaflets dropped over population centers, which announced that columns of rebel troops were advancing toward the capital. This news was accentuated by loud and visible air raids on major population centers conducted by agency-trained mercenaries using airplanes procured with CIA funds. They included the June 25 bombing of the Matamoros Fortress in downtown Guatemala City and the sinking of the British freighter, the *Springfjord*, at port in San Jose, for which the agency had to pay one million dollars in restitution later.[31]

On June 27, 1954, under pressure and believing that a US invasion of Guatemala was imminent, Arbenz resigned. A three-member military junta seized power temporarily, eventually relinquishing it to Castillo Armas, who was inaugurated as the new president on September 1, 1954. The total cost of the operation for the CIA had been only three million dollars.[32] The number of operational casualties reported to President Eisenhower in an after-action briefing was an incredible "only one," although dozens of Castillo's supporters had died during the coup.[33]

Thus, PBSUCCESS entered agency lore as a successful operation. Coming on the heels of operation TPAJAX in Iran, it reinforced the premise put forward initially by Project Fiend that regime change could be brought about rapidly and inexpensively through covert operations, combining paramilitary action with robust psychological and propaganda warfare activities.

* * *

The Albanian formula was dusted off again when the agency began planning the next big covert operation—the overthrow of the Castro regime in Cuba. The task of formulating the overall plan of action fell to Group 5412, named after the 1954 National Security Council Directive 5412, which reaffirmed the CIA's responsibility for covert actions abroad. It was composed of a team of senior representatives from the Department of State, Department of Defense, the Joint Chiefs of Staff, the White House, and the CIA, charged to oversee the CIA's high-risk covert operations during the 1950s and in the early 1960s.[34]

Allen Dulles presented the plan to Eisenhower at the White House on March 17, 1960. Its first step was to form a moderate group of

Cubans in exile to serve as the opposition to Castro. Then propaganda would be conducted on behalf of the group, including clandestine and semi-clandestine broadcasts into Cuba from radio stations established on Caribbean islands south of Cuba. Concurrently, a resistance and intelligence-gathering network of disaffected elements would be established in Cuba. Preparations for a paramilitary force would begin outside of Cuba, the first stage being to assemble a cadre of leaders for training. After cautioning against leakages and breaches of security, Eisenhower directed Dulles to go ahead with the plan and the operations.[35]

Richard Bissell, who had replaced Wisner in 1958 as head of the Directorate of Plans, oversaw the detailed planning and execution of the plan, code name JMARC. Bissell was one of the brightest minds in the government establishment at the time. A former economics professor at the Massachusetts Institute of Technology, he earned recognition during World War II for devising a system using index cards to forecast the status of merchant ships hauling troops and supplies "three months in advance with a five percent margin error."[36] He played a key role in the implementation of the Marshall Plan in Europe and then, beginning in late 1954, managed the project that built the U-2 spy plane with astonishing speed (eighteen months from concept to fully operational planes) and for a total cost of nineteen million dollars, three million dollars under budget.[37]

In the summer of 1953, Wisner had invited Richard Bissell as a consultant to review and provide advice on CIA plans being prepared and executed at the time. During his 1953 review, Bissell came across the plans for a coup d'état in Albania. His active mind was engaged by the complexity of planning such an operation.[38] There was something about the scheme to invade Albania that captured his imagination; he was still turning it over his mind when he organized the Cuban operation in 1960.[39]

The Cuban plan went through a myriad of changes and mid-course corrections by the time it ended in the Bay of Pigs disaster on April 17, 1961. Yet, throughout the changes, the basic recipe of the CIA's covert and paramilitary action—formulated in the early days of the OPC with the Albanian plan—remained the same. While the agency thought that operations in Iran and Guatemala had validated that recipe, its fundamental flaws were revealed by the Cuban operation. When the strategy was played out to its full extent, it produced a spectacular failure that caused the United States and its young president enormous embarrassment and cost Bissell his job.

* * *

So, then, what is the legacy of the Project Fiend? What lessons can be drawn today from that experience?

From a narrowly focused perspective, the immediate and visible end of the story was certainly not a happy one. The CIA and MI-6 did not accomplish the goals they had set for the operation. The Sigurimi and the KGB turned the tables on them and used the killed and captured agents for propaganda purposes for years to come. The Albanians who participated in the operations suffered terrible losses. Dozens perished, and several more who were captured spent the rest of their lives in Communist prisons or hard labor camps. The regime uprooted their families and persecuted them for decades, generation after generation. Families of Albanian exiles, especially of the leaders of the National Committee for Free Albania, suffered similar treatment and were often used as hostages to entice them to return to Albania or to stop activities against the Communist regime.

As an example, in November 1952, Skënder Konitza, first secretary of the Albanian Legation and Sigurimi's legal resident in Rome, approached Hasan Dosti with an offer coming directly from Enver Hoxha. In return for Dosti's defection, members of his family then enduring persecution would receive preferential treatment. Dosti might even be made president of the Albanian courts if he were to return to Albania. Dosti had the fortitude of mind to reject the offer and suggested to Konitza that the Hoxha regime would do better to follow Tito's example and break with Moscow.[40]

Not long after, his entire family was sent to a newly drained swamp in central Albania, near Gradishta, where they joined Abas Kupi's wife and six children. Together with other persecuted families, they founded a village inhabited by internal exiles and opponents of the regime for the next thirty-seven years. One of Dosti's sons married Kupi's daughter[41] there, thus creating a stronger bond between the two families suffering under the Communists than their fathers had been able to create as leaders of the NCFA in exile.

It is easy then to understand the sense of bitterness against their sponsors that a few of the Albanian participants in the US-British operation expressed in interviews they gave in the mid-1980s to Nicholas Bethell for his book *Betrayed*, the earliest account of their activities. Abas Ermenji, a member of the NCFA's military junta, told Bethell in 1983: "We were deceived by the British and Americans. They promised to provide us with the means to liberate our country. In actual fact, they only trained a handful of people. . . . [T]he British and Americans were treating Albania like a guinea-pig. If it had succeeded, they would have tried another country and another people."[42]

Bethell carried the banner of reproach to the British and Americans for using the Albanians for their own purposes. At least as far as the American side of the operations goes, three reproachable moments are: (1) not sharing with the NCFA the decision to remove the elimination of the Hoxha regime from the scope of the operations; (2) prolonging the reconnaissance stage of operations despite the mounting casualties; and (3) incompetence of some of the case officers who ran the operations.

However, going a little deeper in the analysis, it is easy to see that the presence of the United States in the region and its active involvement in the Balkans at the time contributed to maintain the stability in the region. Its forceful diplomacy in support of Albania's territorial integrity and continued independence, especially with the British, Greek, and Yugoslav governments, most likely assured the continued existence of the Albanian state after World War II, just as it had guaranteed it after World War I.

One final perspective to consider is the relative inexperience of the Albanian political leaders who were involved in the operation. Of them, McCargar said:

> There is no way by which the Albanians, under their own steam, could have ever mounted any kind of an operation which would have had any hope of liberating their own country. They had to address themselves to some larger power which would provide the necessary assistance. There's an advantage to being a supplicant if you know

how to play that role. The Albanians representing the political groups were not naïve and, in fact, some of them were very good operators. They knew how to intimate a little blackmail here and there. They just were not as good at the supplicant role as some. They didn't have the experience.[43]

McCargar's statement is not necessarily an indictment of the individual NCFA leaders per se. It is rather an indication that the level of political maturity that the Albanians as a nation enjoyed in the middle of the twentieth century, embodied in their political leaders in exile, was not high enough to convince a major power like the United States to support them all the way. Moving the dial of history forward by sixty years reveals that Albanian politicians at the beginning of the twenty-first century have learned how to be much better "supplicants." They aligned themselves firmly with the United States in the 1990s when the Balkans came again at the forefront of the US national and security interests. Through key events, such as the transition to democracy in Albania, the conflict in Bosnia in 1995, and the war in Kosovo in 1999, politicians from Albania and Kosovo were able to keep their ever-present internal differences in check and articulate with a united voice their national interests before the international community. Since the attacks of September 11, 2001, against the United States, the predominantly Muslim Albanians have given unwavering support to the US in the war on terror and shown in practice the benefits that religious tolerance can bring to a nation like theirs. Because of the increased maturity of their political class, and with the strong support of the United States, the Albanians have been able to attain two significant accomplishments for their nation: Albania's admittance to NATO and the recognition of Kosovo as an independent state.

* * *

Looking at the experience from a broader geopolitical perspective, it is hard to miss the implications of Project Fiend and its outcome. Although its initial goal was to overthrow the Hoxha government, the Albanian operation never developed beyond the reconnaissance and intelligence-gathering stage. It was from the outset and remained throughout its existence a probe to see if covert operations could break a Soviet satellite away from Moscow's orbit. The results of the experiment showed that it was extremely hard, if not impossible, to achieve this goal. The Communists had established a firm chokehold on their countries that could not be broken with the type and magnitude of covert actions that the US and Great Britain were prepared to engage in, without risking an all-out war with the Soviet Union. Rolling back the Iron Curtain was too hard. Rather than spending resources in countries already under Communist rule, the agency had better chances of success trying to stop Communism from spreading in countries still outside the Soviet umbrella, primarily Italy and France in Europe and especially countries in Latin America and Indochina.

Disengagement from Europe was hard and painful to accept, especially when Soviet tanks crushed spontaneous challenges to Communist rule, first in Berlin in 1953, then in Hungary in 1956, and later in Czechoslovakia in 1968. For the people trapped on the other side of the Iron Curtain, it often felt like they were abandoned, forgotten, and lost without a hope. Yet, considering the events from today's viewpoint, it is not hard to see how that disengagement led to an unprecedented period of peace in the continent. When the conditions were right, Europe experienced the most significant reversal of fortunes in recent history, with a relatively peaceful and jubilant replacement of diametrically opposed economic, political, and ideological systems throughout the continent. Communism came to Europe with a roar in 1917, but left with a whisper in the late 1980s to early 1990s.

Thus, while the botched CIA activities to roll back the Iron Curtain in Europe may have seemed a failure at the time and for decades afterward, in the end they contributed to the peaceful establishment of pro-Western democracies in most of the continent. Operations like those in Guatemala and Iran, held as spectacular successes initially, turned out to be preludes to disasters. Guatemala sank into a civil war that lasted for decades and cost the lives of hundreds of thousands. The shah of Iran was run out of power in 1979, and the fervently anti-American theocracy that has ruled the country ever since remains today one of the major challenges confronting the United States foreign policy.

With the benefit of hindsight then, one can make a reasonable argument that the world today is a better place because of efforts spent on Project Fiend and lessons learned from its failures, despite the terrible price in lost lives, pain, and suffering that a lot of participants had to pay.

Epilogue

F rank G. Wisner, the catalyst and inspiration of the early days of Office of Policy Coordination, continued through the mid-1950s to pour his heart and mind into directing actions against the Soviet Union and the Communist threat around the world. During one of his frequent tours of stations overseas, he was in Europe when the Hungarian Revolution exploded in 1956. The CIA had not instigated the spontaneous uprising, but Wisner strongly felt they ought to support it. When the White House decided not to intervene, Wisner obsessed about and suffered at a personal level the brutal Russian crackdown of the revolution in November 1956. Shortly after, he experienced a nervous breakdown. Upon his return to the United States, he took a leave of absence from the agency to treat his depression. He returned to service in 1959, no longer as deputy director of plans but as chief of station in London. He retired from the CIA in 1962 and moved to his farm on Maryland's Eastern Shore, where he spent many hours working in his garden and hunting. He also did some consulting and engaged in a number of business ventures, some of which were focused in Laurel, Mississippi, the town where he was born and where a number of his relatives still lived. These activities were interrupted more and more frequently by bouts of depression, during which he felt deeply despondent. On October 29, 1965, Wisner lost his battle against depression and committed suicide. He was fifty-five years old when he died.

His son, Frank G. Wisner, Jr., joined the Foreign Service in 1961 and became one of the nation's preeminent diplomats, serving as the United States ambassador to several countries. In 2005, Secretary of State Condoleezza Rice appointed Ambassador Wisner as the special representative of the United States to the Kosovo Status Talks, where he played a crucial role in negotiating Kosovo's independence from Serbia.

James McCargar transitioned from clandestine work back into the diplomatic service in 1950 and then resigned from the Foreign Service in 1953. In 1955 he joined the Free Europe Committee in Paris as director of European political, social, and cultural programs.[1] In this capacity, his path crossed again with that of Abas Kupi and other former NCFA members when they attempted to create an Albanian Committee within the FEC.[2] In later years, he worked for the National Endowment for the Humanities and the US National Commission on UNESCO. McCargar wrote and published articles, books, and works of fiction under his name and as Christopher Felix. He briefly described his experiences in the early days of the OPC and on Project Fiend in *A Short Course in the Secret War*, first published in 1963. In 1985, when asked if he regretted anything about his role in the Albanian operation, he said: "Obviously if I were doing it over again today, I'd do it differently. I'd do it much more hesitantly, much more cautiously, but that comes with age. I don't regret the operation itself. I certainly regret the outcome for an awful lot of people. Some of those stories are pretty shattering. But the operation was a valid attempt. I think it could have been done much more prudently than it was."[3] James McCargar died in 2007 at the age of eighty-seven.

Robert Low went back to the State Department after leaving the CIA, where he handled Congressional relations. After moving to New York City in 1954, he entered local politics, serving two terms on the City Council during 1961 to 1969. He moved to San Francisco in 1996.[4]

Michael Burke gave up clandestine work in 1954, after five years with the CIA. At a ceremony in Washington, Allen Dulles awarded him the Distinguished Intelligence Medal with the following citation:

For the performance of outstanding services in planning and direct- ing operations of the Central Intelligence Agency while serving as a senior officer in a foreign country. Through his unusual vision and foresight, his broad area and technical knowledge, skill in maintaining delicate liaison relationships, and outstanding qualities of leadership, he inspired a high level of performance on the part of his subordinates and contributed greatly to the successful conduct of operations in the foreign area.[5]

In the private sector, Burke took executive positions with the Ringling Brothers and Barnum and Bailey Circus, CBS, the New York Yankees, and Madison Square Garden. He retired to Ireland in 1981. In 1984 he published his memoir, *Outrageous Good Fortune*, in which he provided a discreet and heavily sanitized version of his experience in Project Fiend. Burke was seventy years old when he died in 1987.

Gratian Yatsevitch followed in the footsteps of Kim Roosevelt, with whom he became acquainted in the early days of the Albanian operation. Yatsevitch was assigned to Teheran as the CIA station chief in Iran in the late 1950s. After retiring from government service in 1969, he went on to private business before retiring to Maine. His harrowing childhood experiences of the havoc brought upon Russia and the imperial family by the Bolshevik Revolution remained with him over the years. He remained decidedly opposed to everything Communist and sympathized over the years with the royal families he became acquainted with during his career in the military and the CIA. Yatsevitch maintained contact with the families of the king of Bulgaria, the shah of Iran, and King Zog, not as a CIA officer but as an individual and on a personal level. He corresponded with Queen Geraldine up to the end of his life in 1997 at the age of eighty-six.[6]

Joseph C. Lieb's last act as the CIA liaison with the National Committee for Free Albania was in early May 1954, when he and Archibald Lyall, his British counterpart, read a joint announcement to the NCFA leaders in Rome informing them that they were leaving by the end of the month and would not be replaced. "It is the wish of our superiors that the Committee should henceforth conduct its own affairs, so far as possible, and it is their firm conviction that it is now capable of doing so," they said.[7] Lieb returned to Washington and in July 1954 the agency offered to hire him as an employee for a delicate assignment where he would apply his public relations skills toward helping the shah of Iran consolidate his power. Lieb would join the shah's cabinet as a minister, but there was a twist: he would have to serve openly and, therefore, had to renounce his US citizenship. Lieb didn't find the idea wise and declined the offer. He returned to New York, where he resumed his advertising career, which later would lead him to become the worldwide advertising director for Pepsi. He moved his family to Northern California in the 1970s, where he semi-retired. Lieb passed away in March 1986 at the age of seventy-four.[8]

Alfred C. Ulmer returned to Washington in 1955 where he worked in the Far East division of the CIA before going back to Europe to head the CIA Paris station, always under diplomatic cover as first secretary of the embassy and special assistant to the ambassador. He retired from the CIA in 1962 and worked for several years for the Greek shipping tycoon Stavros Niarchos before launching his own investment company called Devon Securities. The company floundered for the first couple of years and he found himself heavily in debt, having sent four children to college, but he would say later that he had managed to pay off all his debts and maintain his good name and reputation. He ended his career working for Lombard, Odier and Company, a Swiss private investment bank, out of Geneva and Bermuda. In the late 1990s, he suffered a stroke that left him paralyzed but not defeated— he remained mentally engaged and continued investing in the market despite his severe speech impairment until he died in 2000 in Virginia Beach at the age of eighty-four.[9]

John H. Richardson took Ulmer's place as chief of station in Athens in 1956, where he helped resettle some of the last remaining agents of the CIA Albanian operations. In 1958 he moved to the Philippines to head the CIA station in Manila and then took the assignment as chief of station in Saigon in early 1962. His CIA career there came to an abrupt end in October 1963, when Vietnamese newspapers blew his cover and identified him in print as the CIA station chief.[10] In the early 1970s he retired and moved to Mexico. When the Berlin Wall came down in 1989, he was thrilled to see the accomplishment of the goal he had pursued throughout his career and amused at how quickly it all ended. "All that effort," he told his son ruefully, "and the damn thing flops over like a cake."[11] Richardson died in Mexico in 1998 at the age of eighty-five.

E. Howard Hunt participated in the planning and conduct of the CIA operations against Castro, which led to the Bay of Pigs landing in 1961. After that, he became chief of covert action in the CIA's newly formed Domestic Operation Division in charge of subsidizing, as a form of covert propaganda, the publication of books and articles in the United States and internationally. Hunt retired from the CIA in 1970 and was hired in 1971 by Nixon administration officials as one of the "plumbers" assigned to stop the leaks of government secrets.

In 1972, Hunt received orders from the White House to bug George McGovern's campaign headquarters near Capitol Hill and the Democratic National Committee Headquarters in the Watergate complex in search of evidence that "DNC was receiving illegal contributions from the North Vietnamese."[12] Hunt selected a handful of Cuban exiles from Miami he had known since Bay of Pigs days to carry out the operation. On May 26 and 27 they tried twice to break into the DNC offices at the Watergate without success because the Cubans could not pick the locks. One of them flew down to Miami on the 28th and returned with the right tools. That evening, the men entered the DNC offices, where they took pictures of files and bugged phones. It turned out that they had not installed the bugging devices correctly, so they were ordered to break in again. On the night of June 16, 1972, the burglars went in for the fourth time, only to be spotted by a security guard who notified the DC police. From the Howard Johnson Hotel across the street, where he had mounted watch, Hunt saw the police load his guys in a white paddy wagon and drive off to the DC jail.[13] The next morning, a young reporter from the *Washington Post* by the name of Bob Woodward learned that Hunt's phone number had been found in the address book of one of the burglars, next to the initials "W. H." It was the thread that led Woodward to unravel the Watergate scandal and ultimately forced President Nixon to resign rather than face impeachment and an almost certain removal from office. Hunt served thirty-three months in prison for his burglary, conspiracy, and wiretapping actions. A prolific writer throughout his life, he published dozens of spy novels and several memoirs. Hunt died in Florida in 2007.[14]

* * *

King Zog never returned to the United States. After the Egyptian government allowed him to leave the country, Zog moved to France in July 1955 and settled in an almost empty villa on the French Riviera, with no servants and refusing all invitations. He sold his estate in Long Island, which had remained unoccupied since 1952 and had been vandalized by treasure hunters in search of Zog's riches to such an extent that the next purchaser simply razed it to the ground and turned it into parkland.

As their financial reserves were depleted, Zog and Geraldine resorted to selling jewelry from their personal collection in order to provide for Zog's dependents and his retinue. The Ostier Jewelers of New York put up for auction on April 1959 seventeen jewelry pieces that they had custom-designed in 1938 for Geraldine's wedding. Among the items auctioned was the diamond diadem that Geraldine had worn at her marriage ceremony topped with the heraldic crest of Albania—a helmet surmounted by the head of the white Albanian mountain goat.[15]

Zog spent his days in France writing the story of his life, which Geraldine translated from Albanian into French. He had planned four volumes but was reported to have finished only two. His lifelong habit of chain smoking caused his health to deteriorate quickly. He died on April 9, 1961, in the Foch Hospital in Suresnes, a suburb of Paris, at the age of sixty-five.[16] He was buried in a Paris cemetery, where he remained for over fifty years. In November 2012, as part of the commemorations of Albania's one-hundredth anniversary of independence, Zog's remains were repatriated from France. He was buried with state honors in the newly built Royal Mausoleum in Tirana.

Hasan Dosti remained in the United States after the dismantling of the NCFA. He kept a low public profile in the hope that the Communist regime would stop persecuting the seven children he had left behind in Albania. All of them suffered in prisons and deportation camps until the fall of the Communist regime. Dosti died on January 31, 1991, in Los Angeles at the age of ninety-six.[17]

Abas Kupi settled in 1955 in the south of France, close to King Zog. A few years after Zog's death he immigrated to the United States, where he settled in Queens, Long Island, in 1967. He always remained attached to the .38 Colt revolver given to him by Colonel Low in the summer of 1949. In 1971, he caused a minor incident at Kennedy International Airport when he brought the revolver on board an American Airlines plane. To the Port Authority policemen who searched and detained him, he described his occupation as unemployed.[18] Kupi died in Freeport, Long Island, in 1976 at the age of seventy-five.[19]

Abas Ermenji and Said Kryeziu were the only member of the original NCFA leadership who lived to see the fall of the Communist regime in 1991. Kryeziu settled in the United States in 1959 and lived in New York until 1993, when he died at the age of eighty-two.[20] Ermenji, after breaking away from NCFA, moved to Paris where he created the National Democratic Committee for a Free Albania. He returned to Albania in 1991 and reconstituted the Balli Kombëtar, which he tried, unsuccessfully, to promote into a political force in the Albanian post-Communist scene. He died in Paris in 2003 at the age of ninety.

The three principal leaders of the Blloku Kombëtar Indipendent remained in Italy. Gjon Markagjoni died in 1966. Ismail Vërlaci died in 1985. Ernest Koliqi continued to teach at the University of Rome, write, and translate until his death in 1975. His works did not become available in Albania until 1991. Xhafer Deva moved to the United States in 1956, where he lived in obscurity until his death in 1978. An obituary in the *Palo Alto Times* on May 27, 1978, said that Deva was assistant supervisor in the mailing service department at Stanford University, where he had worked between 1959 and 1971.[21]

* * *

After resigning from MI-6 in July 1951, Kim Philby spent several years fending off inquiries and investigations by MI-5 and MI-6 into his activities as a Soviet agent. He was officially cleared in October 1955 when the British Foreign Secretary Harold Macmillan publicly exonerated him in a speech in the House of Commons. In August 1956 he moved to Beirut as a correspondent for the *Observer* and the *Economist*, where he resumed collaboration with MI-6. His contacts with the KGB, which had been suspended since his return from Washington in 1951, were renewed shortly after.

As years went by, additional evidence surfaced that removed any doubts in the eyes of the British SIS of Philby's KGB connections. On January 1963, Nicholas Elliott, an old friend of Philby's and former

SIS chief of station in Beirut, confronted him with the evidence. Offering him immunity from prosecution, he was able to extract a verbal confession on January 10, 1963. They were supposed to meet again at the British embassy to formalize the deal, but on the night of January 23, 1963, Philby boarded the Russian freighter *Dolmatova* destined for Odessa.[22]

Far from giving him a hero's welcome in the Soviet Union, the KGB kept Philby at arm's length. One faction within the KGB had always suspected him of being a British double agent. Even those who genuinely trusted him knew that his value as an intelligence officer was over once he was recalled from Washington. He spent his years in Moscow translating for the Russians and training intelligence officers they were preparing to send to the West. In 1968 he published his memoir, *My Silent War: The Autobiography of a Spy*, in which he recounts his involvement in the early days of the Albanian operation without providing any indication that he had played a role in the failure of these operations, which was attributed to him later.

Recollections of those who knew him in Moscow show that Philby's Soviet reality was very different from the rosy utopia he had imagined during his Cambridge years. He found solace in the bottle, although it seems his drinking prowess hit its limits in Moscow. Vladimir Lyubimov, a Soviet spy who had trained with Philby for an assignment to London, recalled: "I met Philby quite a lot and drank more than one bottle of whisky with him, although all the talk about him being a terrible drinker are exaggerated."[23]

Philby died in Moscow on May 11, 1988, at the age of seventy-six. In death, he received the recognition he was not awarded in life. He was buried with full military honors and in 1990 was depicted in a commemorative stamp of the USSR postal service. The Soviet Union, the country to which Philby devoted fifty-five years of his life, ceased to exist in 1991.

* * *

Enver Hoxha remained the absolute ruler of Albania until his death in 1985. His first ten years in power, between 1944 and 1954, were a prolonged and tenacious fight for the survival not only of his regime but also of his own physical self. The pressure traumatized him psychologically and fed the obsessive paranoia that would drive his behavior for the rest of his life. Among the obsessions impressed by the experiences of those years were his hatred for Tito and the Yugoslavs; his absolute certainty that the Americans and the CIA were actively working against him; and his adoration for Stalin.

When Khrushchev came to power in 1954 and embarked on a course of de-Stalinization, rekindling relations with Tito, and peaceful coexistence with the United States, Hoxha was the only leader of the so-called people's democracies in Europe who refused to follow his lead, forcing Khrushchev to break all ties with Albania in 1961. Thus, the CIA's goal of removing Albania from the Soviet orbit was accomplished, albeit not exactly as Wisner and Kennan had envisioned in 1949. Hoxha aligned himself with China against both the Soviet Union and the United States during the years of the Cultural Revolution. When Mao Zedong, Zhou Enlai, and Deng Xiaoping began the course of rapprochement with the United States, Hoxha broke off the relations with China too, leaving Albania completely isolated in the late 1970s.

Each one of these major realignments was preceded and followed by Hoxha's infamous purges of real, perceived, and imaginary enemies, which sent dozens of his fervent followers in front of the firing squad and thousands of innocent Albanians to prisons and hard labor camps. It is still not clearly understood what pushed Hoxha to turn repeatedly against his closest collaborators and eliminate them without mercy. Explanations have ranged from his mental imbalance and Stalin-like paranoia to succession battles orchestrated in the background by his wife, infamously known as Lady Macbeth of Tirana. Yet another hypothesis can be advanced in light of the psychological warfare operations that the CIA carried out as part of Project Fiend. Did Hoxha fall victim to the "poison pills" the CIA may have sent him over the years, directly or through intermediaries from other intelligence services? Did Communist personalities who were purged become the victims of calumnious letters against them or "compromising" documents planted deliberately for the Sigurimi to find and report to Hoxha? It is a hypothesis that may well be proven if and when CIA declassifies operational records of their activities after 1960.

Mehmet Shehu became prime minister of Albania in 1954 and retained this position until his death on the night of December 17–18,

1981. The authorities declared the official cause of death a suicide during a nervous breakdown, although an autopsy was not performed and suspicions of murder have remained unanswered ever since. Although the true cause of Shehu's death remains a mystery, it is generally accepted that he was the victim of the succession struggle that heated up in the early 1980s, as Hoxha's health was deteriorating. After Shehu's death, Hoxha declared him enemy number one and a "poly-agent" of the American, Yugoslav, and Soviet secret services. Hoxha alleged that Shehu had been recruited in the American service as early as the mid-1930s by his former schoolteacher, Harry T. Fultz, with whom Shehu had maintained contact over the years, according to Hoxha's tale.

Kadri Hazbiu became minister of interior in 1954, a post he retained until 1980, when he became minister of defense. Although he had been a protégé of Shehu all his life, Hazbiu was one of the most vocal supporters of Hoxha in the attacks that led to Shehu's downfall in 1981. Ten months after Shehu's demise, Hoxha turned on Hazbiu as well, accusing him of being a key member of Shehu's spy ring. Within a matter of weeks, Hazbiu was stripped of all the positions in the Party and government structures, arrested, and jailed. He was tried, sentenced to death, and shot in September 1983.

* * *

After Hoxha's death in 1985, Albania continued on the path he had set for her as the only Stalinist country in Europe, completely isolated from the West and from the East. The first visible cracks in the armor of the regime appeared in July of 1990, when thousands of Albanians scaled the fences and the walls of Western embassies in Tirana, requesting asylum from the Communist government. The grounds of the United States legation, which at the time housed the Italian embassy, became a place of refuge for hundreds of men, women, and children of all ages and from all backgrounds, united by their desire to escape to the West. Popular discontent grew despite the government's efforts to quell it. The first opposition parties were created in December 1990. A swelling of demonstrations culminated in the toppling of statues of Hoxha and Stalin in Tirana and other major cities in Albania in February 1991. The Communists were voted out of power in March 1992.

The United States and Albania reestablished diplomatic relations in 1991, sixty-two years after they were interrupted by the Italian occupation. Albania joined NATO in April 2009, thus accomplishing the goal of establishing a democratic Albania friendly to the West, which Operation Fiend had tried to achieve sixty years before. Albania today maintains friendly relations with the United States, the United Kingdom, Italy, Greece, and the half-dozen countries that sprang up after the collapse of Yugoslavia.

As of 2014, Greece continues to maintain on the books the anachronistic law declaring a state of war between Greece and Albania, passed by the Greek parliament after Italian forces in Albania attacked Greece in October 1940.

Notes

Prologue

1 "First Team Drop into HBPixie, 11–12 November 1950," BGFIEND documents, November 13, 1950.

2 Gregory W. Pedlow and Donald E. Welzenbach, "The Central Intelligence Agency and Overhead Reconnaissance: The U-2 and OXCART Programs, 1954-1974," History Staff, Central Intelligence Agency. 1992.

3 "First Team Drop into HBPixie, 11–12 November 1950," BGFIEND documents, November 13, 1950.

4 Ibid.

5 Ibid.

6 Major D. H. Berger, USMC, "The Use of Covert Paramilitary Activity as a Policy Tool: An Analysis of Operations Conducted by the United States Central Intelligence Agency, 1949–1951," Federation of American Scientists, Intelligence Resource Program, May 22, 1995.

Chapter 1: The Office of Policy Coordination

1 William Colby and Peter Forbath, *Honorable Men: My Life in the CIA* (New York: Simon & Schuster, 1978), 70.

2 Ibid., 71.

3 Mark F. Wyatt, interview, *Cold War*, CNN, 1998.

4 Gianni Agnelli, interview, *Cold War*, CNN, 1998.

5 Mark F. Wyatt, interview, *Cold War*, CNN, 1998.

6 "NSC 4-A, NSC Minutes, 4th Meeting," NSC documents, December 17, 1947.

7 "NSC 10/2," NSC documents, June 18, 1948.

8 Christopher Felix (pseudonym for James McCargar), *A Short Course in the Secret War* (Lanham, Maryland: Madison Books, 2001), 280.

9 Ellis Wisner and Wendy Hazard, interviews with author, June 2013.

10 Ibid.

11 "Current Status of Project BGFIEND, with Particular Reference to OPC Organization," BGFIEND documents, August 16, 1949.

12 "History of OPC/EE-1," BGFIEND documents, n.d.

13 "James G. McCargar," UNESCO in the Spotlight, May 31, 2007.

14 Evan Thomas, *The Very Best Men* (New York: Simon & Schuster, 1995), 71.

15 E. Howard Hunt and Greg Aunapu, *American Spy* (Hoboken, NJ: John Wiley and Sons, 2007), 40.

16 Thomas, *The Very Best Men*, 40.

17 Hunt and Aunapu, *American Spy*, 50.

18 Thomas, *The Very Best Men*, 63.

19 "Current Status of Project BGFIEND, with Particular Reference to OPC Organization," BGFIEND documents, August 16, 1949.

20 Peter Grose, *Operation Rollback: America's Secret War Behind the Iron Curtain* (New York: Houghton Mifflin, 2000), 154.

Chapter 2: Albania between 1912 and 1949

1 "Former King Zog of Albania Dead," *New York Times* (1923–Current file), April 10, 1961.

2 Nicholas C. Pano, "Albania: The Last Bastion of Stalinism," *East Central Europe, Yesterday, Today, Tomorrow* (Stanford, CA: Hoover Institution Press, 1982), 188.

3 US House of Representatives, 83rd Congress, 2nd Session Select Committee on Communist Aggression, *Communist Takeover and Occupation of Albania*, 1954.

4 "Former King Zog of Albania Dead."

5 "King Zog's Wedding Celebrations in Tirana," *The West Australian*, April 30, 1938.

6 Owen Pearson, *Albania in the Twentieth Century, A History*, vol. I: *Albania and King Zog* (London, New York: Center for Albanian Studies in association with I. B. Tauris, 2004), 401.

7 "King Zog's Wedding Celebrations in Tirana."

8 "CIA Information Report No 00-B-8501-49," BGFIEND documents, n.d.

9 Grose, *Operation Rollback*, 154.

10 Pearson, *Albania in the Twentieth Century*, 483.

11 Peter Lucas, *The OSS in World War II Albania* (Jefferson, North Carolina: McFarland and Company, 2007), 22–24.

12 Lucas, *The OSS in World War II Albania*, 140.

13 "OSS Biographies of Albanian Leaders," NARA, Tirana US Mission General Records, 1945.

14 "Midhat Frasheri, Albanian Ex-Aide," *New York Times* (1923–Current file), October 4, 1949.

15 Julian Amery, *Sons of the Eagle* (London: Macmillan & Co., 1948), 189.

16 Robert Elsie, *Historical Dictionary of Albania* (Lanham, Maryland: Rowman and Littlefield, 2010), 116.

17 Amery, *Sons of the Eagle*, 57–58.

18 Ibid., 65.

19 Dosti Family, *Hasan Dosti: Një Jetë për Çështjen Shqiptare* (Tirana: Botart, 2008), 122–123.

20 Amery, *Sons of the Eagle*, 190.

21 "Albanians Seize Briton," *New York Times* (1923–Current file), February 16, 1944.

22 Leigh White, "Guerrillas of Albania," *New York Times* (1923–Current file), March 13, 1949.

23 Robert Elsie, *Historical Dictionary of Kosovo* (Lanham, Maryland: Rowman and Littlefield, 2004), 106.

24 Owen Pearson, *Albania in the Twentieth Century, A History*, vol. II: *Albania in Occupation and War* (London, New York: Center for Albanian Studies in association with I. B. Taurus, 2005), 388.

25 Amery, *Sons of the Eagle*, 337.

26 Bernd Jürgen Fischer, *Albania at War, 1939–1945* (West Lafayette, IN: Purdue University Press, 1999), 229.

27 Lucas, *The OSS in World War II Albania*, 150.

28 Ibid., 182.

29 "J.E. Jacobs Telegram No. 163," NARA, Tirana US Mission General Records, June 27, 1946.

30 Paolo Benanti, *La Guerra Piu Lunga* (Rome, Italy: Mursia, 1964), 257.

31 Adam B. Siegel, "The Use of Naval Forces in the Post-War Era: US Navy and US Marine Corps Crisis Response Activity, 1946–1990." The Navy Department Library. n.d.

32 Owen Pearson, *Albania in the Twentieth Century, A History*, vol. III: *Albania as Dictatorship and Democracy, 1945–99* (London, New York: Center for Albanian Studies in association with I. B. Tauris, 2006), 32.

33 "Corfu Channel (United Kingdom v. Albania)" The Hague Justice Portal, February 15, 2013; and "Albania expected to resume secret talks with Britain" CREST Database, August 26, 1985. Currency conversion based on calculator at www.fxtop.com. Conversion to today's dollars based on the website US Inflation Calculator at www.usinflationcalculator.com.

34 Karen Mingst, "International Court of Justice (ICJ)," Encyclopædia Britannica Online. n.d.

35 Tony Barber, "6.5m in war gold returns to Albania after 49 years," *Independent*, February 23, 1996.

36 Lucas, *The OSS in World War II Albania*, 160.

37 Milovan Djilas, *Conversations with Stalin* (New York: Harcourt, Brace & World, 1962), 181–182.

38 "The Albanian Operation," BGFIEND documents, March 21, 1949.

39 Ibid.

40 Ibid.

41 Pearson, *Albania in the Twentieth Century*, vol. III, 38.

42 Djilas, *Conversations with Stalin*, 143.

43 Cyrus L. Sulzberger, "Exiles Map Fight on Tirana Regime," *New York Times* (1923–Current file), August 29, 1949.

44 Raymond Zickel and Walter R. Iwaskiw, editors, "Albania: A Country Study," Country Studies, Federal Research Division of the Library of Congress, 1994.

45 Sulzberger, "Exiles Map Fight on Tirana Regime."

46 Cyrus L. Sulzberger, "West Held Easing Stand on Albania," *New York Times* (1923–Current file), March 27, 1950.

47 "Summary of MacLean Profiles for Albanian Politicians," BGFIEND documents.

48 "Albania Plan—Meeting between Abdyl Sula and State Department and OSO Representative," BGFIEND documents, April 28, 1949.

49 "Proposal to Overthrow Present Regime in Albania," BGFIEND documents, January 11, 1949.

50 "Albania Plan—Meeting between Abdyl Sula and State Department and OSO Representative," BGFIEND documents, April 28, 1949.

51 Ibid.

52 "The Albanian Operation," BGFIEND documents, March 21, 1949.

53 "Plan for Albania," BGFIEND documents. June 15, 1949.

Chapter 3: Genesis of Operation Fiend

1 "Proposal to Overthrow Present Regime in Albania."

2 Kim M. Juntunen, "US Army Attachés and the Spanish Civil War, 1936–1939: The Gathering of Technical and Tactical Intelligence," (The Defense Technical Information Center, May 4, 1990), 16–17.

3 "Proposal to Overthrow Present Regime in Albania."

4 Barry had been the director of the State Department's Office of African, South Asian and Near East Affairs, since 1947.

5 "Albania: Possibility of Overthrowing Present Regime," BGFIEND documents, May 27, 1949.

6 Ibid.

7 "The Albanian Operation," BGFIEND documents, March 21, 1949.

8 "History of OPC/EE-1," BGFIEND documents, n.d.

9 "The Albanian Operation," March 21, 1949.

10 "Memorandum of a Conversation with Mithat Frasheri," BGFIEND documents, April 30, 1949.

11 "Memorandum of a Conversation with Ahmet Zogu," BGFIEND documents, May 5, 1949.

12 "Memo for the record of Conversations with King Zog," BGFIEND documents, June 17, 1949.

13 "Outline for Operational Plan for Albania," BGFIEND documents, n.d.

14 Grose, *Operation Rollback*, 155.

15 James McCargar, interview by Jr. Thomas McNiff, McCargar Collection, Howard Gotlieb Archival Research Center at Boston University, May 2, 1985.

16 "Project BGFIEND," BGFIEND documents, July 1, 1949.

17 Stanley Weintraub, *11 Days in December* (New York: Free Press, 2006), 7–8.

18 Felix [McCargar], *A Short Course in the Secret War*, 280.

19 "Meeting on Albania," BGFIEND documents, May 4, 1949.

20 "Project Outline BGFIEND," BGFIEND documents, n.d.

21 "Operation Valuable," BGFIEND documents, n.d.

22 Ibid.

23 Ibid.

24 "Albania," BGFIEND documents, May 23, 1949.

25 "Reasons for Conducting OPC Albanian Operation on Joint Basis with British," BGFIEND documents, July 11, 1949.

26 Ibid.

Chapter 4: The National Committee for Free Albania

1 "A Look Back . . . The National Committee for Free Europe, 1949," CIA. gov. May 29, 2007.

2 Stephen Dorril, *MI6: Inside the Covert World of Her Majesty's Secret Intelligence Service* (New York: Free Press, 2000), 373.

3 Felix [McCargar], *A Short Course in the Secret War*, 280.

4 "Memorandum of 27 September 1949," BGFIEND documents, September 27, 1949.

5 "Conference with [REDACTED] on 16 and 17 September 1949 re Albanian operation," BGFIEND documents, October 3, 1949.

6 Ibid.

7 "Offie's Memo, 6 July 1949," BGFIEND documents, July 6, 1949.

8 "Summary of MacLean Profiles for Albanian Politicians," BGFIEND documents.

9 Pearson, *Albania in the Twentieth Century*, vol. III, 351; Nicholas Bethell, *Betrayed* (New York: Time Books, 1984), 58.

10 John Prados, *Safe for Democracy* (Chicago: Ivan R. Dee, 2006), 61; Bethell, *Betrayed*, 59.

11 "Telecon Conference," BGFIEND documents, July 24, 1949.

12 "Translation of French text handed Colonel Fiske by emissary of Yarborough," BGFIEND documents, July 26, 1949.

13 "The Albanian Operation," BGFIEND documents, March 21, 1949.

14 "Danger of GNA continuing pursuit of guerrillas across Albanian border," BGFIEND documents, July 21, 1949.

15 "Memo from B.Y. Berry to General Van Fleet and General Jenkins," BGFIEND documents, July 25, 1949.

16 "Aide-Memoire 21 July 1949," BGFIEND documents, July 21, 1949; "Memorandum," BGFIEND documents, July 27, 1949; and "Letter to Pilgrim," BGFIEND documents, August 10, 1949.

17 "NCFA Declaration," BGFIEND documents, n.d.

18 "Free Albania Unit Named," *New York Times* (1923–Current file), August 27, 1949.

19 "Memorandum of 27 September 1949," BGFIEND documents, September 27, 1949.

20 "Text of proposed telegram to US diplomatic missions," BGFIEND documents, August 25, 1949.

21 "Letter to Pilgrim," BGFIEND documents, August 10, 1949.

22 "Memo of 2 September 1949," BGFIEND documents, September 2, 1949.

23 Prados, *Safe for Democracy*, 61.

24 Ibid.

25 *The Cost of Treachery*, BBC, 1984.

26 Amery, *Sons of the Eagle*, 96.

27 "Albanian Operation—Activities of Personnel of the Committee for Free Albania," BGFIEND documents, November 15, 1949.

28 "Memorandum of Meeting 10 September 1949," BGFIEND documents, September 12, 1949.

29 "Albanian Operation—Activities of Personnel of the Committee for Free Albania," BGFIEND documents, November 15, 1949.

30 "Conversations with Albanian Leaders in the United States," BGFIEND documents, October 4, 1949.

31 "Midhat Frasheri, Albanian Ex-Aide," *New York Times* (1923–Current file), October 4, 1949.

32 "Telegram from Middle East," BGFIEND documents, November 3, 1949.

33 "Meeting of Joint Policy Committee," BGFIEND documents, November 3, 1949.

34 "Meeting with Lord Jellicoe and Mr. Joyce," BGFIEND documents, November 12, 1949.

35 "Telegrams 1, 2, 3," BGFIEND documents, November 18–19, 1949.

36 McCargar interview, 1985.

37 Ralph Blumenthal, "Axis Supporters Enlisted by US in Postwar Role," *New York Times* (1923–Current file), June 20, 1982.

38 "Albanian Operation—Activities of Personnel of the Committee for Free Albania," BGFIEND documents, November 15, 1949.

Chapter 5: Philby in Washington

1 "Memorandum of 21 September 1949," BGFIEND documents, September 21, 1949.

2 "Memorandum of 28 October 1949," BGFIEND documents, October 28, 1949.

3 Kim Philby, *My Silent War: The Autobiography of a Spy* (New York: Modern Library, 2002), 153.

4 Felix [McCargar], *A Short Course in the Secret War*, 282–284.

5 Ibid.

6 Ibid.

7 Ibid.

8 Philby, *My Silent War*, 146.

9 "Harold 'Kim' Philby and the Cambridge Three," *NOVA*, PBS/WGBH, January 2002.

10 Robert L. Benson, "The Venona Story," NSA.gov. January 15, 2009.

11 Philby, *My Silent War*, x.

12 Ibid., 10.

13 Ibid., 204.

Chapter 6: First Infiltrations of 1949

1 Dorril, *MI6*, 371.

2 Philby, *My Silent War*, 154.

3 "Conference with [REDACTED] on 16 and 17 September 1949 re Albanian operation," BGFIEND documents, October 3, 1949.

4 "Operation Valuable," BGFIEND documents, n.d.

5 "Greek Knowledge of Albanian Operation," BGFIEND documents, August 6, 1949.

6 "Transmittal of BGFiend Documents," BGFIEND documents, April 12, 1950.

7 Bethell, *Betrayed*, 67–68.

8 Robert Lacey, *Monarch: The Life and Reign of Elizabeth II* (New York: Simon and Schuster, 2008), 169.

9 Bethell, *Betrayed*, 61.

10 "Operation Valuable," BGFIEND documents, n.d.

11 "Transmittal of BGFiend Documents," April 12, 1950.

12 "Operation Valuable," n.d. Currency conversion based on calculator at www.fxtop.com. Conversion to today's dollars based on the website US Inflation Calculator at www.usinflationcalculator.com.

13 "Memorandum of 27 September 1949," BGFIEND documents, September 27, 1949.

14 "Albanian Operation—Fate of VALUABLE Teams in Albania Ref. SO DB-20024," BGFIEND documents, n.d.; "Albanian Operation—Fate of VALUABLE Teams in Albania SO DB-20064," BGFIEND documents, November 4, 1949.

15 Ibid.

16 Thomas, *The Very Best Men*, 39.

17 "Report of Interview between Colonel Smiley and Zotos," BGFIEND documents, n.d.

18 "Albanian Operation—Fate of VALUABLE Teams in Albania Ref. SO DB-20024," BGFIEND documents, n.d.; "Albanian Operation—Fate of VALUABLE Teams in Albania SO DB-20064," BGFIEND documents, November 4, 1949.

19 Bethell, *Betrayed*, 92.

20 Ibid., 75.

21 Felix [McCargar], *A Short Course in the Secret War*, 284.

22 Genrikh Borovik, *The Philby Files* (New York: Little, Brown and Company, 1994), 262.

23 McCargar interview, 1985.

24 "Albanian Operation—Albanian IS Activities in Connection with the Committee for Free Albania," BGFIEND documents, December 21, 1949.

25 "Albania Seeks to Resume Trade with Italy," CREST Database, July 19, 1950.

26 "Albanian Operation—Fate of VALUABLE Teams in Albania Ref. SO DB-20024."

27 "Employment of Albanian Refugees for Intelligence Purposes," BGFIEND documents, February 21, 1949.

28 "Procesi i Tiranes," *Gazeta Shqiptare*, May 14, 2012.

29 Sarah-Jane Corke, "US Covert Operations and Cold War Strategy: Truman, Secret Warfare and the CIA, 1945–53," *Studies in Intelligence* (London and New York: Routledge, 2008), 93; "Procesi i Tiranes," *Gazeta Shqiptare*, May 14, 2012.

30 "Report of Interview between Colonel Smiley and Zotos," BGFIEND documents, n.d.

31 "Memorandum of 27 September 1949," BGFIEND documents, September 27, 1949.

32 "Draft Memorandum of 21 October 1949," BGFIEND documents, October 21, 1949.

Chapter 7: Reevaluation of Project Fiend

1 "Albanian Operation—Fate of VALUABLE Teams in Albania Ref. SO DB-20024," BGFIEND documents, n.d.; "Albanian Operation—Fate of VALUABLE Teams in Albania SO DB-20064," BGFIEND documents, November 4, 1949.

2 Felix [McCargar], *A Short Course in the Secret War*, 124.

3 "Meeting of the Joint Policy Committee for Operation BGFIEND," BGFIEND documents, November 21, 1949.

4 Ibid.

5 Ibid.

6 Ibid.

7 "Transmittal of BGFiend Documents," BGFIEND documents, n.d.

8 "Fiend-Valuable 25 September 1951," BGFIEND documents, n.d.

9 "Memorandum on FIEND-VALUABLE Operation," BGFIEND documents, December 6, 1949.

10 Cyrus L. Sulzberger, "West Held Easing Stand on Albania," *New York Times* (1923–Current file), March 27, 1950.

11 "OPC Cable 1424," BGFIEND documents, March 28, 1950.

12 Felix [McCargar], *A Short Course in the Secret War*, 93.

13 "Meeting on FIEND on 27 February 1950," BGFIEND documents, March 1, 1950.

14 "OPC Liaison with Other Intelligence Services," BGFIEND documents, March 7, 1950.

15 "Intelligence Operations against Albania from Italy and Greece," BGFIEND documents, May 3, 1949.

16 "E vranë apo e helmuan Alush Lleshanakun?" Zeri Yt! Media Sociale Shqiptare, April 16, 2011.

17 Agim Gashi, "Ja e vërteta për vrasjen e deputetit Bardhok Biba," *Akllapi Net*, September 6, 2009.

18 They were Preng D. Kola from Oroshi, Pjetër D. Vila from Kaçinarri, Dod M. Biba from Malaj, and Pjetër Paloka from Kaçinarri.

19 They were: Llesh Mëlyshi, Nikoll Bardhok Bajraktari, Bardhok Dod Lleshaj, Gjergj Keq Beleshi, Dod Marka Biba from Kthella; Ded Preng Gjomarkaj, Nikoll Llesh Nikolli, Preng Shkurti, Gjin Kaçi, Ndoc Gjet

Palaj, Frrok Mata, Marka Ndrec Marku, Ded Paloka and Zef Vila from Mirdita.

20 Agim Gashi, "Postvrasja e deputetit Bardhok Biba/Përkujtohet 60-vjetori i vrasjes së 14 burrave," *Akllapi Net*, September 6, 2009.

Chapter 8: Labor Services Company 4000

1 Gratian M. Yatsevitch III, interview with author, July 1, 2013.

2 "Harvard University's Obituary and Death Notice Collection," Genealogybuff.com, January 18, 2011.

3 Colonel Gratian M. Yatsevitch, interview by William Burr, Iranian-American Relations Oral History Project, November 5, 1988.

4 Gratian M. Yatsevitch III, interview.

5 Bethell, *Betrayed*, 144.

6 "OPC Plans and Operations in Albania," BGFIEND documents, May 17, 1950.

7 Gratian M. Yatsevitch III, interview.

8 Michael Burke, *Outrageous Good Fortune* (Boston: Little, Brown and Company, 1984), 121.

9 Burke, *Outrageous Good Fortune*, 123.

10 Ibid., 141.

11 Ibid., 135.

12 Ibid., 140.

13 Ibid., 145.

14 Ibid., 147.

15 Ibid.

16 Ibid., 143.

17 "Memorandum of Understanding on Establishment of Pixie Base in Germany," BGFIEND documents, January 31, 1951.

18 Walter Elkins, "Labor Service Division List of Units," *US Army in Germany*, February 20, 2013.

19 Siegbert Mann, "Labor Service Einheiten (Units)," History of the US Force in Germany: Labor Service and Civilian Support Organization, February 20, 2013.

20 "Letter to Chief of Mission in Frankfurt," BGFIEND documents, August 14, 1953.

21 "Alleged AIS Training Camp for Albanian Agents at Munich," BGFIEND documents, December 10, 1951.

22 "Loeb Estate Covert Site," BGFIEND documents, n.d.

23 "Memorandum for the Record," BGFIEND documents, July 21, 1952.

24 "Brief Summary of Medical Activities in HBBASIS from May 15 to 1 September 1951," BGFIEND documents, n.d.

25 "Memorandum for the Record," BGFIEND documents, July 21, 1952.

26 "Alleged AIS Training Camp for Albanian Agents at Munich," BGFIEND documents, December 10, 1951.

27 "Cable FRAN 9580," BGFIEND documents, December 13, 1952.

28 "Albania Deception Operation," BGFIEND documents, November 13, 1954.

Chapter 9: Odyssey of the First CIA Paramilitary Team

1 "Meeting in Frankfurt on BGFIEND," BGFIEND documents, May 2, 1951.

2 "Relations between CHARITY and BGFIEND," BGFIEND documents, August 21, 1950.

3 "Discussions of 9 May 1950," BGFIEND documents, May 11, 1950.

4 "Relations between CHARITY and BGFIEND."

5 "CIA Information Report No 00-B-8501-49," BGFIEND documents, n.d. F meant that the source reliability could not be judged; 6 meant that the veracity of content could not be judged. OSO used the following rating of source reliability: A=Completely Reliable; B=Usually Reliable; C=Fairly Reliable; D=Not Usually Reliable; E=Not Reliable; F=Cannot Be Judged. OSO used the following rating of content veracity: 1=True; 2=Probably True; 3=Possibly True; 4=Doubtful; 5=Probably False; 6=Cannot Be Judged.

6 "Appraisal of Intelligence Material," BGFIEND documents, January 4, 1951.

7 "Reconsideration of OSO's Operations Against Albania," BGFIEND documents, n.d.

8 "Air Support Aircraft," BGFIEND documents, June 9, 1950.

9 Michael Alfred Peszke, *The Polish Underground Army, the Western Allies, and the Failure of Strategic Unity in World War II* (Jefferson, North Carolina: McFarland & Company, 2005), 76.

10 "Composition of Polish Aircrew—BGFIEND," BGFIEND documents, August 29, 1950.

11 "Events Leading up to the Premature Arrival of BGFIEND Covert Aircraft in Greece," BGFIEND documents, October 9, 1950.

12 "Training of Pixies for BGFIEND," BGFIEND documents, January 19, 1951.

13 "Resistance Situation," BGFIEND documents, August 21, 1950.

14 "Report of Halil Nerguti," BGFIEND documents, February 8, 1952.

15 "First Team Drop into HBPixie, 11–12 November 1950," BGFIEND documents, November 13, 1950.

16 "Report of Halil Nerguti," BGFIEND documents, February 8, 1952.

17 Ibid.

18 Bethell, *Betrayed*, 157

19 Dashnor Kaloci, "Si na stërvisnin oficerët amerikanë në Gjermani," *Dashnor Kaloci Blog*, February 20, 2013.

20 Nicholas Bethell, "Profits and losses of treachery," *Independent*, September 6, 1994.

21 "First Operational Commo Flight—HBPixie," BGFIEND documents, November 16, 1950.

22 "Report of Halil Nerguti," BGFIEND documents, February 8, 1952.

23 Ibid.

24 Ibid.

25 "Letter from Red Team," BGFIEND documents, April 24, 1952.

26 Ibid.

27 "CIA Museum Directorate of Science and Technology," CIA.gov. July 23, 2012.

28 "25 October Report," BGFIEND documents, n.d.

29 "Debriefing of Pine Tree Team—Part I—BGFiend," BGFIEND documents, July 7, 1952.

30 "Note to Military Junta on Situation of Red and Green Team Members Who Took Refuge in Yugoslavia," BGFIEND documents, April 15, 1953.

31 Ibid.

32 "Cable DIR 03050," BGFIEND documents, May 5, 1953.

33 "Cable 2306," BGFIEND documents, May 9, 1953.

34 "Note to Military Junta," BGFIEND documents, July 17, 1953.

Chapter 10: Philby's Exit

1 "Fiend-Valuable 25 September 1951," BGFIEND documents, n.d.

2 Philby, *My Silent War*, 159.

3 Ibid., 156.

4 Burke, *Outrageous Good Fortune*, 147.

5 Ibid., 152.

6 "Venona: Soviet Espionage and the American Response 1939–1957," CIA.gov. March 19, 2007.

7 Benson, "The Venona Story," 27.

8 Ibid., 20.

9 Philby, *My Silent War*, 170.

10 Ibid., 171.

11 Dorril, *MI6*, 396.

12 Philby, *My Silent War*, 184.

13 "Liaison with the British in Washington on Projects FIEND and VALU-ABLE," BGFIEND documents, August 28, 1951.

Chapter 11: Propaganda and Psychological and Economic Warfare

1 "From 'Sons of the Eagle' to Michael Burke," Burke Collection, Howard Gotlieb Archival Research Center at Boston University, n.d.

2 "Letter from Burke to Abaz Kupi," Burke Collection, Howard Gotlieb Archival Research Center at Boston University, n.d.

3 Jon L. Lieb, interview with author, January 2014.

4 Hunt and Aunapu, *American Spy*, 46.

5 "BGFIEND STATUS REPORT, 9 January 1951," BGFIEND documents, January 9, 1951.; "Extract from Report of Operations for the Quarter Ended 31 March 1951," BGFIEND documents, n.d.

6 "Disposal of Yacht 'Juanita,'" BGFIEND documents, box 48, volume 12, February 28, 1955.

7 "Monthly Project Status Report, September 1951," BGFIEND documents, n.d.

8 "The Albanian Operation," BGFIEND documents, March 21, 1949.

9 "Progress Report BGFiend/BGFlume for May and June 1951," BGFIEND documents, July 10, 1951.

10 "LCBATLAND Leaflet Material," BGFIEND documents, August 7, 1951.

11 "Conversation with Department of State on 18 October 1951—Current Status of BGFIEND," BGFIEND documents, October 17, 1951.

12 "Leaflet Drop Schedule to Albania," BGFIEND documents, n.d.

13 "BGFIEND-OPC Action against Shipping in Albania," BGFIEND documents, May 19, 1950.

14 Richard Stolz, "Assignment Trieste: A Case Officer's First Tour," CIA Center for the Study of Intelligence, February 19, 2013.

15 "Intelligence Summary No. 10," BGFIEND documents, April 4, 1951.

16 "Meeting with OSO Re: Current Situation in Albania," BGFIEND documents, April 11, 1951.

17 "Albania," BGFIEND documents, June 7, 1951.

18 "Conversation with State Department Representatives concerning Albanian and Bulgarian Operations," BGFIEND documents, April 3, 1951.

19 "Albania," BGFIEND documents, June 7, 1951.

20 "Scheduled Airdrop to Albania—Instructions of the Director of Central Intelligence," BGFIEND documents, April 18, 1951.

21 "The People of the CIA . . . The First Community DCI: Walter B. Smith," CIA.gov. October 17, 2007.

22 CIA History Staff, "DCI's First 100 Days," Central Intelligence Agency, April 14, 2007.

23 "Extract from Monthly Progress Report For EE-1 for May 1951," BGFIEND documents, n.d.

24 "Fiend Daily Report 2 June 1951," BGFIEND documents, n.d.

25 "Apostol Tenefi," BGFIEND documents, March 23, 1953.

26 "Albania," BGFIEND documents, June 7, 1951.

27 "Extract from Report of Operations for the Quarter Ended 30 June 1951," BGFIEND documents, n.d.

28 "Policy—Albania," BGFIEND documents, July 6, 1951.

29 "Extract from Monthly Progress Report For EE-1 for May 1951," BGFIEND documents, n.d.

30 "Yugoslav Plan for the Invasion of Albania," CREST Database, July 23, 1953.

31 "The Independence of Albania," BGFIEND documents, June 20, 1951.

32 Ibid.

33 "Basic Policy—Department of State," BGFIEND documents, n.d.

34 Ibid.

Chapter 12: Adverse Developments in the Infiltration Program

1 "Attached Letter," BGFIEND documents, May 21, 1951.

2 "Meeting in Frankfurt on BGFIEND," BGFIEND documents, May 2, 1951.

3 Kaloci, "Si na stërvisnin oficerët amerikanë në Gjermani."

4 "Meeting in Frankfurt on BGFIEND," BGFIEND documents, May 2, 1951.

5 "Attached Letter," BGFIEND documents, May 21, 1951.

6 Ibid.

7 "Daily Report—Tuesday 3 July 1951," BGFIEND documents, n.d.; "EE-1 Daily Report, Tuesday July 24, 1951," BGFIEND documents, n.d.

8 "Annihilation of BGFiend Olive Team," BGFIEND documents, August 14, 1951.

9 "EE-1 Daily Report, Wednesday 15 August 1951," BGFIEND documents, n.d.

10 Pearson, *Albania in the Twentieth Century*, vol. III, 436.

11 Bethell, "Profits and losses of treachery."

12 "EE-1 Daily Report, Tuesday 7 August 1951," BGFIEND documents, n.d.

13 "24 October Report," BGFIEND documents, n.d.

14 "Cypress Debriefing," BGFIEND documents, August 31, 1951.

15 Robert Elsie, "1983 Abaz Ermenji: Overthrowing the Communist Regime," Texts and Documents of Albanian History, n.d.

16 "Extract from Monthly Progress Report, EE-1, for May 1951," BGFIEND documents, n.d.

17 "Extract from Monthly Progress Report, EE-1, for April 1951," BGFIEND documents, n.d.

18 "BGFIEND Daily Progress Report June 16/17 1951," BGFIEND documents, Box 49, n.d.

19 "OSO/OPC Infiltration, Albania, 24 June 1951," BGFIEND documents, June 26, 1951.

20 "Memo 28 June 1951," BGFIEND documents, box 49, volume 17, file 1 of 2, n.d.

21 "EE-1 Daily Report, Monday July 30, 1951," BGFIEND documents, n.d.

22 "BGFIEND Status Report for Consultants Meeting," BGFIEND documents, August 15, 1951.

23 "Monthly Project Status Report, September 1951," BGFIEND documents, n.d.

24 "BGFIEND Daily Progress Report, 10 September 1951," BGFIEND documents, n.d.; BGFIEND Status Report for Consultants Meeting 1951.

25 Dorril, *MI6*, 398.

26 "Daily Progress Report 10 October 1951," BGFIEND documents, n.d.

27 "EE-1 Daily Report, 16 October 1951," BGFIEND documents, n.d.

28 Ibid.

29 "Agenda for Rome Conference," BGFIEND documents, n.d.; "Minutes Fiend/Valuable Conference Rome, 22–24 October 1951," BGFIEND documents, n.d.; "22 Oct 51 FIEND/VALUABLE Meeting," BGFIEND documents, n.d.

30 "25 October Report," BGFIEND documents, n.d.

31 Klajd Kapinova, "Hamid Toshi (Saiti)," Shqiperiaetnike.de, n.d.

32 "25 October Report," BGFIEND documents, n.d.

33 "BGFIEND HSTEIN Status Report," BGFIEND documents, May 20, 1952.

34 "Projected 1952 OPC and OSO Operations in Albania," BGFIEND documents, December 12, 1952.

35 "Monthly Project Status Report, October 1951," BGFIEND documents, n.d.

36 Dorril, *MI6*, 397.

Chapter 13: A Bucket of Diamonds and Rubies

1 "King Zog Here for Visit," *New York Times* (1923–Current file), July 27, 1951.

2 "Zog Hired Press Agent," *New York Times* (1923–Current file), September 21, 1951.

3 "Report of the Attorney General to the Congress of the United States on the Administration of the Foreign Agents Act," 1952, 88.

4 "Telephone Conversation Concerning visit of ex-King Zog (Albania) to Department," BGFIEND documents, August 1, 1951.

5 "Conversation with King Zog of Albania," BGFIEND documents, August 23, 1951; "Meeting with Ex-King Zog," BGFIEND documents, August 20, 1951; "Report of Conversation with King Zog," BGFIEND documents, August 23, 1951.

6 "Conversation with King Zog of Albania on 17 August 1951," BGFIEND documents, August 23, 1951.

7 "Conversation with King Zog of Albania on 30 August 1951," September 24, 1951.

8 Ibid.

9 "When 'Knollwood' Was For Sale," *Old Long Island*, August 5, 2009.

10 "Ex-King Zog Buys Syosset Estate with 'Bucket of Diamonds, Rubies,'" *New York Times* (1923–Current file), September 19, 1951.

11 "Nassau Will Sell Ex-King Zog's Estate; Tax Lien to be Offered Dec. 1 for $2,654," *New York Times* (1923–Current file), November 7, 1952.

12 "Zog's Taxes Paid, L.I. Palace Saved," *New York Times* (1923–Current file), November 12, 1952.

13 "Zog Ousts Police Station," *New York Times* (1923–Current file), March 23, 1953.

14 "Conversation with King Zog at Meeting on Wednesday, 12 September 1951," BGFIEND documents, September 18, 1951.

15 "Conversation between King Zog and [REDACTED] on 26 and 27 October," BGFIEND documents, n.d.; "Excerpt from Top Secret Cable 10 December 1951," BGFIEND documents, box 47, volume 6, file 1 of 2, n.d.

Chapter 14: A Rich Harvest of Bitter Fruit

1 Margueritte Ulmer-Power, interview with author, January 3, 2014.

2 "Security Review of Willow Team Operations," BGFIEND documents, March 9, 1954.

3 "SGAA-5441," BGFIEND documents, August 14, 1953.

4 "Apple Team Operational Plan—BGFiend," BGFIEND documents, April 29, 1952.

5 "APPLETREE BGFIEND/SHAM," BGFIEND documents, June 1952.

6 "Security Review of Apple Team Operations," BGFIEND documents, October 21, 1953.

7 Ibid.

8 Ibid.

9 "Apple CE Review," BGFIEND documents, November 13, 1953.

10 "APPLETREE BGFIEND/SHAM," BGFIEND documents, June 1952.

11 "Apple Security 19 March 1954," BGFIEND documents, n.d.

12 "Materials for Consultants Meeting," BGFIEND documents, July 9, 1952.

13 Ibid.

14 "Apple Security 19 March 1954."

15 "Apple Security Feb 10 1954," BGFIEND documents, n.d.

16 "CE Review of Apple Trial," BGFIEND documents, May 18, 1954.

17 "Soviet Military Mission to Albania," CREST database, July 16, 1953.

18 Ferdinand Dervishi, "Radioloja," enver-hoxha.net, n.d.; and Mark Dodani, interview by Fatos Veliu, "Në verën e '52-it . . . ," *BalkanWeb*, August 16, 2012.

19 Ibid.

20 Dervishi, Radioloja n.d.; Mark Dodani, interview by Fatos Veliu, "Zbarkimi i Hamit Matjanit . . ." *BalkanWeb*, August 17, 2012.

21 Ibid.

22 Ibid.

23 "SHAM/OBOPUS Transmittal of RNCASTING Message," BGFIEND documents, May 1, 1954.

24 Dervishi, Radioloja n.d.

25 "Apple CE Review."

26 Dervishi, Radioloja n.d.

27 "Apple CE Review."

28 "Security Review of Apple Team Operations."

29 "Apple CE Review."

30 Ibid.

31 "Security Review of Apple Team Operations."

32 Dervishi, Radioloja n.d.

33 "Apple CE Review."

34 Ibid.

35 Ibid.

34 Ibid.

37 "Communications Comments re APPLETREE CE Review," BGFIEND documents, January 13, 1954.

38 "Apple Tree Team Resupply Missions," BGFIEND documents, September 12, 1952.

39 "Apple CE Review."

40 Ibid.

41 "BGFIEND Apple W/T Traffic," BGFIEND documents, October 21, 1952.

42 "OBOPUS Security Review of Apple/2—Part I," BGFIEND documents, December 10, 1953.

43 "Security Review of Apple Team Operations."

44 "Apple Resupply Briefing," BGFIEND documents, January 31, 1953.

45 Dervishi, Radioloja n.d.

46 "Apple Resupply Briefing."

47 "Security Review of Apple Team Operations."

48 "Apple Resupply Briefing."

49 "Security Review of Apple Team Operations."

50 Ibid.

51 "OBOPUS. Security Review of Apple/2—Part I."

52 "Review of Apple/3 W/T Contacts." BGFIEND documents, August 18, 1953.

53 "Security Review of Apple Team Operations."

54 "Review of Apple/3 W/T Contacts."

55 Ibid.

56 Ibid.

57 Ibid.

58 Ibid.

59 "Security Review of Apple Team Operations."

60 Ibid.

61 "Apple CE Review"; "OBOPUS Security Review of Apple/2—Part I."

62 "Cable 2306Z 6 Nov 53," BGFIEND documents, November 6, 1953.

63 "Testimony of E. Howard Hunt, 10 Jan 1976," Church Committee boxed files hosted by Mary Ferrell, January 10, 1976.

64 "Local Reaction to Apprehension of Zejnel Shehu Group," BGFIEND documents, n.d.

65 "Tirana Trials of CIA Agents," BGFIEND documents, April 1954; "CE Review of Apple Trial," BGFIEND documents, May 18, 1954.

66 Ibid.

67 Ferdinand Dervishi, "Mehmet Shehu vrer për Kadri Hazbiun: Pi raki e puthet me diversantët," *Infoarkiv: Arkiva Mediatike Shqiptare*, May 29, 2010.

68 "CE Review of Apple Trial," BGFIEND documents, May 18, 1954.

69 "Special Leaflet, April 20 1954," BGFIEND documents, n.d.

70 Ibid.

71 "Special Leaflet devoted to RNPUTLOG," BGFIEND documents, June 12, 1954.

72 "Possessions of Deceased Agents," BGFIEND documents, March 31, 1955.

Chapter 15: King Zog Overstays His Time in Egypt

1 "King Zog's Offer to Help Penetrate the Muslim Brotherhood in Egypt," BGFIEND documents, September 23, 1952.

2 "King Zog of Albania," BGFIEND documents, July 24, 1953.

3 "Status of Former King Zog of Albania," BGFIEND documents, December 24, 1953.

4 Currency conversion based on calculator at www.fxtop.com.

5 Conversion to today's dollars based on the website US Inflation Calculator at www.usinflationcalculator.com.

6 "Status of Former King Zog of Albania," BGFIEND documents, December 24, 1953.

7 Ibid.

8 Ibid.

9 "Situation Report and Recommendations for Action," BGFIEND documents, December 3, 1953.

10 "Intelligence Report No. 5635.140," BGFIEND documents, November 18, 1953.

11 "Status of Former King Zog of Albania," BGFIEND documents, December 24, 1953.

12 "Daily Log, 5 January 1954," BGFIEND documents, n.d.

13 "Daily Log, 8 January 1954," BGFIEND documents, n.d.

14 "OBOPUS Status Report, January 1954," BGFIEND documents, n.d.

15 "RNCASTING Correspondence, 16 March 1954," BGFIEND documents, n.d.

16 "Daily Log, 8 February 1954," BGFIEND documents, n.d.

17 "OBOPUS Status Report, February 1954," BGFIEND documents, n.d.

18 "OBOPUS Status Report, March 1954," BGFIEND documents, n.d.

19 "OBOPUS Status Report, May 1954," BGFIEND documents, n.d.

Chapter 16: Planning the Fondest Dream

1 "Foreign Relations, 1950–1955, The Intelligence Community," US Department of State Archive, December 21, 2007, 225.

2 "Foreign Relations, 1950–1955," 379.

3 US Senate Select Committee to Study Governmental Operations with Respect to Intelligence Activities (Church Committee). *"Supplementary Detailed Staff Reports on Foreign and Military Intelligence, Book IV,"* 1976 , 35.

4 "Pros and Cons of Proposal to Detach Albania from the Soviet Orbit," BGFIEND documents, June 4, 1952.

5 Ibid.

6 "Foreign Relations, 1950-1955," 379.

7 "Annex C Plan for Albanian Coup." BGFIEND documents, n.d.

8 "Paramilitary Plans for Coup d'Etat(s) in Albania," BGFIEND documents, February 6, 1953.

9 "Operations against Albania," BGFIEND documents, February 2, 1953.

10 John H. Richardson, "My Father, the Spy," *Esquire*, January 29, 2009.

11 Ibid.

12 Hunt and Aunapu, *American Spy*, 67.

13 "Aggression Actions," BGFIEND documents, June 30, 1953; and "Request for Authorization for Reproduction of the Albanian," BGFIEND documents, n.d.

14 "Albanian Operations," BGFIEND documents, August 31, 1953.

15 "Albania, 8 August 1953," BGFIEND documents, August 8, 1953.

16 Dr. Donald Wilber, "Overthrow of Premier Mossadeq of Iran, November 1952–August 1953" (The National Security Archive, The George Washington University, March 1954), 78–79.

17 Ibid., 81.

18 "Albania, 31 August 1953," BGFIEND documents, August 31, 1953.

19 "Development Concerning Albanian Plan," BGFIEND documents, September 4, 1953.

Chapter 17: The American Backers Are Obliged to Withdraw

1 "Recapitulation of OBOPUS Operations, 1 January to 31 December 1953," BGFIEND documents, February 18, 1954.

2 "Guidance for 1954 Operational Season," BGFIEND documents, February 18, 1954.

3 "1954 Operations," BGFIEND documents, February 1, 1954; Guidance for 1954 Operational Season 1954.

4 Ibid.

5 "Termination of AIRBRAKE, AIRWORTHY, and RNDEPLOY," BGFIEND documents, April 9, 1954.

6 "Foreign Relations, 1950-1955," 538.

7 "Foreign Relations, 1950-1955," 591.

8 "FY 1953 Program," BGFIEND documents, n.d.

9 "Fiscal Year 1954 Operational Program for Albania," BGFIEND documents, n.d.

10 "Fiscal Year 1955 Operational Program for Albania," BGFIEND documents, n.d.

11 Elsie, "Abaz Ermenji."

12 "The Possibility of an appeal to Senator McCarthy for investigation of the NCFA," BGFIEND documents, May 15, 1953.

13 "BGFIEND/Rome Monthly Survey Report 28 November 1952 to 6 January 1953," BGFIEND documents, January 6, 1953.

14 Ibid.

15 "Assembly of Captive European Nations, Records, 1953–1972," University of Minnesota Immigration History Research Center, October 5, 2012.

16 "Operational Review, OBSTACLE/OBDURATE," BGFIEND documents, January 31, 1955.

17 "Project OBDURATE (Aproval)," BGFIEND documents, August 26, 1954.

18 Ibid.

19 "Operational Review, OBSTACLE/OBDURATE," BGFIEND documents, January 31, 1955.

20 Ibid.

21 "Renewal of Project OBDURATE," BGFIEND documents, August 29, 1955.

22 "Kraja-Shyti-Mersini D/A Operation," BGFIEND documents, December 20, 1954.

23 "Renewal of Project OBDURATE," BGFIEND documents, August 29, 1955.

24 "Cable 2354Z 30 Apr 56," BGFIEND documents, 1956.

25 "Formal Statement," BGFIEND documents, n.d.

26 "Cable 2354Z 30 Apr 56," BGFIEND documents, 1956.

27 "Red and Green Team Commitments," BGFIEND documents, June 9, 1956.

28 "Cable 2037Z 5 Jul 56," BGFIEND documents, n.d.

29 "Agjenti 91-vjecar i CIA: Misioni per te rrezuar Hoxhen," *Forumi Shqiptar*, August 19, 2009.

30 "Termination Approval for OBHUNT," BGFIEND documents, January 31, 1958.

31 "OBTUSE Routing Sheet," BGFIEND documents, January 8, 1960.

Chapter 18: Lessons and Legacy of Project Fiend

1 "Identification of W/T Operators," BGFIEND documents, November 17, 1952.

2 "Release of Apple Case for Use by Office of Training," BGFIEND documents, April 20, 1954.

3 "CE Review of Apple Trial," BGFIEND documents, May 18, 1954.

4 "Current Status of Project BGFIEND, with Particular Reference to OPC Organization," BGFIEND documents, August 16, 1949.

5 Brian Latell, *Castro's Secrets* (New York: Palgrave Macmillan, 2012), 3, 10.

6 Markus Wolf with Anne McElvoy, *Man Without a Face* (New York: Time Books, 1997), 285.

7 US Senate Select Committee to Study Governmental Operations with Respect to Intelligence Activities "Church Committee," 1976, 129.

8 Testimony of E. Howard Hunt, January 10, 1976.

9 Ibid.

10 "Church Committee," 130.

11 McCargar interview, 1985.

12 The KGB, or *Komitet Gosudarstvennoy Bezopasnosti* (Committee for State Security), came to life in 1954. Like the CIA, it evolved over the years through a series of acronyms, such as Cheka, NKVD, NKGB, and MGB.

13 "Soviet Use of Assassination and Kidnapping," CIA Center for the Study of Intelligence, February 1964.

14 "Albanian Operation—Plans for Assassination of Members of the Committee for Free Albania," BGFIEND documents, December 2, 1949.

15 "EE-I Daily Report, Friday, 27 July," BGFIEND documents, July 27, 1951.

16 Jon L. Lieb, interview with author, January 2014.

17 "Monthly Project Status Report, September 1951," BGFIEND documents, n.d.

18 "BGFIEND Talks with [REDACTED] and [REDACTED] in Athens on 19 June and 2 July 1951," BGFIEND documents, August 3, 1951.

19 "Operational Plan and Operational Clearance Request for Coup-de-Main Team Members," BGFIEND documents, July 16, 1952.

20 "BGFIEND/Operational Hamdi Bogdani," BGFIEND documents, December 11, 1952.

21 Hunt and Aunapu, *American Spy*, 112.

22 Ibid., 63–64.

23 "CIA's Role in the Overthrow of Arbenz," CIA Freedom of Information Act, May 12, 1975.

24 Ibid.

25 Nicholas Cullather, *Secret History: The CIA's Classified Account of Its Operations in Guatemala 1952–1954* (Stanford, CA: Stanford University Press, 2006), 108.

26 "CIA's Role in the Overthrow of Arbenz."

27 Cullather, *Secret History*, 82.

28 Siegel, "The Use of Naval Forces in the Post-War Era."

29 "Guatemala Briefing," CIA Freedom of Information Act, June 5, 1954.

30 Cullather, *Secret History*, 110.

31 Ibid., 99.

32 "CIA's Role in the Overthrow of Arbenz."

33 Cullather, *Secret History*, 103.

34 W. Thomas Smith Jr., *Encyclopedia of the Central Intelligence Agency* (Facts on File, 2003), 99.

35 "Memorandum of a Conference with the President, White House, Washington, March 17, 1960, 2:30 p.m." (*Foreign Relations of the United States, 1958–1960*), March 17, 1960.

36 Thomas, *The Very Best Men*, 95.

37 Ibid., 166–167.

38 Ibid., 88.

39 Ibid., 213.

40 "Daily Progress Report for Monday, 24 November 1952," BGFIEND documents, November 24, 1952.

41 Brenda Fowler, "Banished for Their Fathers' Sins," *New York Times* (1923–Current file), May 17, 1992.

42 Elsie, "Abaz Ermenji."

43 McCargar interview.

Epilogue

1 "James G. McCargar."

2 Felix [McCargar], *A Short Course in the Secret War*, 299.

3 McCargar interview.

4 "Robert Low," The New York Preservation Archive Project, July 16, 2002.

5 "Michael Burke Distinguished Intelligence Medal Citation," Burke Collection, Howard Gotlieb Archival Research Center at Boston University, n.d

6 Gratian M. Yatsevitch III interview.

7 "SHAM/OBOPUS Announcment by RNLUMPIT re His Withdrawal," BGFIEND documents, April 29, 1954.

8 Jon L. Lieb interview.

9 Margueritte Ulmer-Power interview.

10 Richardson, "My Father, the Spy."

11 John H. Richardson, *My Father the Spy* (New York: HarperCollins, 2005), 282.

12 Hunt and Aunapu, *American Spy*, 202–203.

13 Ibid., 235.

14 "The Watergate Story; Key Players: Howard Hunt," *Washington Post*, n.d.

15 Joan Cook, "Exhibition and Sale of Royal Jewels to Start Today," *New York Times* (1923–Current file), April 1, 1959.

16 "Former King Zog of Albania Dead," *New York Times* (1923–Current file), April 10, 1961.

17 "Hasan Dosti, 96, Dies; Ex-Official in Albania," *New York Times* (1923–Current file), January 31, 1991.

18 "Ex-Albanian Envoy Seized with Revolver on Plane," *New York Times* (1923–Current file), March 1, 1971.

19 "Abas Kupi, 75, Was Leader of Resistance in Albania," *New York Times* (1923–Current file), January 11, 1976.

20 "Said Bey Kryeziu," *New York Times* (1923–Current file), May 19, 1993.

21 Jozo Tomasevich, *War and Revolution in Yugoslavia* (Stanford University Press, 2001), 155.

22 Neil Tweedie, "Kim Philby: Father, husband, traitor, spy," *Telegraph*, January 23, 2013.

23 Will Stewart, "One of the greatest of Soviet spies," *Daily Mail Online*, December 12, 2011.

Bibliography

BGFIEND Documents

The CIA has declassified a large amount of operational documents related to its operations in Albania, ranging between 1947 and 1960. They are available at the National Archives and Records Administration, Archives II, at College Park, Maryland, under the heading *"Records of the Central Intelligence Agency, Record Group 263, OBOPUS/BGFIEND."* The documents are located in boxes 45 to 52 and grouped thematically in thirty-two volumes, based on the project or subproject that they cover. The following list provides a brief overview of the volumes.

Volume 1:   Country plan for Albania.

Volume 2:   Project outline, reviews, termination.

Volume 3:   Subproject OBLIVIOUS related to the National Committee for Free Albania.

Volume 4:   Subproject JBPARSON related to the Albanian Labor Services Company 4000 and the CIA cover training facility in West Germany.

Volume 5:   Activities of the first BGFIEND team parachuted in Albania in November 1950.

Volume 6:   Activities of the BGFIEND Apple Team infiltrated in Albania in May 1952. Its members were arrested by the Sigurimi shortly after and played back against the CIA between June 1952 and October 1953.

Volume 7:   Activities of the BGFIEND Willow Team, which operated in Albania with minor success, but without major losses between 1952 and 1953.

Volume 8:   Activities related to BGFIEND-VALUABLE leaflet drops.

Volume 9:   Subproject OBTUSE related to the propaganda campaign, including the NCFA newspaper *Shqipëria*.

Volume 10:   Subproject OBTEST related to broadcasts into Albania from Greece of clandestine radio Voice of Free Albania.

Volume 11:   Subprojects OBHUNT and OBSIDIOUS, which were minor infiltration missions that the CIA continued to conduct in 1954 after the debacle of Apple Team became public.

Volume 12:   Subproject BGSPEED, related to purchasing and fitting a yacht in the Mediterranean for offshore propaganda missions.

Volumes 13–30: Detailed operational records for BGFIEND.

Volume 31:   Photographs of Albanian agents in training at the CIA covert school in Germany.

Volume   Records of projects OBSTACLE and OBDURATE to
Obdurate: control the BKI political group between 1954 and 1956.

The alphabetical listing of the BGFIEND documents referenced in the book follows.

"1954 Operations." Box 46, volume 2, file 2 of 2. February 1, 1954.
"22 Oct 51 FIEND/VALUABLE Meeting." Box 49, volume 18, file 2 of 2. n.d.
"24 October Report." Box 49, volume 18, file 2 of 2. n.d.
"25 October Report." Box 49, volume 18, file 2 of 2. n.d.
"Agenda for Rome Conference." Box 49, volume 18, file 2 of 2. n.d.

"Aggression Actions." Box 52, volume 25, file 2 of 2. June 30, 1953.

"Aide-Memoire 21 July 1949." Box 48, volume 13, file 1 of 2. July 21, 1949.

"Air Support Aircraft." Box 49, volume 15, file 1 of 2. June 9, 1950.

"Albania." Box 48, volume 13, file 1 of 2. May 23, 1949.

"Albania." Box 49, volume 17, file 1 of 2. June 7, 1951.

"Albania Deception Operation." Box 46, volume 4, file 2 of 2. November 13, 1954.

"Albania Plan—Meeting between Abdyl Sula and State Department and OSO Representative." Box 48, volume 13, file 1 of 2. April 28, 1949.

"Albania, 31 August 1953." Box 51, volume 24, file 1 of 2. August 31, 1953.

"Albania, 8 August 1953." Box 51, volume 24, file 1 of 2. August 8, 1953.

"Albania: Possibility of Overthrowing Present Regime." Box 48, volume 13, file 1 of 2. May 27, 1949.

"Albanian Operation—Activities of Personnel of the Committee for Free Albania." Box 48, volume 14, file 1 of 2. November 15, 1949.

"Albanian Operation—Albanian IS Activities in Connection with the Committee for Free Albania." Box 48, volume 14, file 2 of 2. December 21, 1949.

"Albanian Operation—Fate of VALUABLE Teams in Albania Ref. SO DB-20024." Box 48, volume 14, file 2 of 2. n.d.

"Albanian Operation—Fate of VALUABLE Teams in Albania SO DB-20064." Box 48, volume 14, file 2 of 2. November 4, 1949.

"Albanian Operation—Plans for Assassination of Members of the Committee for Free Albania." Box 48, volume 14, file 2 of 2. December 2, 1949.

"Albanian Operations." Box 51, volume 24, file 1 of 2. August 31, 1953.

"Alleged AIS Training Camp for Albanian Agents at Munich." Box 46, volume 4, file 1 of 2. December 10, 1951.

"Annex C Plan for Albanian Coup." Box 45, volume 1, file 1 of 2. n.d.

"Annihilation of BGFiend Olive Team." Box 49, volume 18, file 1 of 2. August 14, 1951.

"Apostol Tenefi." Box 51, volume 24, file 1 of 2. March 23, 1953.

"Apple CE Review." Box 47, volume 6, file 1 of 2. November 13, 1953.

"Apple Resupply Briefing." Box 47, volume 6, file 1 of 2. January 31, 1953.

"Apple Security 19 March 1954." Box 47, volume 6, file 1 of 2. n.d.

"Apple Security Feb 10 1954." Box 47, volume 6, file 1 of 2. n.d.

"Apple Team Operational Plan—BGFiend." Box 47, volume 6, file 1 of 2. April 29, 1952.

"Apple Tree Team Resupply Missions." Box 47, volume 6, file 1 of 2. September 12, 1952.

"APPLETREE BGFIEND/SHAM." Box 47, volume 6, file 1 of 2. June 1952.

"Appraisal of Intelligence Material." Box 49, volume 16. January 4, 1951.

"Attached Letter." Box 49, volume 17, file 1 of 2. May 21, 1951.

"Basic Policy—Department of State." Box 49, volume 17, file 1 of 2. n.d.

"BGFIEND Apple W/T Traffic." Box 47, volume 6, file 1 of 2. October 21, 1952.

"BGFIEND Daily Progress Report June 16/17 1951." Box 49, volume 17, file 1 of 2. n.d.

"BGFIEND Daily Progress Report, 10 September 1951." Box 49, volume 18, file 1 of 2. n.d.

"BGFIEND HSTEIN Status Report." Box 46, volume 2, file 2 of 2. May 20, 1952.

"BGFIEND Status Report for Consultants Meeting." Box 49, volume 18, file 1 of 2. August 15, 1951.

"BGFIEND Status Report, 9 January 1951." Box 49, volume 16. January 9, 1951.

"BGFIEND Talks with [REDACTED] and [REDACTED] in Athens on 19 June and 2 July 1951." Box 49, volume 18, file 1 of 2. August 3, 1951.

"BGFIEND/Operational Hamdi Bogdani." Box 51, volume 23, file 2 of 2. December 11, 1952.

"BGFIEND/Rome Monthly Survey Report 28 November 1952 to 6 January 1953." Box 46, volume 3. January 6, 1953.

"BGFIEND-OPC Action against Shipping in Albania." Box 49, volume 15, file 1 of 2. May 19, 1950.

"Brief Summary of Medical Activities in HBBASIS from May 15 to 1 September 1951." Box 46, volume 4, file 1 of 2. n.d.

"Cable 2037Z 5 Jul 56." Box 46, volume 3. n.d.

"Cable 2306." Box 46, volume 5. May 9, 1953.

"Cable 2306Z 6 Nov 53." Box 47, volume 6, file 1 of 2. November 6, 1953.

"Cable 2354Z 30 Apr 56." Box 46, volume 3. 1956.

"Cable DIR 03050." Box 46, volume 5. May 5, 1953.

"Cable FRAN 9580." Box 46, volume 4, file 2 of 2. December 13, 1952.

"CE Review of Apple Trial." Box 47, volume 6, file 1 of 2. May 18, 1954.

"CIA Information Report No 00-B-8501-49." Box 48, volume 13, file 2 of 2. n.d.

"Communications Comments re APPLETREE CE Review." Box 46, volume 6, file 1 of 2. January 13, 1954.

"Composition of Polish Aircrew—BGFIEND." Box 49, volume 15, file 1 of 2. August 29, 1950.

"Conference with [REDACTED] on 16 and 17 September 1949 re Albanian operation." Box 48, volume 14, file 1 of 2. October 3, 1949.

"Conversation between King Zog and [REDACTED] on 26 and 27 October." Box 47, volume 6, file 1 of 2. n.d.

"Conversation with Department of State on 18 October 1951—Current Status of BGFIEND." Box 49, volume 18, file 2 of 2. October 17, 1951.

"Conversation with King Zog at Meeting on Wednesday, 12 September 1951." Box 47, volume 6, file 1 of 2. September 18, 1951.

"Conversation with King Zog of Albania." Box 49, volume 18, file 1 of 2. August 23, 1951.

"Conversation with King Zog of Albania on 17 August 1951." Box 47, volume 6, file 1 of 2. August 23, 1951.

"Conversation with King Zog of Albania on 30 August 1951." Box 47, volume 6, file 1 of 2. September 24, 1951.

"Conversation with State Department Representatives concerning Albanian and Bulgarian Operations." Box 49, volume 17, file 1 of 2. April 3, 1951.

"Conversations with Albanian Leaders in the United States." Box 49, volume 14, file 1 of 2. October 4, 1949.

"Current Status of Project BGFIEND, with Particular Reference to OPC Organization." Box 49, volume 14, file 1 of 2. August 16, 1949.

"Cypress Debriefing." Box 49, volume 18, file 1 of 2. August 31, 1951.

"Daily Log, 5 January 1954." Box 52, volume 27, file 1 of 2. n.d.

"Daily Log, 8 February 1954." Box 52, volume 27, file 1 of 2. n.d.

"Daily Log, 8 January 1954." Box 52, volume 27, file 1 of 2. n.d.

"Daily Progress Report 10 October 1951." Box 49, volume 18, file 2 of 2. n.d.

"Daily Progress Report for Monday, 24 November 1952." Box 51, volume 23, file 2 of 2. November 24, 1952.

"Daily Report—Tuesday 3 July 1951." Box 49, volume 17, file 2 of 2. n.d.

"Danger of GNA continuing pursuit of guerrillas across Albanian border." Box 48, volume 13, file 1 of 2. July 21, 1949.

"Debriefing of Pine Tree Team—Part I - BGFiend." Box 51, volume 22, file 2 of 2. July 7, 1952.

"Development Concerning Albanian Plan." Box 45, volume 1, file 1 of 2. September 4, 1953.

"Discussions of 9 May 1950." Box 49, volume 15, file 1 of 2. May 11, 1950.

"Disposal of Yacht 'Juanita.'" Box 48, volume 12. February 28, 1955.

"Draft Memorandum of 21 October 1949." Box 48, volume 14, file 1 of 2. October 21, 1949.

"EE-1 Daily Report, 16 October 1951." Box 49, volume 18, file 2 of 2. n.d.

"EE-1 Daily Report, Friday, 27 July." Box 49, volume 17, file 2 of 2. July 27, 1951.

"EE-1 Daily Report, Monday July 30, 1951." Box 49, volume 17, file 2 of 2. n.d.

"EE-1 Daily Report, Tuesday 7 August 1951." Box 49, volume 18, file 1 of 2. n.d.

"EE-1 Daily Report, Tuesday July 24, 1951." Box 49, volume 17, file 2 of 2. n.d.

"EE-1 Daily Report, Wednesday 15 August 1951." Box 49, volume 18, file 1 of 2. n.d.

"Employment of Albanian Refugees for Intelligence Purposes." Box 48, volume 13, file 1 of 2. February 21, 1949.

"Events Leading up to the Premature Arrival of BGFIEND Covert Aircraft in Greece." Box 49, volume 15, file 1 of 2. October 9, 1950.

"Excerpt from Top Secret Cable 10 December 1951." Box 47, volume 6, file 1 of 2. n.d.

"Extract from Monthly Progress Report, EE-1, for April 1951." Box 49, volume 17, file 1 of 2. n.d.

"Extract from Monthly Progress Report, EE-1, for May 1951." Box 49, volume 17, file 1 of 2. n.d.

"Extract from Report of Operations for the Quarter Ended 30 June 1951." Box 49, volume 17, file 1 of 2. n.d.

"Extract from Report of Operations for the Quarter Ended 31 March 1951." Box 49, volume 16. n.d.

"Fiend Daily Report 2 June 1951." Box 49, volume 17, file 1 of 2. n.d.

"Fiend-Valuable 25 September 1951." Box 49, volume 18, file 1 of 2. n.d.

"First Operational Commo Flight - HBPixie." Box 46, volume 5. November 16, 1950.

"First Team Drop into HBPixie, 11–12 November 1950." Box 46, volume 5. November 13, 1950.

"Fiscal Year 1954 Operational Program for Albania." Box 46, volume 2, file 2 of 2. n.d.

"Fiscal Year 1955 Operational Program for Albania." Box 46, volume 2, file 2 of 2. n.d.

"Formal Statement." Box 46, volume 3. n.d.

"FY 1953 Program." Box 46, volume 2, file 2 of 2. n.d.

"Greek Knowledge of Albanian Operation." Box 48, volume 14, file 1 of 2. August 6, 1949.

"Guidance for 1954 Operational Season." Box 46, volume 2, file 2 of 2. February 18, 1954.

"History of OPC/EE-1." Box 48, volume 13, file 2 of 2. n.d.

"Identification of W/T Operators." Box 47, volume 6, file 1 of 2. November 17, 1952.

"Intelligence Operations against Albania from Italy and Greece." Box 48, volume 13, file 1 of 2. May 3, 1949.

"Intelligence Report No. 5635.140." Box 52, volume 26, file 1 of 2. November 18, 1953.

"Intelligence Summary No. 10." Box 49, volume 17, file 1 of 2. April 4, 1951.

"King Zog of Albania." Box 52, volume 25, file 2 of 2. July 24, 1953.

"King Zog's Offer to Help Penetrate the Muslim Brotherhood in Egypt." Box 51, volume 23, file 1 of 2. September 23, 1952.

"Kraja-Shyti-Mersini D/A Operation." Box 45, volume Obdurate. December 20, 1954.

"LCBATLAND Leaflet Material." Box 49, volume 18, file 1 of 2. August 7, 1951.

"Leaflet Drop Schedule to Albania." Box 47, volume 8. n.d.

"Letter from Red Team." Box 46, volume 5. April 24, 1952.

"Letter to Chief of Mission in Frankfurt." Box 46, volume 4, file 2 of 2. August 14, 1953.

"Letter to Pilgrim." Box 48, volume 14, file 1 of 2. August 10, 1949.

"Liaison with the British in Washington on Projects FIEND and VALUABLE." Box 49, volume 18, file 1 of 2. August 28, 1951.

"Local Reaction to Apprehension of Zejnel Shehu Group." Box 47, volume 6, file 1 of 2. n.d.

"Loeb Estate Covert Site" Box 46, volume 4, file 1 of 2. n.d.

"Materials for Consultants Meeting." Box 51, volume 22, file 2 of 2. July 9, 1952.

"Meeting in Frankfurt on BGFIEND." Box 49, volume 17, file 1 of 2. May 2, 1951.

"Meeting of Joint Policy Committee." Box 48, volume 14, file 2 of 2. November 3, 1949.

"Meeting of the Joint Policy Committee for Operation BGFIEND." Box 48, volume 14, file 2 of 2. November 21, 1949.

"Meeting on Albania." Box 48, volume 13, file 1 of 2. May 4, 1949.

"Meeting on FIEND on 27 February 1950." Box 49, volume 15, file 1 of 2. March 1, 1950.

"Meeting with Ex-King Zog." Box 49, volume 18, file 1 of 2. August 20, 1951.

"Meeting with Lord Jellicoe and Mr. Joyce." Box 48, volume 14, file 2 of 2. November 12, 1949.

"Meeting with OSO Re: Current Situation in Albania." Box 49, volume 17, file 1 of 2. April 11, 1951.

"Memo." Box 49, volume 15, file 1 of 2. April 3, 1950.

"Memo 28 June 1951." Box 49, volume 17, file 1 of 2. n.d.

"Memo for the record of Conversations with King Zog." Box 48, volume 13, file 1 of 2. June 17, 1949.

"Memo from B.Y. Berry to General Van Fleet and General Jenkins." Box 48, volume 13, file 1 of 2. July 25, 1949.

"Memo of 2 September 1949." Box 48, volume 14, file 1 of 2. September 2, 1949.

"Memorandum." Box 48, volume 13, file 1 of 2. July 27, 1949.

"Memorandum for the Record." Box 46, volume 4, file 1 of 2. July 21, 1952.

"Memorandum of 21 September 1949." Box 48, volume 14, file 1 of 2. September 21, 1949.

"Memorandum of 27 September 1949." Box 48, volume 14, file 1 of 2. September 27, 1949.

"Memorandum of 28 October 1949." Box 48, volume 14, file 1 of 2. October 28, 1949.

"Memorandum of a Conversation with Ahmet Zogu." Box 48, volume 13, file 1 of 2. May 5, 1949.

"Memorandum of a Conversation with Mithat Frasheri." Box 48, volume 13, file 1 of 2. April 30, 1949.

"Memorandum of Meeting 10 September 1949." Box 48, volume 14, file 1 of 2. September 12, 1949.

"Memorandum of Understanding on Establishment of Pixie Base in Germany." Box 46, volume 4, file 1 of 2. January 31, 1951.

"Memorandum on FIEND-VALUABLE Operation." Box 48, volume 14, file 2 of 2. December 6, 1949.

"Minutes Fiend/Valuable Conference Rome, 22-24 October 1951." Box 49, volume 18, file 2 of 2. n.d.

"Monthly Project Status Report, October 1951." Box 49, volume 18, file 2 of 2. n.d.

"Monthly Project Status Report, September 1951." Box 49, volume 18, file 2 of 2. n.d.

"NCFA Declaration." Box 48, volume 14, file 1 of 2. n.d.

"Note to Military Junta." Box 46, volume 5. July 17, 1953.

"Note to Military Junta on Situation of Red and Green Team Members Who Took Refuge in Yugoslavia." Box 46, volume 5. April 15, 1953.

"OBOPUS Security Review of Apple/2—Part I." Box 47, volume 6, file 1 of 2. December 10, 1953.

"OBOPUS Status Report, February 1954." Box 52, volume 27, file 1 of 2. n.d.

"OBOPUS Status Report, January 1954." Box 52, volume 27, file 1 of 2. n.d.

"OBOPUS Status Report, March 1954." Box 52, volume 27, file 1 of 2. n.d.

"OBOPUS Status Report, May 1954." Box 52, volume 27, file 2 of 2. n.d.

"OBTUSE Routing Sheet." Box 47, volume 9. January 8, 1960.

"Offie's Memo, 6 July 1949." Box 48, volume 13, file 1 of 2. July 6, 1949.

"OPC Cable 1424." Box 49, volume 15, file 1 of 2. March 28, 1950.

"OPC Liaison with Other Intelligence Services." Box 49, volume 15, file 1 of 2. March 7, 1950.

"OPC Plans and Operations in Albania." Box 49, volume 15, file 1 of 2. May 17, 1950.

"Operation Valuable." Box 48, volume 13, file 2 of 2. n.d.

"Operational Plan and Operational Clearance Request for Coup-de-Main Team Members." Box 51, volume 22, file 2 of 2. July 16, 1952.

"Operational Review, OBSTACLE/OBDURATE." Box 45, volume Obdurate. January 31, 1955.

"Operations Against Albania." Box 45, volume 1, file 1 of 2. February 2, 1953.

"OSO/OPC Infiltration, Albania, 24 June 1951." Box 49, volume 17, file 1 of 2. June 26, 1951.

"Outline for Operational Plan for Albania." Box 48, volume 13, file 1 of 2. n.d.

"Paramilitary Plans for Coup d'Etat(s) in Albania." Box 45, volume 1, file 1 of 2. February 6, 1953.

"Plan for Albania." Box 48, volume 13, file 1 of 2. June 15, 1949.

"Policy—Albania." Box 49, volume 17, file 2 of 2. July 6, 1951.

"Possessions of Deceased Agents." Box 53, volume 29, file 1 of 2. March 31, 1955.

"Progress Report BGFiend/BGFlume for May and June 1951." Box 49, volume 17, file 2 of 2. July 10, 1951.

"Project BGFIEND." Box 46, volume 2, file 1 of 2. July 1, 1949.

"Project OBDURATE (Approval)" Box 45, volume Obdurate. August 26, 1954.

"Project Outline BGFIEND." Box 46, volume 2, file 1 of 2. n.d.

"Projected 1952 OPC and OSO Operations in Albania." Box 46, volume 2, file 2 of 2. December 12, 1952.

"Proposal to Overthrow Present Regime in Albania." Box 48, volume 13, file 1 of 2. January 11, 1949.

"Pros and Cons of Proposal to Detach Albania from the Soviet Orbit." Box 45, volume 1, file 2 of 2. June 4, 1952.

"QKFervor Activities 1951." Box 49, volume 16. n.d.

"Reasons for Conducting OPC Albanian Operation on Joint Basis with British." Box 48, volume 13, file 1 of 2. July 11, 1949.

"Recapitulation of OBOPUS Operations, 1 January to 31 December 1953." Box 52, volume 27, file 1 of 2. February 18, 1953.

"Reconsideration of OSO's Operations Against Albania." Box 49, volume 16. n.d.

"Red and Green Team Commitments." Box 46, volume 5. June 9, 1956.

"Relations between CHARITY and BGFIEND." Box 49, volume 15, file 1 of 2. August 21, 1950.

"Release of Apple Case for Use by Office of Training." Box 47, volume 6, file 1 of 2. April 20, 1954.

"Renewal of Project OBDURATE." Box 45, volume Obdurate. August 29, 1955.

"Report of Conversation with King Zog." Box 49, volume 18, file 1 of 2. August 23, 1951.

"Report of Halil Nerguti." Box 46, volume 5. February 8, 1952.

"Report of Interview between Colonel Smiley and Zotos." Box 48, volume 14, file 2 of 2. n.d.

"Request for Authorization for Reproduction of the Albanian Lek." Box 50, volume 19. n.d.

"Resistance Situation." Box 49, volume 15, file 1 of 2. August 21, 1950.

"Review of Apple/3 W/T Contacts." Box 47, volume 6, file 1 of 2. August 18, 1953.

"RNCASTING Correspondence, 16 March 1954." Box 52, volume 27, file 1 of 2. n.d.

"Scheduled Airdrop to Albania—Instructions of the Director of Central Intelligence." Box 49, volume 17, file 1 of 2. April 18, 1951.

"Security Review of Apple Team Operations." Box 47, volume 6, file 1 of 2. October 21, 1953.

"Security Review of Willow Team Operations." Box 52, volume 27, file 1 of 2. March 9, 1954.

"SGAA-5441." Box 52, volume 25, file 2 of 2. August 14, 1953.

"SHAM/OBOPUS Announcment by RNLUMPIT re His Withdrawal." Box 52, volume 27, file 2 of 2. April 29, 1954.

"SHAM/OBOPUS Transmittal of RNCASTING Message." Box 47, volume 6, file 1 of 2. May 1, 1954.

"Situation Report and Recommendations for Action." Box 52, volume 26, file 2 of 2. December 3, 1953.

"Special Leaflet devoted to RNPUTLOG." Box 52, volume 27, file 2 of 2. June 12, 1954.

"Special Leaflet, April 20 1954." Box 52, volume 27, file 2 of 2. n.d.

"Status of Former King Zog of Albania." Box 52, volume 26, file 2 of 2. December 3, 1953.

"Status of Former King Zog of Albania." Box 52, volume 27, file 1 of 2. December 24, 1953.

"Summary of MacLean Profiles for Albanian Politicians." Box 48, volume 13, file 1 of 2. n.d.

"Telecon Conference." Box 48, volume 13, file 1 of 2. July 24, 1949.

"Telegram from Middle East." Box 48, volume 14, file 2 of 2. November 3, 1949.

"Telegrams 1, 2, 3." Box 48, volume 14, file 2 of 2. November 18–19, 1949.

"Telephone Conversation Concerning visit of ex-King Zog (Albania) to Department." Box 49, volume 18, file 1 of 2. August 1, 1951.

"Termination Approval for OBHUNT." Box 48, volume 11. January 31, 1958.

"Termination of AIRBRAKE, AIRWORTHY, and RNDEPLOY." Box 47, volume 7. April 9, 1954.

"Text of proposed telegram to US diplomatic missions." Box 48, volume 14, file 1 of 2. August 25, 1949.

"The Albanian Operation." Box 48, volume 13, file 1 of 2. March 21, 1949.

"The Independence of Albania." Box 49, volume 17, file 1 of 2. June 20, 1951.

"The Possibility of an appeal to Senator McCarthy for investigation of the NCFA." Box 46, volume 3. May 15, 1953.

"Tirana Trials of CIA Agents." Box 47, volume 6, file 1 of 2. April 1954.

"Training of Pixies for BGFIEND." Box 46, volume 4, file 1 of 2. January 19, 1951.

"Translation of French text handed Colonel Fiske by emissary of Yarborough." Box 48, volume 13, file 1 of 2. July 26, 1949.

"Transmittal of BGFiend Documents." Box 46, volume 4, file 1 of 2. April 12, 1950.

"Transmittal of BGFiend Documents." Box 49, volume 15, file 1 of 2. n.d.

Books, Articles, Online Sources, and Interviews

"A Look Back . . . The National Committee for Free Europe, 1949." CIA.gov. May 29, 2007. https://www.cia.gov/news-information/featured-story-archive/2007-featured-story-archive/a-look-back.html (accessed February 26, 2013).

"Abas Kupi, 75, Was Leader of Resistance in Albania." *New York Times* (1923–Current file). January 11, 1976. http://search.proquest.com/docview/122972189?accountid=34227.

"Agjenti 91-vjecar i CIA: Misioni per te rrezuar Hoxhen." Forumi Shqiptar. August 19, 2009. http://www.forumishqiptar.com/showthread.php?p=2165894 (accessed March 1, 2013).

Agnelli, Gianni. Interview by Pat Mitchell and Jeremy Isaacs. *Cold War* (Episode 3: Marshall Plan). CNN. 1998.

"Albania expected to resume secret talks with Britain." The CIA Records Search Tool at NARA II in College Park, Maryland (hereafter CREST Database). August 26, 1985.

"Albania Seeks to Resume Trade with Italy." CREST Database. July 19, 1950.

"Albanians Seize Briton." *New York Times* (1923–Current file). February 16, 1944. http://search.proquest.com/docview/107041264?accountid=34227 (accessed December 22, 2013).

Amery, Julian. *Sons of the Eagle*. London: Macmillan & Co., 1948.

"Assembly of Captive European Nations, Records, 1953–1972." University of Minnesota Immigration History Research Center. October 5, 2012. http://www.ihrc.umn.edu/research/vitrage/all/am/GENassembly.htm (accessed April 19, 2013).

Barber, Michael. "John le Carré: An Interrogation." *New York Times*. September 25, 1977. http://www.nytimes.com/books/99/03/21/specials/lecarre-interrogation.html (accessed January 1, 2014).

Barber, Tony. "6.5m in war gold returns to Albania after 49 years." The Independent, February 23, 1996.

Benanti, Paolo. *La Guerra Piu Lunga*. Rome, Italy: Mursia, 1964.

Benson, Robert L. "The Venona Story." NSA.gov. January 15, 2009. http://www.nsa.gov/about/_files/cryptologic_heritage/publications/coldwar/venona_story.pdf (accessed February 27, 2013).

Berger, D. H., Major, USMC. "The Use of Covert Paramilitary Activity as a Policy Tool: An Analysis of Operations Conducted by the United States Central Intelligence Agency, 1949–1951." Federation of American Scientists, Intelligence Resource Program. May 22, 1995. http://www.fas.org/irp/eprint/berger.htm (accessed April 12, 2013).

Bethell, Nicholas. *Betrayed*. New York: Time Books, a division of Random House, 1984.

———. "Profits and losses of treachery." *Independent*. September 6, 1994. http://www.independent.co.uk/voices/profits-and-losses-of-treachery-victims-of-kim-philbys-betrayals-are-staking-a-claim-to-the-cash-realised-at-a-recent-auction-of-his-effects-says-nicholas-bethell-1447065.html (accessed February 20, 2013).

Blumenthal, Ralph. "Axis Supporters Enlisted by US in Postwar Role." *New York Times* (1923–Current file). June 20, 1982. http://search.proquest.com/docview/121990260?accountid=34227.

Borovik, Genrikh. *The Philby Files*. New York: Little, Brown and Company, 1994.

Burke, Michael. *Outrageous Good Fortune*. Boston: Little, Brown and Company, 1984.

CIA History Staff. "DCI's First 100 Days." Central Intelligence Agency. April 14, 2007. https://www.cia.gov/library/center-for-the-study-of-intelligence/csi-publications/csi-studies/studies/95unclass/100Days.html (accessed April 14, 2013).

"CIA Museum Directorate of Science and Technology." CIA.gov. July 23, 2012. https://www.cia.gov/about-cia/cia-museum/experience-the-collection/text-version/collection-by-subject/directorate-of-science-and-technology.html (accessed February 26, 2013).

"CIA's Role in the Overthrow of Arbenz." CIA Freedom of Information Act. May 12, 1975. http://www.foia.cia.gov/sites/default/files/document_conversions/89801/DOC_0000919933.pdf (accessed May 1, 2013).

Colby, William and Peter Forbath. *Honorable Men: My Life in the CIA*. New York: Simon & Schuster, 1978.

Cook, Joan. "Exhibition and Sale of Royal Jewels to Start Today." *New York Times* (1923–Current file). April 1, 1959. http://search.proquest.com/docview/114673562?accountid=34227.

"Corfu Channel (United Kingdom v. Albania)." The Hague Justice Portal. February 15, 2013. http://www.haguejusticeportal.net/index.php?id=6287 (accessed June 12, 2013).

Corke, Sarah-Jane. "US Covert Operations and Cold War Strategy: Truman, Secret Warfare and the CIA, 1945-53" in *Studies in Intelligence*. London and New York: Routledge, 2008.

The Cost of Treachery. VHS. Produced by BBC. 1984.

Cullather, Nicholas. *Secret History: The CIA's Classified Account of Its Operations in Guatemala 1952–1954*. Stanford, CA: Stanford University Press, 2006.

Dervishi, Ferdinand. "Mehmet Shehu vrer për Kadri Hazbiun: Pi raki e puthet me diversantët." Infoarkiv: Arkiva Mediatike Shqiptare. May 29, 2010. http://lajme.shqiperia.com/lajme/artikull/iden/1046851779/titulli/Mehmet-Shehu-vrer-per-Kadri-Hazbiun-Pi-raki-e-puthet-me-diversantet# (accessed April 14, 2013).

———. "Radioloja." enver-hoxha.net. n.d. http://www.enver-hoxha.net/content/content_shqip/navig-majtas/cont.nga_shtypi_dhe_mediat/radioloja.pdf (accessed April 13, 2013).

Djilas, Milovan. *Conversations with Stalin*. New York: Harcourt, Brace & World, 1962.

Dodani, Mark. "Zbarkimi i Hamit Matjanit, Hazbiu si fshatar në bandat e veriut." Interview by Fatos Veliu. *BalkanWeb*. August 17, 2012.

———. "Në verën e '52-it u futëm në grupin diversionist të Zenel Shehut." Interview by Fatos Veliu. *BalkanWeb*. August 16, 2012.

Dorril, Stephen. *MI6: Inside the Covert World of Her Majesty's Secret Intelligence Service*. New York: The Free Press, 2000.

Dosti Family. *Hasan Dosti: Një Jetë për Çështjen Shqiptare*. Tirana: BOTART, 2008.

"E vranë apo e helmuan Alush Lleshanakun?" Zeri Yt! Media Sociale Shqiptare. April 16, 2011. http://www.zeriyt.com/e-vrane-apo-e-helmuan-alush-lleshanakun-t83541.0.html (accessed April 13, 2013).

Elkins, Walter. "Labor Service Division List of Units." *US Army in Germany*. February 20, 2013. http://usarmygermany.com/Units/HqUSAREUR/USAREUR_LaborSvc.htm#List1977.

Elsie, Robert. "1983 Abaz Ermenji: Overthrowing the Communist Regime." Texts and Documents of Albanian History. n.d. http://www.albanianhistory.net/texts20_3/AH1983.html (accessed March 5, 2013).

———. Historical Dictionary of Albania. Lanham, MD: Rowman and Littlefield, 2010.

———. Historical Dictionary of Kosovo. Lanham, MD: Rowman and Littlefield, 2004.

"Ex-Albanian Envoy Seized with Revolver on Plane." *New York Times* (1923–Current file). March 1, 1971. http://search.proquest.com/docview/119386219?accountid=34227.

"Ex-King Zog Buys Syosset Estate with 'Bucket of Diamonds, Rubies.'" *New York Times* (1923–Current file). September 19, 1951. http://search.proquest.com/docview/111901371?accountid=34227.

Felix, Christopher. *A Short Course in the Secret War*, Fourth Edition. Lanham, MD: Madison Books, 2001.

Fischer, Bernd Jürgen. *Albania at War, 1939–1945*. West Lafayette, IN: Purdue University Press, 1999.

"Foreign Relations, 1950–1955 The Intelligence Community." US Department of State Archive. December 21, 2007. http://2001-2009.state.gov/documents/organization/96783.pdf (accessed April 13, 2013).

"Former King Zog of Albania Dead." *New York Times* (1923–Current file). April 10, 1961. http://search.proquest.com/docview/115358276?accountid=34227.

Fowler, Brenda. "Banished for Their Father's Sins." *New York Times* (1923–Current file). May 17, 1992. http://search.proquest.com/docview/108942151?accountid=34227.

"Free Albania Unit Named." *New York Times* (1923–Current file). August 27, 1949. http://search.proquest.com/docview/105828528?accountid=34227.

"From 'Sons of the Eagle' to Michael Burke." Burke Collection, Howard Gotlieb Archival Research Center at Boston University, n.d.

Gashi, Agim. "Ja e vërteta për vrasjen e deputetit Bardhok Biba." Akllapi Net. September 6, 2009. http://agim.poeticforum.com/t5059-ja-e-verteta-per-vrasjen-e-deputetit-bardhok-biba (accessed April 13, 2013).

———. "Postvrasja e deputetit Bardhok Biba/Përkujtohet 60-vjetori i vrasjes së 14 burrave." Akllapi Net. September 6, 2009. http://agim.poeticforum.com/t5058-postvrasja-e-deputetit-bardhok-biba-perkujtohet-60-vjetori-i-vrasjes-se-14-burrave (accessed April 13, 2013).

Grose, Peter. *Operation Rollback: America's Secret War Behind the Iron Curtain.* New York: Houghton Mifflin, 2000.

"Guatemala Briefing." CIA Freedom of Information Act. June 5, 1954. http://www.foia.cia.gov/sites/default/files/document_conversions/89801/DOC_0000919933.pdf (accessed May 1, 2013).

"Harold 'Kim' Philby and the Cambridge Three." PBS/WGBH/NOVA. January 2002. http://www.pbs.org/wgbh/nova/venona/dece_philby.html (accessed February 15, 2013).

"Harvard University Obituary and Death Notice Collection." Genealogy-buff.com. January 18, 2011. http://www.genealogybuff.com/ma/harvard/webbbs_config.pl/read/27 (accessed February 24, 2013).

"Hasan Dosti, 96, Dies; Ex-Official in Albania." *New York Times* (1923–Current file). January 31, 1991. http://search.proquest.com/docview/108834466?accountid=34227.

Hunt, E. Howard, and Greg Aunapu. *American Spy: My Secret History in the CIA, Watergate and Beyond.* Hoboken, NJ: John Wiley and Sons, 2007.

"J.E. Jacobs Telegram No. 163." National Archives and Records Administration, Archives II at College Park, Maryland, (hereafter, NARA), Tirana US Mission General Records, Record Group 84, Box 7, Folder 800. June 27, 1946.

"James G. McCargar." UNESCO in the Spotlight: Science and Communications. May 31, 2007. http://unescoscience.blogspot.com/2007/05/james-g-mccargar.html (accessed February 22, 2013).

Juntunen, Kim M. "US Army Attaches and the Spanish Civil War, 1936–1939: The Gathering of Technical and Tactical Intelligence." The Defense

Technical Information Center (DTIC). May 4, 1990. http://www.dtic. mil/cgi-bin/GetTRDoc?AD=ADA222347 (accessed April 12, 2013).

Kaloci, Dashnor. "Si na stërvisnin oficerët amerikanë në Gjermani." Dashnor Kaloci Blog. February 20, 2013. http://dashkaloci.blogspot. com/2006_11_01_archive.html (accessed January 4, 2014).

Kapinova, Klajd. "Hamid Toshi (Saiti), Martir i rënë si parashutist në Shqipëri." Shqiperiaetnike.de. n.d. http://www.shqiperiaetnike.de/html/ body_klajd_kapinova.html (accessed January 4, 2014).

"King Zog Here for Visit." *New York Times* (1923–Current file). July 27, 1951. http://search.proquest.com/docview/112175723?accountid=34227.

"King Zog's Wedding Celebrations in Tirana." *The West Australian*, April 30, 1938. http://trove.nla.gov.au/ndp/del/article/41681626 (accessed December 21, 2013).

Lacey, Robert. *Monarch: The Life and Reign of Elizabeth II*. New York: Simon and Schuster, 2008.

Latell, Brian. *Castro's Secrets: The CIA and Cuba's Intelligence Machine*. New York: Palgrave Macmillan, 2012.

"Letter from Burke to Abaz Kupi." From the Burke Collection, Howard Gotlieb Archival Research Center at Boston University, n.d.

Lieb, Jon L. "Reminiscences about Joseph C. Lieb." Interview by Albert Lulushi. January 2014.

Lucas, Peter. *The OSS in World War II Albania*. Jefferson, North Carolina: McFarland and Company, Inc., 2007.

Mann, Siegbert. "Insignia of the Labor Service." History of the US Force in Germany. Labor Service and Civilian Support Organization. February 20, 2013. http://www.usfava.com/LaborService/abzeichen.LS.htm.

———. "Labor Service Einheiten (Units)." History of the US Force in Germany. Labor Service and Civilian Support Organization. February 20, 2013. http://www.usfava.com/LaborService/units.LS.htm.

McCargar, James. "Reminiscences of Operation Fiend." Interview by Thomas McNiff, Jr. McCargar Collection, Howard Gotlieb Archival Research Center at Boston University. May 2, 1985.

"Memorandum of a Conference with the President, White House, Washington, March 17, 1960, 2:30 p.m." Foreign Relations of the United States, 1958–1960, Volume VI, Cuba, Document 486. March 17, 1960. http://history .state.gov/historicaldocuments/frus1958-60v06/d486 (accessed May 4, 2013).

"Michael Burke Distinguished Intelligence Medal Citation." Burke Collection, Howard Gotlieb Archival Research Center at Boston University, n.d.

"Midhat Frasheri, Albanian Ex-Aide." *New York Times* (1923–Current file). October 4, 1949. http://search.proquest.com/docview/105942761?accountid=34227 (accessed December 22, 2013).

Mingst, Karen. "International Court of Justice (ICJ)." Encyclopædia Britannica Online. n.d. http://www.britannica.com/EBchecked/topic/290850/International-Court-of-Justice-ICJ (accessed February 15, 2013).

"Nassau Will Sell Ex-King Zog's Estate; Tax Lien to be Offered Dec. 1 for $2,654." *New York Times* (1923–Current file. November 7, 1952. http://search.proquest.com/docview/112308950?accountid=34227.

"NSC 10/2." NARA, Records of the National Security Council, Record Group 273 (hereafter, NSC documents). June 18, 1948.

"NSC 4-A, NSC Minutes, 4th Meeting." NSC documents. December 17, 1947.

"OSS Biographies of Albanian Leaders." NARA, Tirana US Mission General Records, Record Group 84, Box 7. 1945.

Pano, Nicholas C. "Albania: The Last Bastion of Stalinism." *East Central Europe, Yesterday, Today, Tomorrow*. Edited by Milorad M. Drachkovitch. Stanford, CA: Hoover Institution Press, 1982.

Pearson, Owen. *Albania in the Twentieth Century, A History: Volume I: Albania and King Zog*. London, New York: Center for Albanian Studies in association with I. B. Tauris, 2004.

———. *Albania in the Twentieth Century, A History: Volume II: Albania in Occupation and War*. London, New York: Center for Albanian Studies in association with I. B. Taurus, 2005.

———. *Albania in the Twentieth Century, A History: Volume III: Albania as Dictatorship and Democracy, 1945–99*. London, New York: Center for Albanian Studies in association with I. B. Tauris, 2006.

Pedlow, Gregory W.; Welzenbach, Donald E. (1992). *The Central Intelligence Agency and Overhead Reconnaissance: The U-2 and OXCART Programs, 1954–1974*. Washington, DC: History Staff, Central Intelligence Agency. http://www.gwu.edu/sites/www.gwu.edu/files/downloads/U2%20%20history%20complete.pdf (accessed December 21, 2013).

Peszke, Michael Alfred. *The Polish Underground Army, the Western Allies, and the Failure of Strategic Unity in World War II*. Jefferson, North Carolina: McFarland & Company, 2005.

Philby, Kim. *My Silent War: The Autobiography of a Spy*. New York: Modern Library, 2002.

Prados, John. *Safe for Democracy: The Secret Wars of the CIA*. Chicago: Ivan R. Dee, 2006.

"Procesi i Tiranes." Gazeta Shqiptare Online. May 14, 2012. http://www.balkanweb.com/gazetav5/newsadmin/preview.php?id=115856 (accessed February 23, 2013).

"Report of the Attorney General to the Congress of the United States on the Administration of the Foreign Agents Act." 1952, 88.

Richardson, John H. *My Father the Spy*. New York: HarperCollins, 2005.

———. "My Father, the Spy." *Esquire*. January 29, 2009. http://www.esquire.com/features/father-spy-0399#ixzz2MD4EBRgt (accessed March 17, 2013).

"Robert Low." The New York Preservation Archive Project. July 16, 2002. http://www.nypap.org/content/robert-low (accessed February 24, 2013).

"Said Bey Kryeziu." *New York Times* (1923–Current file). May 19, 1993. http://search.proquest.com/docview/109154495?accountid=34227.

Siegel, Adam B. "The Use of Naval Forces in the Post-War Era: US Navy and US Marine Corps Crisis Response Activity, 1946–1990." The Navy Department Library. n.d. http://www.history.navy.mil/library/online/forces_cold.htm#table6 (accessed May 1, 2013).

Smith, W. Thomas. *Encyclopedia of the Central Intelligence Agency*. Facts on File, 2003.

"Soviet Military Mission to Albania." CREST Database. July 16, 1953.

"Soviet Use of Assassination and Kidnapping." CIA Center for the Study of Intelligence. February 1964. https://www.cia.gov/library/center-for-the-study-of-intelligence/kent-csi/vol19no3/html/v19i3a01p_0001.htm (accessed May 6, 2013).

Stewart, Will. "One of the greatest of Soviet spies." Daily Mail Online. December 12, 2011. http://www.dailymail.co.uk/news/article-2073234/British-traitor-Kim-Philby-praised-new-book-1-greatest-Soviet-spies.html (accessed February 27, 2013).

Stolz, Richard. "Assignment Trieste: A Case Officer's First Tour." CIA Center for the Study of Intelligence. February 19, 2013. https://www.cia.gov/library/center-for-the-study-of-intelligence/kent-csi/vol37no1/html/v37i1a04p_0001.htm.

Sulzberger, Cyrus L. "Exiles Map Fight on Tirana Regime." *New York Times* (1923–Current file). August 29, 1949. http://search.proquest.com/docview/105951953?accountid=34227.

————. "West Held Easing Stand on Albania." *New York Times* (1923–Current file). March 27, 1950. http://search.proquest.com/docview/105951953?accountid=34227.

"Testimony of E. Howard Hunt, 10 Jan 1976." Church Committee Boxed Files Hosted by Mary Ferrell. January 10, 1976. http://www.maryferrell org/mffweb/archive/viewer/showDoc.do?docId=1353 (accessed May 5, 2013).

"The People of the CIA . . . The First Community DCI: Walter B. Smith." CIA.gov. October 17, 2007. https://www.cia.gov/news-information/featured-story-archive/2007-featured-story-archive/first-community-dci.html (accessed February 26, 2013).

"The Watergate Story. Key Players: Howard Hunt." *Washington Post*. n.d. http://www.washingtonpost.com/wp-srv/onpolitics/watergate/howard-hunt.html (accessed May 11, 2013).

Thomas, Evan. *The Very Best Men: Four Who Dared: The Early Years of the CIA*. New York: Simon & Schuster, 1995.

Tomasevich, Jozo. *War and Revolution in Yugoslavia, 1941–1945*. Stanford, California: Stanford University Press, 2001.

Tweedie, Neil. "Kim Philby: Father, husband, traitor, spy." *Telegraph*. January 23, 2013. http://www.telegraph.co.uk/history/9818727/Kim-Philby-Father-husband-traitor-spy.html (accessed February 27, 2013).

Ulmer-Power, Margueritte. "Reminiscences about Alfred C. Ulmer." Interview by Albert Lulushi. January 2014.

US House of Representatives, 83d Congress, 2nd Session Select Committee on Communist Aggression. *Communist Takeover and Occupation of Albania, Special Report No. 13*. Washington, DC: United States Government Printing Office, 1954.

US Senate Select Committee to Study Governmental Operations with Respect to Intelligence Activities (Church Committee). "Supplementary Detailed Staff Reports on Foreign and Military Intelligence, Book IV." US Senate Select Committee on Intelligence. 1976. http://www.intelligence.senate.gov/churchcommittee.html (accessed April 27, 2013).

"VENONA Documents - October 1951." NSA.gov. January 15, 2009. http://www.nsa.gov/public_info/declass/venona/oct_1951.shtml (accessed February 27, 2013).

"Venona: Soviet Espionage and the American Response 1939-1957." CIA.gov. March 19, 2007. https://www.cia.gov/library/center-for-the-study-of-intelligence/csi-publications/books-and-monographs/venona-soviet-espionage-and-the-american-response-1939-1957/venona.htm (accessed February 27, 2013).

Weintraub, Stanley. *11 Days in December*. New York: Free Press, Simon & Schuster, 2006.

"When 'Knollwood' Was For Sale." *Old Long Island*. August 5, 2009. http://www.oldlongisland.com/2009/08/when-knollwood-was-for-sale.html (accessed May 12, 2013).

White, Leigh. "Guerrillas of Albania." *New York Times* (1923–Current file). March 13, 1949. http://search.proquest.com/docview/105720547?accountid=34227.

Wilber, Dr. Donald. "Overthrow of Premier Mossadeq of Iran, November 1952–August 1953." The National Security Archive (The George Washington University). March 1954. http://www.gwu.edu/~nsarchiv/NSAEBB/NSAEBB28/.

Wisner, Ellis, and Wendy Hazard. "Reminiscences about Frank G. Wisner." Interviews by Albert Lulushi. June 2013.

Wolf, Markus, with Anne McElvoy. *Man Without a Face: The Autobiography of Communism's Greatest Spymaster*. New York: Time Books, a division of Random House, 1997.

Wyatt, F. Mark. Interview by Pat Mitchell and Jeremy Isaacs. *Cold War* (Episode 3: Marshall Plan). CNN. 1998.

Yatsevitch III, Gratian M. "Reminiscences about Colonel Yatsevitch." Interview by Albert Lulushi. July 1, 2013.

Yatsevitch, Gratian M. "Iranian-American Relations Oral History Project: The Reminiscences of Colonel Gratian M. Yatsevitch." Interview by William Burr. November 5, 1988.

"Yugoslav Plan for the Invasion of Albania." CREST Database. July 23, 1953.

Zickel, Raymond, and Walter R. Iwaskiw, editors. "Albania: A Country Study." Country Studies, Federal Research Division of the Library of Congress. 1994. http://countrystudies.us/albania/index.htm (accessed April 12, 2013).

"Zog Hired Press Agent." *New York Times* (1923–Current file). September 21, 1951. http://search.proquest.com/docview/111934723?accountid=34227.

"Zog Ousts Police Station." *New York Times* (1923–Current file). March 23, 1953. http://search.proquest.com/docview/112835804?accountid=34227.

"Zog's Taxes Paid, L.I. Palace Saved." *New York Times* (1923–Current file). November 12, 1952. http://search.proquest.com/docview/112237522?accountid=34227.

Index

Agnelli, Gianni, 5
Agolli, Rrapush, 206
Albanian Communist Party, 34, 141, 213
Albanian Fascist Party, 38
Albanian Guard Company, 106. *See*
    Labor Service Company 4000
Albanian National Assembly, 20, 47, 182
Albanian National Bank, 20
Albanian National Renaissance, 23
Albanian refugees, 36, 43, 45, 103, 141,
    232, 234
Albanian Social Democratic Party, 27
Aliko, Turhan, 81
Aliu, Përparim, 82
American Sixth Fleet, 226
Amery, Julian, 25, 26, 59, 60
Andoni, Vasil, 68, 78
Angleton, James, 6, 85, 90, 96, 109, 110
Animal Farm (Orwell), 11
Apple team, 174–178, 184–196,
    200–207, 230, 231, 244–245
Arbenz, Jacobo, 229
A Short Course in the Secret War (Felix), 261
Asllani, Xhemal, 82

Balkans, 1, 10, 12, 45, 62, 94,
    active involvement of the US in,
    256–257

coverage by CIA, 9, 43, 64–67, 95,
    130, 223, 225
coverage by State Department, 139,
    144, 229
during World War II, 21, 24
Balli Kombëtar (BK), 23–25, 26, 36, 45,
    50, 53, 54, 58, 68–72, 107
Balli Kombëtar Agrarian (BKA),
    234–236
Balli Kombëtar Organization (BKO),
    234, 235
Barcz, Janusz. *See* Polish aircrew,
    members of
Bardho, Sami, 82
Basho, Çaush, 104, 105
Berisha, Rexh, 114, 121
Berry, Burton Yost
    meeting with Frashëri, 45–46
    meeting with Van Fleet, 62
    meeting with Zog, 46–49, 59–61
    and Pipinelis, 62–63
    report on Albanian situation,
    41–44
Bethell, Nicholas, 85
Betrayed (Bethell), 85, 256
BGFIEND. *See* Project Fiend
Biba, Bardhok, 97
Bissell, Richard, 254

BK. *See* Balli Kombëtar

BKA. *See* Balli Kombëtar Agrarian

BKI. *See* Blloku Kombëtar Indipendent

BKO. *See* Balli Kombëtar Organization

Blloku Kombëtar Indipendent (BKI), 38, 46, 47, 58, 86, 109, 234, 236, 266

Bloshmi, Xhevdet, 96

Blunt, Anthony. *See* Cambridge Five spy ring

Bradley, Omar, 142

Branica, Halil, 173, 192, 199, 200
  capture by the Sigurimi, 185–187
  failed first attempt to infiltrate, 176–177
  trial and sentence, 204–206

Brundel, Władimir. *See* Polish aircrew, members of

Bryan, Joe, 66

Burgess, Guy, 128, 129
  member of Cambridge Five spy ring, 75

Burke, E. Michael, 99, 109, 110, 125,
  communication failures, 116–117
  in Hollywood, 102
  interactions with Philby, 102
  as liaison with NCFA, 102–103, 131–132,
  life after the CIA, 261–262
  with OSS, 101–102
  preparing first Albanian infiltration, 111–115
  targeting Albanian leaders, 249

Buryn, Władysław. *See* Polish aircrew, members of

Butka, Petrit, 82

"Buza e Bredhit" operation, 87

C–47 aircraft, 1, 96, 112, 202, 221

Caffery, Jefferson, 210, 211, 212

Cairncross, John. *See* Cambridge Five spy ring

Çako, Ethem, 87, 88

Cambridge Five spy ring, 75

Campbell, John C., 139

Carney, Robert, 218

Cena, Dalip, 107

Cenaj, Ramadan, 114, 121

Central Intelligence Agency (CIA)
  creation of, 4
  first paramilitary team, 1–3, 109–122, 241–242
  influencing Italian election, 5–7
  mission, 4
  Office of Confidential Funds, 52
  operation BGFIEND against Albania. *See* Project Fiend
  operation JMARC against Cuba, 253–255
  operation PBSUCCESS against Guatemala, 250–253
  operation QKSTAIR against Bulgaria, 95
  operation TPAJAX against Iran 228–229
  plan for a paramilitary coup in Albania, 217–229
  and playback operation by Cuban intelligence, 245–246
  and playback operation by East German intelligence, 246

Central Intelligence Group, 4, 225

CHARITY, project, 96, 109, 110

Chisholm, Elizabeth, 8

Christian Democrats, 5, 6

Church, Frank, 246

Church Committee, 246, 247

Churchill, Winston, 228

Chuvakhin, Dimitri, 35

Ciano, Count Galeazzo, 18, 19

Clay, Lucius, 169

Cloak and Dagger (movie), 102

Colby, William, 272n1

Cold War, 1, 7, 9, 10, 128, 217, 218, 243, 245

Collins, Bill, 79

Communist Information Bureau (Cominform), 33, 35, 40, 51, 69, 89

Cooper, Gary, 5, 102

Copeland, Miles, 214

"Coup-de-Main liquidation team," 249

covert aircraft
  for agent drops, 1, 96, 115, 150, 152–154, 199, 200

covert aircraft (continued)
  attempt to bring down by
    Sigurimi, 202
  for communications with
    agents, 117
  for leaflet drops, 133, 140, 253
  planned use during coup in
    Albania, 221
  transfer from US Air Force to the
    CIA, 112–113
Cuba, 125, 243
  CIA operation in, 253–255
  intelligence operations against the
    CIA, 245–246
Cypress team, 150, 161

Daci, Selim, 114, 116, 118, 156
Daci, Zetan, 114
Dalliu, Sali, 114, 121
Dani, Safet, 81
Dapćević, Peko, 142
Dauti, Ago, 82
Davies, Edmund F., 25
DDP. See Deputy Director for Plans
De Gasperi, Alcide, 6
Democratic Front of Albania, 28,
  29, 213
Denfeld, Louis E., 52
Deputy Director for Plans (DDP), 225
Deva, Xhafer, 37, 238, 266
Dilo, Jani, 79, 80, 82
Diomedes, Alexandros, 63
Director of Central Intelligence (DCI),
  6, 140, 214, 217, 250
Djilas, Milovan, 34
Dodani, Mark, 182
Donovan, William J., 6, 101
Dora project, 135
Dosti, Hasan,
  defection offer from Enver
    Hoxha, 255
  during World War II, 23, 26
  early life, 23
  election as NCFA president,
    68–72

  late years, 265
  as leader of Balli Kombëtar, 68, 234
  telegram to Enver Hoxha, 136
  termination of contacts with the
    CIA, 240
Drejtoria e Sigurimit të Shtetit
  (Directorate of State Security).
  See Sigurimi
Dulles, Allen, 57, 140, 253, 261
Dwyer, Peter, 56, 73

Egyptian-British-Israel issues, 212
El Combate (The Fight). See Guatemala,
  CIA operation in.
El Ejército de Liberación. See
  Guatemala, CIA operation in
Elliott, Nicholas, 266
Enlai, Zhou, 268
Ermenji, Abas, 36, 58, 68, 70, 104,
  151, 266
  arguments with CIA case officers, 146,
    147, 151, 234–235, 256
  in British Operation Valuable,
    78, 80
  splinter from reorganized NCFA,
    235–236

Farouk (king of Egypt), 37, 45, 208
Fiske, Norman E., 40–41
Foreign Branch B Section I (FB–I), 9
Frashëri, Mehdi, 37
Frashëri, Mithat, 39, 44, 49
  agreements with Berry, 45–46
  death of, 68, 247
  during World War II, 23–26
  early life, 23
  leads BK, 36, 37
  leads the NCFA, 58, 60, 63–64
  in London, 66
  in Paris, 63
  in the United States, 66–68
Free Europe Committee, 261
Fuller, Horace W., 215
Fultz, Harry T., 22, 29, 66,
  67, 269

Gaba, Haki, 82
Geraldine Appony, 17, 18, 19, 46, 60,
    164, 191, 210, 212, 213,
    262, 265
Gerveshi, Bardhyl, 82
Gjolena, Zenun, 198, 204, 205
Gjonmarkaj, Ndue Pjeter, 97
Gjurra, Adem, 114, 116, 121
Gjyla, Haxhi, 173, 178, 179, 198,
    204, 205
Gogo, Gaqo, 151
Gradishta, 152
Greek civil war, 32
Greek claims on Southern Albania, 14,
    32, 61, 143, 167
Greek Foreign Office, 142
Greek National Army (GNA), 43, 61,
    62, 88
Gromyko, Andrei, 30
Guatemala, 229, 233, 243, 255, 258
    CIA operation in, 250–253
Guzman, Jacobo Arbenz, 250

HARDROCK BAKER. See Guatemala,
    CIA operation in
Hataj, Ramiz, 81
Hazbiu, Kadri, 181, 183, 196, 205,
    206, 269
Higgs, Randolph H., 139
Hila, Ded, 159
Hillenkoetter, Roscoe H., 7
Hitler, Adolf, 18, 20
Hoxha, Enver, 42, 105, 142, 221,
    223, 225
    decides the fate of CIA agents, 206
    first five years in power, 26–36
    in World War II, 22–26
    late years, 267–269
    plan for defection in place of, 226–227
    telegram from Hasan Dosti, 136
Hoxha, Muhamet, 149, 150, 156
Hudson, Charles, 169
Hunt, E. Howard, 133, 202, 204, 225,
    246, 250, 264
Huntington, USS, 29

International Relief Organization (IRO),
    36, 78, 93, 158
Isufi, Hysen, 81
Iran, 223, 233, 243, 253, 255, 258,
    262, 263
    CIA operation in, 228–229
Italian Communist Party, 5, 86
Ivanaj, Mirash, 67

Jacobs, Joseph E., 28
Jacomoni, Francesco, 19
Jellicoe, George, 56, 69, 70
JMARC, project, 254
Joint Chiefs of Staff (JCS), 4, 12,
    51, 52, 73, 132, 142,
    217, 253
Joint Policy Committee, 69, 129
Joyce, Robert, 51, 56, 61, 69, 73, 139
Juanita, 134
Juka, Musa, 37

Kaiku, Dalip, 120
Kalaja, Abdul, 138
Kennan, George F., 8, 9, 44, 51
Khrushchev, Nikita, 239
Klissura, Ali, 23, 26, 37, 68, 234
Koçi, Dule, 120
Kokalari, Musine, 27, 28
Koliqi, Ernest, 38, 266
Komiteti i Maleve (Mountains'
    Committee), 97
Konitza, Skënder, 255
Kosmo, Sotir, 86
Kosovo, 21, 25, 27, 39, 140, 238, 241,
    242, 257, 261
Kotta, Nuçi, 66
Kovaćić, Karel, 30
Kraja, Iliaz, 237, 238
Król, Stanisław. See Polish aircrew,
    members of
Kruja, Mustafa, 37
Kryeziu, Gani, 25
Kryeziu, Hasan, 25
Kryeziu, Said, 25, 58, 66, 88, 104, 119,
    146, 266

Kuka, Ahmet, 81
Kuka, Bido, 81
Kukësi, 2, 220
  Kukësi team, 114, 116
Kulla, Fuad, 138
Kupi, Abas, 37, 103
  late years, 265–266
  in London, 66
  in the NCFA, 58, 60, 70, 86, 88, 104,
    146, 235
  relationship with Burke, 103, 131–132
  in the United States, 66–68
  during World War II, 20, 22, 23, 25, 26
Kupi, Petrit, 66
Kusa, Mustafa, 80

Labor Service Company 4000, 99–108,
  125, 158, 232. See Albanian Guard
  Company
  assessment of Albanian personnel
    in, 146
  covert training, 105–107
  funds, 104
  members of, 104
Lamçe, Ibrahim, 206
Landing craft utility (LCU) boats, 221
Landon, Truman H., 112
La Voz de la Liberación. See Guatemala,
  CIA operation in
LAWBOOK, project, 239
League of Albanian Refugees, 142, 155,
  220, 226
Legitimacy (Legaliteti), 24, 25, 26, 36,
  37, 47, 50, 58
Lepenica, Hysen, 81
Lepenica, Sami, 81
Leshanaku, Alush, 96, 97
Lëvizja Nacional Çlirimtare (LNÇ),
  22–26, 72
Lieb, Joseph C., 132, 137, 141, 146, 147,
  151, 154, 262–263
Lika, Zyber, 87
Lindsay, Franklin, 10, 12, 50, 52
Liqeni i Vajkalit operation, 181
Liquid potassium cyanide (L–pill),
  2, 175
Lleshi, Aqif, 182

Lleshi, Haxhi, 182
Lombard, Florentino Aspillaga, 245
Low, Bob, 88
Low, Robert, 52, 53, 57–60, 66, 69, 261
Luarasi, Sefer, 82
Luce, Henry, 53
Lutfiu, Llukman, 87
Lyall, Archibald, 262

MacArthur, Douglas, 169
Maçi, Halil, 68
MacLean, Donald, 127, 128
  member of Cambridge Five
    spy ring, 75
MacLean, William, 25, 26, 37, 59, 60
Malushi, Gani, 195, 204, 206
Mançe, Zihni, 82
Mangelli, Thomas, 105, 106, 113
Markagjoni, Gjon, 38, 58, 69, 237, 266
Markham, Reuben H., 66
Marshall, George C., 140
Marshall Plan, 5, 254
Martaneshi, 2, 3, 173, 179, 180, 188
Martini, Sotir T., 40
Mason, Gordon, 173, 174, 176, 179,
  187, 190, 193
Matamoros Fortress, bombing of. See
  Guatemala, CIA operation in
Matiani, Hamit, 179, 180, 230, 244, 248
  1951 operations, 152–154, 161
  1952 infiltration of Apple team,
    174–178
  capture by the Sigurimi, 195–198, 200
  trial and sentence, 204–207
McCargar, James, 9, 12, 77, 88, 94, 247
  describes Philby, 73–74
  describes British Operation
    Valuable, 86
  early years, 10
  late years, 261
  launching Project Fiend, 49, 52, 56,
    59, 65
  participates in reevaluation of Project
    Fiend, 90–93
  role in Dosti's selection to lead NCFA,
    69–71
Mëlyshi, Ndue, 97

Menzies, Stewart, 129
Miner, Robert G., 45, 47, 49
Molotov, Vyacheslav, 34, 35
Mugosha, Dushan, 140
Muka, Koço, 37
Muslim Brotherhood, 209, 214, 215
Mussolini, 18, 19, 20
My Silent War: The Autobiography of a Spy
   (Philby), 124, 267

Nadj, Kosta, 142
Naguib, Muhammad, 208
Nasser, Gamal Abdel, 208, 214
National Committee for Free Albania
   (NCFA), 2, 110, 117, 220, 233–234,
   239, 241, 242, 255
   election of Frashëri's successor, 68–70
   formation of, 63
   goals of, 64
   information leaks on operational
      activities, 158
   members of, 63–64
   operational activities for 1951, 146
   operational and security aspects, 156
   operational teams for 1951, 148
   propaganda materials, 136–137
   reconstruction of committee, 155–156
   training of agents, 77–79, 147, 158
National Committee for Free Europe
   (NCFE), 57, 66
National Front. *See* Balli Kombëtar (BK)
National Independent Bloc. *See* Blloku
   Kombëtar Indipendent (BKI)
National Liberation Movement. *See*
   Lëvizja Nacional Çlirimtare (LNÇ)
National Security Act, 4
National Security Council (NSC), 4, 51,
   229, 247, 253
   directive 4–A, 6
   directive 10/2, 7
   directive 10/5, 218
NCFA. *See* National Committee for
   Free Albania
Nerguti, Halil, 114–119, 121, 241
Nichols, Arthur, 25
Nikolla, Pal, 198, 199, 204, 205
Nixon, Richard, 225

Noah, USS, 29
Noli, Theofan S., 15, 16, 19
Northern Epirus. *See* Greek claims on
   Southern Albania
Northrop, Anthony, 154

Oak team, 159
OBTURATE, project, 237
OBTUSE, project, 242
Office of Policy Coordination (OPC),
   3, 41, 43, 44, 51, 73, 138, 217
   budget, 11, 12
   creation of, 7
   issues between OSO and, 109, 111
   merger with OSO, 140
   operation against Bulgaria, 95
   organizational structure, 9
Office of Special Operations (OSO), 5,
   6, 11, 38, 45, 51
Office of Strategic Services (OSS), 6, 8,
   10, 21, 22, 27, 53, 67, 101, 102
Offie, Carmel, 51, 52, 59, 69, 70, 71,
   94, 103
Olive team, 148–149, 159
One–time pads (OTPs), 120, 126–127
Orwell, George, 11
Ottoman Empire, 12–16, 37
Outrageous Good Fortune (Burke), 125, 262

Pali, Zef, 66, 68, 70, 71
Papagos, Alexandros, 20, 61, 62
Paris Peace Conference of 1919, 14, 23
Pasha, Muhammad Ali, 37
Pavlov, N. J., 35
PBSUCCESS project, 251, 253
Peposhi, Liman, 120
Perkins, Harold, 154
Peza, Myslim, 182
Philby, Harold Adrian Russell "Kim,"
   85, 86, 90, 91, 266–267
   Burke's description of, 102
   exit from Washington, 129
   involvement in Albanian operation,
      124–125
   McCargar's description of, 73–74
   as SIS liaison officer, 73–76
   and Yatsevitch, 101

Pine Tree team, 120–121
Pipinelis, Panayiotis, 62
Plaka, Nuri, 198, 204, 205
Planeja, Myftar, 114, 121
Plan Fontana, 87
plausible deniability, 50, 57, 226, 252
Pleshti, Sherif, 176
Policy Coordination Group, 73
Policy Planning Staff, 9, 44, 61
Polish aircrew, 1, 3, 130
    members of, 112
Polygraph tests, 151
Popović, Koća, 142
Premçi, Tahir, 173, 178, 181, 183, 187,
    189, 190, 191, 204, 205
Prifti, Thoma, 154
Program Branch 7 (PB/7), 246, 247
Project Fiend
    1951 infiltrations in Albania, 146
    asymmetrical warfare, 245
    British-American operations in,
        53–56, 93–94
    defunding of, 233
    economic warfare activities, 137
    objective of, 52, 89
    phases of operation, 50–52
    propaganda warfare program,
        132–134
    psychological warfare program,
        134–136
    radio communication, 243
    reevaluation of, 89–98
Psychological Strategy Board (PSB),
    217, 218, 219, 228, 229,
    232, 251
Psychological warfare activities, 11, 227
Pupe, Servet, 148, 149

QKSTAIR project, 95

Radio Tirana, 50, 64, 118, 138, 156, 159,
    161, 171, 204, 205, 206, 213
RAKI operation, 80
Reka, Hatip, 104
Richardson, John, 225, 230, 231, 263

Rockefeller Foundation, 17
Roosevelt, Kermit, 69, 90, 228
Rrapushi, Nijaz, 149
RS–1 radio sets, 120, 186, 243
Ruddock, Merritt K., 94
Rudkowski, Roman. See Polish aircrew,
    members of
Rusta, Azis, 159
Rustemi, Avni, 14, 15

Sadat, Anwar, 212
Sakollari, Xheladin, 154, 174, 178, 179
Sallku, Hysen, 159
Saumarez, HMS, 30
Seaman, H. Bogart, 170
Secret Intelligence Services, 55, 73,
    123, 155
    operations in Albania. See Valuable
    Soviet penetration by Cambridge Five
        spy ring, 75
Selmani, Hysen, 169, 173, 175, 202
Senaj, Belul, 82
Shehi, Myslim, 180
Shehi, Zenel, 173, 179, 192, 194, 244
    infiltration in Albania, 175–178
    capture by the Sigurimi, 180–182
    trial and sentence, 204–207
Shehu, Kasem, 149, 156
Shehu, Mehmet, 34, 35, 36, 181, 204
    cruelty of, 27, 97–98
    decides the fate of CIA agents,
        205–206
    early years of, 26–27
    late years, 268–269
    plan for defection in place of, 226–227
Sheno, Zogoll, 81
Shqipëria, 139
Sigurimi, 68, 86, 87, 97, 107–108, 115,
    116, 120, 125, 138, 149, 156, 157, 248
    "Buza e Bredhit" operation by, 87
    capture of Branica, 185–186
    capture of Matiani, 195–198, 200
    capture of Shehi and Premçi, 180–182
    help from Soviet intelligence in elimi-
        nating Frashëri, 68, 247–248

"Liqeni i Vajkalit" operation by, 181
Simcox, Tony, 25
Sinatra, Frank, 5
Sinclair, John A., 228
Sino, Abdyl, 79
Skënderbeg, Gjergj Kastrioti, 13, 18
Smiley, David, 78, 79, 80, 85, 87, 88
Smith, Walter B., 12, 129, 139, 140, 217, 227
Sons of the Eagle (Amery), 59
Special Operations Executive (SOE), 21, 25, 37, 78
Special Projects Group, 9
Spets Byuro #1, 247
Spiru, Nako, 34
Springfjord, 253
Spycraft techniques, 243
Stalin, Joseph, 27, 32–35
State Department, 7, 8, 51, 94, 137, 164, 211
  expected role in coup against Hoxha's regime, 220, 229
  influencing composition of NCFA, 45, 58
  post World War II mission in Albania, 28–29
  supports territorial integrity of Albania, 33, 143–145
Stevens, Leslie C., 217
Stolz, Richard, 137
Sula, Naum, 195, 196, 204, 206
Sulzberger, Cyrus L., 94

Tempo, Svetozar Vukmanović, 142
Tenefi, Apostol, 141
Thompson, Llewellyn, 51
Thurston, Ray, 229
Tidmarsh, Harold A., 113
Tiger team, 148–149
Tito, 10, 40, 42, 51, 69, 89, 95, 156, 218, 223, 255
  influence over Albanian Communists, 22, 33–35, 268
  plan to invade Albania, 142
  sponsoring the Albanian League of

Political Refugees, 141–142, 155
Toptani, Essad Pasha, 14, 15
Toptani, Iliaz, 114, 116, 118, 156
Toshi, Hamid, 159
TPAJAX, project, 228, 253
Trebova, Ali, 80, 81
Truman, Harry S., 4, 140

Ulmer, Alfred C., 173–176, 179, 190, 197, 263
US Army European Command (EUCOM), 103

Valuable
  1949 infiltrations, 77–83
  1951 Fiend–Valuable meeting in Rome, 154–159
  American decision to disengage Fiend from Valuable operations, 93–95
  decision to coordinate with American plans, 53–55
Van Fleet, James A., 62
Vassiliev, Nikolai, 35
Vata, Tahir, 120
Veliu, Fido, 149, 159
Venona, 126–127
Vërlaci, Ismail, 38, 39, 45, 58, 63, 69, 96, 266
Vërlaci, Shefqet, 19, 20
Vlora, Nuredin, 68
Voice of Free Albania, 135, 233, 242, 250
Volage, HMS, 30
von Blomberg, Baron William Frary, 163, 164, 169

Watergate scandal, 246, 264
Weckerling, John, 219
Wehrmacht, 24
Wied, Prince William of, 14
Wilson, Woodrow, 14
Wisner, Frank Gardiner, 52, 53, 64, 73, 139, 140
  dampens Greek desire to cross Albanian frontier in 1949, 61–62
  early life, 8

Wisner, Frank Gardiner (continued)
  late years, 260
  meeting with Philby and others to
    review Project Fiend, 90–92
  and OPC, 9–12
  opinion on plans for a paramilitary
    coup in Albania, 217–218, 225
  report from Berry on Albania, 41–43
  reevaluates Project Fiend, 93–95
  in World War II, 8
Wisner, Frank G. Jr., 261
Wolf, Markus, 246
Wyatt, F. Mark, 6
Wysiekierski, Zbigniew. *See* Polish
  aircrew, members of

Xhaferri, Arif, 82
Xiaoping, Deng, 268
Xoxe, Koçi, 27, 28, 34, 35, 42, 141

Yatsevitch, Gratian M., 109, 111, 117,
    137, 177, 189
  early life, 99–100
  late years, 262
  meeting with Zog, 164–169, 171
  meeting in Rome to review Fiend–
    Valuable, 154–159
  military and intelligence career, 100
  opinion on the 1953 plan for a
    paramilitary coup in Albania,
    223–224
  and Philby, 101, 129–130

Yugoslav Federative Republic, 143
Yugoslav plan to invade Albania, 152

Zedong, Mao, 268
Zhupa, Kasëm, 87
Zog, Ahmet, 182, 191, 192
  agreements with Berry, 45–47, 49,
    60, 61
  bank balance in Egypt, 216
  early life of, 15
  Egyptian government against,
    208, 213
  in exile, 19, 20
  and Fiske, 40–41
  late years, 265
  marriage celebrations of, 17–19
  meeting with Fuller, 209
  meeting with Yatsevitch, 164–169
  as president of Albania, 16–17
  purchase of property in U.S.,
    169–170
  recognition of government, 38
  relationship with King Farouk, 37,
    44–45, 208
  relationship with Muslim Brother-
    hood, 214
  team in Albania, 173
  trip to New York, 163–164
Zotos (colonel in Greek Army
    Intelligence), 87, 88
Zyberi, Rifat, 159
Zyberi, Riza, 149, 159